Trial and Error

Trial
and Error

THE DETROIT
SCHOOL SEGREGATION CASE

Eleanor P. Wolf

WAYNE STATE UNIVERSITY PRESS
DETROIT   1981

Library of Congress Cataloging in Publication Data

Wolf, Eleanor Paperno.
  Trial and error.

  Bibliography: p.
  Includes index.
  1. School integration—Michigan—Detroit—Case
studies. 2. Discrimination in housing—Michigan—
Detroit—Case studies. I. Title.
LC214.23.D6W64   370.19'342   80-25025
ISBN 0-8143-1673-5

This book is for Leo
who knows about schools and cares
about the children who live in them

Contents

Preface

Some old friends have, upon occasion, expressed misgivings about this study of the Detroit school segregation case and the issues involved in its litigation. A few thought that the book might harm the cause of civil rights, but most, knowing how difficult I would find it to endure this charge, were concerned for me on that account. I have decided that the first of these concerns is not valid. My reaction to the second can be expressed, I find, in the words of a great scientist. I offer the admonition of Albert Einstein: "The right to search for truth also implies a duty. One must not conceal any part of what one has recognized to be true."

The original research was made possible by the Ford Foundation, to which I am grateful for support. Wayne State University granted me sabbatical leave to continue the study, and the university Center for Urban Studies freed me to work on the manuscript for an additional term.

In addition to help from colleagues in my own and related disciplines, I am indebted to attorneys and law school professors of widely varying views. Special thanks go to Theodore Sachs, attorney, and to Professors Paul Carrington, John Coons, David Kirp, and Robert Sedler. Their efforts to explain some aspects of constitutional law were extremely helpful. Thanks are also due Rebecca Warfel for assistance with library research; to my friend Rennette Elder, for her unique editorial-secretarial help during the early stages of manuscript preparation; and to the publisher's editor, Jean Owen, whose skill and taste contributed so much.

I owe a special debt of appreciation to Evelyn Weissman, research associate, who not only collaborated in writing the school violations chapters but also continued to provide the constant assistance, ad-

9

vice, and encouragement without which this project could not have been completed.

This study would have been impossible without a complete copy of the trial record. Although such transcripts are public documents, they are virtually inaccessible. For months the only copy of *Bradley v. Milliken* available to the public was to be found at the Sixth Circuit Court of Appeals in Cincinnati. When the transcript did return to Detroit, I learned that a copy would cost about ten thousand dollars, but I was saved by the kindness of Donald Miller, the court trial reporter. He allowed me to take his copy of the proceedings, a few volumes at a time, to reproduce and return to him. I mention these difficulties to call attention to the fact that there is something wrong with a system that makes it so difficult for scholars and the public to read the record of important judicial proceedings.

Some of the ideas in this book were developed originally in articles for *The Public Interest* (No. 4, Winter, 1976) and for the 1977 volume of *The Supreme Court Review*. Portions of Chapter 19 were first presented in a paper, "Courtrooms and Classrooms," at the 1976 conference on law, education, and the social sciences organized by the National Institute of Education. That paper appeared in the May, 1977, issue of *Educational Forum*. The conference papers were edited by Ray C. Rist and Ronald J. Anson and published first by the N.I.E. and later in *Education, Social Science, and the Judicial Process*, edited by Rist and Anson (New York: Teachers College Press, 1977).

Introduction

IN 1869 the Michigan Supreme Court ruled that racial exclusion violated the state's constitution and ordered the Detroit Board of Education to admit a black child to a school from which he had been turned away.[1] Thus ended de jure segregation in the state of Michigan—but over a century later, in *Bradley v. Milliken*, the Detroit system was once again found guilty of the same offense: maintaining schools that were segregated de jure.[2]

One must look back in time a bit to understand how such a ruling was possible. Until about twenty-five years ago mingling of the races in public facilities in the South was generally forbidden by state law. In May of 1954, the United States Supreme Court, in the famous school case *Brown v. Board of Education*, ruled that laws imposing racial separation in the public schools were unconstitutional.[3] This decision was the culmination of a series of rulings that had gradually eroded the power of government to enforce such separation. The Supreme Court holding was soon extended to all public facilities such as parks, libraries, and public transportation. The era of Jim Crow, the laws which codified the system of racial segregation, was over. But a prolonged period of bitter struggle, often marked by terror and violence, followed before the court decision was clearly established and implemented throughout the country.

The end of state-imposed racial segregation meant open access, but even when honestly enforced, open access, generally speaking, neither produced nor maintained a substantial degree of actual racial mixture. For instance, the main library in a Southern city, drawing upon the entire population, would typically have a mixed clientele. But local branches, neighborhood-based, tended to reflect the racial composition of the surrounding area, just as they did in the North. De facto segregation, in the sense of racial concentration not imposed by law, ordinarily prevailed in facilities which drew upon users in this

11

fashion even though compulsory separation of the races was no longer the law in the South. During their oral argument before the Supreme Court in *Brown* the National Association for the Advancement of Colored People attorneys did not define this as a problem. When questioned about it specifically, they seemed to emphasize that their goal was to end racial exclusion, not racial concentration. Counsel repeatedly stated that their objection was to state-imposed racial classification: "do not deny any child the right to get to a school of his choice on the grounds of race or color within the normal limits of your districting system . . . do not assign him on a basis of race. . . . If you have some other basis . . . any other basis, we have no objection. But just do not put in race or color as a factor."[4]

The process of dismantling racially segregated public schools in the South proved to be more difficult and complex than desegregating other facilities. There was a period of official defiance on the part of some states, which, proclaiming the doctrine of interposition, opposed federal "intervention."[5] Many of us recall vividly such scenes as that of the nine black children trying to enter a Little Rock high school; the sight of one lone black student, James Meredith, attempting to enroll at the University of Mississippi; and Governor Wallace standing "in the schoolhouse door" at the University of Alabama to dramatize his defiance of the Court's decision. In addition to terror, intimidation, economic reprisals, and the actual closing of schools to avoid desegregating them, subtler mechanisms were used to bar black students from schools to which they were admissible by law.

The turbulence of these years of resistance to school desegregation diverted public attention from the underlying social fact that even if Southern school systems had promptly moved to a policy of assigning children to the school nearest their homes, the creation and maintenance of racially mixed classrooms would have been as difficult in the South as in the North. (The experience of the Washington, D.C., system makes the point.[6]) It is true that there were a few racially mixed residential areas in the South, some rural, some in old cities. These instances of residential "integration" were not a manifestation of racial equality, however. Geographic proximity was often acceptable to whites when the blacks concerned were subservient, when all forms of interaction between the groups were under white control, and when blacks were barred from white facilities in the area. Dramatic illustrations of the injustice of such a dual system were numerous, as black children were compelled to walk or to be transported past a nearby white school to a more distant black one. In later years, as the desegregation of facilities proceeded, these racially mixed residential areas in the South began to vanish.

Although the issue was not clearly articulated during this period, there was another and deeper reason why simply ending racial exclusion and moving to a Northern-style neighborhood assignment system seemed to many civil rights supporters to be an inadequate response to the promise of the *Brown* ruling. The reference in the Supreme Court decision to the inherent inequality of "separate educational facilities," and the citation of social science research in the famous footnote 11 to support this view, suggested to some that it was actual racial mixture, not merely an end to state-imposed exclusion, which was being mandated.[8] Although most constitutional scholars disagree with this inference, and few contend that ending invidious racial classification requires such an interpretation, much of the media coverage suggested that *Brown* would create "integrated" (i.e., substantially mixed) schools, that this mingling would ensure "equal education" (a term that was rarely defined), and that it would eventually create better racial understanding throughout the nation.

The failure of much of the South to comply with the judicial mandate to cease racial discrimination in the schools was to have enormous consequences for the country as a whole, for in the process of devising tests of compliance with desegregation orders a new approach, the "test of numbers," developed. The federal courts in the South were overwhelmed by charges that this or that school system had not been desegregated, that one device or another was being used to assign children to schools on a racially discriminatory basis. Judges struggled with what has been described as the "great mystery"[9] of desegregation law: what is the evidence needed to prove that a dual system has been made unitary? The proof that open access had been established in a school previously closed to them seemed to require the presence of black children as confirmation. Adults tested the newly ordered desegregation of beaches, golf courses, parks, and public transportation, but it was children, usually in small numbers, who so often had to confront the jeering crowds or the physical assaults of segregationists. Because usually (even when open access was instituted in good faith) most children lived in racially concentrated neighborhoods, the black children reassigned to formerly white schools were often a small and vulnerable minority.

The federal judiciary's response to the problem of determining that the process of desegregation had indeed been carried out in a given school system was eventually to become itself the instrument for attacking racial imbalance in Northern school systems such as Detroit's. In 1966 in a famous Southern case in Jefferson County, Judge John Minor Wisdom moved toward viewing the actual degree of racial mixture within schools as evidence that a district had been desegregated.[10] He offered as a rationale for the use of such a yardstick its acceptance by the courts as evidence of non-discrimination in jury selection.[11] The analogy was erroneous. Names for jury duty, if picked at random from a pool of eligible persons, will of course yield proportionate samples from this universe. But families do not arrange themselves randomly, like slips of paper shaken in a hat or fishbowl. They are clustered residentially by income, life style, social ties, custom, discrimination in the housing market, or some combination of these and other forces. A more reasonable statistical test would have been to examine the extent to which the racial composition of the school matches the racial composition of the area it claims to serve. The court made a rather feeble effort to forestall such an objection by declaring that racial separation in residence was a consequence as well as a cause of racially concentrated schools,[12] but the opposite is closer to the truth, for separate schools had made the occasional Southern pattern of mixed residential areas possible. In 1968, in the *Green* case, the Supreme Court upheld the use of school racial proportions as the prime indicator that a formerly dual system had indeed been desegregated.[13]

Implications for the North

The possibility of using this new doctrine to compel the creation of racially mixed schools in the North soon became apparent. For a number of years after *Brown*, racial separation in this region had been defined as de facto and beyond the reach of court action. But after *Jefferson County* and *Green* Southerners were quick to point out that if racial proportions were taken as the prime indicators of desegregation many schools in Detroit and Chicago were almost as segregated as those in the South. As long as desegregation was defined as open access, the Northern systems were generally in conformity with *Brown*. Pro-integration groups in the North, therefore, attempted to achieve more racial mixture in schools by voluntary action, administrative policy, or state laws. In the early 1960s, a time of great public attention to urban problems, these efforts were bolstered by claims for the educational and attitudinal benefits of racially mixed classrooms.[14] Despite a generally favorable reception in the press to such studies the public was not persuaded by the arguments of the researchers, and efforts to require better racial balance through legislative or school board action failed to gain popular support. For example, in 1963 James Allen, New York State Commissioner for Education, ruled that no school should be composed of more than half "minority" pupils, but this requirement was not implemented.

The judiciary was not generally responsive to the contention that the condition of racial "isolation" itself constitutes a denial of constitutional guarantees of equal protection.[15] The question of whether the use of geographic school assignment, untainted by state acts of discrimination, is permissible has only indirectly been addressed by the Supreme Court, but the answer seems to be that it is. However, the Constitution's sure protection against racial separation as a consequence of official actions has emerged as the most dependable legal approach. There is some difference of opinion among legal scholars as to whether this constitutional protection against official (de jure) segregation rests only on the impermissibility of the invidious use of racial classification or whether it necessarily involves some imputation of harm (a denial of equal protection) from the racial isolation which results—and, if the latter, whether the alleged harm must be proved empirically. These difficult questions have been sidestepped by court decisions that simply find school systems to have practiced, openly or surreptitiously, some form of racial discrimination.

The judicial rulings that eventually ordered busing programs to achieve racially mixed schools were not based on an interpretation of *Brown* to mean that predominantly black or one-race schools, regardless of cause, were illegal. Had this been the case, there would have been no need for trials such as the one in Detroit. Instead, adhering to the legal doctrine that evolved in the South, plaintiffs seeking Northern school integration were required to show that a given system was segregated as a result of deliberate state action, so that (albeit covertly) the state was maintaining dual school systems. Proponents of school integration, who were convinced that racially mixed schools would enhance the education of black children and contribute to interracial harmony, now had an instrument through which they could secure in court what they had failed to achieve through legislation or school board action. The NAACP, which had been pushed into the background during the civil rights and anti-poverty activism of the late 1960s, was superbly equipped for this sort of struggle. It set about to develop a strategy and to amass evidence to show that the severe racial imbalance in Northern schools was not really de facto, but was the outcome of government action. If, through a judicial finding of de jure segregation, school desegregation could be defined as the existence of a reasonable racial mixture, *Brown* could at last be read to require racially mixed schools regardless of residential patterns. The essential "predicate" was a prior finding of de jure segregation. The Supreme Court ruling in the *Swann* case, issued soon after the Detroit trial began, supported this approach: "absent a constitutional violation there would be no basis for judicially ordering assignment of students on a racial basis."[16]

The Detroit Case and the Trial Judge

The Detroit ruling, as affirmed by the opinion of the Sixth Circuit Court of Appeals in 1973, was the triumph of the NAACP strategy: if the Detroit school system were found guilty of deliberate racial segregation, it was hard to see how any system could escape a similar ruling. Detroit had been losing population since 1955, but its black community had been growing very rapidly, from 9 percent in 1940 to 45 percent in 1970. In 1964 a liberal-labor coalition won control of the school board, and, as William Grant said: "In the years that followed the Board had changed school boundaries to promote integration, hired black teachers and administrators and demanded from publishers textbooks giving a fairer portrait of the races. Every decision, every appointment, every statement reflected the board's over-riding commitment to the goal of racial integration."[17] This attitude made the judgment in *Bradley v. Milliken* puzzling or shocking to the public, although I think that many observers believed at the time that the courts had found the condition of racial concentration itself to be illegal, rather than finding that the system had deliberately created or contributed to it. (This widespread confusion stems in part from the double meaning of the term "segregation," which can refer to the fact of racial concentration or to acts of discrimination to create racial separation.) Both the superintendent of schools, Norman Drachler, and the most recent president of the Detroit School Board, A. L. Zwerdling, had been honored by the NAACP for their accomplishments on behalf of school integration (T, pp. 4269–4303). The deputy superintendent, Arthur Johnson, one of whose chief duties was to scrutinize school boundary shifts and all changes in student assignments, had been the director of the Detroit chapter of the NAACP for most of his career and later was associate director of the Michigan Civil Rights Commission. By 1971 a program designed to encourage students to transfer to schools in which they would be a racial minority had resulted in about eight thousand transfers of black pupils to predominantly white schools.[18] In addition to these attempts by the Detroit School Board, many citizens' groups had been attempting to maintain integrated neighborhoods and schools since the late 1940s. This goal was not achieved, of course, but in view of the fact that the public school population had become over 50 percent black eight years before the Detroit trial began, these efforts were noteworthy. With the benefit of hindsight, I do not see how any attempt to achieve stable biracial schools could have succeeded, given the demographic and economic conditions that prevailed, but this was not clear at the time.

The size and scope of the remedy mandated in *Milliken*—massive interchanges between Detroit and fifty-two suburban school districts—was, until struck down by the Supreme Court, by far the most ambitious plan for racial dispersion the nation had ever seen. Despite this remedy, however, the Detroit case is in no important way unique. It simply affords the best opportunity to see with greater clarity the issues and the judicial processes involved in the school segregation cases. Much of the testimony was quite similar to that offered in other cities; indeed, some of the same expert witnesses were called upon in Detroit: the lengthy testimony on constitutional violations by school authorities, in support of the charge that what appeared to be de facto segregation was really de jure, was given by the same person who had appeared for the NAACP in most of these cases, Dr. Gordon Foster. *Milliken* may have been startling, but it was not a fluke.

Bradley v. Milliken was precipitated into the courts as a consequence of a movement aimed in the opposite direction, the push for "community control" of schools. (See Appendix B for a chronology of the Detroit case.) In 1969, responding to the Detroit version of the black power demands which then had the New York city school system in an uproar, the Michigan legislature passed a law which partially decentralized educational authority by providing for the election of regional school boards. Coleman Young, who was then a state senator, played a major role in its passage. In the ensuing struggle over how the boundaries of those regions might be drawn, the pro-integration majority of the Detroit Board of Education, fearing an institutionalization of racial divisions, adopted a "benign gerry-mander" of half of the city's high school attendance areas to improve their racial mix, the so-called April 7 Plan. The state legislature responded to powerful public pressure by action (shortly thereafter declared unconstitutional by the Sixth Circuit Court of Appeals) which nullified this plan, and the Detroit electorate responded with a swift and unprecedented recall of the School Board members who had voted for the boundary changes.[19]

At some point during this period the national staff of the NAACP decided upon a course of action which went far beyond their previous attempt to compel implementation of the April 7 Plan. The organization filed a suit charging both the Detroit School Board and state officials with maintaining a deliberately and "officially" (i.e., de jure) segregated school system (T, pp. 10–12).

The trial began in April, 1971, a time of unprecedented conflict and turbulence in the public schools. Shortly before the trial started, many schools within the city and in nearby towns and suburbs were closed by disorders. In suburban Willow Run the school principal was tarred and feathered after he attempted a reconciliation between blacks and whites.[20] In a number of places militant groups took over school offices and held staff members hostage. Demonstrations forced the closing of Mumford, Pershing, Mackenzie, Cooley, Ford, Osborne, and Northwestern high schools in Detroit.[21] The University of Detroit, a private Jesuit institution, was troubled by violence; a strike at the University of Michigan the year before was sparked by demands that the school enforce a quota of at least 10 percent black enrollment within three years.[22] There was an atmosphere of urgency difficult to recapture now, a prevailing mood that these extraordinary events called for an extraordinary response by society.

The assignment of Judge Stephen Roth to the case appeared at the time to be an unlucky choice for the plaintiffs. He was a conservative among Michigan Democrats, had no previous associations with civil rights efforts, and was a most unlikely candidate to formulate the most sweeping busing order ever issued. In 1970 his views on the involuntary reassignment of students—even those of high school age—to improve racial mixture were strongly negative, as can be seen in his rejection of the comparatively modest April 7 Plan. Since this is the only indication I have of his pre-trial opinions on the subject, I quote a substantial portion of the ruling in which he selected, instead, a "voluntary magnet plan" proposed by an anti-busing School Board member:

. . . Child raising, that is, education, is the first and largest industry of every species, including man. . . . Fortunately . . . there is something in the nature of man which drives him to develop his peculiar endowments. A school system is . . . perhaps the most important way in which the human society discharges its responsibility to its young and to its survival. When we do this well the educator calls it "quality education." In a heterogeneous society . . . such an education cannot be attained without integration. Our objective, then, as the Court sees it, is not integration in itself—which, if achieved in the wrong way, can be counter-productive—but the best education possible, with its sine qua non: integration. Integration for integration's sake is self-defeating; it does not advance the cause of integration, except in the short haul, nor does it necessarily improve the quality of education. To put it simply, a good education, to say nothing of the best education, cannot be achieved without integration. . . . [Later] There is within each child an innate force pressing upon him to fulfill whatever potentials he possesses. . . .

. . . The April Plan's . . . principal aim is to improve integration by the "numbers." . . . it does not offer incentive to or provide motivation for the student. Instead of offering a change of diet it provides forced feeding. The MacDonald [voluntary magnet plan] offers the student an opportunity to advance in his search for identity, provides stimulation . . . and tends to establish security. . . . based on the experience in the same school system, i.e. Cass Technical High School, it holds out the best promise of effective long-term integration. . . . [Later] If to integrate is "to combine a form, a more complete, harmonious or coordinated entity" then the plan we have chosen is . . . the most likely to be productive. It places the emphasis not on "desegregation" (representing the legal rights of Blacks) but on "integration" (an ideal of social acceptability). . . . whether the Constitution . . . not only prohibits discriminatory segregation, according to race, but also requires integration, has not yet been decided [but] we believe that consistent with the [Supreme] Court's ruling, where a school district has taken steps enhancing integration . . . it may not reverse direction. . . . any action or failure to act, by the Board of Education designed to "delay, obstruct or nullify" the . . . April 7 step toward improving racial balance . . . is a prohibited State action.

It is our judgment that the MacDonald [voluntary magnet] plan is superior . . . in advancing the cause of integration. . . . in this way the students, in their quest for identity and in their inherited drive for realizing their potentials, will bring about such integration as no coercive method could possibly achieve.[23]

Judge Roth, it would appear, was considerably less positive about compulsory school integration than the leadership of the system on trial before him. Less than a year later, conferring with counsel after he had rendered his decision against the Detroit system, he said: "the task we are called upon to perform is a social one which our society has been unable to accomplish. In reality, our Courts are called upon in these school cases to attain a social goal through the educational system, by using the law as a lever."[24]

Within six months, Judge Roth had ruled out any desegregation plan limited to Detroit as ineffective and ordered a metropolitan remedy involving approximately 780,000 children, from kindergarten through high school. He died two weeks before the Supreme Court, by a single vote, struck down this remedy on the grounds that since only Detroit had been found guilty of de jure segregation, the remedy, too, must be confined to Detroit.[25] Thus it came about that the city was, in 1975, required to desegregate its public schools, then 75 percent black, and must continue this effort today, although the latest count shows that the proportion black has increased to almost 85 percent.

Not many people have a clear understanding of the basis for the decisions in the Northern school segregation cases; when I began this study I was no exception. The District Court's ruling made no references to educational effects—to harm from racial concentration or to benefits of racial mixture. It was dominated by an emphasis on the city's demography and on the severity of residential segregation. From this the judge moved, with what seemed to me a puzzling lack of logic, to the conclusion that the actions of the school system had been a substantial cause of segregated schools. But as much space was devoted to praise of the system's efforts on behalf of integration as to a recital of its constitutional violations. Judge Roth expressed regret that any fault or blame had to be found, for if "segregation . . . is an evil it should make no difference whether we classify it as de facto or de jure."[26]

What had Judge Roth heard during the lengthy trial to reach conclusions so at variance with his former belief that involuntary mixture was undesirable? Did considerations of educational effectiveness truly play no part in his change of heart? What kind of evidence had been presented on residential behavior to cause him to identify government complicity in housing discrimination as the major source of segregated patterns? On what basis had he concluded that in a city where neighborhoods were so segregated, actions of school authorities had made such a difference in the racial composition of neighborhood schools? And had he been told that the racial dispersion of students would change patterns of residence? Or did he intend a permanent system of racial quotas in the assignment of children to schools?

I wanted to discover what kinds of expert testimony from the social sciences had been utilized in these proceedings, to evaluate the quality and inclusiveness of these materials, and to estimate their impact and influence. This last was a hazardous and speculative undertaking. But the verbatim transcript of the proceedings, recording all of Judge Roth's comments and questions over a period of many weeks, should offer some insight into his response to the testimony, it seemed, and I think that it did.

The first part of this book focuses on the details of the Detroit case itself. Chapters 1 through 5 deal with the key portions of the courtroom testimony on various aspects of residential segregation, pointing out some of the shortcomings of the testimony and indicating what I think the Judge should have heard, in addition, to give him an adequate summary of social science knowledge on this topic. An attempt is also made to discern from his questions and comments the influence of this material upon his thinking. Chapters 6 through 11 approach the testimony on education in a similar fashion. The next five chapters deal with the testimony on school violations, the basis on which *Milliken* was affirmed by the Court of Appeals. Chapter 17 deals with the social science testimony used during the hearings on desegregation remedies over which Judge Roth presided in 1972. In the remaining chapters some of the issues raised by *Milliken* that I believe apply to the present school segregation cases as a whole are considered: a layman's view of the legal basis of these school cases is presented; the problems involved in the use of social science evidence in judicial proceedings are discussed; and, finally, this judicial effort is considered from a social policy perspective.

I have not attempted to evaluate alternative policies to improve race relations or to enhance the educational achievement of children who are not doing well in school. I have not tried to specify the proper role for the judiciary in a democratic society, nor to formulate in any definitive way better procedures for the use of social science in the courts. Any one of these topics would require a separate book, and this one is long enough.

Overview

The most unusual feature of the district court decision in the Detroit case was its emphasis on residential patterns and demographic trends. Almost one-third of the text of the opinion was devoted to these subjects. Judge Roth identified "public and private" discrimination in housing as the chief cause of racial separation in residence, although economic factors and black preferences may have played some part.[1] The perspective of the ruling was generally assimilationist: congregation of other ethnic groups was a thing of the past; own-group preference of blacks was minimized; and all such concentrations, regardless of cause, were viewed as unfortunate.[2]

The opinion was a faithful reflection of the testimony offered during the trial and revealed the indoctrination which the court had received on these subjects. The principal expert witness had begun by carefully defining "segregation" in the neutral language of demography, as a mathematical construct that measured the extent of departure from a random distribution of the races, without regard to cause. But the stress on racial exclusion so dominated the testimony that within a few days Judge Roth phrased an inquiry he put to an expert witness thus: "Are the forces of good overcoming the forces of evil? That's what it comes down to as far as housing segregation is concerned" (T, p. 772). Later, the Sixth Circuit Court of Appeals avoided references to residential patterns and population changes and explicitly repudiated this basis for affirmance of the district court ruling.[3] The constitutional violations by school authorities alone became the basis for declaring the city's schools segregated de jure. It was as if a wobbly superstructure had been placed atop a considerably firmer foundation—and the foundation then removed. That foundation—racial exclusion as the chief cause of residential patterns—had been carefully laid by the plaintiffs at the start of the trial. The essence of their strategy was stated by NAACP counsel J. Harold Flannery: "racial containment of blacks in Detroit . . . is not a fortuitous phenomenon, but it is in fact a result of private and public . . . discrimination which permeated our generation and those before it and . . . further, there is an interlocking relationship between the racial composition of schools and discrimination with respect to housing opportunities" (T, p. 139).

It was a strategy designed to erase the distinction between school segregation de jure and de facto, a distinction that had blocked past efforts to attack Northern school imbalance through the courts. The plaintiffs stated their aim of making new law early in the trial: "the dichotomy between so-called de facto and de jure school segregation is simplistic to the point of naivete" (T, p. 460). They would show that despite the pro-integration sentiments of the system's leaders,[4] school assignment policy rested on residential patterns produced by discrimination in which government was so deeply involved that the segregation was de jure: the consequence of state action. And if present government policies seemed to belie this, the heritage of past actions remained.

Flannery's language also presaged the outline of the lengthy testimony that was to follow. Residential patterns were either fortuitous, i.e., produced by accident, or were created by discrimination. There were no experts during either the trial or the remedy hearings that followed to challenge or enlarge this distorted perspective. It would have been difficult enough to present research findings on residential patterns, a complex and multi-faceted area of behavior, in the format of a two-sided courtroom presentation; in this case the adversary framework produced no counter-testimony of any kind. Since there was no conceivable advantage to the defendants in disputing or amending the evidence on residential segregation or its causes, they simply took the legal position that (in line with a precedent case in the Sixth Circuit) school authorities were not responsible for racial imbalance resulting from residential patterns.[5] Therefore, the only testimony the court heard on this topic came from witnesses selected by the plaintiffs.

The testimony on residential segregation consumed most of the first seven days of the trial, and the witnesses were well-chosen to fulfill Edmond Cahn's famous requirements for effective advocacy in a path-breaking case:

if you wish a judge to overturn a settled and established rule of law, you must convince both his mind and his emotions, which together in indissociable blend constitute his sense of injustice. . . . His mind must see not only that the law has erred but also that the law itself proffers a remedy. Then he can feel free to correct the error without betraying the consistency and continuity of the legal order because he will only be replacing mistaken law with correct law. . . . all this he may determine to do—if you are able to arouse the propulsive force in his sense of injustice, i.e., the excitement of glands and emotions that any man may experience when he witnesses the inflicting of injustice.[6]

Karl Taeuber, the well-known sociologist from the University of Wisconsin, who laid the basic framework for the testimony with the definition and measurement of housing segregation in terms of departure from a random distribution, offered some historical background and a causal analysis in which discrimination overshadowed all other factors. Most of the other expert witnesses were either attorneys or staff members from civil rights agencies accustomed to the advocacy style used in courtroom presentation. (In addition to these experts Patricia Cousens supplied demographic data on Detroit, and Harold Black documented the past distribution of restrictive covenants.) Martin Sloane, a lawyer with an extensive civil rights background, who had worked for the Housing and Home Finance Agency (later to become the Department of Housing and Urban Development, or H.U.D.), documented the past complicity of government in housing discrimination. Robert Tucker, an attorney whose race brought an element of personal authenticity to his material and who had directed the fair housing division of the H.U.D. office for the region, also testified on the contribution of government, as well as private market components, to racial discrimination in housing. Both men stressed the inadequacy of present government efforts to overcome the effects of past actions. William Price, also an attorney and former director of the Detroit Urban League, recounted government involvement in racial discrimination in public housing and urban renewal. Richard Marks, senior staff member and former director of the Detroit Commission on Community Relations, presented considerable historical material on Detroit, and James Bush and James Bauder (from local civil rights agencies) testified on the severity and ubiquity of discrimination in housing. Their descriptions of various techniques of exclusion and intimidation documented a history of injury and injustice.

The force of this testimony was powerfully supplemented by the personal accounts of a number of black real estate brokers, whose plain-spoken accounts of their experiences when they attempted to operate in white neighborhoods clearly made a deep impression on the judge.

In addition to the presentation of these materials at the start of the trial, expert witnesses on other topics also offered their views on residential behavior during the weeks that followed.[7] Dr. Robert Green, chief education expert for the plaintiffs, described (at some length) suburbanization as white flight caused by racism, itself a consequence of "the failure of the schools," (T, pp. 966–9, 1025–28). Dr. Stuart Rankin, expert witness for the defendants, informed the court that to overcome racism the suburbs must be included in a desegregation plan because "that is where it (racism) is" (T, p. 4228). The departing school superintendent, Norman Drachler, after presenting copious statistical materials on the incidence of disease, poverty, crime, etc., attributed the departure of middle-class families from the city to "racial stereotypes" (T, deposition of June 28, 1971).

Taken as a whole, the message of the testimony on residential patterns was this: segregation is measured as concentration, but this concentration is caused by exclusion and discrimination motivated by racial prejudice. Economic factors are of minor importance, and since blacks are not an ethnic group in the way in which foreign-born families once were, voluntary congregation is unlikely except as a response to intimidation. Thus racial concentration is largely compelled, and government has been such a potent force in this compulsion that its outcome can be described as de jure segregation, the product of state action. The outlook for housing integration is bleak. Racial separation in residence is severe, widespread, unresponsive to economic improvement, worsened by the passage of time, and impervious to the assimilative processes that dispersed other groups.

In the chapters that follow we will see that the trial process, to some extent through distortions but mainly through omissions in the testimony, produced a picture of residential behavior that was gravely defective. It nevertheless played a crucial role in determining the outcome of the trial and in influencing Judge Roth's appraisal of a desegregation remedy.

CHAPTER 1
The Contribution of Government Action

Judge Roth: "Perhaps I shouldn't ask this but I am intrigued by it. We had a witness here from, I think, Washington, and I gathered from his testimony that there was some validity to the conclusion that the more government efforts expended the more segregation you get" (T, pp. 743–44). It is not difficult to understand the basis for the judge's comments. In an effort to show the complicity and responsibility of government, expert witnesses gave lengthy testimony to show how various government agencies and policies had contributed to racial segregation in residence. This testimony constituted the legal heart of the plaintiffs' case offering the courts new ground for a finding of de jure segregation in the Detroit school system.[1] Children assigned on a neighborhood basis were subjected to de jure segregation once removed because neighborhood segregation had been substantially caused by government action. And if, as the judge observed in his ruling, much of the state action had taken place in the past, these effects continued, for, he added, somewhat ambiguously, "the choice of a house is a relatively infrequent affair."[2]

The expert witnesses came from federal, state, and local agencies. Martin Sloane and Robert Tucker testified on policies of the federal government. According to Sloane, both the Federal Housing Administration and the Veterans Administration, but especially the former, had been "formidable factors in developing the patterns of racial residential separation that exist in metropolitan areas today (T, p. 454). He continued: "FHA had done so much to sow the seeds of housing discrimination and lay the foundation for racial separation in metropolitan areas, to harden the patterns of residential segregation, that

27

thirty-five years later we are still reaping the results of what FHA did in its first decade of existence" (T, pp. 453–54). He described how, until the Supreme Court's 1948 decision, F.H.A. had accepted and supported the use of racially restrictive covenants. The federal program of public housing, which began in 1937, was, he said, "a very strong factor in the development of racial residential patterns" (T, p. 457). Local option in tenant selection was the rule, which meant that in most instances (at least until after 1954) tenant assignment followed racial lines.

Later, Robert Tucker testified in similar fashion. While acknowledging the influence of the total experience of black people, especially that of slavery, he singled out the role of government among the forces that "contribute to both the existence and continuation" of residential racial segregation: "the first force . . . is the entry of the U.S. government into the housing scene in the 1930's" (T, pp. 765–67).

Richard Marks, from the Detroit Commission on Community Relations, described the way in which local agencies of government implemented federal programs. In its early years the Detroit Housing Commission followed customary racial lines in both the siting and tenant selection processes (T, pp. 153–56, 171–97). Later, as Marks pointed out, the Detroit Common Council refused to approve sites for public housing that were in "other" neighborhoods. It was not until 1959 that some public housing projects became racially mixed. Although one such project was to have been integrated from its opening in 1952, it attracted only forty-four white tenants as compared with approximately two thousand blacks.

Much of the testimony from officials of local civil rights agencies dealt with the racial discrimination practiced by the real estate industry and emphasized the failure of government to restrain such operations. Real estate firms were cited both for organizing neighborhood associations to prevent or discourage black in-movement and for fomenting panic selling by whites to blacks (T, pp. 169–70, 536–39, 563–69, 572–84). Their newspaper advertisements designated certain properties as "Colored" (T, p. 547). Witnesses read into the court record the written policy statements of the Detroit Real Estate Board's Code of Ethics from the year 1926; it stressed the obligation of the realtor to avoid introducing "undesirable" or "unharmonious elements" into a neighborhood (T, pp. 643–59). (Judge Roth appeared uneasy at hearing testimony going back almost half a century and at one point asked whether the realtors were supposed to have known of the judicial rulings that were to come far in the future.) It was only in 1950 that F.H.A. began to refuse insurance for loans on property covered by restrictive covenants filed after that year (T, pp. 191–95, 452). Many such covenants remained, but after the Supreme Court ruling of 1948 their restrictions were unenforceable.

There was also much testimony concerning acts of intimidation and vandalism directed against black families who ventured into white areas; by implication, government, and especially, of course, the police, in their failure to protect black citizens, shared culpability with lawless whites (T, pp. 191–95).

An example of the way in which government was identified as responsible for residential segregation was Detroit's first downtown urban renewal project, Lafayette Park. William Price testified that the failure of the city to find adequate substitute housing for black families who had been living in the area was due to the absence of an "open occupancy policy" (T, p. 696). Most of them, he said (quite accurately), moved into adjacent (also black) neighborhoods.

The testimony here concerning the role of government in the creation of racial residential separation would suggest that a policy of laissez-faire in the housing market would have produced integrated, or at least less racially concentrated, neighborhoods. This is highly unlikely. Some areas in old Southern cities were more mixed than most Northern urban neighborhoods, but this was a holdover from the era of white supremacy. When blacks were excluded from all facilities used by whites, their residential proximity was of no consequence and might even be convenient.[3] In the North, black residential segregation was of very long standing, far antedating government-assisted housing or the use of restrictive covenants strengthened by judicial enforcement. As Leon Litwack puts it:

The vigorous exclusion of Negroes from white residential neighborhoods made escape from the ghetto virtually impossible. . . . As early as 1793 the attempt to locate "a Negro hut" in Salem, Massachusetts, prompted a white minister to protest that such buildings depreciated property, drove out decent residents and generally injured the welfare of the neighborhood. Some years later, New Haven petitioners complained that movement of Negroes into previously white neighborhoods deteriorated real estate values from 20 to 50 percent. . . . the Negro had to be contained in his own area. . . . By 1847 the residents of South Boston could boast that "not a single colored family lived among them."[4]

Karl and Alma Taeuber make a similar point:

The most consistent finding in these historical investigations for various cities is a sharp increase in residential segregation between 1910 and 1930 in every city, both Northern and Southern, for which we have data. For most of the Northern cities this was their first period of large scale in-migration . . . and . . . the initial development of large racially homogeneous areas of Negro residence. . . . We are not claiming that residential segregation originated during this period. . . . we would argue that Negroes in cities have always been residentially segregated to some extent. . . . from the Civil War to World War II there was probably a general tendency for residential segregation to increase with the growth of the Negro population.[5]

Government did not enter the housing market until long after these patterns had been established. The F.H.A. program so stressed by the expert witnesses began in 1935 (public housing did not begin until 1937), but in Detroit, for example, the 1940 segregation index was almost 90![6] The V.A. program began, of course, after World War II. Home ownership accounted for little of the pre-1940 housing expenditures of Detroit's small black population, and it is inconceivable that barely five years of F.H.A. programs or three years of public housing programs could have had any perceptible effect on the patterns reflected in the 1940 index. In fact, although expert witness Marks had declared that until 1920 Detroit blacks lived "all over the city," the segregated residential patterns of black Detroiters had been established in the previous century: "Detroit's near east side absorbed the city's increase in black population in the late nineteenth century. Throughout the period the . . . census recorded no less than 85 per cent of all blacks in Detroit living within this area. . . . [they] were even more concentrated than ward statistics would indicate."[7]

It is clear, then, that racial residential separation existed long before government intervention in the housing market began during the New Deal. It also appears that racial residential clustering similar to our own has occurred in England in recent years, a country with no history of government support to maintain the racial character of neighborhoods.[8] What our patterns of residence would have been if the federal government had vigorously supported a nondiscriminatory policy can only be a matter of conjecture. If the advocates of these programs had insisted upon such a requirement during the New Deal, the legislation could not have been enacted. A favored strategy used by opponents of public housing at the time, for example, was to attach an open-occupancy requirement to the enabling legislation. The absence of such a regulation in legislation which was passed reflected majority public sentiment, and it is clear that even organizations devoted to Negro equality gave much higher priority to housing assistance than to integration. Would there have been more racial mixture in residence if these programs of housing assistance had not been enacted? What of the long-term effects on the movement for racial equality of programs that enhanced black economic capacity within the traditional framework of the dual housing market? I know of no way to make such calculations. A study of race and housing in a midwestern city shows that there was virtually no black homeownership before F.H.A. was created, and that that program (or, later, V.A. financing) freed blacks from the severe economic liability of the land contract.[9]

The expert witnesses characterized government policy after 1955 as one of failure to give adequate support to the concept of open occupancy. There would have been much more residential mixture, they declared, if prohibitions against discrimination had been vigorously enforced. But they offered no evidence to support this assertion. In their evaluation of the F.H.A. and the V.A. programs, Eunice and George Grier conclude:

discrimination per se was only a small factor in the impact of federal policies and practices. . . . The beneficiaries of these programs were "modal families" able and willing to commit themselves to home ownership with a mortgage. . . . a certain minimum of present earning and good prospects for future income were paramount, as well as some evidence of faithful repayment of past obligations. Households which did not fit these criteria—smaller families, older couples, single persons, people with low or precarious earnings, families who sought dwellings for rent rather than for sale, even families dependent upon the wife's employment for an adequate income—all were required to satisfy their needs chiefly through the older housing left vacant by people moving to new homes in the suburbs. Prominent among those left behind, of course, were Negroes.[10]

Although studies done in the 1950s reported that mixed occupancy in public housing was having a helpful effect on racial attitudes,[11] most public housing projects occupied by young families became heavily black during the decades that followed. In large cities the pool of applicants was largely black, and the public housing alternative was often rejected by many white (as well as black) households who did qualify. The Jeffries project in Detroit, for example, had been "integrated" by Wayne State University students in the early 1960s, but crime and violence brought about rapid white attrition.

During the past several years there have been numerous attempts to promote racial dispersion in residence by vigorous affirmative programs. Some have been conducted by citizens' fair housing groups seeking to attract prospective white homebuyers to racially mixed areas or to entice black homebuyers to traditionally white neighborhoods. Most of these attempts have had scant success.[12] An elaborate program to encourage blacks to seek assisted housing in predominantly white neighborhoods in the San Francisco Bay Area comes closest to being a test of the validity of charges that if government would offer both financial subsidies and skillful placement services, many blacks would prefer such areas. In 1973 a program, conducted by the National Committee against Discrimination in Housing as a pilot or demonstration project, was financed by H.U.D. Based on a carefully designed, rather elaborate program of research and data collection, education, publicity and staff training, it sought black tenants for rental units within 102 projects in the Bay Area. Eight professionally trained staff members (two full-time, six part-time) worked on the pilot project for seven months. Despite these efforts only twenty-one families chose such areas, and only fourteen of these families were black.[13]

During the trial William Price claimed to show that desperately poor black families without any housing subsidies whatever—without (during the period he described) even a moving allowance—could have been "placed" in white areas if the Detroit Housing Commission had only made vigorous attempts to implement open occupancy. There is virtually no evidence to support such testimony. Those displaced would not have been living in the worst slums in Detroit if they could have afforded something better. Studies of the relocation of such families reveal them desperately searching for a place to live with incomes no larger than they had before urban renewal began.[14] The searcher for housing under such harsh conditions gives very little consideration, if any, to finding a racially mixed neighborhood. The contention that government intervention produced a pattern of resettlement any different from that routinely produced by forced moves ordered by private landlords or for any number of other reasons was without foundation.

The great emphasis the plaintiffs placed upon government as a causal factor in the development of racial separation in residence was not the result of a review of research on the matter but was offered to support their legal rationale for a finding of school segregation de jure. To attribute residential patterns to government action is very much a lawyers' argument; it provides a justification for the demand that government now undo what "it" has done and lends plausibility to the belief that this is possible. Instead of a conjunctural phenomenon involving the acts of millions of households over many years, patterns of residence were viewed here as the outcome of discriminatory acts by government. The implication is that what one policy has done, an opposite policy should and can undo. Although there were references to the present failure of fair housing legislation to achieve racial dispersion, this was explained as a failure to provide adequate support and commitment to the task. The facts that a standard of random distribution was inappropriate and that law was relatively ineffective in altering residential concentrations created in such large part by white avoidance were not considered. By identifying government as the prime offender in the creation or intensification of racial concentration, a government-imposed remedy of student dispersion was legitimated, prospects for the stability of such a remedy were inflated beyond any reasonable expectation, and the illusion was created that this dispersion, once established, could thereafter exist without permanent racial quotas. Vigorous government action can indeed protect the right to open occupancy, that is, access to housing on a non-discriminatory basis. But substantial racial separation in housing can exist without any racial discrimination, with or without state action. If some of the groups involved have even a moderate preference for living in neighborhoods where they are a majority, concentrations will develop.[15]

CHAPTER 2
Own-Group Preference of Blacks

In 1970 Karl Taeuber wrote: "there is much room for disagreement as to how much residential segregation would occur in the absence of economic or discriminatory restrictions on Negro housing choice. Whether that segregation would be greater or less than that of Catholics or Jews from Protestants, or of various prosperous ethnic groups from one another, is unknown."[1] But during the Detroit trial he stated: "I believe the choice argument is easily exaggerated, in part because of too easy an analogy of what is believed to have happened to some of our nationality groups in the past" (T, p. 358). He went on to say, "I don't think the choice factor is very relevant" (T, p. 363).

Perhaps Taeuber was pushed into an advocacy role by the adversary nature of the courtroom proceedings. There was little offered during the trial to suggest that since its impact is unknown, the factor of choice might be an important influence. Nor was there any reference to the problem of establishing a clear distinction between voluntary and involuntary residential behavior. In his book of six years earlier, *Negroes in Cities*, Taeuber, the principal expert witness on this topic, said that "it seems impossible to separate coercive and voluntary components of residential segregation,"[2] but neither he nor anyone else made this point during the trial. I have raised the issue thus:

How do you maintain, with sufficient clarity to use it in law, an analytic distinction between voluntary ["unrestricted choice"] and involuntary residential decision? If a Negro, Jew, or Mexican-American rarely attempts to buy or rent in a certain area where he could afford to do so, is this because no others of his group live there? Or because he has heard of others who were

34

refused? Or because he dreads exposing his family to a cold or hostile reception? If this presumption is correct (how to know this in advance?) has this decision been "involuntary"? What if his calculation was, in fact, inaccurate? If one is unwilling to take the risk, even if statistically slight, of provoking hostility, is this a "voluntary" choice?[3]

Although the defendants offered no housing testimony, some of their attorneys did crossexamine the experts presented by the plaintiffs. In one such instance Assistant Attorney General Eugene Krasicky disputed Richard Marks' assumption that if a census tract had under 5 percent black occupancy, this figure showed that it was "difficult or impossible" for blacks to find housing there. Pressed on this point, Marks conceded that he could recall only one complaint from the area in question, and added: "I can only conclude that [a hostile reaction] was or would have been typical of the reception of any black family in this area." (This and quotations that follow are from T, pp. 159–73.) Krasicky pressed further (T, p. 162):

Q: When was that complaint received?

Marks: That was about five years ago.

Q: Have you had any complaints since that time?

Marks: There have been no further move-ins that have involved violence that I know of.

Q: No, no. Have you had any complaints?

Marks: I can't testify to any further complaints that our office has had in that area.

Another counsel pursued this same line of questioning, asking Marks to define the term "containment," which he used so frequently (T, pp. 163–71):

Marks: . . . when a pattern, not just of individual refusals but a pattern that exists throughout a total area, we call that containment.

Q: . . . Let me see if I have you right. . . . The policy of containment goes into effect where we have the case of a black purchaser willing, ready and able to purchase a house of his choice but unable to find a [seller] willing to sell to him . . . ? . . . Let's refer to the map of 1960. . . . how many blacks were in the position of being being able to buy homes . . . anywhere in the city . . . ?

Marks: I don't believe I can give you a specific figure. But blacks in Detroit led the nation . . . in the increases in home ownership. . . . [*Later*] I do not have that data [on sales to blacks between 1950 and 1960] immediately available.

Q: . . . getting back to . . . the word containment . . . how many blacks . . . in that decade attempted to buy a home in any of the areas of the city which we might characterize as white, but were refused the opportunity?

Marks: That statistic would not be available to me either. . . .

Q: . . . would it not be correct to assume that many . . . who bought homes . . . chose to live in [a] particular area?

Marks: I am sure that some people choose to live precisely where they feel they can buy a house. . . . This period . . . was one in which many black people . . . believed that there was in fact open opportunity . . . it was only the evidences . . . at the outskirts of those movements, of violence, that convinced . . . some of the black people in our city that there was literally containment . . . that made almost impossible the movement of black people into any area other than that which was viewed as eligible for black residents. Some areas were designated . . . black.

Q: . . . you have made . . . a categorical statement regarding a state of mind of large numbers of people in the city. . . . how do you know this to be true? . . . you tell me you don't know how many blacks bought homes . . . from 1950 to 1960, and you do not know how many were refused a home in one of the so-called white neighborhoods, nor do you know the number who bought homes in black neighborhoods as a matter of choice. . . . You say there were incidents of violence when blacks purchased a home or attempted [this] in a white neighborhood. . . . How many incidents occurred in that decade?

Marks: I do not have the records in my office available at this point.

Q: And you do not have records of those cases where blacks bought into white neighborhoods and there were no incidents?

Marks: . . . Most of the housing exchanges which did occur, occurred in that fashion. . . . in most of those incidents there was no crossing of a psychological line, it was simply filling in a pattern . . . already . . . established. . . . The theory on which our office was operating was that it represented simply a decision to expand the areas of black occupancy by people . . . involved in the real estate business. . . . But any time that a black family sought to move beyond that newly defined psychological and brick line . . . there was violence. . . .

Q: . . . would you say that . . . in every instance that a black was the first . . . to move into a white neighborhood that an incident occurred?

Marks: No. . . . Very often they were met by persons of goodwill. . . .

Q: Would you have any way to . . . generalize about this . . . whether the latter . . . was as typical as the former . . . ?

Marks replied that he could not, and instead offered, as a "very gross generalization," statistics on the Detroit vote on a homeowner's ordinance, "Showing that a good one-third of whites . . . are fully prepared to accord black citizens a welcome" (T, p. 172).

It should be noted that evidence for the existence of a "psychological line" is completely circular; the manifestation of violence is taken to be proof of the line's existence. The concept, however, seemed to impress the judge, who asked whether "studies have been made of . . . the communities which build the psychological line." The witness said he knew of none (T, p. 172–73).

The theme of Marks' testimony was that fear of violence (or the existence of a real estate conspiracy) was the explanation for the failure of those blacks who could afford to buy homes in white areas to do so. This explanation is persuasive up to a point, but leaves many questions unanswered. For example, during cross-examination Marks conceded that many census tracts which he characterized as all-white had in fact some resident black families (T, p. 160). Tracts with less than 5 percent black occupancy were classified as white in the exhibit he used. How can this scattering of a few black families throughout Detroit—and the fact that they were not joined by others—be reconciled with the fear-of-violence thesis? Clearly, episodes of violence or other manifestations of hostility have important effects, and fear of experiencing such dangers is an understandable basis for avoidance—whether it be black avoidance of white neighborhoods for fear of racially motivated attack or rebuff, or white avoidance of black neighborhoods for fear of crimes of violence. Such fears are not groundless or unimportant. But certainly the fact of racial concentration is too complex to be explained adequately by this single factor.

While acknowledging that blacks' apprehensions about their reception in all-white neighborhoods act as a deterrent, Taeuber emphasized discrimination and exclusion, overt and covert, as the major obstacles to greater residential dispersion:

Q [from Intervenor-Counsel Alexander Ritchie]: . . . what is the problem of the black lawyer [or judge] finding . . . houses in the suburbs . . . ?

Taeuber: . . . there has been a traditional pattern . . . restrictive covenants . . . notations on multiple listing services . . . indicating blacks are not wanted. . . . [M]any black would-be purchasers have encountered many kinds of resistance, either not being shown homes that they know are on the market, having a difficult time securing financing, . . . and other mechanisms of this sort that are detailed in the McEntire volume and other works.

Q: You do not think that the fact that they do not live in these particular suburbs is because of preference on their part?

Taeuber: Preference . . . may be a factor. . . . But that preference is . . . influenced by the degree to which they know that other blacks have encountered difficulties . . . have had their children taunted or encountered other . . . experiences that make it . . . unhappy . . . for them. . . . I am unwilling to speak of choice as if it's a perfectly free choice in a society in the way in which neighborhood choices tend to be a free choice for the white person.

Q: In other words, it's quite possible that they would be able to purchase a home in one of these areas without any difficulty, but they are restricted from doing so because the experiences they and their families would have after they moved in would make residency in that . . . area undesirable.

Taeuber: It's possibly a contributing factor in many cases, yes.

Q: And it will be the most contributing, might it not, in this day and age?

Taeuber: I tend to doubt it.

Q: I would offer this to you: where the money is available there is no reason today that you cannot move freely around and get financing and buy a house. . . . If a person wants to buy a house in the suburbs or anywhere else, he can buy it. But . . . he is restrained by the fact that he knows that his subsequent living in that dwelling will be very unpleasant. Is that not a fact?

Taeuber: . . . I cannot say . . . that's a fact. It's an opinion with which I would disagree. I simply don't believe that that is the major reason these days, or that blacks . . . despite the legislation [and] the social climate you mentioned, have a completely free choice of homes that would be shown to them . . . that would be made available to them, where every effort will be made on the part of the sellers to make it as comfortable to purchase . . . as it would be for the prospective white purchaser.

Soon thereafter the judge intervened (T, pp. 386–91):

Q: Am I to understand . . . that you do not consider as a . . . noticeable factor the alleged reluctance of some people to embark upon a move which might subject them and members of their families to discomfort?

Taeuber: Yes, I consider it a real factor. The question I thought I was trying to answer . . . was [if] it was the most important factor in the current housing market. . . . There are . . . various kinds of subtle mechanisms. One of the . . . deterrents is simply the notion that there will be trouble, or you may not be able to easily finish your housing search if you have to resort to various kinds of legal mechanisms in order to exercise your rights. This puts a great burden on the individual. [*Later*] . . . not only that he may subject his family to the ill-will of living in a white neighborhood where people will be . . . uncordial, but . . . also that the search itself may subject him to various kinds of demeaning responses on the part of the whites . . . and he may prefer to avoid that also.

This appraisal was supported by later testimony from several black real estate brokers, who recounted their experiences of humiliation and rebuff when they tried to get listings or inspect property in white areas. Defense and intervenor-counsel joined in expressions of disgust: "a shameful record"; "a tale of horror . . . of degradation and dehumanization" (T, pp. 605–7).

Black Residential Preferences

Taeuber supported his assessment of black choice as "not very relevant" by citing opinion data: "on a national basis, polls by the Louis Harris organization in 1963 and 1966, after some of the Black Power rhetoric had become quite common, . . . showed 64% and 68% respectively of the black population sample saying they prefer integrated neighborhoods and only one-fifth or less saying they preferred to live in black neighborhoods" (T, p. 326). The Brink-Harris poll question offered respondents a choice between a "neighborhood with whites and Negroes" (proportions unspecified) or an "all-Negro neighborhood."[4] Even so, if the "Not Sure" category is evenly allocated between these two positions, the proportion favoring an all-black areas approaches 30 percent, a figure which, if reflected in residential behavior, would make a considerable contribution to segregation, defined as concentration. But of greater significance is Brink and Harris' explanatory remark that nearly half of the 64 percent who favored the first alternative said that "it is not so much their wish to live near whites as having the right to do so." They add: "Negroes were specifically asked to choose which was more important to them—equal treatment or 'a lot of mixing of the races.' By a margin of better than 8 to 1 they chose equal treatment."[5] This qualification was not mentioned in the courtroom testimony. The constant confusion between the commitment to equal rights and associational preferences and behavior was a feature of this entire trial, as will be seen in the discussion of white attitudes and residential behavior.

Taeuber's presentation of the Brink-Harris data is an example of the way in which social science materials were often utilized during the trial. If, in a scientific paper, there had been a discussion of the bases for black housing choices which gave some attention to opinion data, the author would have made some reference to contrary evidence. There is a considerable amount available. For example, Gary Marx found little sentiment in favor of a neighborhood that was "mostly white," a condition that would prevail nationwide if one adopted the standard of Taeuber and others; i.e., a segregation index of 0 would exist if each area were composed of blacks and whites in the same ratio as that of the total population.[6] Even if one uses the metropolitan area as a basis rather than the nation as a whole, a random distribution would yield "mostly white" neighborhoods. Entrance into new areas means entrance into areas which are mostly white. The following table provides a sharp contrast to the presentation of the Harris material by Taeuber.

Residential Preference, by Region

Type of neighborhood preferred, if all are equally well kept up
(in percentages)

	Metro.	N.Y.	Chicago	Atlanta	Birmingham	Total
Mostly Negro	55	52	68	74	69	62
Mixed, or no difference	38	35	25	18	27	31
Mostly white	4	9	5	5	1	4
Don't know	3	3	4	2	3	3

Source: Marx (1967), p. 176.

Part of the divergence in these opinion studies may be the result of the wording of the questions. The Marx material avoids the use of the ambiguous term "integration," which has two sharply contrasting meanings: the absence of racial exclusion (as in a reference to James Meredith's having "integrated" the University of Mississippi) and the existence of varying degrees of racial mixture. The Marx study, further, has the merit of attempting to separate the wish for decent housing from the concern with mixture; the Harris question does not do this. Yet it is well known that both black and white assessments of predominantly black neighborhoods are affected by the social-class characteristics of such areas. Just as questions put to whites on the subject of race mix are generally prefaced with: "If a Negro family with about the same income and education as you have were to move into your neighborhood," so a question searching for the degree of interest by blacks in race mixture must attempt to screen out other concerns.

There are other poll data which might have been brought out by opposing experts (had there been any) or revealed in the course of crossexamination. In 1967, a National Opinion Research Center survey of Negroes living in the north and west of the United States indicated that almost two-thirds preferred to live in neighborhoods that were mostly or totally black, regardless of whether or not they currently lived in integrated neighborhoods.[7] A study of racial attitudes in fifteen cities in 1968 by Angus Campbell and Howard Schuman showed only 1 percent of the black respondents wanting to live in "mostly white" neighborhoods; 48 percent reported that they preferred neighborhoods in which the racial mix was about fifty-fifty; 37 percent said that the racial composition of the neighborhood made no difference to them.[8] Schuman and Hatchett found similar preferences in the Detroit Area Study; fewer than 1 percent of the black respondents wanted to live in a "mostly white" area.[9]

Albert I. Hermalin and Reynolds Farley have suggested that whites who express support for integrated housing may be defining an integrated neighborhood as less than 20 percent black, while blacks who speak of their preference for integrated areas may be thinking of an area 30 to 40 percent black, or "mixed half and half," as the data for 1971 are reported by the Duncans and Schuman for Detroit.[10] This interpretation would be consistent with the poll data cited, which show black rejection of mostly white areas.

These data give little support to any expectation of random dispersion even under conditions of completely open access. If blacks continue to show virtually no preference for mostly white areas, and whites tend to reject areas which are not predominantly white, prospects for stable residential mixtures seem dim. But these verbal expressions of preference cannot be equated with actual residential choices, which are subject to many other influences.

Studies of Black Residential Behavior

The willingness expressed by whites in opinion polls and attitude studies to live in racially mixed areas is often viewed with suspicion and cynicism. A generally increasing willingness to accept black neighbors and a considerable expression of tolerance or unconcern at the prospect, as shown in these studies,[11] are not reflected in a comparable decline in racially concentrated housing. Actions, it is claimed, speak louder than words. These actions may have various meanings attached to them, as will be seen later. However, if we accept for the moment the warning about verbal expressions of support for housing mixture, the warning has to be attached to the verbal expressions of both races. If we must look at white behavior (instead of opinions), we must also look at black behavior. It was this perspective which was recommended in Taeuber's testimony: "blacks who lead the invasion . . . to white areas . . . tend to be wealthier and better educated. . . . I interpret this as indicating that those who can afford to do so among the black population try and escape the worst housing and seek better housing. One of the things they seek is housing that is less segregated, so this is an expression in their behavior of their choice" (T, p. 362).

The fact that blacks who move into all-white areas are more prosperous and of higher status does not prove that most prosperous blacks share this priority. Nathan Kantrowitz interprets the departure of prosperous blacks from existing black areas as caused by their wish to remove themselves from contact with the poor of their own race, rather than a wish to be near whites.[12] Anthony Downs has described the task of convincing Negro families that it is desirable to live in an area where they are in a minority as a "significant problem."[13] Gans asserts that "even if blacks had freedom of choice, not many would now choose predominantly white areas"[14] and found in his study of Levittown that there were more listings of willing white sellers than black buyers.[15]

Research that casts further doubt on Taeuber's assessment, and which might well have been cited, includes a study of residential behavior of middle-income blacks in the Boston area who were displaced by urban renewal:

Unlike most families in the [Washington Park] community those we studied have the economic means to move into the suburbs and the more prosperous parts of Boston. . . . We began the study in the belief that Roxbury's Negroes would rush to embrace any opportunity to escape from their relatively segregated and declining neighborhood. Integration is in the air and the longed-for appears at last to have become the possible. . . . One of the issues we considered was the availability of housing outside of Washington Park to middle-income Negro families. . . . We can conclude firmly . . . that while there is not completely free choice, there is considerable housing for sale without discrimination in and around Boston. . . . To our minds everything pointed to an exodus from the ghetto to the . . . white parts of Boston.[16]

The authors go on to recount their surprise at their findings on the relocation of those who had chosen to leave the area:

we were so surprised at the low proportion of families who had moved to a less segregated area that we wondered if we had allowed sufficient time to elapse. . . . Therefore . . . sixteen months from the time that we began to study these middle-income Negro families we again ascertained where they resided. . . . Less than four percent had chosen to live among families in predominantly white communities. Less than five percent of the families in a ten month period actually inspected a dwelling outside of Roxbury. . . . it is quite clear that if this group of families continues to integrate to such a limited extent the possibility of more residential heterogeneity in the Boston area is most limited, in spite of the considerable efforts of many civic organizations to develop racially mixed communities. . . . It must be borne in mind that *non-discrimination is not the same thing as integration*. Often . . . the two are confused.[17]

Another study which raises questions about the extent to which self-segregation can be minimized as a factor in the residential behavior of blacks was conducted in St. Paul. All households displaced by expressway construction, whether black or white, were traced. About 90 percent of the displaced white families relocated outside of the predominantly black area where they had been living, while only 15 percent of the black households relocated outside of this black area. However, in contrast to the testimony offered during the Detroit trial by William Price, who attributed the relocation pattern of displaced black families to discrimination (T, pp. 696–98), interviews revealed that the majority of these displaced blacks had not tried to find replacement housing outside of the surrounding black area. As F. James Davis reports it, "Most of the reasons given for not trying were in terms of satisfaction with the area, attachment to friends and family, desire to stay close to work or other facilities and lesser costs." Only 7 percent reported experiencing overt or covert actions in their search for alternate housing which were, or could be, suspected to be discriminatory.[18]

Fair housing committees have had some success in enticing prosperous black families into white areas, but the usual report is of more oportunities than customers, despite substantial efforts. Since comparable high-quality dwellings can usually be bought for less in a racially mixed urban area than in a white suburban area, there would have to be a very strong interest in the latter to overcome this disadvantage. As secure, middle-class, predominantly black neighborhoods become more common, these housing opportunities may even tend to weaken the tendency of high-income black households to seek homes elsewhere.[19]

Bradburn, Sudman, and Gockel report a large number of residential areas in various parts of the country where blacks are present and constitute 5 percent or less of the households. Many of these neighborhoods do not, they report, increase in black proportion.[20] Yet the ice has been broken, and the risks associated with being the "first family" no longer exist. One can therefore consider it a reasonable hypothesis that the proportion of black families seeking such an area is not large. A comparable house in a mostly black neighborhood usually costs less, is easier to find, and avoids even the possibility of an unfriendly social climate.

Blacks as a Distinctive Subculture, Social Network, or Both?

We have quoted Taeuber's warning against the too easy analogy between the residential behavior of blacks and that of other nationality groups in the past. However, some believe that such comparisons are instructive. The U.S. Advisory Commission on Civil Disorders stated: "The experience of other ethnic groups indicates that some Negro households would be scattered in largely white residential areas. Others—probably a larger number—would voluntarily cluster together in largely Negro neighborhoods. The Integration Choice would thus produce both integration and segregation. But the segregation would be voluntary."[21] And Philip Hauser writes: "It is clear that internal social and economic pressures would prompt Negroes to . . . live in enclaves for some time to come even if there were no barriers to their movement. . . . The descendants of 19th century immigrants, German, Irish and Scandinavian, not to mention 20th century immigrants and their offspring, still live in voluntary enclaves."[22] Chester Rapkin and W. Grigsby also make this point: "The tendency to move to areas in which Negroes are already in residence is due in part to the desire to obtain satisfactory housing without the risk of rebuff and in part to a positive desire to live in an area in which there is an appreciable number of other Negroes. This phenomenon has been observed among other ethnic groups such as Jews and Italians who attach considerable value to the comfort and ease of communication with people of like culture and heritage."[23]

The argument over the extent to which black Americans are one of a number of minority groups, generally subject to the same influences and processes of social change, or to which they represent a unique sociocultural phenomenon within American society has a long history. The currents of intellectual thought, as well as political argument, sometimes run strongly in the direction of similarity-continuity, sometimes more strongly in the "blacks are a special case" direction. The more strongly one leans toward the perspective of some kind of Negro uniqueness, the more legitimation there is for programs which single him out for differential treatment or assistance, whether in schools, housing, or employment.[24]

The most explicit reference to black uniqueness during the housing testimony in the Detroit case came when housing expert witness Robert Tucker offered the following response to a question on the causes of residential segregation (T, pp. 766–77):

The causes of racial segregation . . . are multi-faceted . . . but . . . the essential cause is the only life that we as black and white people . . . have known. . . . The cause is related to the origin of the problem . . . the original system of chattel slavery which we have never overcome. The . . . state of black people . . . derived principally from that experience and has been different. The development educationally, socially and culturally has been different and I would have to add the fact of . . . blackness itself, rendering black people highly visible, is a very crucial cause.

Whether Tucker agreed with the earlier traditional civil rights position that black Americans were set apart only by racial prejudice and, unlike other minorities, had no distinctive subculture, was not revealed. His reference to a "different cultural development" hints at some disagreement, but we cannot even be sure what he, a lawyer by profession, meant by the term "cultural." He seemed to be saying that the black experience was completely different from that of other groups, a position once challenged by Thurgood Marshall arguing for the NAACP in *Brown,* before the Supreme Court:

> The only way this Court can decide this case in opposition to our position is that there must be some reason which gives the state the right to make a classification that they can make in regard to nobody else, in regard to Negroes. . . . the only way to arrive at this decision is to find that for some reason Negroes are inferior to all other human beings.
>
> Nobody will stand in this Court and urge that . . . in order to arrive at the decision they want us to arrive at there would have to be some . . . reason why, of all the multitudinous groups of people in this country, you have to single out Negroes and give them this separate treatment. It can't be because of slavery in the past, because there are very few groups in this country that haven't had slavery some place back in the history of their group. It can't be color, because there are Negroes as white as the drifted snow, with blue eyes, and they are just as segregated as the colored man.[25]

During the Detroit trial Karl Taeuber put forth the traditional position of American sociology, once widely shared and still held by many respected scholars: blacks are virtually indistinguishable in all important respects (save physical appearance) from whites of similar social class and region. Any behavioral differences that might exist, in this view, are responses to victimization and could be expected to disappear when that victimizing ceases. The designation of blacks as an ethnic group was not customary in the earlier sociological literature.[26] By contrast, white ethnics of European origin, Orientals, and Spanish-Americans clearly maintained, in varying degrees, a foreign cultural heritage, although the more common sociological judgment was that this was a transitory phenomenon which would soon vanish through dispersion and social mobility.

It was not until the 1960s that the perspective of blacks as a racial, rather than an ethnic, group was challenged with any success. Milton Gordon has clarified the concept of assimilation by distinguishing between its cultural and structural components. Groups may become more similar to the host society in their culture while retaining a strong sense of belonging to the group and maintaining a structure of social relationships with other group members.[27] Lester Singer called attention to the process of ethnogenesis, the social construction of ethnicity; black Americans, having shared a distinctive set of historical experiences and circumstances, were generating an ethnic identity.[28]

The potential significance for the trial of this seemingly theoretical controversy did not entirely escape the court. The issue arose in the course of Taeuber's presentation of the segregation index he had computed for the residential distribution of Poles in Detroit. Intervenor-counsel, Ritchie, put the question:

Q: There would . . . be . . . a great difference between a study of European ethnic groups and an Afro-American ethnic group, would there not, by virtue of the fact that the European groups had brought a culture to this country which after one generation would become somewhat meaningless because it no longer has any roots in the country of its origin . . . ? On the other hand (with Afro-Americans) you would have a group who actually has created its own culture right here and would still be . . . creating a culture. . . . Would that not be a difference . . . between . . . the two groups?

Taeuber: I don't follow that distinction. . . . [T]he Afro-American group has been in the country for . . . several hundred years and any distinctive culture that they may have is of the character that may differentiate people of a different region or may differentiate farmers from people who live in the cities or something of that sort, whereas the Polish example would be people who do have ties to a group with a distinctive culture that is outside the United States and not enmeshed in our particular American tradition.

Q: Do I infer from your answer that when we speak of an Afro-American ethnic group . . . we are not really talking about a true culture group . . . as a Polish ethnic group is a culture group . . . ?

The court then entered the discussion:

Roth: . . . is it your position, Professor, that there is no such thing as an Afro-American culture?

Taeuber: I would like to give a straight answer but I find it very hard to know what different people include in the concept of culture. There may be many blacks who, if you do a statistical study, have preferences in food, music or styles of speech or matters of that sort, and would come out with a different average than that of some other group.

Judge Roth persisted:

The reason I ask that, without getting into the semantic problem as to what you might mean by culture, and what Mr. Ritchie and I might mean . . . I got the impression that most black people think there is such a thing. . . . Now, as a sociologist, I was interested in what you had to say about it.

Taeuber: This is a curious development, I think, in recent years. There has been a feeling among the prominent black civil rights agencies of trying to push the notion that blacks were basically Americans in terms of basic aspirations and life-styles. They prefer and value monogamy, freedom of the individual to develop his own career . . . . There is this extent to which blacks in our society in many cases, and more so now than they would have, say ten years ago, before it became part of the . . . intellectual climate, that they in some ways feel easier among other blacks, feel free from a certain threat, but I don't believe in terms of fundamentals of what defines a culture, fundamentals of life style, aside from some of these peripheral [items], whether you want a coffee break, or what you want to eat, or what kind of entertainment, I don't believe there is a distinctive black culture in the United States. (T, pp. 393–96)

This assessment was offered on the third day of the trial. No further testimony on the subject emerged until an expert witness on education, James Guthrie, many weeks later, made a passing reference to the recent growth of black consciousness, which he felt had resulted in some "differences in blacks and whites at all levels up and down the SES continuum . . . some things associated with being black" (T, p. 4160). He said no more on this matter. Near the close of the trial there was a brief presentation which conflicted with Taeuber's views. Statements concerning the existence of a distinctive "black perspective" came in the course of Lawrence Doss' defense of community control (discussed in Chapter 11 below). The black leader criticized a curriculum based on the imposition of "white middle-class culture on the black inner-city kid": "as a consequence of American history . . . we have different cultures . . . today . . . we must deal with these cultural differences" (T, pp. 4418–20).

Doss, however, was unable to make an adequate exposition of the "blacks as an ethnic group" perspective. While the influence of intragroup association on black residential behavior was virtually ignored, the subject of ethnic differences in behavior received only scant mention, and Karl Taeuber, the most prestigious of the expert witnesses, had discounted its existence. This resulted in an incomplete view of residential behavior, particularly with reference to white responses to these differences, and was to become a handicap in considering the educational testimony as well.

There is a considerable literature that could have been cited to support the sparse and rather uncertain assertions that a distinctive black ethnicity might have been generated by shared historical background and contemporary experience. Some of these writings are based on survey data: "Our analysis of Negro and white responses to thirty-two questions from ten national opinion surveys leads us to conclude that there are important Negro-white differences in attitudes that cannot be explained by differences in educational level or regional distribution. [The items covered a wide range of topics, from child-rearing to the role of the United Nations.] . . . we believe our findings support the view that there is a unique Negro subculture in the United States. Furthermore, our finding that several of the Negro-white differences were greater at the younger ages suggests that the Negro subculture is persisting."[29] Others are based on direct behavioral observation: "Taken together, all of these conditions [the reference is to a complex of social and economic circumstances] produce a distinctive style of life. Whether it is a unique culture shared by Negroes alone, or an amalgam of Americanisms seems beside the point. All cultures are an amalgamation of elements stolen, borrowed or inherited from diverse sources."[30]

Although the quotation above is taken from a study of a slum area where the existence of distinctive subcultures of Negroes, Italians, Mexicans, and Puerto Ricans is clearly documented, evidence of some discernible life-style differences is also forthcoming from studies of middle-income areas:

In South Shore not only do authentic social and demographic differences exist between the white and black populations, but there are also more subtle differences in virtually all black-white confrontations. A few examples may be cited. Whites and blacks in South Shore sound different; among whites, speech varies with length of residence in Chicago, family status background and ethnicity. Blacks have an analogous internal pattern of speech differentiation—in addition to a common touch of Southern Negro dialect, not quite absent even among many middle-class Chicago-born blacks. Young blacks walk differently from young whites; many, boys especially, use a swagger which sets them apart from their white schoolmates. Without carrying out a complete inventory of black and white habits and folkways, we know these differences exist and that, whether they speak of them or not, both blacks and whites in South Shore are sensitive to them.[31]

No one at the trial spoke of these differences, and none of those who testified utilized the distinction set forth by Gordon between cultural distinctiveness and in-group association. This would have been helpful in showing the court how it comes about that a group— e.g., middle-class blacks—can be quite similar to other groups at similar occupational and educational levels in much, though not all, of its behavior, yet can maintain a high degree of interpersonal relations with own-group members. The latter characteristic could be expected to influence residential choice significantly.

The discussion of whether black Americans constitute a group comparable in some ways to white ethnic groups was couched by Taeuber and those who questioned him only in terms of the extent of their cultural distinctiveness, but the sorting, grouping, clustering, and dispersion processes involved in residential behavior involve chains of social relationships. Studies of migration streams reveal the ways in which ties of kinship and friendship direct the movements of people into particular locations within a region. The huge piling-up of blacks from the South in certain Northern cities (a condition which Myrdal, for example, saw as so undesirable) could not possibly be explained solely by reference to exclusion.[32] It is but one expression of the operation of the network of social relations which links persons and households, a network of social relations which makes up human society.[33] To speak of a random distribution within it is a sociological absurdity, yet this (the segregation index) has become the standard by which the degree of housing discrimination is often measured.

As with white ethnics, the mechanism which results in clustering need not involve a conscious decision to seek a dwelling near others of one's own group. The fact that a disproportionate number of one's friends and virtually all of one's relatives are fellow ethnics is an important element in developing a cognitive map of "places to live." Molotch observes that there is less black demand for areas which are distant from existing black areas because "black demand . . . increases with propinquity: blacks can locate in such areas without losing contact with existing black institutions and old friends, and in a more general way proximity presents intervening opportunities which inhibit a search for housing in white areas further distant."[34]

During the trial no mention was made of Jewish residential distribution in the Detroit area. Jews have become both prosperous and culturally assimilated, yet Jewish residential patterns in the Detroit metropolitan area, as in many other places, are noticeably concentrated. This pattern, however rooted historically, now appears to be voluntary; it thus suggests a comparison to the future distribution of black Americans. It is worth noting, too, that the strong support given by most Jews to the principle of open occupancy is quite unrelated to their actual distribution in metropolitan space. Right of access is a necessary but far from sufficient condition to create dispersion in residence, and belief in civil rights seems relatively unrelated to contact-interaction. This last distinction is one that was never made during the trial.

The clustering tendencies of groups other than blacks are relevant in still another way which went unnoticed. If other groups manifest strong own-group preferences in residence, this process alone will produce some degree of spatial isolation of blacks. This subject is considered in the next chapter.

CHAPTER 3
Residential Behavior of White Ethnic Groups

The only reference to white ethnic groups in *Bradley v. Milliken* was to their ties as being "of the past." This is followed by the sentence: "The ghetto is at once both a place of confinement and a refuge. There is enough blame for everyone to share."[1] It is not clear whether the reference to the ghetto is to the present black concentrations or is intended to encompass the white ethnic enclaves of the past as well. In any case, the description uses language which casts such clustering in negative terms: "confinement," "refuge," and "blame." Both the sparseness of the reference and its tone reflect the perspective of the expert witnesses.

Virtually all of the testimony on residential segregation (like that on education) was based on comparisons between blacks and whites. The use of the category "white" as a group parallel to "black" for the purpose of comparison both reflects and perpetuates the lack of sensitivity to the fact that "white" is a composite residual category, made up of all those persons who are not black. Yet it is obvious that in no sense is almost 85 percent of our population an ethnic group (as are blacks), and we cannot hope to understand residential behavior in these gross terms. The perspective offered at the trial, which ignored this diversity, remains more common in contemporary social science than mine. But some exposure to a contrasting orientation to residential decisions (and, later, to educational achievement) might have moderated the oversimplified, moralistic explanation of an immensely complex set of motives, wishes, pressures, constraints, and concerns that underlie the residential choices of millions of individual households.

It is not necessary to elevate clustering tendencies among white ethnic groups to the status of an ideology in order to recognize the contribution of this factor to residential patterns. The concept of structural pluralism is used here as description, not as prescription or philosophy.[2] Social relations are shaped by social class variables. Economic resources limit housing choices. Occupation, education, and life style influence housing and neighborhood tastes and preferences. The stage of the life cycle affects family needs for space and facilities. And for many, ethnic background guides residential location through interpersonal networks of kinship and friendship. Word-of-mouth knowledge about specific neighborhoods, vacant flats and apartments for rent, and houses for sale is passed on in this way. Persons in metropolitan areas have a mental map; their geography is generated in the course of interpersonal contacts in which ethnic background has been shown to play an important part. These cognitive maps have large gaps; much of metropolitan space is unknown territory. The most important steering is done not by brokers, but through interpersonal contact prior to contact with realtors whose advice generally strengthens preexisting inclinations.[3]

Material on ethnicity as a factor in housing choice would have contributed to Judge Roth's understanding of residential patterns. First, some amount of black residential concentration is the consequence of the own-group clustering of white ethnics, which operates whether or not there are blacks in the community. A ruling by Judge Roth had the effect of excluding consideration of this factor (T, pp. 208–10). When counsel for an intervenor-party challenged the expertise of a housing witness from Detroit's Commission on Community Relations, contending that he lacked knowledge of the cultural patterns of Detroit's ethnic groups, plaintiffs' counsel responded that such knowledge was unnecessary; the witness was being presented as "an expert in the causes of residential segregation . . . not the sociological character of various groups." The questioner persisted. His rationale for consideration of such materials was expressed in everyday speech, but the viewpoint is in keeping with much current sociologial research: "As I see the causes of racial segregation, I don't look upon that as being only a limited aspect of the question of prejudice as it relates to the claims of this party plaintiff and I would like to know what exactly Mr. Bush's background is in . . . the cause of discrimination as it relates to the white population . . . of . . . Detroit" (T, pp. 209–10). Judge Roth intervened at this point to say that the witness was "not being presented as a sociologist [but] only . . . to reveal the causes of the pattern [of segregation] which was established," and overruled the objection.

By so ruling, the court made a social science determination through the use of judicial authority. It stated, in effect, that sociological analysis is not involved in the discovery of the causes of segregated housing patterns, and, further, that the residential behavior of white ethnics is not relevant to an understanding of the causes of the pattern of racial segregation. The first of these claims is absurd, and is perhaps a matter of unfortunate phraseology. But the declaration that the topic is irrelevant is the more significant example of the resolution of social science controversies by judicial fiat. There is ample evidence to suggest that own-group preferences of white ethnics contribute to the spatial isolation of blacks. Even in the absense of other factors, if Polish-Americans, Jewish-Americans, Italian-Americans, and others exhibit any degree of own-group clustering, this will tend to leave others—blacks or other groups of whites—more concentrated residentially than would otherwise have been the case. There was no mention of this consequence of white-ethnic clustering at any point during these proceedings.

Better evidence on white ethnics' housing behavior might have contributed to a different orientation on the part of the court. We have noted that the text of Judge Roth's decision reveals an assimilationist ideology which assumes that all ethnic enclaves are, at best, unfortunate. Nationality concentrations, however, were seen as fast disappearing, whereas racial segregation was seen as getting worse. There was scarcely a hint from any source during either the trial or the remedy hearings to challenge the notion that there is a qualitative difference in white ethnic residential patterns, as compared with those of blacks, or to question the general assumption that blacks were an altogether unique group within American society, requiring, therefore, unique treatment by law and social policy.[4]

There were three segments of testimony on the residential behavior of white ethnic groups. The first came on the day the trial began and occurred as a result of questions interjected by Judge Roth during crossexamination of the expert witness Richard Marks (T, pp. 174–77):

Court: Historically, wasn't much of your pocketing of population nationally and ethnically based?

Marks [using the map]: . . . For years this section right in here, ethnic . . . Eastern Europe, it replaced itself. It had great holding power, there was very little movement at the edges, but increasingly the pressure of population . . . does involve the transfer of properties to black families at the edges of these ethnic pockets.

Court: I have one other question along that same line. . . . some of the pattern of housing in the more distant past, not 1940, but well before that time, so far as . . . Detroit is concerned, was an outgrowth of the pockets of immigrants that came here and settled and they did it for their own protection because they didn't know the language, for one thing, nor the customs nor the ways, and wasn't it natural for them to collect in a group so they might better conduct their business and social intercourse?

Marks: True.

Court: But passing from those ethnic groups, are there pockets of . . . people who have . . . followed a segregated pattern in other parts of the country and who have come here?

Marks: I'm afraid I don't know. . . . Give me an example.

Court: Let's put it bluntly. Are there big pockets of people, historically or at present, who have come up from the South?

Marks [not understanding this, for some reason, as a reference to blacks]: No . . . all of the groups that you have mentioned . . . Poles, Italians, Germans, all of the ethnic groups have been, as you described, first to hit a city and to have a primary area of occupancy but as that population group moves over time, say ten years, and people get involved in the life of the community, get jobs . . . and their families grow they have the need to move on. They want to have a bigger house or need a little more room or want a newer house. This is part of the American ethic. . . . All of the groups . . . including the Southern white, . . . he has an initial point of entry, and then . . . as soon as those roots are down, he is established as part of the community and he begins to move. He moves where his job and his emerging status takes him, which has been to housing elsewhere. . . . We watched persons of Italian, German, Jewish, Russian and other extractions . . . move to secondary concentrations . . . and watched the Negro make the effort to cross the line, only to be . . . held in as a contained population.

No further questions on this subject were asked of this witness by either the court or the defense attorneys. Yet this testimony could well have been challenged or modified by existing evidence well known to social scientists. Some examples follow.

1. Concentrated pockets of ethnic settlement in Detroit are not, as

Judge Roth put it, of "the more distant past," well before 1940, but were very marked indeed thirty years ago and persist in varying degrees today.

2. Cultural assimilation (learning the new language, the customs and ways) is only one aspect of the assimilation process. This process is uneven, varying for different groups because of a large number of variables, involving both the ethnics' own cultural heritage and the responses of the host society to them, the period at which the person arrived in this country, and so on. In any case, cultural assimilation apparently proceeds more rapidly than does structural assimilation, a parallel process which has to do with social relations and thus is closely related to where people live.[5]

3. The social networks in migration, as far as we know, are heavily influenced by pre-existing ties of friendship and kinship and would indeed affect the residential behavior of people coming up from the South.

4. There is no evidence of which I am aware to suggest that the usual, average, or typical time period of new ethnic groups to remain in the "clustering stage" is, as Marks has it, ten years.[6] The assertion that an individual member of an ethnic group, after about ten years, "moves to where his job and emerging status takes him" is soon contradicted in Marks' own testimony by the statement that "those people move to secondary concentrations." Which is the accurate description? Movement to secondary concentrations is also characteristic of blacks and has little impact on segregation unless accompanied by dispersion.

Studies that would have been enlightening to the court, in considering the issues raised by Marks' testimony, include the work of Stanley Lieberson, showing that departure from original areas of white ethnic settlement does not necessarily mean an end to ethnic clustering: while ethnic segregation in both city and suburbs "appears to be declining," says Lieberson. "If there is something distinctive about suburban living for these ethnic groups it is not found in terms of sharp deviations from the propensities of their central-city compatriots to segregate residentially. . . . suburbs appear to approximate ethnic patterns in the central city."[7]

Rosenthal has documented the persisting residential concentration of American Jews as they move outward to suburban areas.[8] These new clusters represent, for the most part, Jews of the second or third generation. In a study of Detroit Jews, 70 percent reported they were living in neighborhoods characterized as half or mostly Jewish, and other research reveals Jewish residential concentration almost as intense as that of blacks.[9] What was once partly involuntary may become largely voluntary. Dennis Clark reported the persistence of ethnicity among various groups in what he termed the "echo ghettos of the suburbs."[10] Michael Parenti, summarizing some of this literature, concluded that "geographical dispersion, like occupational and class mobility, has been greatly over-estimated. Movement from the first settlement actually may represent a transplanting of the ethnic community to suburbia."[11] (The same erroneous assumption—that suburbanization and integration were synonomous—was often made in the past with regard to blacks. Now that there are more suburban areas occupied by blacks, the error is less common.) A study of this process in New Haven found that "as the years have passed the immigrants and their descendants have moved in varying numbers into the middle class. This economic mobility did not result in equivalent geographic dispersion, in part . . . because of the continuing comforts of ethnic proximity. . . . ethnic differences . . . continue to be a major organizing principle in the city's social structure."[12]

Studies of the Detroit metropolitan area conducted under the sponsorship of the Wayne State University Center for Urban Studies report that

until recently, much of the scholarly and popular literature suggested that ethnic communities are quickly disappearing from the urban landscape as the perceived homogenization process proceeds. . . . there are many ethnic concentrations throughout the metropolitan area, some recent in origin and other that have persisted for a long period of time. . . . immigrant groups are still forming in the central city, and to a lesser degree in suburban areas as new groups arrive in Detroit. . . . At the same time, stable second and third generation ethnic communities such as those established by blacks, Poles and Italians remain in the city and older suburbs.

But ethnic concentrations involving Poles, Jews and other groups have also developed in the rapidly growing new suburbs. . . . Little is known . . . about the nature of the older second and third generation neighborhoods, or about the new suburban concentrations. . . . Many of these communities have been subjected to processes that have resulted in the movement of ethnic populations away from old neighborhoods and the development of new communities elsewhere.[13]

Herbert Gans, in his foreword to Neil Sandberg's study of Polish-Americans in the Los Angeles area,[14] expresses a position perhaps most typical of the dominant view in American sociology at present:

Acculturation is concerned with the giving up of the ethnic culture in favor of mainstream American culture. It has proceeded at such a rapid pace that the majority of ethnics have already adopted American ways of life by the second generation. . . . Assimilation, which refers to social and other relationships with people of non-ethnic background, has also proceeded, but far more slowly and many ethnics still socialize with and marry people of the same national origin, and live in urban neighborhoods and suburban subdivisions in which a plurality of the residents are from the same ethnic group.[15]

Gans sees no force at work against the long-term trend toward structural assimilation, but this does not mean that such assimilation has already taken place, nor is it clear when it will occur.

The reader is reminded that none of the above researchers was seeking to minimize the greater degree of black residential concentration, nor to discount the role of discrimination in accounting for its severity. Some of these studies did not even compare clustering tendencies of various groups, a topic to which we now turn.

Although another housing expert, Robert Tucker, when asked about black self-segregation at the Detroit trial, stated that it was "only a minimal factor," he added that it would "certainly not be to a greater degree than would determine the housing choice of other groups" (T, pp. 349–50). For some groups, as has been noted, self-segregation is a strong influence, but Tucker said nothing more on the subject.

The only detailed reference to white ethnics' residential patterns at the trial was offered by Karl Taeuber, who compared them with those of blacks:

Segregation indexes . . . have been calculated for . . . ethnic groups of European origin. . . . we can compare residential patterns of one nationality group with . . . another or with all native whites. . . . this has been done for a large number of such comparisons and the segregation indexes, depending on the . . . groups involved tend to be ten, twenty or very rarely about thirty, compared to these indexes of seventy, eighty, or ninety for the black versus white comparison . . . [In] 1910 there was not that great difference . . . but the nationality segregation measures diminished very rapidly. (T, pp. 349–50)

Later in the trial, Taeuber compared blacks and white ethnics in more detail. He had prepared material on Polish residential distribution, in response to the issue raised during the cross-examination of Richard Marks. But before he could offer it, the counsel for the Detroit School Board, George Bushnell, objected on grounds of "relevancy and materiality. . . . I just can't understand what the Poles have to do with this litigation" (T, p. 374). It would be difficult to find a better example of the advantage enjoyed by the plaintiffs in this lawsuit. The NAACP team was well aware of the possibilities inherent in the comparison of black residential patterns with those of other groups. Not only was such testimony relevant (and the court so ruled), but it also had the potential (never exploited) of arousing some doubts about the accuracy of the picture of American society being drawn in the courtroom.

The objection to his testimony overruled, Taeuber went on. He calculated the Polish segregation index in Detroit to be 52 (T, p. 376), as compared with that of 75 for Negroes (T, p. 351), adding that the figure of 52 was probably too high, since only the first two generations of Poles in this country were classified as Polish (T, 376). He did not guess at what the black segregation index might be if residential distributions were compared only between those blacks who had been born—or were the children of those born—in the North, although some scholars have suggested that the old South may be considered a different social world.[16] When asked whether he had been able to discover any ethnic group which retained an ethnic community into the second or third generation, he replied, "not to a degree more extensive than that found for the Polish group here" (T, 393). In view of what is generally regarded as the high residential concentration among American Jews, the failure to mention them as a possible example is surprising. Although Taeuber noted that black segregation created as a byproduct some degree of Polish segregation (T, pp. 376–77), he did not add that the reverse, as noted above, is also true, i.e., that own-group clustering of white ethnics is part of the process by which black concentration comes about.

Outstanding recent research on the residential distribution of white ethnics has been done by Nathan Kantrowitz. He astonished both social scientists and the public in 1969 with his findings that in northeastern and midwestern cities interethnic segregation remains high well into the present, changing little between 1930 and 1950. Moreover, in the New York metropolitan area, which, his data indicate, resembles the pattern found in some other cities, 1960 data reflected a continued high interethnic segregation.[17] In his study, Kantrowitz showed that an old, well-accepted ethnic group, the Norwegians, had their lowest degree of segregation (45.4) from Swedes, and that their degree of segregation from Russian Jews, 70.7, approached the figure for segregation from Negroes, 87.7. He concluded:

If we assume that residential segregation numbers reflect the degree of cultural acceptance we think it is a fair speculation that Norwegian segregation from Negroes differs in degree but not in kind from their separation from Slavic Jews. . . . if Protestant Norwegians hesitate to integrate with Protestant Swedes, and Catholic Italians with Catholic Irish, then these groups are even less likely to accept Negroes as neighbors.[18]

Kantrowitz's work in this area was expanded and refined in a book published in 1973, in which he concluded that little decline in either interethnic or racial segregation can be expected in the foreseeable future.[19] There was no reference to his earlier work during the trial, although Taeuber was familiar with it.[20] The Harvard-M.I.T. Joint Center for Urban Studies recently found that 75 percent of all adults in Boston were living in the sector of the city in which they had lived as teenagers. A similar pattern was found in Houston, where "nearly three-fourths of those interviewed were living in the same sector as their neighborhood of previous residence. The next neighborhood to which they were thinking of moving was again in the same sector."[21] (When such residential movement involves blacks, it is called the extension of the ghetto.) As for Kansas City, "as members of each [ethnic group] . . . have prospered and deserted the city center, movements of individual group members . . . have been predictable according to where the lead-edge of the group's members have moved."[22]

In summary, in the Detroit trial the testimony on the absence of black subculture and the contention that segregation in housing is entirely caused by discrimination (with rather minor adjustments for economic ability), together with the scant testimony on white ethnics, reflected a view of blacks as a wholly unique, qualitatively different group within American society. There is evidence to support such an assessment, but there are also studies which show that a portion of the separation of blacks and whites results from the fact that within the "white" category are groups characterized by ethnic bonds. We know that groups may develop distinct patterns of residential clustering which persist long after exclusionary practices have ended. There is also an alternative perspective which was not presented: clustering need not be defined by the group in question, or by others, as an evil if it is not imposed by exclusion or by any other form of discrimination.

CHAPTER 4
Blacks' Socioeconomic Status and Residential Choice

The expert witnesses discounted the influence of blacks' socioeconomic status as a cause of residential segregation: in the words of the principal witness, Karl Taeuber, "the role of economic status is minimal" (T, pp. 359–60). Taeuber supported his assessment by comparing median rentals of black- and of white-occupied units, as well as the estimated value of owner-occupied dwellings. The comparison showed black expenditures on rent to be somewhat higher, although neither the size of the unit nor the size of the household was taken into account. Taeuber concluded that economic status accounted for perhaps one-fourth of the racial segregation in Detroit (T, p. 362). Not enough information was presented on economic comparisons of owner-occupied dwellings, by race, to allow an evaluation of this material, although in 1970 half of Detroit's black households were homeowners.

Taeuber is not alone in minimizing the role of economic ability[1] but, in contrast, many studies do attribute major importance to the limitations of black purchasing power, and these were not mentioned in the testimony. Among highly regarded authorities who stress the influence of this factor are George and Eunice Grier, who conclude that "economic incapacity is the central obstacle to desegregation."[2] Herbert Gans, attempting to determine why only small proportions of blacks in past years lived outside of central cities, emphasizes that "only a tiny proportion of ghetto residents can even afford to live in the suburbs."[3] Anthony Pascal, a housing economist, estimates that about half of racial separation in residence can be accounted for by socioeconomic factors.[4] Raymond Zelder, also an economist, calculates that between 30 percent and 50 percent of housing segregation is accounted for by demographic and economic differences.[5] Anthony Downs, in an analysis of black residential behavior, emphasizes that any substantial program to encourage black dispersion would require extensive financial subsidies.[6]

The comparison of housing expenditures Taeuber offered to support his thesis is not a very satisfactory measure of economic status, especially as it relates to home purchase. As another study put it: "Negroes are at an economic disadvantage because of their low assets as well as their low incomes. The extent of their disadvantage in assets is indicated by the fact that their average net worth is less than a fifth of that for the population as a whole. Young Negro families are likely to be unable to obtain gifts and loans from their parents to finance the down payment on a home as well as limited by their own resources."[7] Duran Bell's study of indebtedness shows current income and expenditures to be inadequate indicators of blacks' ability to sustain long-term economic commitments.[8] Donald Warren, comparing black and white households in Detroit at similar income levels, found differences in both family composition and occupational status that suggest a far more precarious middle-income status in the black group.[9] A study of neighborhood change in northwest Detroit showed that, despite the common belief that the first wave of black in-movers are prosperous professionals, almost 40 percent of the household heads in the new area had blue-collar jobs.[10] Taeuber, along with many others, has noted that the first black families to enter an area are usually more prosperous than those who come later, suggesting that economic ability is a necessary, though insufficient, prerequisite for residential dispersion. Therefore, the larger the pool of potential entrants, the greater the probability that some will move into previously all-white areas.

Current efforts by advocates of housing integration to curb zoning restrictions reflect their recognition that being priced out of the market is much more than a minimal factor in residential integration. A study of black families entering twenty-four suburban communities found that "although they clearly surpassed central-city blacks in income, education, job status and home ownership," they did not attain parity with their white suburban neighbors on a variety of indicators of socioeconomic status, including current income.[11] Such conclusions, if derived from the observations of white suburbanites, would probably be dismissed as "prejudice," yet they reflect a stubborn reality.

Neither the present nor the past economic status of Detroit's black households was adequately described during the trial. Richard Marks opened his testimony on the history of residential segregation in the city by offering this picture of the past: "in the black community there were people who were employed year-round at full-time jobs as teachers, as doctors, some lawyers, some business men. There was plenty of range of economic level in the black community, a range that made these individuals eligible to purchase housing anywhere. . . . The explanation of why Negroes live where they live fails us if we apply strictly an economic test" (T, p. 151). This last was a straw man. No ethnic group is distributed solely on the basis of economic ability, and discrimination in the sale and purchase of housing has been and remains a crucial factor in black residential location. But Marks' presentation was also distorted in another way. Housing patterns in Detroit were formed many years ago; this was the plaintiffs' rationale for entering into the record the 1926 policy statements of the Detroit Real Estate Board, extensive testimony on the prevalence of pre-1948 restrictive covenants, and other historical material. Karl Taeuber himself gave 1940 as the year by which patterns of racial residential segregation in Detroit had crystallized (T, p. 347). If one accepts this statement, the data on black income and occupational distribution as late as 1955 are instructive. According to a University of Michigan survey of that year, only about 4 percent of Detroit-area black (male) household heads were in white-collar occupations: professional, managerial, clerical, or business.[12] That this fact would not have a powerful effect on residential choices of both blacks and whites is inconceivable. Such a skewed distribution not only explains much of black residential behavior, but also suggests that the common white perception at the time that a black neighborhood is a poor neighborhood was generally accurate. Twenty years later there was considerable economic improvement, but there were still striking differences in the proportion of the very poor among the two groups. In a recent study of Chicago, Brigitte Erbe concludes: "Middle class blacks . . . live in much closer propinquity with the lower class than do middle class whites simply because the black lower class is larger than the white lower class. . . . It is . . . the presence of a much larger poor population in the black community than in the white community that accounts for the differences in the socio-economic composition of black and white neighborhoods at each socio-economic level."[13]

A neighborhood that changes in racial composition—i.e., becomes predominantly black—is likely to change in its socioeconomic character as well, and the knowledge that this is so is not confined to sociologists.

There are two ways in which black socioeconomic status affects residential segregation; directly, by limiting the housing options of blacks themselves, and indirectly, by influencing the housing choices of whites. The first of these effects got some consideration in the Detroit trial, chiefly by Karl Taeuber. The effect on housing choices of whites was completely ignored.

If one compares the testimony on housing with the testimony on education (and later, on desegregation plans), a fundamental inconsistency between these two bodies of evidence becomes apparent. During the presentations on housing and residential patterns, the social class distribution of blacks was taken to be of little consequence. During the testimony on education, it was to emerge, together with racial concentration, as the central explanation for the underachievement of black children. Later, during the remedy hearings, it became an essential part of the rationale for seeking a metropolitan remedy. The proportion of poor (black) children had to be kept low enough to ensure a helpful classroom climate for them and to inhibit white attrition. The further contention was that the correlation between being poor and being black was so high that race could serve as a proxy for poverty. (Thus the absence of precise data on the social class of students was viewed as no problem.) But if, as was so frequently said during the remedy hearings, the probability of being poor, if black, was so high that the experts fashioning a desegregation plan needed only to know race in calculating the proper socioeconomic mix, might not ordinary citizens proceed on the same assumption?

An assertion frequently heard during both the trial and the remedy hearings was that a substantial degree of racial integration could not be attained without social class mixture, given the socioeconomic characteristics of the black population: there simply were not enough middle-class blacks to go around. Yet the implications of this fact for past, present, and future residential movements were not considered—not even mentioned. If it were so crucial a factor in assuring an advantageous learning environment that the defendants' educational experts were willing to embrace a massive program of student transportation to achieve it, it clearly would be an important factor in the residential decisions of middle-class parents, black and white, who were knowledgeable about such matters.

· Just as we cannot tell with certainty where blacks would live if they were free from both overt and covert forms of discimination, so we are uncertain about white response to black residential propinquity in the absence of differences in socioeconomic status and life style. A number of social scientists have tried to distinguish between racial prejudice and calculations based on the assessment of real differences. In his study of the economics of housing discrimination, Anthony Pascal was compelled to confront this issue early on:

It is perhaps useful to examine in somewhat more detail what we mean by the word prejudice. Those phenomena which in the context of this study are assumed to explain the residual observed segregation after socio-economic differences have been taken into account might, in fact, be occasioned by those very differences. More clearly, prejudice, particularly in the residential context, might be a response to class differences. It might be the case, for example, that most families favor behavioral standards in their neighbors (in terms of decorum, pride in the home's appearance, child rearing practices, etc.) which are similar to their own standards. Then because information is costly, the household is probably behaving efficiently when it seeks a neighborhood in which the residents display socio-economic characteristics not widely different from its own. Thus the desire for neighborhood homogeneity might result in skin-color prejudice but might also simply reflect prejudice against different and particularly "lower-class" behavioral standards. . . .

Alternatively, consider a hypothesis which assumes more sophistication on the part of majority group respondents. The initial residents of a neighborhood can be expected to look some distance into the future. . . . Suppose then that the initial residents suspect that opening inflow of members of a minority group, even if the invaders are of a similar class to the original residents, signals the eventual arrival of households of the minority group but with different, "lower," class characteristics. In that case, a knowledge of the distribution of households by class within each minority group should affect the resistance that the initial residents feel towards the entrants coming from any particular group. Thus, members of groups in which the proportion of "lower" class households is high would anticipate more difficulty in entering a neighborhood currently segregated against them.[14]

Many who are insistent in pointing out the severity of persistent black poverty are unwilling to recognize that if this is so, avoidance by others may be a response to poverty rather than race. Although some social scientists have attempted to show that chronic poverty is not associated with behavioral or life style characteristics, differences of many kinds, including family composition and stability, consumer behavior, certain types of deviance—and educational achievement— undeniably exist as a result of both class and ethnic background.

In the text of Judge Roth's ruling the inclusion of references to crime and health problems in central-city neighborhoods[15] would suggest that such conditions were the subject of considerable oral testimony. This was not the case. They were drawn from an exhibit offered in the deposition of the departing school superintendent as an explanation of the poor academic achievement of the city's black students. That these data might have a powerful influence on the residential decisions of other people, white and black, was not mentioned by anyone. Indeed, Superintendent Drachler himself, after reporting, for example, that the homicide rate in a center-city area was twenty-five times as great as that in an outlying district, appeared to find nothing inconsistent in attributing white avoidance of black schools and neighborhoods to "ingrained attitudes" (T, pp. 131–36, 153).

Even a tiny proportion of readily identifiable persons whose behavior creates fear and concern causes others to avoid such areas, in the same way that instances of intimidation or harassment, even if statistically rare, inhibit black attempts to enter all-white neighborhoods. There are obvious implications for social policy here. While the strictest enforcement of anti-discrimination provisions is essential, efforts to achieve any substantial amount of racial mixture are unlikely to succeed in the face of gross inequality and associated differences in life style. As Herbert Gans puts it:

once the majority of nonwhite people are on the way to affluence, they will no longer be so threatening to their white fellow citizens. When they do not need to resort to the desperate acts that stem from poverty, color will no longer be a symbol of poverty, the stereotype of the slum dweller will disappear and so will many of the current objections to racial desegregation. Non-whites will be able to move to the suburbs . . . and opposition to a constructive city-suburb relationship will die down. I suggest that if unemployment and other causes of poverty can be eliminated, segregation will eventually begin to disappear by itself. This does not mean giving up the struggle for integration *but national strategy ought to emphasize the abolition of poverty in this generation so that the children of today's Negro poor will be able to move into the mainstream of American society economically, socially and politically. If these children can obtain decent jobs and incomes, so that being nonwhite is no longer viewed as being lower class much of the white support for segregation would begin to crumble. Once color is no longer an index of poverty and lower-class status it will cease to arouse white fears, so that open-housing laws can be enforced more easily and ultimately may even be unnecessary. Real integration could then be achieved, possibly even through voluntary means.[16]*

Not only was this a perspective wholly absent from any of the proceedings, but quite the opposite view was presented to the court, as though it were the consensus of expert opinion.

There is a considerable body of sociological work to show the strong and persistent preference for social class homogeneity in residence among households whose ethnic ties may be weak. There is little evidence that such inclinations or wishes were less widespread in the past, but the ability to implement them is greater now: "When people become more affluent and can choose where they want to live, they choose to live with people like themselves. . . . in the last generation or two . . . the opportunity . . . to live among compatible neighbors . . . previously available only to the rich, has been extended to people in the middle and lower-middle income brackets."[17] Anthony Downs contends that white concern for being the majority in residential situations stems from the wish to "be sure that the social, cultural and economic milieu and values of their own group dominate their . . . residential and . . . educational environment."[18] The testimony on residential segregation, in addition to minimizing the effects of even gross past and present black-white differences in income, never mentioned the associated characteristics to which Downs refers. In some kinds of behavior, such as family instability and juvenile crime involving violence, they are considerable, even at roughly comparable income levels. To omit consideration of such class and subcultural differences leaves a vacuum that tends to be filled by attributing white avoidance entirely to irrational prejudice. What portion of this avoidance is attributable to realistic evaluations and what portion to irrational fears or exaggerated estimates of the prevalence of disliked behavior is difficult or impossible to determine. But the possibility that there is any realistic basis whatever for avoidance was never acknowledged.

Preference for social class, life style, or even ethnic homogeneity has little to do with suport for open occupancy. "They have a right to live wherever they can afford to—and so do I" seems to be the message found in recent opinion surveys: attempts to exclude on account of race have lost legitimacy.[19] It is the double meaning of the terms "segregation" (concentration or exclusion) and "integration" (stable mixture or open access) that confuses the interpretation of these data and the general discussion of these issues. Opponents of civil rights try to use evidence that most blacks seem to lack interest in racial mixture per se as a justification for exclusionary practices. Integrationists try to use blacks' intense concern about the right to open occupancy as equivalent to the wish for racial mixture. Both are wrong, for these are quite different dimensions. One is a matter of the basic rights of citizenship; the other is a matter of associational preference.

Although there are a few rather expensive enclaves where prosperous households of both races live together, they have constituted up to now (in large cities) too small an area to fill even a single high school.[20] Unless they plan to use private schools, therefore, upper-income black and white families avoid or abandon such areas at this stage in the life cycle. With the exception of these enclaves, the typical racial residential process in metropolitan areas has been that of racial transition, the subject of the chapter that follows.

CHAPTER 5
Changing Neighborhoods

The Testimony

Most schools in Detroit which are now black were once entirely white; it follows that there were some years during which both school and neighborhood were racially mixed. Thousands of people in Detroit personally experienced these years of change, which I suspect is the chief reason why they are puzzled by the judicial finding that their schools were segregated de jure. The neighborhood changed, and schools, like other facilities serving the public—stores, parks, libraries, and post offices—reflected that change. The process of racial transition was the most immediate cause of a school system which was two-thirds black at the time of the Detroit trial. How does this change come about? And will neighborhoods continue to change after schools have been immersed in the "cleansing bath" of the desegregation remedy—defined as the elimination of racially identifiable schools, and achieved by making each school roughly similar to others in its racial proportions?

In view of the fundamental importance of these questions, one would have expected substantial testimony on this topic. Instead, what was offered was sparse and of poor quality. The chief witness on residential segregation, Karl Taeuber, whose testimony was far superior to the other social science evidence offered during the trial, described the expansion of black settlement. He cited the number of census tracts that had experienced racial transition over the years, but carefully noted that this was a "mechanical interpretation . . . not what caused it" (T, p. 366). His judgment that discrimination was the chief factor in housing segregation was, by inference, his explanation of racial transition, but this explanation was not explicitly offered. The closest he came to such a diagnosis was in response to a question by an intervenor-counsel, who, referring to Taeuber's statement that the movement of prosperous blacks into white areas shows their desire for integrated living (T, p. 373), asked why, if that were true, other blacks did not avoid already well-mixed areas in favor of greater dispersion. Taeuber's explanation was almost wholly in terms of discrimination, overt and covert. He gave valuable insight into the operation of subtle forms of constraint (T, 387-92), but he left much unexplained. In many areas with small percentages of black families, others have not followed. Something other than discrimination must account for this, but nothing further was said about the matter in the testimony.

Richard Marks viewed racial transition as the result of decisions of the real estate industry (T, p. 170), and the explanation offered by another civil rights agency staff member also suggested a deliberate plan: "When the areas in which black families have already been permitted to reside no longer supply enough houses for the housing demand in the black community, well, then, block by block, square mile by square mile, the periphery of the areas in which black people reside is expanded and the white families residing therein are induced to move and sell their homes to black families" (T, pp. 568–69). The assertion that neighborhoods change because real estate brokers have the power to induce people to sell their homes to blacks (not whites?) and leave was the only explanation offered.[1]

At one point during the testimony Judge Roth asked whether there is more segregation in Detroit now (1971) than there was in 1967. Both his question and the reply to it show the confusion caused by the inconsistent use of terms. Taeuber responded: "There are more black areas than there were. . . . the all-white areas remain all-white. There isn't a neighborhood in Detroit which has stabilized in terms of black and white proportions" (T, p. 743). The reference to the all-white areas of 1967 remaining all-white was simply inaccurate. The issue of stable mixed areas had been raised earlier, when Taeuber was asked: "In your knowledge and experience . . . do you know of any occasions where large numbers of whites and . . . blacks . . . live together in a completely desegregated area?" He replied: "No. The only comment I want to make is that that has to be observed over a period of time to differentiate a desegregated area from one of those peripheral areas that is in the process of [changing]" (T, p. 392, referring to a map). Here Taeuber seemed to be defining "desegregated" as permanently stabilized at some unstated racial proportion, while in the preceding quotations the distinction between open access and stability of mix seems to have been completely lost. In any case, he offered no reasons for the instability to which he refers.

While the experts on residential patterns generally ignored the topic of racial transition, the education experts referred to it frequently, usually as "white flight." Dr. Robert Green, the plaintiffs' chief witness on education, explained that white flight was caused by lack of contact with blacks and the racial prejudice developed as a consequence. Describing his trip from Lansing to Detroit for his court appearance, Green said (T, pp. 965–66):

From Southfield all the way down to 8 Mile we counted about three black faces. And I see the schools as being directly related to that. We did not educate the white adults who went to the Detroit public schools who are now living in Livonia. We did not educate young whites who were educated at Central. I can remember when Central was predominantly white. . . . I can remember when Eastern was about 60% white. . . . All the whites have fled.[2] Northwest Detroit has fled to Oak Park, Livonia, Bloomfield Hills. I see that flight as being significantly related to what we have not done in our public schools. . . . Livonia was sticks and stones when I was a kid. That suburban community was built because the Detroit public school system did not perform its function. It was built because we had all-white elementary schools, all-white junior high schools and all-white high schools.

But Green offered the same explanation for flight from racially-mixed schools and neighborhoods: "The whites ran, whites fled [northwest Detroit] . . . because of fear" (T, p. 966). He went on later to say that the flight occurred "because the schools have failed to play their proper role in socializing and humanizing young people to be fair and non-prejudiced in . . . how they view people of color" (T, p. 1025).

Another expert witness on education, Dr. Stuart Rankin, having characterized the suburbs as racist (T, p. 4228), later attributed this to lack of contact with blacks: "the most basic problem we are dealing with . . . is the problem of racism and poor race relations among people and the fact that the ghetto has been created . . . and maintained by the white community . . . the large portion of that white community resides in the suburbs. . . . therefore a plan which doesn't make any inroads on that, that does not provide a desegregated experience for the children in the surrounding [suburban] areas will . . . fail" (T, DR, p. 584). Yet he warned that if only the Detroit schools were desegregated, there would be rapid white flight, which seems inconsistent with the hypothesis that lack of contact with blacks was its cause (T, DR, p. 586). Indeed, he predicted that middle-class blacks might also leave the city.

During the lengthy remedy hearings there were constant references to the problem of racial stability. The tipping point concept was used as though it were a well-established explanation for neighborhood change. For example, defense expert Dr. James Guthrie defined the tipping point in this way: "It is asserted to be that percentage point after which when the number of blacks exceed that point, whites begin to leave. . . . I would be willing to place it in a band . . . somewhere between 35 and 50 or 55 percent black. When a school is more than that, then somewhere in that band whites become fearful for some rational and some irrational reasons and when [they] can [do so] they leave" (T, DR, p. 458). Although poor white families tended to be more intolerant than others, he explained, "high socio-economic families are the first ones to leave if there is a movement to desegregate" because they know that predominantly black schools will probably have their resources cut (T, DR, p. 463). They ask: "Where will the money come from to make it run now that we are being discriminated against?" (T, DR, pp. 463, 509).

In Guthrie's explanation of the residential movement that would be stimulated by changes in school racial composition there is no reference to concomitant changes in socioeconomic status and associated lower levels of academic proficiency. (He himself, during the trial, offered low SES as a key reason for substandard black achievement but appeared to think that parents would be blind to these changes.) In similar fashion, another expert witness on education related how, when racial transition in northwest Detroit produced a mostly black elementary school, test scores dropped one "or possibly two full grade levels within three years" (T, DR, pp. 568–70). But he seemed not to realize that the original residents would be at least as aware of this change as he (he was the assistant principal at the time of the transition) had been, and that other consequences of the drop in socioeconomic status would be manifest in the neighborhood as well as in the classroom. His characterization of the suburbs as the location of "racism" suggested a lack of understanding that if an area and its school changed as he had described, there were real reasons for parents to avoid or leave it if they could. Indeed, he even observed that in changing neighborhoods the cost of housing does not screen out social class changes, noting that "these same houses were being used but the . . . families . . . were generally of a lower economic status" (T, DR, pp. 568–70).

Rankin's passing reference (there was nothing more) to the relationship between racial transition in neighborhoods and concomitant changes in socioeconomic status associated with changed behavior patterns in and out of school was made during the remedy hearings. During the trial only the plaintiffs' experts offered testimony on residential segregation, and their purpose in so doing was to make a case for government action as a substantial cause of racial separation in housing. The causes of neighborhood change were virtually ignored, despite Judge Roth's concern with this topic from the very start of the proceedings. The reason for his concern was obvious, and he made no attempt to conceal it: a feasible desegregation remedy depended upon avoiding the seemingly inexorable process of racial transition, and the judge from the beginning was preoccupied with the question of whether a lasting remedy for segregation could be secured by judicial power. When Intervenor-Counsel Ritchie asked Martin Sloane whether, based on his experience in Washington, D.C., he thought that an attempt to desegregate a school system which was two-thirds black would result in Detroit schools becoming almost entirely black, Sloane seemed unwilling to reply. He said that he was not familiar with the Detroit situation and that "it's awfully hard, even if I worked here, to make predictions" (T, p. 508). There then followed a series of attempts by Judge Roth to get an answer:

Roth: . . . I'm interested in pursuing Mr. Ritchie's thought. . . . You and the [Civil Rights] Commission have made extensive studies on the impact of segregated housing on the school system and segregation there, or lack of integration, whichever way you want to . look at it. Now, based on your studies—when we talk about Detroit, we're talking about a typical metropolitan area, so that what might be true of Detroit would be true of many cities, perhaps including Washington. . . .

This is a suit alleging segregation in the Detroit school system. . . . Without knowing all the specifics of the Detroit situation, but taking it as a good example of a large city with a mixed population . . . 46 . . . percent black . . . what would happen to what are . . . now white areas? Would [it] . . . really lead to abandonment in large numbers by white folks so that when you ended up you'd have a city that was no more integrated than it was when you started? . . .

Sloane: . . . There is one school of thought that talks about a tipping point theory, both in terms of education and in terms of housing, as some magical percentage, say 35, 40 or 50 per cent black, suddenly the entire school, or school system or the entire area will turn completely black. This is a matter of conjecture and it's very difficult to say yes or no to it. And I believe you said . . . that the Detroit school system is 46% black.

Ritchie: No. That's the city population.

Sloane: The same principle has been discussed . . . with respect to residential population. Experience in Washington is perhaps instructive. The Washington metropolitan area has not changed more than one percentage point . . . in the last 70 years. It's always been roughly 75% white, 25% black. The distribution of the population by race . . . has changed very dramatically, to the point where northern Virginia suburbs have something like 6% black and 94% white. . . . Montgomery County has something like 4% black, 96% white, whereas 60, 70 years ago there was an even distribution. . . . Washington public schools are now in excess of 90% black and it's very difficult to talk about achieving school integration with that kind of a percentage. But . . . in terms of the metropolitan area . . . the problem becomes a good deal less difficult because then we're dealing with a school [and] residential population which is 75% white and 25% black. . . . In a situation like that you have to talk in terms of metropolitan-wide desegregation, residentially as well as in education. . . . it is . . . an exercise in futility to think in terms of integrating a school system which is already so predominantly black as to make racial integration an impossibility. . . .

Roth: . . . fortunately or unfortunately, this lawsuit is limited to the city . . . and we're not talking about the metropolitan area.

Sloane: I feel uneasy making a pronouncement or prediction about a city which I'm really not that familiar with.

I surmise that the reason for Sloane's reluctance was that the NAACP, on whose behalf he was appearing, consistently avoided any rejection in principle of a remedy confined to Detroit (see Chapter 17 below for further discussion of this point). Judge Roth persisted in attempting to get an answer to his question:

Roth: Well, but I'm suggesting to you that the problem would be no different, whether you're talking about Detroit or some other city. If you take just the essential elements of what . . . I stated as a hypothesis here, based on your experience and training, what is your opinion as to the effect of it and the outcome?

Sloane: . . . I had reports of experiences in other cities . . . not . . . as large as Detroit . . . like Berkeley . . . or Evanston . . . where the reports are that desegregation has been accomplished completely and successfully as measured by such factors as school attendance, achievement scores. . . .

Roth: I don't want to keep pressuring, but . . . suppose you and I were to meet ten years from now, could you give me an opinion . . . that you think would be valid as to an effect . . . ten years from now?

Judge Roth's earnest attempt to discover what this expert on racial patterns of residence believed would be the effect of making Detroit schools, in a district already two-thirds black, approximately uniform in racial composition is obvious. I believe this was a critical juncture in this case, although it was but the fourth day of the trial. He received an answer for which there is little substantiating evidence:

Sloane: In our experience with the Commission . . . one of the reasons why in some cities desegregation has not worked is that the people involved have felt that the only obligation is to bring the children together and that is that, whereas there is a good deal of preparation that has to be done, a good deal of work after the physical desegregation has been accomplished to make sure it works. So it would depend, I would hope that the city of Detroit . . . would be sufficiently enlightened so that [the people involved] would take the steps necessary to make sure that desegregation works and that it is quality education for children of all races. But that would depend on what was done following the act of simple desegregation.

Roth: Well, it's a phrase I've used before, maybe I can use it again and maybe it expresses your view. I take it, if I can paraphrase your answer, that you (can't) achieve integration of the schools in this city or any other simply "by the numbers."

Sloane: You can accomplish desegregation simply by the numbers. But just ticking off the numbers doesn't necessarily mean that it's going to work and that education is going to be as good as it should be for all children or that you can avoid problems. You've got to take the steps necessary to avoid the problems and to . . . improve the quality of education. That is, the act of physical desegregation is the first thing. It is an essential precondition to successful desegregation because without it you don't have desegregation at all. But it's only a first step. (T, pp. 508–15, passim)

Judge Roth's efforts to learn what a housing expert thought about the prospects for future racial transition were thus completely frustrated, although by the end of the colloquy he appears to have been diverted from realizing this. But in the course of efforts to get a response, the court was given some highly dubious information.

1. There is no evidence for a tipping point formulation which holds that after a certain percentage is reached an area or school system will suddenly become 100 percent black. (It was unfortunate that the hypothesis was put forth in such ludicrous terms.)

2. The statement was made that Evanston and Berkeley are successful both as to attendance and achievement. A layman would, I think, assume, from the context of the inquiry, that neighborhood racial change had been halted and black achievement substantially improved. There is little evidence of this, and the applicability of these two experiences to Detroit is very doubtful.

3. The overall racial proportions of the Washington metropolitan area have not changed, according to Sloane, but the races have redistributed themselves. The most plausible explanation for the shift— that after schools were desegregated most white households using public schools avoided the city in favor of heavily white suburbs—was not mentioned.[3]

4. Most misleading was Sloane's suggestion that a public school system already composed of two-thirds (mostly poor) black children could be "successful" if quality resources were provided after "the act of simple desegregation."[4] There is no evidence whatever to suggest that in a system where each school is about 65 percent black steady progression to all-black schools which arises from residential change would be halted by any kind of educational program. If Sloane meant that from an educational point of view there could be "success" whether or not white families remained in the city, it would have been instructive, and surprising, for an NAACP witness to say so plainly. But this would not have been responsive to the court's questions.

What the Court Should Have Heard

An adequate presentation of research findings on racial transition would have provided Judge Roth with a basis for questioning some of the unsupported generalizations that were offered repeatedly during the subsequent weeks of the trial and the remedy hearings the following year. Among them I shall mention six.

1. It has not been established that unusually high rates of outmovement ("white flight") are typical of racially mixed neighbor-

hoods. Many studies of turnover show average rates of residential mobility, but most families who leave are white, while most who enter are black. The contribution of real estate brokers to this process is very difficult to estimate. Fair housing committees have not been able to persuade many white buyers to enter such areas.[5]

2. Neither white avoidance nor departure have been associated with higher intensities of "prejudice"; that is, those who reject racist beliefs and support equal rights have not remained longer in most racially mixed areas, nor are they more likely to enter them, according to existing studies.[6]

3. There has been no empirical demonstration of the existence of a tipping point or band, that is, acceleration of white departure after a certain black proportion is reached.[7] In part, this is due to the fact that residential transition is the result of increased avoidance of the area rather than departure from it, in part to the fact that residential decisions are made on a basis of calculations about the future character of a given neighborhood, not its present composition. The question posed by Judge Roth, "What would the city be like in ten years?" is precisely the one which prospective residents consider as they attempt to project the future of a neighborhood in which they are contemplating a house purchase. Scholars are uncertain about the proximate future of racially mixed areas, but, unlike prospective purchasers, they are not required to make a large financial investment on the basis of their predictions. Home buyers are cautious and strive to minimize risks in making the largest investment most families ever make. They therefore try to avoid areas whose future is comparatively uncertain.

The rate of home sales is strongly affected by housing market conditions, both in the transition area and elsewhere in the region where alternative housing must be secured; the wish to leave (or avoid) an area is not the same as the ability to do so. The effect of various percentages of blacks on whites' residential choice is much affected by the social class composition, present and anticipated, of the black population. These variables have a different effect on renters and buyers, on those thinking of leaving a neighborhood and those thinking of entering it, and on those who use area facilities, including schools, and those who do not.[8]

4. Racial transition occurs in suburban neighborhoods much as it has in cities and can be expected to increase as the proportion of blacks in these areas grows. Racial attitudes in "suburbs" (they vary

greatly in their socioeconomic characteristics) are not unlike those in cities.[9] There is no basis for the expectation that a political boundary would generate (or be associated with) an attitudinal difference. The assumption that suburban growth in the metropolitan area came from people in flight from Detroit was never questioned during these proceedings, although there is evidence to show that between 1965 and 1970 only a minority came from the city.[10] Most arrivals came from other Detroit suburbs or other parts of the country.

5. There is little substantial evidence to show the effect of racial residential mixture upon social interaction or racial attitudes. Differences in social class and life style appear to be greater barriers to interaction than race.[11] It would be difficult to demonstrate that those who have lived in racially mixed areas have become more tolerant as a consequence.[12] Physical proximity and social distance often coexist, so that the spatial distribution in a mixed area may tell us nothing about sociological reality. The effect on lower-status households of contact with those of higher status is as uncertain in the neighborhood as it is in the classroom. The best estimate seems to be that if objective status differences are small and the wish to acquire the behavior of upper-status groups is strong, the latter are helpful models. The assumption that the attitudes of whites would be improved by their children's contact with predominantly poor blacks and that this change in parental attitude would then promote stable mixed neighborhoods is entirely unsupported either by empirical data or any body of theory on intergroup relations (see Chapter 10 for a discussion of the effects of such contact). This article of faith was never challenged throughout the trial proceedings by any expert witness.

6. Racially mixed areas have been more likely to experience changes in social class composition than white areas of comparable housing stock because the supply of securely middle-class blacks has been so small (as we have noted in the earlier discussion of black economic status).[13]

Empirical research on residential choice and behavior in areas of racial transition is not as substantial as one might expect, given the importance of the issue. Available materials indicate that housing decisions involve complex cost-benefit calculations and that the socioeconomic characteristics of an area, as well as some clustering tendencies by both blacks and white ethnics, are paramount.[14] Interviews with whites leaving racially changing areas reveal fear of street crime and delinquency involving violence, objections to the larger proportion of children who are not doing well in school or who misbehave there, and the conviction that, based on their previous experience and observation, the mixed area will become predominantly black and will probably become more lower class as well. Middle- and upper-class blacks (the latter are a tiny group) express similar concerns and are found to have left their previous neighborhoods for much the same reasons.[15] Their cost-benefit calculations are somewhat different, in that (as we have noted) about half-black is a favored proportion; their risk or cost calculations accord a negative value to an all-white area (with more expensive housing), which is distant from friends or relatives and where they expect to feel unwelcome or worse.

Later in the trial, education experts repeatedly stressed that social class mixture as well as racial mixture was not only educationally desirable but inevitable if schools were to be a rough reflection of the area's population proportions. In order to create racially mixed classrooms some white students would have to be reassigned elsewhere and replaced by black children whose average social class status was considerably lower. Racial mixture thus entailed social class mixture. If this were true for schools, it would be true (although to a somewhat lesser degree) for all but the most costly neighborhoods when they became mixed. But none of the testimony on residential segregation reflected this fact, and the finding that racial mixture was most likely to endure when both races were of middle-class (or higher) status was never made clear to Judge Roth.

Legal advantage led the plaintiffs to focus their testimony on discrimination in housing and former government complicity in the denial of open access in the sale and rental of homes. Such evidence was abundant, and a compelling case was made to support the contention that these restrictions, now mainly covert, inhibit the residential movements of black families. But why do some white households leave, and why do so many refrain from entering neighborhoods that have become racially mixed, thereby maintaining the typical pattern of racial transition? Since no party in the case calculated that testimony analyzing this process was vital to its legal position, no such testimony was offered. Thus it came about that the most obvious explanation for the absence of stable racially mixed schools in Detroit got no consideration, although an understanding of the issues involved had such clear implications for the probable success of any desegregation remedy.

PART II: EDUCATIONAL ISSUES

Overview

Like the testimony on residential segregation, the educational testimony was marked by distortions and omissions. The impact of both bodies of evidence on Judge Roth was, I think, profound and greatly influenced his eventual finding of de jure segregation and the metropolitan remedy that followed.

The testimony on residential segregation had aroused the judge's sense of injustice and, by stressing the role of government, rationalized the use of judicial power to undo the effects of past state action. Now the testimony on education converted him from his pre-trial belief that involuntary reassignment for integration was a misguided policy and persuaded him that racially mixed classrooms were essential for educational success.

Although there were no references to educational issues in Judge Roth's ruling, testimony on these topics during the trial had been extensive. Unlike the presentation on residential segregation, which was offered only by the plaintiffs, both sides offered expert witnesses on education. Dr. Robert Green, an educational psychologist from Michigan State University, Paul Smith, from the School of Education at Harvard University, and Dr. Gordon Foster, from the School of Education of the University of Miami, were the principal NAACP experts. (Foster dealt mainly with specific acts of segregation but frequently also discussed the educational consequences of such practices.) In addition to a number of local people who testified on specific events and policies, the defense presented as chief experts Dr. James Guthrie, of the University of California at Berkeley School of Education, Dr. Stephen Lawton, of the Ontario Institute for Study in Education, and Dr. Stuart Rankin, associate superintendent for research in the Detroit public school system.

81

On most educational issues, plaintiffs and defendants were not adversaries, and on the crucial matter of the educational necessity for racial mixture they were in complete agreement. Virtually no negative evidence on this subject was presented during the trial. I think that this unanimity of expert opinion was the factor that caused Judge Roth to alter his pre-trial opposition to involuntary school integration. The defendants' expert witness testimony was consistent with the Detroit School Board's ideological commitment to integration and its hope that the Detroit case would make "new law," i.e., an eventual ruling that school racial concentration regardless of cause was a constitutional violation because it deprived children of equal educational opportunity. But the experience of the past ten years, when the public school population of Detroit increased from one-half to two-thirds black, had convinced them that city-only busing would be a disaster. Defense witnesses therefore allied their advocacy of racial dispersion with insistence on the need for a middle-class majority in the classroom, which, they stressed, was attainable only through suburban participation in the remedy.

Taken as a whole, the message of the testimony on education was that school resources could not be equalized, learning could not be effective, background disadvantage could not be overcome in the absence of racial (plaintiffs' emphasis) or race-class (defendants' emphasis) mixture in the classroom. Mandatory reassignment to create such a mixture would improve the academic achievement of blacks, would not harm (and probably would help) whites, would stimulate black aspirations, enhance black self-esteem, heighten teachers' expectations, and improve interracial relations in both schools and society.

CHAPTER 6
Social Background and Academic Achievement

The relationship between individual social background and academic achievement is by now well known, although there are important controversies and unanswered questions about the precise nature of the causal links involved. Whatever their nature, there is no doubt of their existence. Nancy St. John, in her synthesis of research on the subject, states the generally accepted view: "Regardless of the relative contributions to academic aptitude of genes, of home environment, or of the interaction of these two, their joint effect on school progress is powerful. The Coleman Report documented dramatically the already well-established relation between socioeconomic status and achievement."[1] There are no research data of substance to challenge this conclusion, which is supported by findings from other modern societies.[2] School entry level data on children in the United States (and elsewhere), as well as comparisons of academic achievement between children of varying social background within the same school, confirm the predominance of what the child brings over anything the school gives, including association with other children.[3] (This does not mean that the impact of the student's socioeconomic status might not be much modified in the future by special strategies of educational intervention.)

Unfortunately, this basic social science knowledge was not adequately conveyed to the court during *Milliken*. Although defense experts frequently asserted the existence of the relationship, they failed to consistently stress its strength or its implications. The plaintiffs' expert on education first denied the influence of social background on school performance and then retreated in confusion and obfuscation.

83

At some points the very existence of group differences in achievement was denied; at others, differences (reluctantly conceded to exist) were declared to be the outcome of school factors such as resource discrimination, teachers' expectations, and racial homogeneity.

Plaintiffs' Testimony

The NAACP position on the question of the impact of student socioeconomic status on academic success has generally been cautious, for two important reasons. First, the Constitution forbids discrimination on the basis of race but offers little protection against the consequences of economic inequality. Second, emphasis on the overwhelming impact of the individual child's social background would suggest that all school factors may be of comparatively minor importance in accounting for present achievement differences. In line with this general orientation—i.e., minimizing the role of social background factors—the plaintiffs' expert witness on education, Dr. Robert Green, offered some of the most surprising testimony given during these proceedings. The excerpts that follow are taken from his direct examination by NAACP counsel Louis Lucas (T, pp. 873–76):

Lucas: . . . do you have an opinion as to the entry level of black children and white children in terms of their achievement?

Green: There is a major national body of data from such men as Otto Klineberg, Dr. Havighurst at the University of Chicago, and Kenneth Clark in New York and many others which support the point very very strongly that there tends to be little discrepancy between black and white youngsters at the point of entry into the public school system, namely at the first grade level. This discrepancy begins to appear once the youngster is involved in an educational program. It becomes increased over time. Sometimes it is referred to as a systematic decline in achievement over time on the part of blacks and increase in achievement over time on the part of white youngsters. So what we find is very little discrepancy at the point of entry, and the discrepancy comes over time as the youngster moves through the academic program. . . . One could infer that the Detroit data probably approximates a national body of educational achievement data . . . very little discrepancy at the point of entry . . . or if there was a discrepancy, it was minimal, but the discrepancy by the eighth grade is very dramatic and tends to increase over time. This data . . . approximates the kind of data that can be nationally referred to in terms of the discrepancy between black and white achievement in segregated schools over time.

Judge Roth interrupted to ask: "Am I to understand that you are satisfied, based on your own experience and studies and those of other experts . . . that, speaking generally, there is no achievement difference, scholastically speaking, between white and black children at the entry level?" (T, p. 877). Dr. Green then began to alter his response somewhat, as well as to add further inaccuracies:

Green: In general there is a body of data that supports the point of view that the discrepancy between black and white students at entry level tends to be minimal, very small. There are some differences as a function of geographic region. I can very safely predict that the entry-level differences between black and white youngsters in . . . Detroit are much smaller than the entry-levels between the black and white youngsters in Wilcox County, Alabama. I could also safely predict that the entry level between black and white youngsters in . . . Flint . . . and Pontiac . . . and Benton Harbor, Michigan . . . are probably minimal at the point of entry to the public schools. . . . This is not to say that they are exactly similar. This is not the case at all . . . but generally speaking, the differences at the point of entry . . . tend to be minimal and in many instances they tend to not be statistically significant, if I might be that precise.

Judge Roth persisted: "Is this supported by studies made of pre- but almost-school age children? I am thinking of the four . . . or five year old who has not yet entered the school system" (T, p. 878). Green then retreated still further, and at the end of this response was answering an altogether different question than the one first put to him (T, pp. 878–79):

In general the differences are much, much smaller and in some cases minimal than one would find at the second grade level. Again there are other complicating factors. If we take black youngsters three and a half years of age who have been afforded a very impoverished upbringing . . . and compare their educational achievement with white affluent three and a half year olds, the differences, of course, would be much larger.

But if we take comparable groups in a sense that we could control socioeconomic status, take comparable groups of black and white youngsters, we would find that even at year three the differences are very small, very minimal.

Judge Roth by now appeared somewhat confused. Instead of pointing out that Green had not been asked to compare the entry level proficiency of black and white children of similar socioeconomic status, he remarked (T, p. 880):

Well, this is an intriguing subject. . . . I have no doubt that education is much more than . . . formal education in school and I would be surprised to find that a youngster out of a household where the parents are college gradu-ates, as against a household where the . . . parents are . . . at the 6th grade level of education . . . I would find it surprising to have you support the position that at the pre-entry level those children start out at the same place.

Note that the courtroom's procedures do not permit the prompt correction of a series of inaccurate statements, nor do they allow an adversary-counsel or expert witness to intervene with questions that, if properly formulated, could have determined whether Green was at this point changing his testimony on entry level differences. Instead, the expert continued with his non-answer to Judge Roth's original question (T, pp. 880–81):

Green: Sir, I said that socio-economic status does play a role here, and if we take a youngster from a very essentially poor background . . . who is three and a half . . . and . . . compare that youngster with another three and half year old from an affluent background, the differences are larger. But if we control that factor, if we take black and white youngsters from essentially the same background, the differences would be very minimal. Again, if we place a black youngster in a segregated school system and a white youngster in a segregated school system then the differences would be reinforced and would begin . . . to . . . become very dramatic.

Roth: Would become enlarged then?

Green: Very much so. So your point is a good one. If we take different groups of youngsters and compare them, the differences would be larger at year three and a half than they would be if we took similar groups of youngsters using race as a factor for comparison purposes.

Roth: Pardon the interruption.

With Green's last virtually undecipherable response, all is now confusion in this testimony, and defense counsel's cross-examination failed to clarify it (T, p. 931):

Bushnell: You do acknowledge that some experts . . . whose work you have referred to in your own publication . . . contend that home environment . . . influences the child's probability of success in school . . . ?

Green: I will support the point of view that it has been argued that the home plays a role, can play a role in how a youngster performs in an academic setting. I will also add that there is data and I can cite and refer you to several studies which can be made available to you, that the overwhelming influence on the youngster's achievement in a school setting is the school itself and not necessarily the home.

Bushnell: All right. Now, you are not absolutely throwing out . . .

Green: No, I'm not throwing out the influence of the home. I'm maximizing the influence of the school, though.

The defense counsel pressed him to specify what factors were included in references to "background" or "socioeconomic status" (the terms were being used interchangeably).

Green: The major criteria I use . . . is income. Once we have moved past that criteria the other is debatable about values and whether or not you love the library and so forth.

Bushnell: You reject the other?

Green: They are not as significant in the correlations we find between educational achievement and in the breakdown of socio-economic status the most crucial factor is income. Income will account for 90 per cent of the variance.

Bushnell: You give little or no value to an index of possessions or index of values or education or access to books in the home?

Green: Sir, the reason I use income as a major criteria invariably is because education correlates highly with income, books in the home correlates with income; values do not refer to income. We only have to reflect on values in America today to reflect on that. . . . Income is socio-economic status. . . . Other matters tend to be superfluous.

Bushnell: . . . you tell me the rich have a higher socio-economic status than the poor?

Green: I am saying that in America the rich have more money than those who are not necessarily rich, and that income, the amount of income correlates highly with the other facts you picked out, books in the home, educational levels and so forth, but not necessarily with attitudes and values. (T, pp. 926–27)

Bushnell did not ask Dr. Green for his explanation of how income differences make an impact on academic achievement—if indeed the expert was willing to say that they do. Although Green declared that several studies showed that the school, rather than home background, was the "overwhelming influence" on a child's academic achievement, the cross-examining counsel failed to ask for the names of these works or the data presented in them.

Defense Testimony

The defense experts' testimony on this subject was quite different from that of the plaintiffs, although, as we shall see, they arrived at many similar conclusions. After all, they relied heavily on the influence of social class differences to account for the marked disparity in black and white academic achievement in Detroit's schools. Yet, taken as a whole, their testimony was sometimes confused, often inconsistent, and generally incomplete. It was incomplete because they avoided the fact of black-white differences at roughly comparable income levels and on occasion denied their very existence. It was confused because they so frequently merged the presumed (and weak) effect of classmates' SES with the undeniably powerful effects of the individual child's own social background. Further (perhaps because of their enthusiasm for race-class school mixture), they constantly tended to reduce SES differences to the "attitudes and values" of parents, teachers, and children rather than consistently emphasizing the more concrete differences in life circumstances—unemployment and chronic insecurity, illness, family size, household instability, levels of education, styles of verbal interaction, and methods of child socialization—some of which are closely related to academic proficiency and others of which pose special problems for classroom management.

The testimony was often inconsistent and lacking in clarity because of the obvious reluctance of defense experts associated with the public school system to say anything that might be interpreted as harboring "low expectations" for disadvantaged children. This was especially true during a period of overblown rhetoric and exaggerated expectations for various kinds of reform. The schools were publicly committed to a belief in their virtually unlimited power to equalize educational outcomes regardless of social background. An institution so committed finds it almost impossible to acknowledge fully the powerful impact of the student's background upon his academic performance. For example, Dr. John Porter, the state superintendent of instruction, when asked directly which school districts in the state had the highest academic achievement, declined to answer, saying that such comparisons were meaningless because districts had different needs. He added: "When certain kinds of changes are made . . . [the] results are that students respond equally well" irrespective of their social background (T, Porter Deposition, pp. 2101–7).

James Guthrie, from the Berkeley School of Education, was relatively free of such pressures and could have conveyed to the court a summary of existing research findings on this topic if this had been his aim. But (as later chapters will show) his devotion to the goals of metropolitan integration and his profound belief in the power of schooling to overcome societal inequities in the lives of children caused him to mute or soften those conclusions that might have served as a rationale for a do-nothing policy. He began with an extended statement on the causes of marked social class differences in academic proficiency at the time children enter school, referring to prenatal factors, possible nutritional deficiencies, the greater incidence of health defects among poor children, parents' educational level, less vocabulary development, insufficient educational stimulation, and unfavorable neighborhood influences (T, pp. 4085–4100). This valuable material, well supported in the literature, refuted the plaintiffs' expert testimony on this subject, although its effectiveness in the courtroom was diminished because two months had elapsed since the plaintiffs' witnesses had appeared.

But the important fact of entry level disparity, having been explained so admirably at the start of Guthrie's testimony, was virtually ignored thereafter. Instead, the testimony that followed emphasized a series of factors that greatly altered the nature of the relationship as originally presented. Teachers have "lower expectations" for such children; this contributes to low achievement (T, pp. 4114–15). (Was there a serious gap in entry level scholastic skills—or did teachers mistakenly estimate that there was? Or is the disparity something only scholars are permitted to notice?) Soon the original presentation was further confused by Guthrie's insistence that "the quality of school services a child receives is a function of his social and economic status"; this, he said, was one explanation of why black children in predominantly white schools were doing better (T, p. 4105). He went further: school resources are allocated in a discriminatory manner; children from high-income families get "good" schools; poor children get "poor" schools, and "as a consequence" perform poorly. Then he suggested that the general understanding that the Coleman Report found that resource variation did not explain achievement variation was due to the public's "misinterpretation." School achievement is "tied to the social class of the child because of this discriminatory pattern in the allocation of school resources" (T, pp. 4116–18). The child's social background as the major influence in the development of academic aptitude, an influence that is strikingly apparent before the child has been in school for a day, and which continues to exert its many-faceted influence thereafter, had faded into the background by mid-morning.

Guthrie's further testimony continued to call into question the strength of the relationship he had set forth so well in his opening statement. The stark realities of disadvantaged life circumstances were gradually dissolved into differences in "attitudes," "values," and "expectations" that could be altered by contact with the proper proportion of classmates from advantaged circumstances, perhaps to bolster his support of school integration (T, pp. 4123–55). "I don't want a record . . . that it's unalterable," said the defense expert (T, p. 4150). The testimony emphasized how background factors that influenced the child could be overcome by changing pupil composition, finances, and school offerings.

Guthrie explained his criticisms of the Coleman Report's methodology in arriving at its conclusion that student social class composition was virtually the only school factor that was associated with achievement (T, p. 4110). This testimony was marred by two serious defects that further vitiated the helpful insights he had earlier given to Judge Roth. One, the constant reference to peer effects, as if contact with classmates had been established as a cause of academic success or failure, rather than simply an associated condition, is discussed in Chapter 9 below. Second, the constant use of the phrase "social class" to refer either to the individual child's own social background or to that of his classmates was so confusing as to place the entire meaning of Guthrie's testimony on this topic in doubt. For example, his assertion that the Coleman Report was wrong in "weighing the social class of the child more heavily in influencing school achievement than school services" came directly after a discussion of the relative weight of classmates' social class as compared with other school factors. In view of Guthrie's earlier clear insistence on entry level disparity, it seems hardly conceivable that he would want to so alter his position. Perhaps he was referring to the impact of classmates, but his reference to the social class of the child makes this doubtful. And later, he declined to challenge counsel's summary of research showing that "achievement differentials are . . . caused by . . . differences in delivery of school services" (T, p. 4168), although such a statement is in obvious contradiction to his statement on entry level disparity, as well as to so much other research showing great differences in achievement within the same school.

Toward the end of his testimony, Guthrie had so far departed from his earlier stress on the negative impact of poverty that he attributed the poor school work of black children from a Detroit public housing project to the effects of an unfavorable classroom mix: "racial integration without sufficient . . . socio-economic balance" (T, p. 4209). And the high achievement of pupils in the small Chrysler school, then serving a mixed neighborhood, a prosperous enclave of luxury housing, was characterized as illustrating the thesis that "socio-economic status is a significant component of integration" (T, p. 4212). I would surmise that the enlightenment on the effects of social background that he had offered Judge Roth at the beginning of the day had been greatly dissipated. Whether the contradictory and ambiguous nature of the testimony reflected Guthrie's own ambivalence and uncertainty or whether it was the outcome of his apparent desire to serve the cause of integration and educational compensation is not clear. At one point, for example, he urged that advantaged children who began school with well-developed academic skills be given advanced work "to maximize" their accomplishments—this without acknowledging that such a program would widen the gap between them and the under-achievers (T, pp. 4109–11).

Toward the end of Guthrie's testimony Judge Roth asked him whether a chance to attend a "good school" starting in fifth grade could reverse the damage to a child from a background of "social and economic deprivation" who had also received poor educational services until that time. Instead of pointing out that the effects of poverty and other background conditions would continue to influence such children and that there is as yet inadequate evidence to support a prediction of success, Guthrie said: "I find it difficult to project any . . . immutable damage to him . . . should he henceforth have the opportunity to attend good schools" (T, p. 4188). The "miracle," Guthrie declared, would be that such a child would have a chance to go to a "series of classes which are of a different order" (T, p. 4188). Thus the expert witness who began by emphasizing the impact of social background upon the development of academic proficiency concluded by minimizing its effects, except as they are a barrier to attendance at "good schools."

Dr. Stuart Rankin, like Guthrie, effectively countered early testimony concerning the absence of group differences at the time of school entry. Rankin, however, offered no data to support their existence, although school-wide distributions were available. Two years earlier Lebeaux and I, for example, compared entry-level scores in a poor black school with those in the Chrysler school (a school whose population was of high income and racially mixed) in the mid-sixties. Almost 40 percent of the low-income black children had D or E scores, while at Chrysler only 3 percent of the students had such ratings.[4] Statistics such as these from the Detroit schools might have clarified the nature and dimensions of the issues on which the court was hearing testimony. Like Guthrie, Rankin fully acknowledged the strength of the correlation between social class and achievement (T, pp. 3822–26, 3831–32), but, also like Guthrie, in his further testimony he stressed attitudes and value differences concerning education as factors that most affected school work. "The factor that may be behind social class differences," he explained, "is the parents' communication to the child that he is important, that he can learn, that education is important." In poor areas there are "few students to bring those values we are interested in bringing and those expectations" (T, p. 4247). Poor families, he said, often do not "prize education as highly" (T, p. 3802). (It should be noted that social science studies do not support these characterizations of poor blacks.)

Rankin too placed less emphasis on real differences in life circumstances outside of school: family size, economic insecurity, conditions of life in deteriorated and crime-ridden neighborhoods, and the verbal styles of interaction among people with little education. More serious, perhaps, as far as Judge Roth was concerned, was that during crossexamination disadvantaged children somehow became deficient schools, strongly suggesting that eliminating the latter (by making all schools of uniform composition) would help the former (T, pp. 4241–43). Instead of disentangling school resources, peer influences, and the social background of students, these factors were constantly muddled. When asked whether "you are of the opinion that a school which has a predominantly low income and in this case it coincides highly with black and you prefer the term SES, that there [are] some educational deficiencies in such schools as a result of these factors?" Rankin responded "Yes."

Once it was conceded that the schools were deficient (although this deficiency consisted only of the disadvantage of the children) the direction of a remedy was indicated (T, p. 4241):

is it better to leave these black children in schools which you concede have educational deficiencies rather than to put in students with higher SES, who in this case are mostly white, in those schools and remove thereby the . . . separation of identification between schools which are high-SES because of their concentration of white population, and between those that are black and therefore deficient schools because of low SES concentrations?

If a mix of proper proportions could be secured, "high-SES white students" should be "put in," the expert agreed. Thus what began as an explanation of the impact of a child's life circumstances upon his schoolwork was transformed into a policy recommendation supporting the planitiffs' requirement that schools be made racially unidentifiable. Rankin also failed to maintain a sufficiently clear separation between a student's own social background and the indirect and weaker impact of his classmates' social background upon him:

Q: . . . you say that the more potent factors such as SES, income level, are those over which the school has no control . . . ?

A: Yes. . . . It may be that society could control in some way the SES of a school. The mix of that in a school. (T, p. 3806)

If at this point he had added that, of course, compared to the effect of a child's own life circumstances, the influence of the children he meets in school seems, not surprisingly, to be quite slight, the relative importance of these two sets of influences would have been clarified. Neither he nor Guthrie did this. Instead, by using the same term (SES) for both, they suggested, whether intentionally or not, that both factors were extremely powerful.

Ethnicity—Unmentioned (or Unmentionable?)

"Social background," as the term was used during the testimony on education, did not include any consideration of ethnic subcultural differences. The earlier testimony on residential patterns had given some consideration (inadequate though it was) to ethnicity. There had been a degree of attention to the clustering tendencies of various (white) ethnic groups, and the chief expert witness had presented an index of segregation among Detroit Poles. Judge Roth himself had raised the question of whether there is such a thing as black culture. Yet the possibility that ethnicity (apart from discrimination based on race) might exert an influence on school performance was never raised. All others were considered as a homogeneous mass divided only by social class.

A matter-of-fact acceptance of the marked differences in academic achievement between a number of ethnic groups might have made it possible to acknowledge that black scholastic achievement also differed from that of some other groups even when social class is held constant. But the failure to recognize such differences made it appear that any instance of black underachievement which cannot be readily explained by social class disparity must be the result of racial discrimination or concentration. It was simply assumed that the only alternative to such explanations implied some assumption of innate racial inferiority. In one of the few references in these proceedings to the educational history of other groups, the experience of immigrants' children was presented as a sharp contrast to that of blacks. Speaking of the large numbers of young blacks in Michigan prisons, Dr. Green said (T, pp. 963–64):

I cite this as a failure of the Detroit public schools to a great extent and not . . . the community. Because the schools can play a significant role. If you refer to Drake's book, *History of American Education*, Drake points out very clearly when the waves of immigrants came to this country. . . . from 1914 through 1927 and 1928 the school was very responsive. . . . look at the Philadelphia school system from . . . 1918 to 1923. . . . you will find very special programs designed for after school for adults, for children, to offset the disadvantages that they brought to America. . . . in the Boston school district Drake cited . . . a very systematic, carefully tailored school program to offset the crime rate among the Irish in the Boston area.

This misinformation (it does not appear in Drake[5]) was not challenged. The general assessment of public school concern and compensatory offerings to meet the needs of immigrant children is not widely shared by contemporary social scientists. In his introduction to Colin Greer's *The Great School Legend*, indicting the public schools for their failure, Herbert Gans, for example, characterizes as "legend" the belief that the public school "was an effective antipoverty agency that took poor immigrant children and taught them so well that eventually they became affluent Americans. . . . the public schools of the late nineteenth and early twentieth centuries instead failed them in large numbers and forced them out of school."[6] Diane Ravitch has estimated that during some periods as many as 40 percent of New York's immigrant students were academically retarded.[7] Oscar Handlin has described the frequently cold and hostile atmosphere, the harshness and ridicule of many teachers, and the alien content of the curriculum of the schools attended by these pupils.[8]

The defendants' experts on education emphasized throughout these proceedings that disparities in academic achievement between black and white pupils were caused by social class differences or by "segregation." As we have seen, they explained that socioeconomic status exerted its influence either directly, through the differences in "values and aspirations" associated with the various social class groupings, or indirectly, through various kinds of differences in schools. Both Guthrie and Rankin took every opportunity to explain to Judge Roth that the achievement gap between black and white students was wholly caused by the disproportionate number of black students found at the lower SES levels. Thus, for example, Dr. Guthrie declared that "income level is consistently more highly correlated with achievement than [is] race" (T, pp. 4095, 4097, 4214–15); "the white child from poor circumstances will tend to perform low whereas the black child from more fortunate . . . circumstances, other things being equal, would tend to perform successfully (T, p. 4100); "the disproportionate number of black people . . . at the lower end of the economic and social continuum tends to confuse us and makes it look . . . as though this was a racial phenomenon" (T, p. 4100). Guthrie may not have been aware of differences in academic proficiency between children at similar social class levels but varying ethnic backgrounds; he may have thought it impolitic to acknowledge them; or he may not have accepted the evidence of their existence. The last explanation may well be the right one. When asked by plaintiff's counsel whether he agreed with the contention that "there is no such thing as a test free of cultural bias," he replied, "that's a true fact." The statement that the presence of such bias was "like giving part of a test in a foreign language" he characterized as "a second true fact" (T, pp. 4146–47). In a different setting a questioner might have asked whether these observations suggested the existence of some ethnic as well as class differences that might affect academic proficiency.

Dr. Rankin ignored all differences in the academic success of various white ethnic groups. He too explained to Judge Roth that the appearance of black underachievement was entirely the result of the skewed social class distribution of blacks, i.e., their disproportionate numbers at poverty levels. He noted that in Detroit there were some black schools, such as Bagley and Hampton, "near the top" SES levels, while Burton and Franklin schools, although predominantly white, were "very near the bottom" (T, p. 4242). The implication was that academic achievement in these schools would match their SES rankings, and during the remedy hearings he made this point (T, DR, p. 577). In fact, in 1972, during those hearings, in Burton school, with almost 80 percent of the families on A.F.D.C., 51 percent of the fourth-graders were reading at or above grade level, while in more prosperous black Bagley (10 percent on A.F.D.C.) only 34 percent were reading at or above grade level. In Franklin school (34 percent on A.F.D.C.) about half of the fourth-graders were reading at or above grade level. To cite another example, in heavily black Pasteur school (about 11 percent on A.F.D.C.) only 30 percent were reading at or above grade level.[9] As associate superintendent for research in the Detroit school system, Rankin might be expected to be aware of these or other scores showing black underachievement in areas where most children were not poor. He had also been an administrator at the Pasteur school and must have known that its academic achievement did not match its SES level.

The discrepancy in the schools named is not unusual. When academic achievement scores are available together with data on race and social class of each child, the average for blacks can be seen to be below that of whites (ignoring ethnic divisions within the white group) even when children at similar SES levels are compared. Data reported by the U.S. Commission on Civil Rights show that when only high school seniors, for example, are compared, white students in the lowest social class grouping do better than blacks in the highest.[10] David Goslin calls attention to the fact that "rural Southern whites, who have the lowest average scores of any white group, outscore midwest urban Negroes, who have the highest average scores of any Negro group, on every single test given from grade one to grade twelve."[11]

Not only did Guthrie suggest that, for the sole purpose of alleviating the underachievement of the low-SES black students, placement with "a majority of higher-SES black students" would be effective, but during the remedy hearings he declared that "putting low or medium SES white students in a school where the blacks ranged from middle to high SES" would probably elevate the achievement of the white students (T, p. 4127; T, DR, pp. 450, 465–66). These statements were, of course, consistent with his frequent assurances that social class, not race, was the best predictor of academic achievement. During the trial no one challenged this. Later, lawyers for the suburbs tried to do so, but lacked sufficient familiarity with the literature to dispute, for example, Rankin's assurances that there is "little, if any difference in achievement between black and white students at similar socio-economic status levels" (T, MR, p. 584).

There are three alternative explanations, not mutually exclusive, for the troubling and perhaps not widely known finding that even middle-class black children in this country were not, as a group, doing as well in school as one would have expected. I find explanations based on genetic differences in mental ability so unconvincing that this hypothesis is not even considered. The marked variation between various black cultural groupings in Africa (like the success of West Indian immigrants in the United States) is but one of many bodies of evidence to counter such a claim. An early and much favored causal hypothesis was that underachievement resulted from unequal school resources. Evidence for this hypothesis is now hard to find, especially since the appearance of the Coleman Report, and it is further challenged by data from schools that have had busing programs for several years. A variant of this hypothesis, popular a few years ago during the community control movement, is that when the schools are controlled by whites racist attitudes or cultural disharmony stunt the intellectual development of black children.[12] With the passage of time and the appearance of more and more predominantly black or black-controlled school systems, this explanation seems even weaker than before. (The hypothesis that racial concentration itself explains underachievement is considered in a later chapter but is questionable, in view of achievement data from schools integrated either by busing or by residential integration.[13])

The second hypothesis is that our measures of social class or socio-economic status are too crude to capture the more elusive components in the position of a stigmatized minority, and that they do not give enough weight to the cumulative effects of social and economic disadvantage that is of long standing. Goslin, for example, attributes black underachievement to "the residue of deprivation."[14] Herzog et al. point out that within whatever category is designated as "poor" some will be poorer than others and that poor blacks are often clustered toward the bottom of the continuum.[15] Stinchcombe explores the cumulative effects of the interaction among a number of environmental factors.[16] When social background factors include consideration of the social climate of family life and the volume and style of parent-child interaction (especially as these relate to cognitive development), much more is being included than the usual objective measures of income, occupation, and education of parents. Such analyses merge into the third alternative explanation, which is that if behavioral similarities exist within all ethnic groups—blacks included—one should not be surprised to learn that some of these group characteristics help or hinder the development of certain kinds of academic skills. Jencks et al. estimated that "economic differences explain less than a third of the test score differences between blacks and whites. Cultural differences may explain far more."[17] For example, given the importance attributed to the amount and complexity of verbal interchange among adults and children, the race differences in family size and composition may be quite relevant. Treiman and Terrell recently reported that 40 percent of never-married black women, as contrasted with 3 percent of never-married white women, have children in the household.[18] Is this demographic fact to be classified as a SES or "cultural" difference? Disentangling ethnic from social class characteristics is not easy, and no one should claim certainty or precision. The problems are partly semantic: how should "culture" be defined; what components are included in socioeconomic status? We know, too, that some group characteristics that may have originated as a response to exclusion or hostility can become incorporated into patterns of group behavior that are later perpetuated by other factors.

In the past, some behavioral characteristics of black Americans were often explained as an outcome of their racial, i.e., biological, inheritance. The prevalence of this racist ideology, which now has few adherents,[19] gave a bad name to any consideration of behavioral traits that could not be entirely explained by social class or by current discrimination. (Lawrence Doss, a black leader then working on Detroit's school decentralization plan, was the only witness who men-

tioned the possibility that there might be a distinctive black subculture that was made up of something more than reactions to present
victimization [T, p. 4423].) It was not until behavior came to be
generally viewed as the product of sociocultural influences (a development in which sociologists and members of allied disciplines in the
United States played a major role) that the taboo against the discussion of group differences in behavior began to disappear. Even now,
although in public life (and the public schools are very public) some
deference is paid to "ethnic diversity," the subject is a delicate one in
a multigroup society. Americans who return from their travels speak
freely about their negative and positive responses to nationals encountered abroad but do not speak so freely about ethnic groups in
this country. A group may be cautiously praised for high academic
achievement, but one who refers to the lower academic achievement
of an ethnic group without blaming someone or something for it is on
dangerous ground.

These constraints apply with special force to the discussion of black
subcultural characteristics, including academic proficiency. Before
World War II blacks were so small a proportion in most Northern
cities and, for the most part, so poor and so recently drawn from the
underschooled South that questions about their classroom achievement seemed to answer themselves. After World War II civil rights
forces made a generally successful effort to prevent keeping public
records by race. Until the 1960s most people of good will who were
aware of the disproportionate rate of failure among black students did
not speak about it openly. If there had been more discussion about
school achievement and other differences among various white and
Oriental ethnic groups, a more enlightened perspective concerning
black school performance might have been developed. Well-established differences among other ethnic groups have been found in a
number of behavioral areas: political attitudes and behavior, occupational distribution and social mobility, consumer behavior, incidence
of various illnesses, and many more.[20]

Ethnic differences in the academic proficiency of various groups
(other than blacks) are also known to exist. Almost sixty years ago
tests of native white "Americans," blacks, Jewish, and Italian pupils
in New York City showed Italians with the lowest scores, although all
subjects were described as English-speaking.[21] A study of school re-
tardation before World War I showed rates varying from a low of 6
percent (children of German background) to a high of 36 percent

(Italian); a 1911 study compared rates of high school graduation ranging from none (children of Italian families) to Russian Jews (16 percent) with native whites at 10 percent.[22] These early studies were
crudely done and, as suggested above, for many years thereafter
tended to be avoided because of connotations of prejudice or stereotyping. Recently, contemporary researchers, using modern techniques of analysis, have demonstrated "the existence of net religio-
ethnic differentials in educational achievement after adjusting for
social origins effect."[23]

Gerald Lesser and his associates show different patterns in cognitive skills between children from different ethnic groups but similar
social class levels; even after some years in school these variant patterns persisted.[24] Morris Gross has demonstrated differences in some
academic aptitudes among two groups of Jewish children at the same
social class level but from different cultural traditions.[25] The remarkable educational achievement of Japanese-Americans has been attributed to a variety of social and cultural factors.[26] Differing patterns
and markedly different levels of academic achievement have been
found to exist among eleven-year-old boys from white Anglo-Protes-
tant, Canadian Indian, French Canadian, South Italian, and Jewish
backgrounds.[27] Rosenberg found considerable variation in self-esteem
between various ethnic groups, with Polish-American students rank-
ing among the lowest, while blacks and Irish Catholics were at about
the same level.[28] The specific socialization practices and subcultural
emphases that account for these differences are often unclear, but the
variations do exist.

Ignoring the differences between groups in the conglomerate category "white" had two unfortunate effects of this case and others like
it. First, in the absence of a similar perspective on other groups,
black underachievement (at comparable SES levels) had to be either
concealed or attributed to racial discrimination of one kind or
another. This becomes a form of scapegoating. Second, the invariable
use of black-white comparisons that ignore the fact that "white" is the
average of a large number of ethnic groups within this composite
category often makes black educational achievement seem worse than
it is. Some inter-ethnic differences, for example, have been shown to
be much more substantial than white-nonwhite differentials. A comparison of second-generation Jewish and Italian women, for example,
revealed that the former had six times the proportion of college
graduates of the latter, a far greater disparity than that which appears

when whites (10 percent) are compared with nonwhites (5 percent). But using only the latter statistic makes it appear that nonwhites are uniquely underachieving.[29] Ira Rosenwaike comments:

the seven-eighths of the American population placed in the white category cannot be considered as monolithic. . . . But when . . . nonwhites are compared with whites in dichotomous tables, as is commonly done, this consideration is overlooked. . . . Negro gains in achievement should properly be compared with those of individual ethnic groups rather than with the aggregate white population, which . . . is an average of many groups.[30]

Thernstrom has suggested that "the truly relevant comparison is not between Negroes and whites as a bloc, but between Negroes and earlier migrant groups at the point at which they entered the urban industrial world": "An index of 'white' mobility or median income, education or anything else is a composite figure which lumps together the illiterate Sicilian peasant or the Kentucky hillbilly just arrived in the city with the seventh generation of Harvard College and various other long-established social types."[31]

Judge Roth was misled by the testimony on the relationship between social background and academic achievement. The plaintiffs' presentation was confused or inaccurate. The defendants' experts acknowledged black underachievement but attributed it in large part to certain aspects of socioeconomic status that could be greatly offset by school resources and integration; their determinedly upbeat stance tended to overstate these effects. All who testified either ignored ethnicity as a component of social background relevant to academic proficiency or specifically denied its influence. Neither side acknowledged that at similar social class levels, when black school performance was compared with that of whites (an inappropriate category), blacks on the average were not doing as well. The failure to recognize that some measure of inter-ethnic variation in academic proficiency can be expected as long as ethnic groups with some degree of cultural distinctiveness exist within our society offered a distorted norm of uniformity to use as a measure for black achievement. Neither the degree of societal inequality nor the present cultural emphases of various ethnic groups is immutable. Both are subject to change—planned and unplanned. But while they exist, both these sets of influences have an impact on academic achievement, and the extent to which schooling alone can overcome them is as yet uncertain.

CHAPTER 7
School Resources and Academic Achievement

The ruling of the district court contained virtually no reference to racial discrimination in the allocation of school resources. Judge Roth said only that school facilities had been furnished in a manner "in keeping generally with the discriminatory practices which advanced or perpetuated racial segregation."[1] It was not clear whether this charge was part of his overall finding that the system had separated children on a basis of race or whether he meant that resources had been unequally allocated on a racial basis.

Considerable testimony was offered on the subject of resource allocation and its relationship to academic achievement, but its overall effect was to confuse rather than enlighten the court. Expert witnesses on both sides offered many unsupported assertions concerning the power of modest increments in educational resources to overcome substandard academic achievement.

Dr. Robert Green, the plaintiffs' educational expert, repeatedly stressed that levels of school achievement were determined by "educational inputs" within the school and that underachievement was caused by "educational deficits" of schools (T, pp. 877, 894, 899). These declarations were made without qualification. It was as though the Coleman Report of 1966, with its data showing that variations in school resources did not account for differences in achievement, had never appeared.[2] Green responded to any suggestion that the effect of educational resources was limited as though it were heresy—an attempt, he declared, to blame "home and community rather than schools for the miseducation of children" (T, p. 930). In his extended testimony he sometimes asserted that school resources were allocated unequally on the basis of race and sometimes only that blacks thought ("perceived") that they were. No distinction was drawn between belief and actuality, and virtually no evidence was offered to support either claim. As an example: "In all-black schools there is a general feeling that the resources in those schools may not be commensurate with resources in white schools. I have not seen cost figures regarding resources . . . per school in Detroit but I do know nationally that this is the case"(T, p. 972). Green offered no support for a statement that differed considerably from another key finding of the Coleman Report.[3] Such statements were not challenged. It seems likely, however, that even if defense counsel had known enough about the content of that much-discussed research to question Green about his assertions, the witness would have merely shifted his emphasis to "what people thought." He stated earlier in his testimony: "North and South, there is a very strong feeling on the part of black parents that whenever a school is perceived as a black school . . . the resources . . . and teaching personnel . . . often placed in that school are substantially different and inferior . . . . This is a general perception on the part of the black community" (T, pp. 869–70). But Green was apparently not suggesting that these "perceptions" were confined to black parents: "You can readily perceive and perhaps justifiably so, that schools that are essentially white will have available greater . . . more adequate . . . more abundant resources than schools that are identifiable as black schools" (T, p. 871).

Resources were unequal. Or blacks perceived them as unequal. Or everyone perceived them as unequal. But even if they were actually equal, and even if most people perceived them as such, they were not equal:

Q: [from counsel]in a segregated area where the school is new and you have compensatory programs and you have a greater per capita expenditure than in white schools . . . does the community still retain the image that it is an inferior school?

A: Yes. Because the black community is well aware of the fact that separate but equal has never been a fact of life and never will be. (T, p. 1056)

Green offered no data to support his assertion concerning the beliefs of "the black community" and was asked for none. From the perspective of the NAACP, even if charges of discriminatory resource allocation are completely unfounded, a school that is "racially identifiable" (defined by the NAACP as markedly disproportionate in racial composition) cannot be equal in school quality. Just prior to Green's appearance, the plaintiffs offered an exhibit and testimony by John Schweitzer to show that the average level of academic achievement in predominantly black schools was considerably lower than at those that were predominantly white (T, pp. 830–56). Schweitzer, presented only as a statistician, offered no explanations. No one pointed out that, as students' scores were not identified and classified by race, it was possible that black children were also doing poorly in predominantly white schools, or that black students in predominantly black (90 percent or more) schools might have been a less advantaged group to begin with. No entry-level data on students' initial scholastic aptitude were offered, nor were they requested. There were no data on students' socioeconomic status, an omission noted at one point (but not pursued) by defense counsel. Most objections related to the plaintiffs' choice of schools, "polar categories" of 90 percent black and 90 percent white. Why, the defense asked, had not some of the more racially balanced schools been selected? Thus the defense lent inadvertent support to the inference that the racial proportions of schools "caused" achievement levels—precisely what the plaintiffs were trying to suggest through use of this material.

The NAACP's most lengthy presentation on school resource inequality was offered by Paul Smith of the Harvard School of Education (T, pp. 1712–1827). He presented a number of exhibits on the distribution to schools (classified by their racial composition) of a large number of items, ranging from acreage per school site to the proportion of staff at various salary ranges and the degree of racial similarity between students and staff (T, p. 1728). But in the 117 pages of testimony, marked by long colloquies on techniques of data analysis, objections to the choice of items, and the absence of measures of deviation, there was no reference to what is known concerning the relationship between these variables and school achievement, a classic example of misplaced precision that ignored the central causal issues which should have been revealed to Judge Roth.

Smith returned for further testimony at the close of the trial and presented some revision and updating of previous material (T, pp. 4643–73). Pupil-teacher ratios in predominantly white and predominantly black schools were about the same (T, p. 4650). Federal compensatory grants had been excluded from these calculations (T, p. 4651). The difference in per capita pupil costs in the mainly black compared with the mainly white schools was $39 (in favor of the white schools), derived largely from the somewhat greater proportion of higher seniority teachers in the latter (T, p. 4652). Smith described the disparity in resource allocation as "systematic discrimination against blacks" (T, p. 4665).

Defense Testimony

Dr. Stephen Lawton, testifying for the Detroit School Board, also offered an analysis of the allocation of educational resources. He too found that a larger proportion of higher seniority teachers were working in predominantly white schools than in black ones (T, p. 3701). The differences were not great, approximately two years of experience, on the average (T, p. 3755). Since a larger proportion of white teachers were long-time employees, this finding was predictable in any system where seniority permits teacher preference to be exercised. Although the union contract in Detroit accepted the goal of racial balance in teacher assignment, it also protected the traditional right of higher seniority teachers (of either race) to retain assignments in the school where they had been working; i.e., if enrollment dropped, lower seniority teachers were more likely to be moved to another school. Lawton also found average class size in predominantly black schools to be slightly lower than in predominantly white ones (T, pp. 3704–5).

Lawton declined to comment on the seniority difference which accounted for the salary differential and thus for the rather small overall financial disparity in pupil expenditure by race, saying that the question of whether higher seniority teachers tend to enhance student achievement was outside his area of competence (T, p. 3757). (Plaintiffs' witnesses had simply assumed that the presence of more experienced teachers contributed to the higher achievement found in predominantly white schools.) Neither Lawton nor any other defense expert who testified on this topic reported research that indicates a reverse relationship: high-seniority teachers do not "cause" high achievement; rather, high-achieving students "cause" teachers who can do so to remain at schools where they predominate because most find such students easier and more fun to teach and because these schools have fewer discipline and behavior problems.[4] Since the Detroit system salary schedule, like that of other cities (and most other institutions), was based on the rationale that higher seniority teachers deserved higher pay because they were more effective, the School Board attorneys were not inclined to challenge this assumption, although Rankin (T, p. 3807) disputed it.

Other witnesses for the system were not as cautious as Lawton, who had avoided the claim that resource differences were a factor in producing achievement differences. Lawrence Doss, for example, completely reinterpreted the findings of the Coleman Report when he suggested that the reason why a majority of middle-class pupils in the classroom enhanced learning was that such parents could "reach the bureaucracies" and thus secure more educational resources for their schools (T, p. 4414). The board's chief expert witness on education, Dr. James Guthrie, declared that the Coleman Report findings of a strong association between students' socioeconomic status and academic achievement is to a considerable extent the result of an intervening variable, discrimination in the allocation of educational resources (T, pp. 4417–18): "Clearly, children who come from high-income households go to good schools and tend to perform well . . . . children from low-income households have waiting for them poor schools and *as a consequence perform poorly*" (T, p. 4117; emphasis added).

What impact this testimony, of which this is but a brief excerpt, had on Judge Roth one can only guess. Guthrie had offered, earlier that day, an extended discussion of the influence of the child's social background on his intellectual development, but the testimony on the impact of school resource discrimination weakened this earlier explanation of differences in achievement. Indeed, Guthrie informed the judge that the central finding of the Coleman Report—that the child's social background rather than differences in school offerings is the chief source of achievement variation—was in error (T, pp. 4164–71). He attributed the mistaken conclusion to faulty methodology, citing his own study of this subject.[5] If even the chief expert for the defendants attributed the low achievement of poor black children to unequal resources ("poor schools"), some form of discrimination must be responsible. Perhaps it could not be proved, perhaps it was not even clear what it consisted of, but both sides seemed to agree that it was there.

None of the other educational experts for the Detroit School Board dispelled this suspicion; rather, their testimony tended to confirm it, not by design but as a consequence of their stress upon the value and power of the resources that they had to offer and with which they were most familiar. Dr. Stuart Rankin (for the defense) stressed the importance of teacher expectations, teaching methods, student participation, staff training, reduction in class size, and the use of such techniques as interaction analysis and the involvement of parents and teachers in curriculum planning (T, pp. 3803–11, 4223–25). Teacher behavior was the "most potent" variable in the educational program. "But it . . . is not anywhere near as significant as far as statistical measuring . . . as socio-economic status" (T, p. 3805). Although he continued to stress that "socio-economic status was a strong variable," he declared that "the educational program was also a strong variable" (T, p. 4245). His assertion, under crossexamination, that "I'm not able to tell you the relative strength of the two" may have suggested that they had equivalent causal power.

Perhaps it is unrealistic to expect school officials and professors of education to cast doubt on the power of schooling to overcome inequalities in children's achievement. Their own self-esteem as well as the rationale for their claims on public financial support are involved. A similar emphasis on school resources as the chief factor in student achievement characterized the testimony of the departing superintendent, Drachler. After presenting a grim list of social and economic problems in Detroit, he went on to declare that a busing program, even if confined to Detroit (then with a two-thirds black school system), could succeed in creating "better education than . . . ever before"—so fine that it would prevent the further attrition of middle-class households (T, pp. 149–53). This miracle could be accomplished if racial dispersion were accompanied by doubling school resources.

The testimony of other school system witnesses, e.g., Dr. John Porter, state superintendent of instruction, Dr. Delmo Della-Dora, of the Wayne County Intermediate School District, and Mary Ellen Riordan, president of the Detroit Federation of Teachers, was similar. They tended to attribute power to school resources beyond the capacity to equalize educational results which they had thus far demonstrated. They seemed not to realize that such declarations lent plausibility to the plaintiffs' contention that discriminatory allocation of school "inputs," as they described them, were at least a partial explanation for the substandard achievement of Detroit's poor black students. This inference might have been countered by a candid admission from someone that there was no evidence available to show that schools can produce equal results for every economic and ethnic group, while there was much evidence to suggest that uniform, i.e., equal, allocation of school resources could not create such an outcome. While Detroit School Board witnesses vigorously denied that there was discriminatory resource allocation, they simultaneously contended that there was a strong causal relationship between such resources and variations in achievement. Their failure to explain or reconcile these explanations left the judge confused concerning this central issue and receptive to the proposition that uniform racial composition within schools ensures against resource discrimination and that equalization of school resources would tend to produce equalization of educational achievement.

The present controversies concerning the relationship between school resource differences and differences in academic achievement did not develop until many years after the *Brown* ruling. To the extent that the substandard academic performance of most black children was recognized—and it was not widely known or widely acknowledged—the prevailing assumption was that the problem was entirely caused by unequal school resources and would disappear with reasonable equalization.

Looking back, it is not easy to see how, with so little supporting evidence, the resources explanation enjoyed such almost universal acceptance. A single example will refresh our recollection. Early in 1966 an elementary school principal in an all-black Detroit neighborhood wrote to then Attorney General Katzenbach objecting to the latter's characterization (quoted in the local press) of one-race schools as "without exception, inferior schools."[6] Mr. Katzenbach did not, in his reply, take the position that racial uniformity in and of itself made such schools inferior. He attributed the deficiency to resource discrimination:

What I intended to convey was that all too often public schools in slum areas are inferior because adequate resources are not put into these schools. And all too often, these are schools attended largely by Negro children. The evidence is entirely clear that the controlling factor is not the race nor the economic situation of the students concerned; it is, rather the will of the community to provide adequate resources with which to teach them.[7]

Studies of black achievement within racially mixed schools in the North would have shown that resource differences did not adequately explain achievement differences, but such research was rarely undertaken and almost never reported to the public. Many years after the fact, for example, Robert Perloff described the opposition he encountered during the 1950s when he tried to investigate racial differences in school achievement.[8] Northern school systems were pressed by civil rights organizations throughout the 1950s to refrain even from maintaining records which identified students or staff by race, and many, among them Detroit, complied with these demands. References to poor academic performance in all-black schools in the North were generally considered (like references to high crime or delinquency rates) a sign of prejudice and were not openly discussed. A study of entry-level differences in scholastic aptitude would have shown that variations exist among children of the same race from various social class backgrounds, as well as among children from some ethnic groups, at roughly similar levels of family income.[9] These initial group differences are followed by variations in academic achievement that tend to persist regardless of present variations in educational resource allocation.

Until the 1960s poor schools were considered by almost everyone to be an adequate explanation for poor schoolwork. One reason for the persuasiveness of this explanation was that many low-income areas *did* have gravely inadequate schools and that many of these same areas *did* produce disproportionate numbers of low-achieving students. Black children in such areas, especially in the South, were subjected to gross educational deprivation in segregated schools. Children who attended school intermittently and quit early, or children whose teachers were themselves poorly educated, could not and did not learn very much. Factors which occur together (poor resources, poor achievement) were assumed to have a cause and effect relationship that fully explained substandard achievement wherever it appeared.

To say that school differences account for achievement differences is to avoid the consideration of touchy subjects that, in the eyes of some, verges on attributions of racial inferiority or directs attention to inequalities of wealth and income far beyond the power of "equal schools" to rectify.[10] (Shortly before the trial began, thirty-nine Michigan school districts had refused to use the new assessment tests that required information on family socio-economic status.[11]) School resource allocations are measurable and more amenable to reform than overall societal inequalities. Campaigns for resource equality enlist strong support from influential groups, such as educators, who directly benefit from the infusion of such funds. Thus self-interest, the more likely prospects for success, avoidance of hard questions about societal inequities, and disregard of delicate issues of subcultural ethnic emphasis all come together in the focus on school resources as the cause and thus the cure of the underachievement of poor black children. Confusion was and still is compounded by a sea of platitudes about "quality education for everyone," "better schools for all children," etc., although it is obvious that improving everyone's education would not diminish the size of the achievement gap.

The Coleman Report shattered this consensus. The social background of the individual student proved to be much more strongly associated with his achievement than any variations in school factors, including the social background (or race) of a child's classmates. The Coleman Report did not, of course, suggest that this proved that educational resources could never play a more important role than they now do. It is quite possible that the range of resource variation was not great enough. Disadvantaged children might greatly improve their academic achievement if their schools were enriched severalfold. Perhaps resources of a different type, carefully tailored to their special needs, rather than simply more of the same, was what was needed to reduce achievment differences. Perhaps, in order to overcome background disadvantages, preschool programs should begin at very early ages and should involve parents as well as their children.[12] It is surprising and unfortunate that, after so many years of programs to improve the academic achievement of disadvantaged children, there has not been even one long-term experiment allocating greatly increased educational resources to a small neighborhood school. Until this is done, and done on a scale commensurate with the level at a very good private school, we will not know the extent to which such a program, together with a comparable preschool program, would enhance achievement. In my own view, however, justice demands that educational resources be allocated on a basis of need whether or not achievement is thereby equalized.[13]

There is a substantial body of excellent scholarship in the field of what is commonly known as compensatory education.[14] Much of this work, both the empirical studies and the general theoretical foundations concerning the sources of educational disadvantage, is far superior to that examining the effects of classroom heterogeneity upon a child's scholastic achievement. Perhaps, as Jencks and others have suggested, it is unlikely that school reforms of any kind will have a substantial impact upon societal inequality.[15] A nation wishing to move in that direction (and the United States shows little public sentiment in support of such a goal) must use more direct strategies to achieve it rather than attempting to reach such an outcome via the schools. But Judge Roth was given neither an accurate account of what was known about the relationship between school resource differences and academic achievement nor a clear statement of divergent views concerning the potential influence of changed resource allocation.

CHAPTER 8
Teachers' Expectations and Ability Grouping

Witnesses for both defendants and plaintiffs were intoxicated with the popular expectancy hypothesis. On the very first day of the trial, a former Board of Education member, describing various reasons for unsatisfactory achievement by poor children, said that "teachers did not have the belief that the students they were trying to teach could perform. . . . they didn't have the expectations for the students that would be necessary if you were expecting the student to perform at his best" (T, p. 58).

The plaintiffs' expert witness on education, Dr. Robert Green, laid great stress on the findings of a much-publicized book on the subject (T, pp. 890–92):

Q: Can you briefly describe the Pygmalion concept as used in the classroom situation?

Green: . . . In a nutshell, the term was initially coined by Professor Robert Merton, a sociologist . . . who talked about the self-fulfilling prophecy.[1] Rosenthal at Harvard picked up this concept and was able to demonstrate both with animals and laboratory studies and later with elementary children that the self-fulfilling prophecy is very much a part of the process that is involved in the classroom which leads to a strong teacher press or a lack of a strong teacher press in terms of how the teacher attempts to reinforce educational achievement. . . .[2]

Q: Can you describe the experiment? I believe it was done in California, was it not, with elementary children?

Green: In a nutshell, what Rosenthal did was to allow teachers to begin to believe that one group of youngsters in the classroom [was] bright, and another in a classroom or, say, in a school, [was] not quite as bright, when, in fact, the data indicated there was very little difference between the youngsters in terms of socio-economic status and past educational achievement.

With this kind of background information, it was found that teachers who were given youngsters who were alleged to be not quite as bright, the youngsters' ability was quite different than those who were alleged to be brighter, which was reflected by actual achievement of the youngsters.

Q: In other words, if the teacher was told these children were bright children, they tended to perform in that fashion?

Green: Yes. . . . Teachers were also told in this particular study that those youngsters categorized as being bright, that in mid-year . . . there would be a spurt upwards in terms of academic achievement. This did, in fact, occur with the bright youngsters, not with those . . . described as being dull. In terms of systematically observing the behavior of teachers, it was discovered that at mid-year . . . the teachers with the so-called bright youngsters spent more time with the class and presented them with more information, more educational data, and they did, in fact, cause the spurt.[3] Again, that spurt was related to what they expected in terms of academic achievement on the part of the children involved. (T, pp. 892–93)

. . . .

Q: . . . Teachers' attitudes have a significant effect . . . on performance as measured by marks, tests, and what have you?

Green: Yes.

Q: . . . Coleman, in his Report, reflected the fact that teacher attitudes are significant with respect to pupil performance, did he not?[4]

Green: Yes. (T, pp. 986–87)

Later Green stated: "Teachers who are assigned to those schools . . . [uni-racial and poor] . . . don't perceive that those children will learn as readily as children in Oak Park . . . Livonia·. . . or Grosse Pointe [suburbs] . . . or from predominantly white . . . middle-income Detroit neighborhoods" (T, pp. 988–89).

Green's fascination with expectation effects led him to some peculiar explanations for the relatively superior performance of white students (T, pp. 1049–51):

Q [by intervenor-counsel, cross-examining]: You stated that this system is also detrimental to white youngsters. Would you particularize exactly how a segregated system affects the academic performance of a white youngster?

Green: I said it has a negative effect. . . . the most obvious one is that it allows white youngsters to grow up with a feeling of superiority. . . .

Q: Does that sense of superiority, false though it may be, is that reflected in the whites achieving a higher academic performance in a segregated school than in a racially integrated school? . . .

Green: It might be due to the fact that teachers . . . in . . . white schools believe that those children can learn and will often work much more effectively to provide good learning experiences for them. So the answer in that regard is yes.

Expert witnesses for the defendant Detroit School Board appeared similarly impressed by the power of positive thinking. Defense Counsel Bushnell, in the course of direct examination of his witness, Dr. Guthrie, said (T, pp. 4114–15):

Let me interrupt and talk about one . . . effect about which there has been some earlier testimony . . . the study conducted at Harvard that has been referred to as establishing the Pygmalion effect. The self-fulfilling process that the teacher thinks the child can't fullfill and he doesn't. The guy that did it begins with "B" [an apparent lapse of memory].

Guthrie: "Pygmalion in the Classroom," by Rosenthal and Jacobson, yes. . . . the research has been one of the most interesting and sophisticated . . . in educational literature. It is one of those times I am proud to be an educator to see the level of that research. It is very sophisticated indeed. In summary, . . . Jacobson and Rosenthal are right, but for the wrong reasons. The research they have done in a San Francisco school or set of classrooms in the . . . Bay area has been found to be flawed so flagrantly that their findings cannot be believed or cannot be generalized. . . . Nevertheless, I believe that their thesis is correct and there are other studies which support it. . . . A study done in Pittsburgh of many classrooms in which the same type of experiment was arranged, that is, teachers were deliberately deceived with regard to information on the ability level of students, the Pygmalion effect was found there and in ways which are scientifically believable.

What we are talking about here is the teacher's expectations for the performance of a child do tend to influence how the teacher behaves toward that child and the teacher's behavior toward that child influences, indeed, how the child performs, such as the low expectation of performance led to the fullfilling of that expectation and high expectations tend to lift children above moderate performance.

In summary, I agree with the thesis but I think the Court should be provided with better evidence in support of it.

Everyone agreed that teachers' expectations were a key determinant in academic achievement. Although defendants' experts had asserted—and plaintiffs' expert had at one point reluctantly conceded—that socioeconomic status was the crucial influence, teachers' expectations were simultaneously accorded great power. No attempt was made to reconcile these alternative causal analyses, although there was clearly a contradictory aspect to this presentation. Was severe disadvantage of various kinds outside of school really a hindrance to intellectual development, or did teachers merely believe—mistakenly—that it was? At some points expert witness Green was unwilling to state that there *were* real differences in achievement levels (T. p. 934):

Q: There is no question but what some kids . . . perform . . . better than others in an academic environment . . . right?

Green: Some teachers rate [some] children more highly than they rate others.

Q: . . . But we can agree, can we not, that some kids do perform better than other kids?

Green: We can agree that some youngsters achieve higher on standardized achievement tests than other children, and we can also agree that some teachers rate the performance of some youngsters higher than they rate the performance of others.

Q: Thank you, Doctor.

Defense witnesses spoke in similar fashion concerning the power of expectations. When Lawrence Doss (see Chapter 11 below) was asked about the reasons for the relationship between social class and educational success, he responded thus: "probably in middle-class schools . . . the teachers expect more than they do in lower-income schools. Where the expectations are low, the students are more apt to meet low expectations. I think this is borne out in an experiment that was made in a California school a year or so ago. . . . we could dig that out for the record if you would like to look at it" (T, p. 4418). Dr. Stuart Rankin (also for the defendants) said: "We have evidence that the extent to which a teacher communicates to a child that the child is capable of learning, will learn, is expected to learn, is an important variable in how well that child learns. . . . Teachers' behavior, including the way he or she expresses his attitudes of expectation to the child, are significant and potent variables" (T, p. 3803). Later, he said: "I believe it is possible for a teacher brought up in a white society to have attitudes about black children that are more likely to group those children along with the poor. . . . In other words . . . it may be there are teachers who don't expect the youngster to learn" (T, p. 3815).

The witness, who had himself emphasized that black children were, in fact, disproportionately poor, apparently saw no contradiction in attributing this knowledge, if held by teachers, to their attitudes and upbringing in "white society." And although he had frequently attributed black underachievement to the unfavorable effects of such poverty, a teacher who shared this understanding, he declared, had impermissible expectations: "Black and white middle-class teachers, some . . . just don't expect poor children to learn very well" (T, p. 3818).

During the metropolitan remedy hearings Rankin warned that it would be essential for suburban schools to meet incoming poor black students from Detroit "with the expectation that they will succeed as well as anyone else" (T, MR, p. 404), although in view of all that had been said so often during the trial about the effects of disadvantage, such a belief seems quite irrational. The chief counsel for the defendants, George Bushnell, joined in the chorus: "A teacher whose emphasis is on tender loving care and providing success experiences . . . he is going to have a whale of a lot better results . . . and the child is going to perform at a higher level, than one who comes in thinking because you are poor you can't make it" (T, p. 993).

No research other than *Pygmalion in the Classroom* was cited in support of assertions throughout the trial and the remedy hearings on the power of teacher expectations to improve levels of academic achievement. Although Guthrie noted its serious flaws, he praised its "methodological sophistication" and, most important, assured Judge Roth of the validity of its findings. There have been some studies that have reported confirmation of various aspects of the expectancy effects hypothesis. But no citations were made to the severe criticisms of the Pygmalion study, although much of it had been published by the time of the trial. For example, Richard E. Snow said that "the research would have been judged unacceptable if submitted to an American Psychological Association journal in its present form. . . . Its reporting . . . stands as a casebook example of many of Darrell Huff's admonitions to data analysts."[5] James J. Buckley commented:

"those who seek proof of the theory about teachers' expectations should continue their search; they will not find it in the *Pygmalion in the Classroom*."[6] In another review, Robert L. Thorndike wrote: "the basic data upon which the structure has been raised are so untrustworthy that any conclusion based upon them must be suspect." He deplored its publication and feared its uncritical acceptance.[7]

A number of attempts to replicate expectancy effects as found by Rosenthal and Jacobson have met with failure. Among them are William Claiborn, who states that the evidence "remains equivocal" and warns against conclusions from such "ambiguous data";[8] Jerome B. Dusek ("teachers are good predictors of children's academic potential") also says that telling teachers that students will perform well has no influence upon their achievement;[9] Elyse S. Fleming and Ralph G. Anttonen ("in the real world of the teacher, using I.Q. test information, the self-fulfilling prophecy does not operate as Rosenthal hypothesizes"[10]); Jean José and John J. Cody ("in general, it appears that 'expectancy' as used in this study had little or no effect on student performance and/or teacher behavior"[11]); and Theodore X. Barber and Maurice J. Silver, who analyzed thirty-one studies which attempted to replicate general experimenter bias or expectancy effects.[12] Most did not succeed. Barber et al. conducted five further attempts to replicate experimenter bias effects; all failed to do so.[13] The expert witnesses did not mention any of these failures to replicate the so-called Pygmalion effect, including the failures reported by Rosenthal and Jacobson themselves in their book.[14]

Despite the slender proof in support of teacher expectations as a strong influence upon achievement, and the abundance of evidence casting doubt upon this hypothesis, no word of caution was expressed. There was a single skeptical reference, offered not in court but in the deposition of the departing school superintendent, Norman Drachler, taken a few days before the trial ended. Commenting on a graph that showed the relationship between family income and average academic levels, he said: "Obviously one is always concerned about how much does teacher attitude, principal attitude, the whole Rosenthal or Pygmalion effect have on it. I am sure it has a little bit to do with it but primarily it is the conglomerate of poverty and health, poor housing and discrimination, which I am sure has a great impact on the quality of achievement" (T, Deposition, p. 137). He did not elaborate. Nor did he observe that a teacher's expectations about a student's performance, like a student's expectations about himself, whether in hitting home runs or doing arithmetic problems, might be more consequence than cause of his achievement. A study of available data by Marshall Smith, for example, led him to conclude that parents' expectations for their children are probably caused by student performance, rather than the other way around.[15]

Those whose duties involve the training of teachers, e.g., academics from colleges of education or administrators, are understandably drawn to explanations of achievement that stress variables subject to teacher control or modification. The practitioner is virtually compelled to adopt a perspective that emphasizes what *can* be done, and since social science generalizations are probability statements that do not apply to all cases, it is appropriate for the practitioner to act initially as if the student before him is in the segment to which the generalization does *not* apply. But the perspective does not thereby acquire causal validity. To assume that someone can excel in arithmetic—or football—is not to make it happen.

Experts told Judge Roth that in classrooms of poor black children teacher expectations were low, and that these attitudes were an important cause of the students' poor schoolwork. The question of whether teacher expectations for such pupils would be any higher if they were a minority in the classroom after reassignment by busing was not raised during the trial. But the idea was conveyed that classroom integration would correct "low expectations" for such children. Why this would be so in a setting where, by comparison with others, their performance would (on the average) be lower was not considered.

There is a seductive quality in the notion that educational achievement can be markedly improved if teachers will maintain expectations of success that fly in the face of their past experience and the major findings of social research. Leonard Fein, commenting on this belief, which figured so prominently in the campaigns in New York and Detroit for "community control," identified its attraction: "The special appeal of this position is that it makes educational quality seem much easier to attain. No longer are we required to worry centrally about the continuing impact of environmental disadvantage; simply create a system which can provide teachers who will say to their students, in effect, that they are getting better in every way, every day and eureka, the gap will vanish—or, at least be narrowed."[16]

The related topic of grouping children on a basis of academic proficiency, thus "institutionalizing" the school's expectations for their performance, was also the subject of testimony.

"[T]he . . . real basic issue, as I said in the beginning, is that what we want from the Court is the striking down of race. . . . the question is made about the educational level of children. . . . They give tests to children so what do we think is the solution? Simple. Put the dumb colored children in with the dumb white children, and put the smart colored children in with the smart white children—that is not a problem."[17] So said Thurgood Marshall in 1955 before the Supreme Court, when he was acting as NAACP counsel in *Brown v. Board of Education.* There were no references to "tracking" or "ability grouping" in any of the court decisions in *Bradley v. Milliken.*[18] Other school segregation rulings, notably *Hobson v. Hansen,*[19] have had many such references, and the practice has been part of the legal basis for some school segregation decisions.[20] Regardless of its use as legal grounds, the testimony on this topic, like the education testimony in general, was an important aspect of Judge Roth's indoctrination. Expert witnesses on both sides provided him with an array of half-truths without presenting any contrary evidence.

There was a surprisingly large amount of testimony on the subject. This material was not part of any formal complaint against the Detroit schools, whose policy and leadership declaimed against ability grouping and whose expert witnesses expounded on its evils in much the same way as the plaintiffs' experts. (There was, however, a reference [see T, p. 893] to the criticisms of the *High School Study Commission Report of 1968* concerning the alternative curricula offered in secondary schools, a practice sometimes characterized as "tracking.") Whether this issue was raised by the plaintiffs simply because it was part of the standard battery of topics in school segregation cases or because the introduction of this material was thought to somehow tarnish the image of the pro-integration school system I do not know.

The content of the testimony was similar in emphasis to the teacher expectations material in that the underlying theme was the same: destructive practices in schools—rather than entry-level deficits deriving from and constantly reinforced by the inequalities of society—caused the poor achievement of black children. Ability grouping was simply the institutionalization of low expectations. Here are some illustrative excerpts from this testimony (T, pp. 889–90). Dr. Robert Green states:

Green: Typically, black youngsters are placed in tracks that reflect a lower academic press. . . . I'm referring to teacher press. . . .

Q: What accounts for this lower placement of black children?

Green: . . . the lower placement of black children is a function of their test performance. Their . . . test performance is highly related to test educational experiences. Black children typically . . . attend very tightly segregated . . . elementary schools. . . . the accumulation of . . . educational deficits will be reflected in the youngsters' test performance, which leads to lower track placement. . . . The test performance is a measure of the educational failure of the school system itself, and the youngster bears the brunt of this as a function of his test performance which leads to lower placement. . . . the basic principle underlying tracking is that youngsters in a certain track were not expected to perform as highly because they had essentially different ability levels, not necessarily different potential for achievement . . . and with this major assumption underlying the whole concept of tracking, almost by definition teachers enter such a setting not expecting youngsters to achieve at a particular level.

Differences in learning were the creation, then, of the schools. An inquiry about the entry-level performance of such children before their exposure to any kind of school experience and a reminder that black children in mixed classrooms often performed less well, on the average, than their white classmates would have directed the court's attention to out-of-school factors.[21] But there was no one who saw the relevance of this information. Defendants' experts, despite their statements about the relationship between academic aptitude and socioeconomic status, seemed not to grasp the implications of this line of testimony or perhaps, since the schools were not specifically charged with using ability grouping to achieve segregation, did not give the matter much thought. James Guthrie's testimony on the subject, under cross-examination, was not much different from Green's (T, pp. 4151–52):

Guthrie: . . . tracking is one of the more subtle and devious devices by which a supposedly integrated setting can be re-segregated. . . . And I find very little justification . . . for homogeneous group tracking. As I have seen it operate it does so to the disadvantage of black and poor students.

Q: They usually end up as expected, in a lower track, don't they?

Guthrie: All too frequently.

Q: And with very little mobility, which is one of the claimed benefits of the exponents . . . that you can move up and down, depending on how well you do?

Guthrie: Too little crossing over to suit me. . . .

Q: Isn't one of the evils of tracking the labelling of children and its effects . . . this identification in the eyes of the teacher of the expectation level, that the child can do X or Y and this is all you should expect of him and in turn the child's own realization of that expectation and of that labelling?

Guthrie: You appear to understand the phenomenon very well. I concur with you.

Q: And this in turn affects the belief-system of the child, his own self-expectation and in turn his parents' . . . ?

Guthrie: Correct.

The plaintiffs' expert on segregation, Gordon Foster, conveyed the impression that it was the perceptions of proficiency differences, not the differences themselves, that were at the root of educational difficulties. Responding to a question as to why he had found ability grouping detrimental to students, he said: "they had this disperception[22] of themselves, and the learning process was pretty poor because of the fact they were perceived by others as slower than the rest. . . . their expectations were therefore lower and the work output was pretty low. . . . it was much more difficult to teach them and to engender a meaningful educational experience" (T, pp. 1376–77). Asked if students would not learn of their own and their classmates' ability if tests were given in a heterogeneous classroom, he replied: "Not necessarily."

Straightforward responses to questions on this touchy subject were hard to come by. Virtually the only persistent attempts were made by Intervenor-Counsel Ritchie, who approached the matter somewhat circuitously. For example, he tried to get State Superintendent of Education John Porter to state "what school district in the . . . Detroit area is the best . . . as defined by . . . the highest test scores" (T, p. 2105). Porter never answered this question, the response to which would have revealed a good deal about the relationship between social background factors and school achievement. He first said that he didn't know, but then added (T, pp. 2105–7):

I don't know of anybody in the nation who would have that information because what is best in the school district that ought to be producing 75% of its students to go . . . into industrial employment is a lot different than where I live in East Lansing, where 97% of the kids go on to college. . . . What is needed in Gogebic [a remote area in Michigan's Upper Peninsula] up there where there are more deer than people is far different than what is needed in Detroit. . . . We are now in the process of developing what the common performance objectives ought to be, assessing the students' needs across the state, and then evaluating . . . the delivery of services to respond to those needs based upon performance objectives . . . and then making some recommendations. This is a whole new concept.

Ritchie did not give up, although why he refrained from repeating his request for the achievement test scores is a mystery. The school district scores were readily available.[23] He asked how, if educational objectives are dissimilar, they can be achieved without different curricula—the much-condemned tracks. Porter's response was vague. After noting that there is a common core of knowledge all students need, he added: "Over and above that there are . . . individual differences that must be responded to . . . based upon local need-assessment, whether it be technical or occupational services or managerial or what have you." Ritchie tried once more: "How could any system of education go about finding out where individual differences lay? . . . I ask that . . . because previous witnesses for the plaintiffs have alluded to the problems related to tracking. . . . I try to resolve their statements with regard to tracking with your statement . . . regarding individual differences and . . . objectives."

Porter's confusing and non-responsive reply is reproduced in full (T, pp. 2107–8):

Well, let's keep in mind that we are talking at two different levels here. You are talking to me as a chief state school officer responsible for not only what happens in elementary schools, but also my concern is what happens to children, what happens to youth and what happens to the adult. So I don't look at the bureaucracy. I look at the individuals that have to be serviced. Our job is to assess what takes place in the elementary schools, public and private, in terms of responding to the needs of children, in terms of children, basically the elementary school component having certain skills, language skills, computation skills, motor skills, social circumstances creating appreciation skills and fine arts skills. We assess . . . whether or not the boys and girls are acquiring these skills within limits or certain bands. Now that's our job. It is up to local school superintendents and local boards of education then to respond to the individual needs of these boys and girls in terms of compensatory education programs, vocational programs, special education, where there are organic mental and physical handicaps. We then look at youth and try to determine whether or not our youth are getting certain kinds of opportunities so that they can become more productive adult citizens. It is up to the local district to respond to the individual needs of the youth. Our job is to assess whether or not the whole system is responding to the needs of the youth and now we are taking a look at adult needs, and we are asking a very comparable question: Are the adults of our great state able to receive within the bureaucracy the kind of educational services they need for retraining, improvement, and becoming more responsible citizens of the society. So our track is slightly different than that of any particular local district.

Ritchie thanked Porter and asked no further questions.

Judge Roth might have been surprised to learn that research findings do not quite support the assertions made by the education experts concerning the harm of grouping. Surveying a number of studies on the effects of ability groups, Jencks found no consistent data on their impact on academic achievement.[24] Other research surveys published in 1968, 1969, and 1971 came to similar conclusions.[25] Walter Borg, in a study done for the Department of Health, Education, and Welfare, found mixed and inconsistent effects on achievement and self-esteem for various groups at different age levels; his findings, he concluded, question "the dire consequences . . . predicted by critics of ability grouping."[26] Henry Dyer found that assignment to classes on a basis of proficiency has virtually no effect, perhaps, he suggests, because "the concept is too semantically soft to penetrate the complexities of the teaching-learning process as it actually operates in the classroom."[27] A recent study described as providing the first empirical analysis of the impact of achievement grouping in desegregated schools in the South found different outcomes for elementary and for secondary schools. It concluded that the practice had unfavorable effects on the racial attitudes of small children, while the "more enculturated" older student tends to associate with those of similar interests whether classes are homogeneous or not.[28] (Why one would try to prevent such an understandable inclination is a puzzle.) The study reported no effects on achievement, but the data on attitudes were viewed as substantial enough for the research team to suggest that the usual prohibition against ability grouping at the secondary school level be carefully reconsidered. Damage to self-esteem from classroom grouping is called into question by Marshall

Smith's finding that large numbers of pupils do not know what track they are in.[29]

The issue of maintaining racial mixture in classrooms ungrouped by proficiency in subject matter was to surface again during the remedy hearings. How would compensatory or remedial programs be offered to students with learning problems? Would parents of children more advanced in their studies be willing to let them remain in a class whose offerings were geared to the needs of those much less proficient?[30] Educational settings that require some standard of academic competence for admission have been the success stories of school integration.[31]

The emphasis on both teacher expectations and the harm of grouping children by subject proficiency were characteristic of the general tone of the testimony on education. Differences in achievement were not accepted as stubborn and real; they were said to represent, in large part, the "perceptions" of teachers, generated by their prejudices. When evidence of marked differences in learning was incontrovertible, it was attributed to prior expectations which had themselves caused underachievement. Even those expert witnesses who stated that socioeconomic status was a predictor of school achievement simultaneously contended that teachers who made a similar prediction did so because of class or race prejudice. If schools would avoid assigning children to any group based on attained level of proficiency, even avoid any assessment of a how a child would do next week based on what he did the week before, a serious handicap to children's progress would be removed. Entirely forgotten was the fact that the Detroit elementary schools had few classes based on ability, yet displayed the same pattern of achievement—highly correlated with social background—as schools that did. Mingling disadvantaged students with others was presented as a helpful corrective, or at least as an inhibitor to the development of "low expectations" and any system of class assignment based on them.

Ability grouping does tend to prevent racial mixture on a large scale at the present time because, unhappily, the formula so forthrightly suggested by Thurgood Marshall twenty years ago results in groups highly patterned by race. If this imbalance is defined as "segregation," it is suspect and in some states forbidden. Thus the California legislature has decreed that "there should not be disproportionate enrollment of any socio-economic, minority or ethnic group in classes for the retarded."[32]

Such a ban, like the ban on other grouping based on ability, does not prevent inequality; it merely conceals it—from some. There was a large element of such concealment in the testimony from both sides on grouping and expectations. Taken as a whole, it tended to strengthen the belief that classroom mixture would help disadvantaged children not only because of the direct effects of peer contact but because of the indirect effects upon teacher expectations and behavior.

CHAPTER 9
Student Mix and
Academic Achievement

I noted earlier that Judge Roth's decision finding Detroit schools segregated de jure made virtually no reference to any educational harm from this condition nor to any benefits that would be forthcoming from racially mixed schools. This was in line with the legal reasoning that because state-imposed segregation violates the Constitution, such considerations are redundant.[1] Yet it is impossible to read the trial record without becoming aware of his intense interest in the testimony on educational subjects and especially, of course, on the issue of integration. He asked questions, challenged statements, requested clarification and further explanation, mused aloud on the implications of materials presented, and, in general, was a very active participant in the proceedings. His final remedy order was such a striking contrast to his expressed pre-trial views on involuntary integration that one must conclude that this testimony had a profound effect upon his thinking.

Everyone involved in the trial supported "integration." Plaintiffs, mindful of the scope of constitutional protection, stressed the requirement of racial mixture. Defendants stressed the need for favorable social class proportions and, as is usual for heavily black school systems in these cases, contended that only a metropolitan solution could truly integrate the city schools. But they expressed their commitment to the goal of integration with as much enthusiasm as did the plaintiffs. Both sides testified that properly mixed classrooms would improve academic achievement, and until the entrance of the suburban systems, long after the trial was over, no one attempted to challenge these claims.

126

Dr. Robert Green, the plaintiffs' expert witness on education, declared that segregated schools "negatively impact on the academic achievement of black youth" (T, p. 862). He defined a segregated school as one whose characteristics the observer can readily identify as "a function of color, as a function of race" (T, p. 865). This suggests that only a rather evenly biracial school can escape being designated as "segregated." But in later testimony Green referred to racial "identifiability" as racial disproportion, i.e., the extent to which a school fails to reflect the racial proportions of the school district (T, pp. 997–1002).

Green's explanation of an exhibit showing high average levels of academic achievement in predominantly white local schools, as compared with those in predominantly black schools, was that the level in the latter was caused by their "segregated character." He simply assumed that black children were achieving at a lower level in such schools, compared with black children in schools that were mostly white (T, p. 872). Since the scores of children within Detroit schools were not identified by race, there was no way of knowing which of the black children were doing better and, if so, how much better. No one pointed this out, nor did anyone ask whether the black children in the mostly white schools were of higher scholastic aptitude at the time they entered. These omissions are all the more astounding in view of a lengthy colloquy later in the day between the expert and the crossexamining counsel on the topic of research methods and interpretation. Bushnell questioned Green about the meaning of a scattergram based on the data described above: does a correlation on a graph prove causation? Green's reply (T, p. 1004):

I checked into that last night. McNamara in his book on psychological statistics indicates that a correlation per se need not imply causation. But a particular individual with a background in the kind of phenomena that is plotted on the graph can very safely infer causation. . . . the correlation does not prove the causation. . . . the correlation can indicate causation provided the individual is an expert in that . . . area. . . . there is a whole field known as inferential statistics and that assumes that the individual who . . . applies a particular statistical concept to a problem is knowledgeable about the problem.

Neither this strange statement (the non-equivalence of correlation and causation is an accepted fact and not attributable to any one author) nor the colloquy that followed it made any reference to the absence of scores and entry-level data disaggregated by race. Instead there was a discussion of trivialities, e.g., the fact that the scores were from 1969, while the racial count was from 1970, and the precise meaning of "predominantly black." Green insisted that in "multi-racial schools one does not find this kind of discrepancy" in the achievement of black and white children (T, p. 1007). The defense counsel's failure to grasp the basic omissions in this testimony, focusing instead on the racial composition of the schools used in the exhibit, simply strengthened the plaintiffs' unsubstantiated claims that the black child's academic performance was determined by the race of his classmates, and that changing the racial composition of these classrooms would improve that performance.

Green assured the court that "data from a number of cities . . . readily suggests that busing . . . black youngsters to white schools and white youngsters to predominantly black schools can, in fact, positively facilitate academic achievement" (T, p. 913). These studies were not identified, nor was the singular claim for the helpful effects of black predominance explained. Later Green offered Riverside, California, as an excellent example of how even serious inadequacies in home conditions can be offset by "multi-racial school settings" (T, p. 939). Black children from "very poor homes" in the Detroit suburb of Royal Oak Township, when put into multi-racial schools in rather prosperous white Oak Park, he said, had done well (T, pp. 939–40, 997). The disparity in achievement between black and white children "tends to become minimal" he said, in systems where a busing program exists, such as Berkeley, California: "The gap closes, in other words" (T, pp. 1007–8). He cited no data and was asked for none.

Green offered no systematic theory to explain the mechanisms by which racially mixed schools enhance academic achievement. (It would be unfair to fault him for this because such theory is generally undeveloped or quite confused.) However, he emphasized a number of factors. Some, such as teachers' expectations and resource discrimination, as well as children's self-esteem and aspirations, are discussed elsewhere in this volume. Although generally reluctant to concede the influence of home and family, he did suggest that parents, "perceiving that the school is not one that facilitates academic achievement," decrease their "support" to it (T. p. 868). Much of Green's testimony simply assumed as self-evident that teachers in mostly black schools did not make a sufficient effort ("teacher press" was the phrase he favored)—that they did not try to get children to learn—and that the children in those schools, because teachers "perceived them as low-status" and "racially isolated," did not make an effort either. Since, as we have seen, he tended to deny the fact of entry-level disparity, Green attributed variations in academic performance almost entirely to factors within the school. He insisted that the effects of racial mixture were so powerful that, even if integration were delayed until high school, black students who had been doing poor work until that time would improve as a result of "the overall press of that school" (T, p. 1059).

Green's occasional statements concerning the impact of school racial composition on white students were confused and contradictory. He declared that segregated schools were harmful and damaging to white children, but in the context of his definition of a segregated school (see above) the nature of the harm he saw is not clear (T, p. 862). His references to the increased discrepancy in the achievement level of white and black children as they move through segregated schools suggest that white students' academic progress was not harmed by these arrangements (T, p. 875). But later he said that black applicants to graduate schools "tend not to perform as well . . . as white students who attended . . . multi-racial schools" (T, p. 876). (He offered no evidence for this statement, the meaning of which is, at any rate, ambiguous.) He also said that a white child attending a segregated school would have his entry-level superiority "reinforced"; it would become "very dramatic" (T, p. 880). Responding to a question, he surmised that the higher achievement of students in all-white schools is caused by their teachers' belief in their learning ability (T, p. 1051). Although his emphasis was, by and large, on the benefits of racial mixture, he also declared: "if you mix very poor white kids with very well-to-do white kids, you will ultimately see a change in [poor white pupils'] academic achievement also" (T, p. 1009). Green was not asked for evidence to support any of these statements.

The tone of the School Board testimony is suggested by the chief defense counsel's declaration: "Racial integration is an absolute essential to the educational experience" (T, p. 982). Counsel was expressing both the official policy and the personal views of the Detroit system leadership. Deputy Superintendent Johnson, for so many years the leader of the local NAACP, testified—of course—that integration was required for quality education. Dr. Drachler, the departing superintendent, said that even a Detroit-only busing program, if coupled with enough additional school resources, could be so successful that it would halt the loss of middle-class families from Detroit's public schools (T, Drachler Deposition, p. 152).

The chief expert witnesses for the defense, Guthrie and Rankin, were equally enthusiastic. Dr. Guthrie declared that his own children had benefited from contact with even the seamiest manifestations of social disadvantage (T, p. 4203):

I was one of the parents that participated in trying to get that area [Berkeley] to racially and socially integrate such that my children for some part of their schooling are bused into neighborhoods . . . less fortunate. . . . I think their view of the world has been broadened. . . . They now see drunks and dope addicts they otherwise would not have seen, or at least they see some drunks and dope addicts not dressed as well as they have seen and I don't think my children have been alienated or are beginning to wander down some . . . path not to my liking. . . . I hope I exercise a great deal of influence over their aspirations.

Defense experts differed with Green in stressing that class as well as racial heterogeneity was a requirement for educationally effective integration: "if both black and white come . . . from the lower end of the socio-economic spectrum there is some possibility [that] integration will lead to no added achievement" (T, p. 4122). But "if it were possible to integrate the school racially and simultaneously . . . across socio-economic status boundaries, the weight of the evidence . . . is [that] the performance of the lower SES black children will increase" (T, p. 4123).

But a majority of students of higher socioeconomic status was required to create a classroom climate where there was a concern for academic achievement, said Guthrie. His description did much to explain his earlier emphasis on values and attitudes as the differentiating features of social class groups, for unlike unequal life circumstances, attitudes might be altered by contact (T, pp. 4123–24): "The majority of the children . . . have been socialized to be successful in school. They know how to behave. . . . They are not frightened. . . . they set a classroom tone which the teacher can cater to, and the students . . . hold in high regard things academic. . . . the reward system is for doing things successfully in school rather than fighting the school."

These peer effects were frequently labeled as effects of socioeconomic status, so that it was often unclear whether, when the term was used, the expert witness was referring to the child's own social background or to the effects of contact with peers of a given SES; for example, to a question, "you say that as between SES and race, SES

is predominant in increasing the learning capacity and ability of the
low-income child" the answer was, "The weight of the evidence is
overwhelmingly in favor . . . of SES being the influencer of performance, as opposed to race" (T, p. 4134).

Guthrie's earlier attention to actual learning deficits at the time of
school entry was not mentioned again. No reference was made to
the continuing effects of inadequacies and disadvantages of neighborhood and family life. Instead, the stress was on the harmful effects
of assigning students to a school whose "value system is dominated
by children from the lower socioeconomic status" (T, p. 4154), "children who reflect their parents' performance expectations" (T, p.
4147). These effects would be much ameliorated if only a middle-
class (usually characterized as "upper-SES") majority could be provided (T, pp. 4128, 4134, 4138–39). The mechanism was described
thus (T, p. 4126):

the value system of the students and the perceptions of the classroom held by
the teacher appear to be influenced by the characteristics of the majority of
the students in the classroom and if there are, let's say, only 20 percent
upper-SES children in the classroom, the tone . . . and the teacher's expectations for it tend to be established by the remaining 80 percent low SES
students. So you take some majority middle, or upper SES students in order
to tip this perceptual value of the teacher, and value among students. . . .
What [does] the majority mean—51 percent or 60 or 70 percent[?] It's very
difficult to define that precisely. But it's at least 51 percent and probably is
more effective the higher above that you go.

Later, speaking of a poor black suburban area, Guthrie stressed the
detrimental effect on academic achievement of the "expectation con-
stellation" characteristic of such school districts (T, p. 4156). Performance is adversely affected by attendance at schools that are "stigmatized by low expectations" and, increasingly, big cities as a whole
suffer from what Guthrie called "reputational stigma" (T, pp. 4157–
59). All of this suggests that the disadvantages of social background
exist more in the eye of the beholder than in reality; the fact that
children begin school with about the same disparity in academic proficiency as they show later was forgotten.[2] Placement among more
advantaged peers doing better work—that is, placement in schools
free of "reputational stigma" —would up-grade the performance of
low achievers.

Much of the defense experts' testimony on the benefits of race-class mixture concerned the need for a metropolitan rather than a Detroit-only desegregation plan in order to secure the proper social class proportions. Guthrie recommended inclusion of all the school districts in the metropolitan area and hoped that there might be some way to compel the inclusion of students attending non-public schools as well: "I don't know what legal levers exist . . . but . . . I would begin to question their tax-exempt status if . . . they seem to follow a pattern of . . . de facto segregation" (T, p. 4133). Educational considerations, rather than "arbitrarily drawn boundaries" (i.e., local school districts), should determine where students attend school (T, pp. 4140–43). Racial and social class integration would increase the academic achievement of black students and improve the attitudes of whites (T, p. 4132). Therefore, "what I am searching for within the city . . . and outside of it [are] those pockets of white and upper-SES students who could be used to achieve social class and racial balance" (T, p. 4133).

Rankin, who returned to the witness stand after Guthrie's departure, had a similar view (T, p. 4228): "if it is possible to place low-income students in a situation where there is a majority of high-income students . . . the low-income students are likely to achieve better and the high-income students are likely to stay at least where they are. . . . I would like to shoot for at least 60% high-income [students] and maybe higher than that." Like Guthrie, he emphasized that to get the classroom mix Detroit needed for improved black achievement the suburbs had to be included (T, pp. 4229, 4249).

The empirical basis for the existence of a majority of public school students of high income under a metropolitan busing plan will be considered in the chapter on the remedy hearings. At this point I want to consider the adequacy of the testimony to support claims that racial mixture (the plaintiffs' contention) or race-class mixture (the defendants' view) improves academic performance.

Guthrie was in the best position to explain to Judge Roth that there was, in 1971, almost no evidence to support claims for improved academic achievement as a consequence of planned race-class mixture. Green did not seem to understand the limitations of the existing data, and an expert witness such as Rankin, an administrator in a school system accused of de jure segregation, might hesitate to express doubts concerning the academic benefits of integration lest such skepticism cast doubt on the sincerity of the school system's efforts to attain it. But Guthrie was free to speak as a scholar, if he chose such a role over that of advocate, and at one point it appeared that he might do so. Commenting on statistics purporting to show that black children attending predominantly white schools were doing somewhat better on the average than black children in predominantly black schools, he pointed out that the former were "probably middle class or above": "If you have a school which is racially integrated in the North, it is probably because it draws upon neighborhoods where there are black children living close to white children and if that's the case the likelihood is good that those are middle-class black children" (T, p. 4104).

Can you bring about higher academic achievement by placing poor black children who (on the average) are doing substandard school work in a classroom of higher achievers? There was virtually no evidence on this issue, although it was the basis for all of the hopes that a desegregation remedy would help poor black students do better in school. Such dispersion had hardly ever been tried; where it had, the results were spotty and inconclusive. But no one pointed this out to the judge. Instead, both sides cited the Coleman Report as though it supplied evidence on the academic effects of integration programs. Guthrie had ample opportunity to correct this misconception and, in the process, to explain to Judge Roth the basic logic of causal inference. During cross-examination Lucas asked whether the Coleman Report did not indicate that when black children are assigned to a predominantly white school black achievement increased (T, p. 4163).

Much would have been clarified if Guthrie had pointed out that the Coleman Report has no before-and-after data to show what happens to poor black children when they are assigned in this fashion, that it is a "snapshot" of what was found in schools across the country at a given time. Instead, Guthrie stated only that the reasons for higher performance of black children attending white schools are in dispute. He went on to explain at some length that in his opinion the reason for their better performance was superior school resources, a factor which, Guthrie insisted, the Coleman team had grossly underestimated because of inappropriate methodology (T, pp. 4164–75). Later, when Lucas asked him whether the Coleman Report contained longitudinal data on the effects of integration, Guthrie, instead of answering simply no, and adding that this omission placed a serious limitation on our ability to talk about the effects of mixture, said: "I don't think there are any. . . . There were some studies . . . of 8 to 10 integrated school districts, some of that could be interpreted as being longitudinal" (T, p. 4186).

In fact, there are no data in the Coleman Report on the academic achievement of individual children before and after assignment to racially mixed classes. Eight or ten school districts must have sounded fairly substantial to the judge. (Later Dr. Rankin answered a somewhat similar question and in his response also omitted to explain the implications of the absence of before-and-after data [T, p. 4250].) The impression that the Coleman Report proved the beneficial effects of *creating* a certain classroom mixture was constantly reinforced by the language used by experts and counsel. They spoke of "taking," "placing," or "putting" poor black students in classes composed mainly of advantaged peers. Further, no one pointed out that, even if the correlation between a child's school performance and that of his classmates was assumed, for the sake of argument, to be the result of that classroom composition, these "effects" were slight indeed compared with the influence of the child's own social background.[3]

Some of the widespread misunderstanding of the Coleman Report findings concerning integration is due to the misleading phraseology of the Report's Summary, written to help soften the blow of a disturbing document.[4] The chief finding of the research was that variations in academic achievement overwhelmingly reflect what the child brings to school rather than anything the schools were offering, including the influence of classmates. In an apparent effort to put the best possible face on these findings and thus discourage their use as a justification for do-nothing educational policies, the Summary (but not the body of the Report) presented the association found between the individual child's academic performance and that of his schoolmates as though a cause-effect relationship had been established.

Those who had read the entire Report were well aware that this was not the case:

The Coleman study contains no data at all on the effects that might accrue from "putting" minority pupils with different kinds of schoolmates. It is one thing to suppose that a pupil's attitudes and behavior reflect those of the peer group in which, because of innumerable circumstances, including possibly his own predilections, he happens to be; it is quite another thing to infer that if he is moved from one group to another, his attitudes and behavior will change in predictable ways. This is not to say that changing the mix of children in a school will not change the children in the mix; it is merely to call attention to the fact that the Coleman data by their very nature are incapable of providing any information at all on what changes will occur or the likelihood of their occurence.[5]

This judgment was made by Henry Dyer in 1968. Coleman himself warned against the inference of causality in 1967, and the *American Sociological Review* symposium on the Report (among others) published in 1967 called its readers' attention to the limitations of the data.[6] Only a study that monitored the achievement of the same students over time could demonstrate the influence of contrasting types of pupil mixtures.[7] The Coleman Report, a cross-sectional survey, did, of course, try to compare students of similar social class, but given the processes of self-selection ordinarily involved in a black household's move to a white area, true matching is almost impossible. Many of the black children found to be attending predominantly white schools (at the time these data were gathered) might well be from families whose presence there was related to certain characteristics not captured by crude socioeconomic indicators.[8] The assumption that the relationship, or correlation, between an individual child's achievement and that of his classmates reflects their influence upon him, rather than his own attributes, was challenged by Levin in 1968: "the achievement score of an individual is as highly correlated with those of his fellow-students at grade one as it is at grade 12. Yet it is not possible to attribute high correlations at grade one to the influence of fellow-students, since the tests were administered at the beginning of the first school year."[9]

In addition to these sources, by the time of the trial Nancy St. John's highly regarded summary of existing research was available. She concluded that the evidence on the effect of classroom mixture on scholastic performance was "inconclusive."[10] Yet the only testimony to question the academic benefits of mixture was a single reference (T, p. 144) in a deposition given by Dr. John Porter, the state superintendent of instruction, a black man, who observed that some studies found that achievement of black students remained low even after classroom integration. But this was in March of 1972, many months after Judge Roth had issued his landmark ruling. I think it is fair to say that Judge Roth was given a misleading picture of the research on the effects of peers on academic achievement, a picture which greatly exaggerated both the strength of the association and the probability that this is a cause-effect relationship.

The research published during the years since the trial has failed to alter the judgment that the results of race-class mixtures on academic achievement are either nonexistent or uncertain.[11] Before the remedy hearings in *Milliken* had even begun, Paul Dimond, a counsel for the

NAACP, wrote that in his opinion the evidence on the educational advantage of integration did not prove "much of anything," and in the years that followed, proponents of busing have more and more deemphasized such claims.[12] Studies of academic achievement in systems under busing programs (even some that were voluntary) have for the most part failed to show the hoped-for effects.[13] St. John's 1975 volume is a comprehensive survey, synthesis, and evaluation of available research on a number of desegregation "outcomes."[14] This work is a model of fairness and objectivity. Although it reveals the author's hope that solid evidence to support the hypothesis of academic enhancement could be found, St. John was not able to alter her earlier verdict of "inconclusive."

General theory in social psychology supports the expectation that some lower achievers might be stimulated to perform better in classrooms dominated by more proficient students. These higher achievers need not, of course, be white, nor need they be of higher socioeconomic status, although the statistical probabilities are that they would be both. Such group effects, when they have been found to exist, have generally been small and would be expected to work in either direction: proficient learners in a classroom dominated by slower learners would be less stimulated, and one would predict their actual gains (as compared with their potential gains in more favorable settings) to be less. In addition, there is probably an optimum range for these differences in school performance. If they are too great, the less proficient learner might be discouraged rather than stimulated to higher levels of achievement.

There is little research to demonstrate the effects of various kinds of classroom composition, uncontaminated by other differences, upon the academic performance of children who begin school at various levels of scholastic proficiency. Some of the busing efforts now in effect should generate such findings, but most attempts to make these programs succeed have incorporated a variety of educational components in addition to greater classroom heterogeneity. This mix makes it difficult or impossible to know the cause of any enhancement in learning that might be found.

CHAPTER 10
Other Integration Benefits: Aspirations, Self-Conceptions, and Race Relations

In addition to the testimony on the helpful effects of classroom mixture upon academic achievement, expert witnesses on both sides told Judge Roth that school integration would have a beneficial impact upon the aspirations and self-conceptions of black students and upon racial attitudes and race relations.

The plaintiffs' expert, Dr. Green, had at one point defined a segregated school as one that was racially identifiable because its racial composition was markedly disproportionate to that of the school system as a whole. He declared that such schools lowered the motivation and aspiration levels of black students and were harmful to their self-conceptions (T, pp. 862–63, 866). Attendance at a predominantly black school (regardless, apparently, of school system proportions) causes the black child to "perceive his status as inferior" (T, p. 920). Blacks who have attended racially mixed schools "have higher levels of aspiration and motivation" (T, pp. 867, 1058). Dr. Green drew from some anecdotal material from his boyhood in Detroit to support these contentions. For example, speaking of attending a heavily black high school, he said: "The general conversation centered around: Why should I struggle to graduate from this high school? Why should I struggle to complete my education when in fact there might be and probably will be little relationship between the education that is being offered me here and opportunities after graduation?" (T, pp. 866–67).

Although such material does not seem to support assertions that it is racially concentrated schools which cause the allegedly low levels of motivation—lack of training for jobs was the theme of his classmates' conversations—crossexamining counsel did not appear to notice this.

Nor was Green asked whether appraisals of the job market after graduation also accounted for reportedly low levels of motivation among children in elementary schools.

Defense expert Guthrie, who stressed the value differences between social classes with regard to education, suggested that the low levels of motivation or aspirations among black children was due to their disproportionate representation among the ranks of the poor and their lack of contact with children from households of higher socioeconomic status. His most detailed explanation of how social class mixture would raise these aspirations came during the Detroit-only remedy hearings, when he was supporting the efforts of the Detroit Board to secure a metropolitan decree (T, DR. pp. 453–54):

Now a child from a disadvantaged home, a low socio-economic status home, who himself has not heard much about college or who has not been instilled with the expectation that he will go to college, when injected into a classroom in which there are several or many students who do hold that expectation for themselves begins to pick up the idea that college-goingness is important and more often than not begins to pick up the value that that is something he wants to do. . . . his life-style or expectation of his own behavior begins to be shaped by the expectation of the students around him.

This is not something he got from his parents. . . . It is not something he would have gotten if he had been isolated in a classroom or school which consisted of students from his own economic level. He never would have caught that new expectation. It is a consequence of being placed in a mixture of students of a higher social and economic bracket.

During the trial Guthrie warned that a mixture of the black and white poor would have an adverse effect on black aspirations and self-conceptions (T, pp. 4121–22):

Q: . . . an integrated lower-class, school, what is the effect of that?

Guthrie: . . . There is some evidence that it will lead to some negative effects for black children particularly. The negative effects have to do with their own levels of aspirations and self-concept and these constellations of things that we call attitudes about oneself. The research for instance, by Gloria Powell . . . demonstrated that both in the North and South black children coming into contact with white children in the absence of nothing else being varied, nothing else changes, that their self-concepts are damaged, their aspiration levels are lowered. They begin to view themselves in a different way and not positive, which was the case previously. I am being careful to qualify my response by saying nothing else is varied, just putting poor black children in with poor white children.

Guthrie told the court that peer-group effects on aspiration were unlikely to work in a reverse direction. Higher-status children would have a beneficial effect on their poor classmates, but this contact was unlikely to hurt the more advantaged students (T, p. 4203):

The effect would probably not be very great . . . as long as those higher socio-economic status children were not made to live in that [poor] neighborhood and totally disassociate themselves with their formerly advantaged neighborhood. As long as they could return home after school, see their parents, see what took place in their own neighborhood, I doubt that their aspirations would be swamped by negative examples.

Neither expert was asked for evidence to support their assertions concerning the low level of black pupils' aspirations, motivations, and self-conceptions, and they volunteered none.

Research on students' "aspirations" is difficult to interpret because the term is not uniformly defined. Are aspirations hopes, wishes or preferences, plans for the future, or "motivation" to succeed in the present? Studies that ask respondents about realistic expectations may produce somewhat different results than those which investigate hopes; the latter may reflect a considerable amount of fantasy. Nevertheless, there are very few studies that support the contentions made by experts during this trial and the remedy hearings that black children have less pronounced wishes to succeed or more modest aspirations for careers than do whites. Most data support the opposite conclusion. Despite the many references to the Coleman Report, its important findings on these matters were never mentioned. According to the Report, high aspirations of black students coexisted with low achievement:

Apart from the generally high levels for all groups the most striking differences are the especially high levels of motivation, interest and aspirations reported by Negro students. These data are difficult to reconcile with the facts of Negroes' lower rate of completion of school and lower college-going rate. They appear to show [that] Negroes are especially strongly oriented toward the school as a path for mobility. This finding is consistent with other research that has shown greater aspirations for college among Negroes than among whites of comparable economic level. But the results suggest . . . a considerable lack of realism in aspirations.[1]

Coleman and his associates observed that the data on black children "give a picture of students who report high interest in academic achievement but whose reported interest is not translated . . . into achievement."[2] Much of the testimony during the trial, however (and during the later remedy hearings), offered a quite different picture. Comparatively little was said about low scholastic proficiency and lack of academic skills; much more was said about lack of motivation, poor self-image, low aspirations, and a lack of interest in education. For example, the description of a classroom of slow learners (T. pp. 1376–78) as children who have a "perception of under-achievement" such that they and others "think of themselves as slower" suggests that their low self-esteem is a primary cause rather than a consequence of poor school work.

Jencks points out that "Blacks at any given economic level have lower test scores than whites. This means that a student at any given ability-level will rank higher in his class if he attends a predominantly black school. . . . blacks have higher aspirations than whites of similar ability and economic origins. This means that students are more likely to have friends who want to attend college if they attend predominantly black schools."[3]

Neither interview data nor participant observation material gathered by black field workers in a poor Detroit neighborhood gave any support to the notion that blacks are characterized by low motivations and aspirations and by lack of interest in education on the part of parents. Summarizing our findings, Charles Lebeaux and I wrote:

Little substance was found in the motion that initial lack of pupil interest or motivation or parental indifference are key factors [in black underachievement]. Negro parents generally revealed great faith in education and were keenly aware of its importance to their children's future. Nor do the learning problems of children from poor Negro families (or those recently from such background) appear to be the result of cynicism based on any long-run calculations about the children's future employment chances . . . as is often alleged. The basic problem is, rather, that many . . . children experience learning difficulties almost at once and that subsequent to this, defensive reactions often develop on the part of both the children and their teachers.[4]

The references to self-conceptions, self-images, and self-esteem (these terms were used interchangeably) also failed to reflect the weight of existing evidence. Percy Zirkel and E. G. Moses found no significant difference between the self-concepts of Negro and white children, or between black self-concepts in segregated and in integrated settings.[5] Morris Rosenberg and Roberta Simmons found that black students generally had higher self-esteem than whites of similar status, and at the high school level the proportion of black youths with low self-esteem was much greater in predominantly white than in predominantly black schools.[6] The Coleman Report found that black self-esteem in general was as high as that of whites but that the self-concepts of black students declined as the white proportion in a school increased, apparently because of their contact with more children who were at higher levels of achievement.[7] Despite the frequent appeals to the Coleman Report in the trial proceedings, this finding, too, was never brought to the court's attention.

John D. McCarthy and William L. Yancey offer an explanation of such findings: under conditions where blacks use other blacks as comparison or reference groups for self-evaluation, esteem is less likely to be threatened.[8] An empirical study by Jerold Heiss and Susan Owens, using a refinement of the McCarthy and Yancey hypothesis, found no support for the view that black Americans have low self-esteem.[9] Rather, their research suggested that when whites are accepted as the relevant comparison group, self-esteem tends to be lower. Similar findings were reported by Stephen Asher and Vernon Allen, who also observed that integration probably leads to increased comparison with whites, a process which, as noted above, is associated with lowered self-esteem.[10] Joyjia Hsia found lower self-concepts among black pupils in Evanston, Illinois, after integration with white children from more advantaged families.[11] Nancy St. John further reported, in 1971, that when levels of academic performance are low, children of both races tend to feel more secure.[12] Later, summarizing forty studies on this subject, she found little support for the belief that desegregation enhances black self-image: "When desegregation involves crossing social-class as well as racial lines, the norm against which pupils evaluate themselves may well be higher. It is not surprising, therefore, that . . . academic self-concept tends to fall with school percentage white."[13]

Gloria Powell, studying adolescents in the South, found that, on the whole, children in all-black schools had significantly higher self-concepts than those in mixed schools, and generally had higher self-concepts than did whites in either type of school.[14] In her study of pre-schoolers Judith Porter found race highly salient for black children, who "overwhelmingly showed preference for white in response to attitude questions," as well as in doll choices.[15] However, she found the effects of racial mixture to be uneven and unclear: middle-class and lighter-skinned Negro children showed "particularly high rates of own-group rejection in desegregated settings," as did the "least-advantaged groups of blacks, who are placed in a doubly difficult situation due to a combination of race and poverty." However, this finding was reversed for darker-skinned children.[16] Porter concludes that her data do not confirm other researchers' findings that black self-image is negatively affected by desegregation and emphasizes the need for more study of this complex subject.[17] I know of no theoretical propositions in social psychology, e.g., reference group theory, to predict that placing children who are not doing well in classrooms of higher achievers will elevate their levels of self-esteem.[18] (This is not, of course, to suggest that the aim of education is to maintain favorable estimates of one's abilities and unrealistic levels of aspiration.)

The testimony from experts on both sides concerning race relations involved a confused collection of shaky assumptions. These were not presented in any systematic manner but underlay many assertions concerning racism, prejudice, discrimination, and the power of interracial schools to overcome these evils. Robert Green, for example, appeared to take for granted the decisive role of school experiences, the beneficial effects of interracial contact on "attitudes" (the term was not defined), and the cause-effect relationship between racial attitudes and a variety of overt acts in diverse situational contexts. At various points he declared that the failure of the Detroit schools to teach the proper attitudes was an important cause of suburbanization (T, pp. 966, 1026–28), racial discrimination in private clubs, and the racial disorders of 1967 (T, pp. 963–64). This failure was due in large measure, he said, to the absence of multi-racial schools: white children who have not had interracial contact grow up with a feeling of superiority toward blacks which can be overcome when racially mixed classrooms are present (T, p. 1050). He cited research to support his assertions (T, p. 960):

Nevitt and Sanford [sic] have done research in which they were able to systematically document in large numbers of undergraduate white students this kind of tacit attitude about people of color and specifically black Americans; that somewhere along the line they are inferior. This is true at the university level, at the Ph.D. level, even regarding blacks who have attained good training at schools. This is true even at schools such as Harvard, Yale, Fordham and so forth. I would like to add that early experiences in the school setting to a great extent could offset this prevailing American attitude.

Dr. Green was the only expert witness to consider the matter of the relationship between verbal responses and overt behavior, but his testimony on this topic was confused and inconsistent. At one point he seemed to be saying that overt behavior may not reveal attitudes: "whites who unconsciously perceive blacks as inferior may strive to overcome this by being very fair" (T, p. 960). But soon he declared that only actions indicate attitudes: "The only way I can determine prejudice is in terms of how people act. . . . the majority of whites in Detroit tend to hold at a conscious or unconscious level attitudes of inferiority about people of color" (T, pp. 969–70).

Although defense experts emphasized that the optimum mix was a classroom with a middle-class (usually described as a "high-status") majority, regardless of race, they were careful to note that racial mixture brought about the "added benefits of racial understanding" (T, p. 4128). The chief defense counsel referred to these benefits as the "aspect of this lawsuit about which I see no argument or disagreement at all" (T, p. 4128). This was true; the many claims for the beneficial impact of interracial contact upon race relations were not questioned during the trial (except for a single comment by Lawrence Doss, reported in Chapter 11 below). Although all the expert witnesses, especially those for the defense, had acknowledged the substandard levels of black achievement, they still insisted that encounters between middle-class whites and lower-achieving blacks in the classroom would correct white students' stereotypes. The lack of logic here was generally overlooked, although at one point Guthrie attempted to reconcile the two positions somewhat: "my own children [in Berkeley's busing program] . . . have begun to see that whereas they entered school being able to read more quickly than most of the black youngsters, there were other things . . . in which they didn't begin to match the sophistication of the black children" (T, p. 4206).

Leaving unspecified the nature of the greater sophistication of disadvantaged children, he went on to suggest that academic competence tends to be specific, rather than general (a view quite unsupported by most evidence): "My daughter has come to see that the brightest child in her class in math happens to be a black girl . . . even though my daughter may be able to read more quickly than the black girl. Individuals possess different abilities" (T, p. 4206). Whether Guthrie's persistent tendency to de-emphasize marked differences in scholastic skills was intentional or not one cannot know, but it is clear that while a black child may be described as the "brightest in the class in math," a white child's superiority in reading becomes only a matter of speed.

Nothing more than anecdotal material was offered to support the experts' assurances that placing substantial proportions of disadvantaged black children in predominantly white middle-class schools will improve racial attitudes. There is virtually no empirical evidence to support this implausible claim and nothing in race relations theory to predict such an outcome. The fact is that the two desired effects of racial dispersion tend to be mutually exclusive: the (largely unverified) peer effects hypothesis suggest that a low-achieving minority will benefit academically from contact with a higher-achieving majority, but interpersonal contact is said to improve intergroup relations only when participants are of relatively equal status. I have noted elsewhere that there is a circular quality to the sociological proposition that the required conditions for favorable interracial contact are "sustained interaction on behalf of common goals by participants of relatively equal status."[19] If these conditions exist, what more needs to be done? The desired ends have already been achieved.

There were several references during the trial (and the later remedy hearings) to the singular success of the Cass Technical High School in Detroit, which then had a majority of black students. Judge Roth himself suggested it as a model in his pre-trial ruling supporting magnet schools (see the Introduction to this volume), but it is not clear that he fully understood the factors underlying Cass Tech's success. There, tracking (so disparaged throughout the trial) created a program for academically talented students, and this, along with attractive special curricula and some scholastic entrance requirements for applicants, drew students on a voluntary basis from all over the city. Disruptive students and chronic failures were not retained. Cass Tech was not a model for system-wide desegregation—it skimmed off the cream from the city's schools—but it did show what factors made such a relatively stable interracial school possible.

The problem of reconciling these two aims of integration (improved school performance of blacks and better race relations) was not defined as such in the courtroom by anyone, at any time, and Judge Roth seemed to be unaware of any conflict between these objectives. Since experts for both sides were as one in stating (unchallenged by counsel) that integration across social class boundaries would simultaneously improve both school performance and race relations, this oversight was not surprising. Later in this book I will consider the question of why testimony on aspirations and self-conceptions, as well as on achievement, is permitted in school cases charging violations of the Constitution. My own view is that even if a mountain of research were available to show, conclusively, that black students in a mostly white public school are injured in every conceivable way, their right to enter that school should not be denied because of their race. But if there is to be testimony on the effects of heterogeneity or its absence, the courts should have something more to go on than vulgarized and platitudinous versions of the contact hypothesis and simplistic presentations of the relationship between opinions and actions.

An adequate presentation of research on the presumed effects of biracial schools upon attitudes and race relations requires some specification of terms: what kind of racial mixture is being studied; of what duration is the contact; what is meant by "attitude," a concept that includes a number of components? Is awareness of race, for example, which, in studies of small children is often taken as an indicator of "prejudice," an appropriate indicator? What *is* "prejudice"? (If black Americans, as a consequence of distinctive historical experiences, today suffer disproportionate rates of school failure, family instabilities, and involvement in certain crimes of violence, are respondents whose answers on opinion surveys reflect these realities "prejudiced"?[20]) Is ethnic own-group preference also to be defined as prejudice? Many studies do so. By "race relations" we ordinarily mean something other than reports by students on their friendship choices in a classroom, or verbal responses on various tests, yet the relationship between these behaviors and actual support for civil rights legislation or willingness to live in a mixed neighborhood for an extended period is in considerable doubt, to say the least.[21] Belief in racial inferiority (a cognitive component in racial attitudes), for example, has declined dramatically, yet racial separation continues, and in some recent years overt interracial conflict has increased.[22] Does this increased conflict bear any relationship to "prejudice"? Sociologists have long observed that the volume of conflict is, in fact, often an indicator of an assertive movement toward greater equality. Do we evaluate improvement in race relations in terms of "justice" (equality of reward or of opportunity)˜or in terms of peace, quiet, and harmony? Is there any relationship between intergroup associational preferences and societal protection of minority civil rights?

American social scientists' almost obsessive fascination with various aspects of the contact hypothesis in race relations has been reflected in a mass of work, far too much to cite here. However, the reader is referred to Nancy St. John's *Desegregation Outcomes for Children* for a fine treatment of one aspect of the subject: the effect of schools upon measurable racial attitudes. After reviewing a substantial amount of research and considering its limitations and methodological problems, she concludes as follows:

Comparative studies of the racial attitudes of segregated and desegregated school children are inconclusive. Findings are inconsistent and mixed regardless of whether students' racial attitudes or friendship choice was the object of study, regardless of whether desegregation was by neighborhood or busing, or voluntary or mandatory and regardless of whether the study design was cross-sectional or longitudinal.[23]

St. John's book was not available at the time of the Detroit trial, of course, but much of the research on which her assessment was made had been done. No reference to those studies is found in the transcript of the trial.

CHAPTER 11
The Issue of
Community Control of Schools

Community control of schools was a highly volatile and controversial issue in 1971, part of a larger surge of "black pride," black consciousness, black nationalism, black power—all in all, a new kind of black assertiveness. The national mood and its manifestations can change so rapidly that it is hard now, less than a decade later, to remember how demands for black participation in school affairs, ranging from administrative decentralization to neighborhood "autonomy," seemed to be sweeping the country. In actuality, only a few cities were involved, and Detroit was one of them, although the struggle there compared neither in scope nor intensity with the convulsions felt in New York City.[1]

Judge Roth was obviously concerned about the conflict between demands for neighborhood control, or even greatly increased participation by black parents, and a desegregation remedy that would disperse students throughout a large metropolitan area. At some points he questioned expert witnesses on this matter, but, with one exception, most of the testimony on the issue was evasive and some was deceptive.

The plaintiffs' expert, Dr. Green, told the court that black parents were demanding community control only out of despair over the lack of integration (T, pp. 910–12):

If the school districts remain segregated along racial lines then we will demand control of our particular schools. This is a political response to a particular situation that very much relates to a geographical structuring of the school district along racial lines and I think the political distinction and edu-

147

cational distinction is very important and crucial. . . . this relates to the argument that is sometimes offered that integration is in opposition to community control. That is not necessarily so. When we refer to the educational concept, irrespective of where a child attends a given school, then the parents of those children should have some input into how that particular school is structured.

Should have some input? This was a long way from the vociferous demands for virtual local autonomy then being heard, but the NAACP counsel, reflecting the organization's ambivalence toward this movement, did not explore these ambiguities, nor did he ask whether the distance from home to school would not make parental participation far more difficult, especially for poor people without cars. When Green was asked whether he saw any conflict between the goals of decentralization and those of desegregation, he responded, "Not at all" (T, pp. 1019–21).

Most of the defense experts were either vague or evasive; clearly, they were reluctant to state in plain language that the black nationalist sentiment sparking much of the local agitation for "control of our own schools" was both ideologically and practically incompatible with metropolitan racial dispersion. School system officials tread warily; they must retain a degree of harmony with all of the important segments of the community. (Dr. Guthrie, from the University of California, was not questioned on this subject.) Thus Dr. Delmo Della-Dora told Judge Roth that local school decisionmaking could mean the "community of people, not the community of geography," suggesting that physical distance between home and school would not necessarily be a barrier to parents' involvement. When pressed by an intervenor-attorney as to whether extreme geographic "attentuation of the community" would not make it very difficult for parents to participate effectively in school governance (would they not have to travel to areas where they "felt alien"?), Della-Dora declared that the problem might perhaps be solved through "regional school boards," although how the existence of such boards would overcome the obstacles to parental participation presented by sheer physical distance was not made clear (T, pp. 3308, 3370). From time to time defense expert Rankin made a number of references to the educational importance of greater local school autonomy and decisionmaking power for parents (school programs "designed by the people who are there") but ignored the difficulties that metropolitan student dispersion would create for such a policy (T, pp. 3803–11, 4223–27). The departing super-intendent, however, was asked whether extensive student dispersion was compatible with "community control." Drachler responded (T, Drachler Deposition, p. 148):

> I think America is pragmatic enough . . . to re-tape what we have called local control, which I believe is a myth, and to squeeze out from Federal planning and thinking and resources the most pragmatic kind of plan which will on the one hand enable the schools to continue to operate in accordance with American democratic values and at the same time leave enough control at the local level, which will be more meaningful control than the kind of local control we thought we had for fifty years.

The tone was reassuring, but the substance was both non-responsive and inaccurate. In the United States public schools have been quite open to citizen pressure in a variety of ways, assessed as desirable or disgraceful according to one's point of view. Localism in American education has been more than a "myth," and metropolitan student reassignment under judicial supervision would clearly alter the locus of power while placing additional spatial barriers between schools and the parents of children attending them.

Because the Detroit case had been initiated on behalf of blacks, and because it was blacks (not the same persons, of course) who were pressing for community control of schools, it was understandable that Judge Roth would be especially concerned with the views of black expert witnesses.[2] He tried to get Deputy Superintendent Arthur Johnson to tell him how serious the conflict was between metropolitan desegregation and what were then militant demands for black community control, but his efforts were not very successful:

Roth: Without indicating where you stand . . . would you say that the drive of perhaps the majority or at least some of the black community of Detroit toward decentralization of the school system in Detroit had its focus on a goal of control of their schools?

Johnson: . . . the drive for school decentralization . . . had its focus on something slightly different or more than control. . . . it was a drive to really connect the black community with the control of the school system in a meaningful way to such an extent that this community could feel that it had an equal stake in the whole system and equal access to the power of the system. . . .

Roth: Well, visualizing hypothetically a . . . metropolitan system, do you see any inconsistencies between trying to achieve integration and yet holding onto community control of the the schools?

Here was a simple question, requiring, one would think, a simple answer. But it was not forthcoming. Johnson replied (T, pp. 4349–51):

Not so much as an inconsistency but as some break in the pattern of community development and thinking around the schools at the present time. . . . I don't think it is totally inconsistent because I would assume even with the metropolitan approach, if that were developed, that with it would go the right of people to move which would give body and substance to this beyond just the movement of students. I'm talking about where people live. . . . there are some hazards in this for school decentralization. . . . whatever people may have in mind, when we talk about control as this process is now conceived and even as it is being implemented there are some real hazards there, and frankly, your Honor, I do think that we are under heavy obligation to serve both needs. There is need in the big urban school system to bring schools in the community back together in a way that they have not been, to reduce the distance and to increase the involvement of parents in the community in the education process. I do think that is essential. . . . Anything that tends to frustrate that . . . imperils the development of a quality program. At the same time I believe that integration is required to have a truly quality educational program for black and white students. . . . our command is to find a way to do both and I know that is extremely difficult.

One wishes that the judge, at this point, had directed the witness to answer the question that had been put to him.

Two witnesses who might have been expected to speak with greater candor were Malcolm Dade, Jr., and Lawrence Doss, coordinators of the Detroit Office of School Decentralization, an agency made possible by financial support from the Ford Foundation. Dade's testimony was lengthy but not very enlightening. Although at one point he stated that "within the black community there was a concern that boundary lines would be drawn in such a way that would afford the greatest potential to elect a black [or majority black] school board" (T, p. 3452), most of his testimony involved so many discreet circumlocutions that it must have been quite hard for the court to follow it. For example, when asked whether there was concern about the racial makeup of the school boards to be elected, he replied (T, pp. 3454–55):

It seems to me as I look back to that point in time there was a concern, I think as there always is, with discussions around the school to be very concerned with what is perceived as their own community and to also be concerned as to whether those that would eventually make the decisions as the law required would give adequate ear to the kinds of things the people in the community were saying and one of the ways in which many people in the community saw as maintaining their voice was this concept of drawing the lines in such as way that allowed them to politically elect [not?] a black board, or a white board, but a board that would be sympathetic to their concepts and their concerns and these concerns I think varied throughout the city. It is even difficult, I think, to define a school community on the basis of the high school boundaries but if one uses that as an artificial boundary then I think you can say for each of the high schools there is probably some difference in the attitude in that very community and it reflects different kinds of problems.

The School Board attorney, obviously trying to reveal to Judge Roth the conflicting ideologies within the black population, questioned his witness as to present "community" sentiment concerning the recently instituted decentralized system. Dade replied (T, p. 3470):

It seems to me that there is a dissatisfaction with schools generally. Dissatis-faction varies in terms of how it gets acted out in thought and deed as you move around the city and there still is this concern on the part of the community as to the degree of involvement that they have. I think as you find a relation to income that as income goes up there is more of a willingness on the part of the community to view in a very positive manner their elected representatives in terms of those various boards and the fact that they are acting in their best behalf, but it is hard, I think, even for the strongest critic to say that there is not a great deal more involvement and certainly it is clear to me that there is every day a greater understanding of what this educational process is. It may not be where it should be but there is more than what was and one has only to pick up the papers to recognize that it even makes news today, things that would not have made news seven or eight months ago and now is making news, and when one makes news one has another way of informing people. This is a significant part of decentralization. So I think that the perceptions of the community as it relates to education still is one of dissatisfaction, but I don't think people have given up hope in terms of the fact that they do believe that there can be improvement.

Defense counsel had elicited from Dade a chronology of the decen-tralization effort, from the public pressure for passage of the enabling state law to the recall of the school board members who were respon-sible for the April 7 high school integration plan. But the underlying

issues and conflicting values were completely obscured. The crossexamining NAACP counsel had no interest in revealing the extent to which
the black community was divided on the issue of racial dispersion,
nor the fact that there was indeed some degree of support for black
control of black schools. Not until Intervenor-Counsel Ritchie (who
had been a spokesman for citizens' groups in some white peripheral
areas of Detroit) questioned Dade was there some sharpening of
these issues (T, p. 3488). Yes, Dade said, black political pressure in
Detroit was primarily responsible for the passage of Act 244 decen-
tralizing the control of schools. And yes, the black community wanted
to select the staff, decide on curriculum, and oversee the "entire
operation of the school"—but, said Dade, this was not only the demand of black areas, but of white ones as well (T, pp. 3488–89). What
priority did black parents place on the attainment of racial integration? Dade's response, shorn of its vague and euphemistic language,
was that their concern was with children's academic progress and that
"unfortunately . . . most people no longer see integration as being
the way to achieve that objective" (T, p. 3491). Ritchie asked whether
Dade agreed with the contention, made by plaintiffs' expert witness
Robert Green, that the black community saw a school which was
racially identifiable as an inferior school. Some of Dade's apparently
evasive responses ("the whole concern of citizen participation is in the
throes of reality") may represent his wish to be extremely cautious on
this issue. Judge Roth rephrased the question: "I think what Mr.
Ritchie wants to know is the perception of the black community
toward schools which are predominantly black in student attendance.
Do they look upon [them] as inferior schools, based on that fact
alone?" Dade replied: "based upon my own personal feeling and my
observation and discussions . . . with people . . . the answer would
be no" (T, pp. 3488–92).

In the process of Ritchie's questioning of Dade, the support of
many black leaders, including that of Coleman Young, then a state
senator, for decentralized control of city schools was put into the
record. Dade noted, too, that some civic leaders had given scant
support to or had even ridiculed the School Board's April 7 Plan,
although he also stated (T, p. 3460) that some did applaud the fact
that "symbolically this represented to many a step in the right direction . . . against racism" (T, p. 3460). But, as noted above, Dade was
not asked directly whether neighborhood control and racial dispersion
could be achieved simultaneously.

Lawrence Doss, a prominent black leader, was the next to testify. At the time of the trial he was president of New Detroit (a privately funded interracial coalition organized after the 1967 riots), but he had been in charge of decentralization plans for the Detroit schools before joining New Detroit. He described his background as that of a systems analyst; he had no academic background in the social sciences, nor was he a professional educator. The plaintiffs challenged his role as an expert witness on educational matters, but the judge made short work of this objection: "I suppose everyone is an expert [in this field]. . . . the witness is well-qualified to answer." Before his involvement in the public schools Doss had been director of the data center of the Internal Revenue Service in Detroit. Under direct examination by defense counsel, Doss made a fairly strong case for decentralization, citing the obstacles to public participation in a school system of great size. It was not just a matter of minority political pressures, he said: "literally thousands of people . . . wanted to be involved" in making policy in the schools their children attended (T, p. 4366). Bushnell asked whether, given the existing racial separation of neighborhoods, a school system could be both racially integrated and "decentralized," as Doss was using the term; would making each Detroit school approximate the then 65 percent black:34 percent white school population of the district be compatible with decentralization? Doss began by saying, rather unequivocally, "No" (T, pp. 4368–70): "It would completely eliminate the notion of parents having control of the boards and the administrators that supervise their children because . . . many children would be going to school outside of the regions in which their parents lived, therefore the parents would be disenfranchised in terms of what their vote meant with respect to . . . community control" (T, pp. 4368–70).

But the defense counsel, unwilling to let the testimony of a civic leader be framed wholly in terms of the legitimacy of the locus of power, unwisely led his witness into a discussion of the academic benefits inherent in a decontralized system. Perhaps unaware of the grave weaknesses in the claims of the community control movement that academic harm came from centralized authority or that academic enhancement came from localized control, Bushnell elicited statements from the witness about the educational benefits from "teamwork" and the "accountability" of school staff to students and the local area. Metropolitan busing would make these educational goals impossible to achieve, Doss declared. During the ensuing crossexamination by Co-counsel Flannery, Doss allowed himself to be drawn ever deeper into a field for which he was quite unprepared. He said he had tried to "read all of the literature on decentralization and the educational questions related" to it and had conferred with "literally hundreds of students, administrators, educators and experts from across the country," as well as local university authorities, etc. (T, pp. 4378–90). He had already warned that compulsory integration in the existing tense social climate would produce school disruption; this was a weak basis for an objection in a school case alleging de jure segregation, and Flannery did not fail to exploit this point (T, pp. 4374, 4380, 4402).

In lengthy colloquies between Doss and counsel, and between Doss and Judge Roth, who evinced a deep interest in this entire issue, Doss did well as long as he was describing the wishes and declared "rights" of some citizens to have certain kinds of power over their schools. The NAACP counsel was on very weak ground in trying to persuade the court that Detroit schools could be both racially integrated and controlled by the area in which they were located. Roth's questions (T, pp. 4398–99) as to whether, under modern urban conditions, city-dwellers knew each other well enough even on a neighborhood basis to create the kind of relationship and exert the type of control Doss envisioned showed his acumen: "Isn't it the rare block . . . in the city . . . where a family who have lived there for ten years knows everybody?" Concerning neighboring patterns in high-rise apartments, he asked: "isn't it a nostalgic desire to return to the little red school house?" Doss' insistence that "it is much more difficult, especially for poor black people," to become involved in school governance without living reasonably close to their school was unanswerable. "You can't . . . gerrymander school attendance areas," he said, "and still have the concept of community control at work." "If the child must go to another school in another region the parents' vote is meaningless" (T, pp. 4385, 4392). The judge agreed: "your views are consistent. . . . I don't quite see how to square community control with so-called integration. As you say, it does disenfranchise, and I can't quite see the community touch between a board member or a ten-man board in the inner city and the students attending there [who] are perhaps 65% from the outside. . . . to me there is an inconsistency" (T, p. 4401). But neither the witness nor those who questioned him confronted the key issue: community control was a mechanism to enable a voting minority to acquire a measure of political power over schools in a setting where they would otherwise be outvoted. Claims for educational benefits as a consequence of "closeness," "teamwork," "avoiding bureaucracy," "accountability," or parents' "sense of control" could not be documented.

Doss was encouraged to declare his preference for voluntary integration. "Pluralism," he called it—the family is to decide whether a child should attend a school in which his own ethnic group predominates. Roth was troubled; didn't *Brown* imply that a preference for attending a school made up of students of one's own racial group was no longer protected by law? (T, p. 4402). At this point Doss stepped into quicksand. Instead of drawing a distinction between constitutional requirements to abolish racial exclusion and racial composition, he reiterated his fear that "involuntary desegregation" would produce interracial conflict. Educational benefits were unlikely because compulsory integration would lead to disruption and bitterness in urban public schools and neighborhoods (T, pp. 4402–7). (He did not seem to realize that these objections to desegregation had long since been rejected by the courts.) Under Flannery's crossexamination, Doss conceded that student transfers should not be permitted if they resulted in increased racial concentration (T, pp. 4405–6). This transfer policy had been instituted by Superintendent Drachler some time earlier, but, Doss continued, given increased citizen participation (via decentralization) and greater progress on urgent social and economic issues, the "problems of racism and the problems of black revenge against racism" could be overcome. People would then "feel much more inclined to voluntarily send their children to schools with children of other ethnic backgrounds" (T, p. 4408). But Flannery could and did easily show that Doss had little factual basis for these expectations in a school system already two-thirds black, and when he allowed counsel to lead him into a discussion of whether these recommendations were consistent with the findings of the Coleman Report, Doss was in deep trouble. Despite his claim to have studied the report "and other analyses of its data," he drew the conclusion that the superior achievement of middle-class children was the result of greater school resources allocated to them (T, pp. 4414–15). To Flannery's obvious delight ("this is an exciting piece of testimony to me"), the defense witness declared that, in Detroit, less money was allocated to inner-city children than to those in outlying neighborhoods (T, p. 4415). When it became clear that the disparity represented the already discussed salary differential, Doss then moved to the contribution of what he called another key factor: "teachers' low expectations" for low-income students (T, p. 4418). From this he moved to some of the distinctive emphases of the then-fashionable community control movement (T, pp. 4419–20):

lower socio-economic people, especially blacks, may have somewhat of a different frame of reference, a different cultural background and may not be as responsive to a white middle-class approach. . . . many poor black kids especially get very turned off because they are not dealing with things that represent the real world to them. . . . He will grow up in an educational climate that is foreign to him if we impose the white middle-class culture on the black inner-city kid. It may not be in his ball park at all.

When the neighborhood had more control over its school, the resulting "teamwork," Doss said, would increase the "encouragement and motivation that the student gets from his home" (T, p. 4420). Flannery pressed him on how such hypothetical academic improvement could be reconciled with the Coleman Report data showing that schools of predominantly higher socioeconomic status students enhance the educational performance of poor children. Doss could simply have replied that the cross-sectional study had not proved a cause-effect relationship, that, in any case, the alleged "effect" was quite small, and so on, but he was not prepared for this kind of rejoinder. Instead, he said: "where we are today is that we have cultural differences and . . . we must deal with those cultural differences in the real world and we must deal with them in terms of what the needs are of each given culture and each person in that culture as each person sees it and as that culture sees it, not as someone else sees the needs for some other culture, which becomes very paternalistic" (T, p. 4422). Flannery pressed on: "you are saying that we find ourselves at the point of . . . cultural differences resulting largely or in part from prior discrimination and your prescription is . . . to ameliorate those differences on the basis of a fundamentally separatist approach . . . ?" (T, p. 4423). Not all differences, Doss objected, were caused by discrimination; some went back to Africa (T, p. 4424). He insisted that voluntary integration was a pluralist, not a separatist, approach; returning to this old theme, he insisted that "forced integration would not be at all possible in today's climate . . . and it would "dampen the spirits if not destroy the participation of many many [powerless] people who for the first time . . . have some feeling of power" (T, pp. 4425–29). Flannery pressed him to admit that given the existing realities in housing patterns Doss's proposals would result in racially separate schools. Doss would say only that additional racial concentration could be constrained and voluntary integration "encouraged." In answer to Flannery's final question, he said that he was not aware that if there is a finding of prior discrimination remedial action may be imposed by court order (T, p. 4424).

The fact that implementing both local neighborhood governance and large-scale student reassignment by race is impossible was concealed or papered over by most witnesses.[3] Had this case occurred in New York City, failure to recognize and confront this contradiction would perhaps have had serious consequences, but in Detroit the militant community control movement was, predictably, short-lived. By the time the busing remedy was implemented, the political leadership of both the city and the school system had become mainly black, and much of the pressure for a mechanism to achieve more minority control had evaporated.[4] The decentralized structure, however, remained.

PART III: CONSTITUTIONAL VIOLATIONS BY SCHOOL AUTHORITIES

Overview

The trial ended late in July. In September of 1971 Judge Roth ruled that Detroit schools were segregated de jure. The extensive testimony he had heard on various educational issues was not mentioned in his decision. The emphasis, as I have noted, was on demographic trends and residential patterns caused by discrimination. After summarizing the record of housing segregation, Judge Roth declared that there was an "affirmative obligation of the defendant Board to adopt and implement pupil assignment practices and policies that compensate for and avoid incorporation into the school system the effects of residential racial segregation."[1] But the Court of Appeals for the Sixth Circuit specifically rejected residential segregation as a basis for finding the Detroit schools segregated de jure and removed from its ruling the references to housing and demography that had been so prominent in the decision of the district court: "In affirming the District Judge's findings of constitutional violations by the Detroit Board of Education and by the State defendants . . . we have not relied at all upon the testimony pertaining to segregated housing except as school construction programs helped cause or maintain such segregation."[2]

The appeals court made no reference to an "affirmative duty" of a school system in a residentially segregated city to abandon the geographic method of student assignment. If such a duty were to be established, every city with a significant percentage of blacks would be obliged to use criteria other than distance from school as the basis for assignment, and litigation to prove specific acts of discrimination and segregation by school officials would not be needed. Perhaps the appeals court reasoned that, given the continued legality of geo-

159

graphic assignment (following a precedent case in this circuit[3]), the emphasis Judge Roth had placed on residential segregation and demographic changes greatly weakened the charges against the schools. Or perhaps the appeals court believed that a finding of segregation de jure based on government complicity in residential segregation and the failure of the school system to abandon geographic assignment was simply too great a departure from legal precedent. The northern school cases have maintained consistency with those in the South through the use, in both instances, of acts by school authorities as a necessary predicate for issuance of a court desegregation order. In the South these "acts" were defined, at first, as the maintenance of an openly dual system and, later, as failure to dissipate the lingering effects of previous compulsory school segregation. In the North the courts have come to consider as equivalent acts various forms of "cheating" to increase segregation beyond that produced by residential concentration by school systems. This evidence of constitutional violations then becomes, to use the language of Owen Fiss, the "trigger" that can fire the "cannon" of mandatory desegregation: dispersed school assignment to make schools as racially "unidentifiable" as is practical and feasible.[4] Fiss, in discussing the *Swann* case, characterized this legal "theory for attributing responsibility" as "contrived," defensible only if "the primary concern of the courts is the segregated patterns themselves, rather than the causal relation of past discrimination to them."[5]

Judge Roth's characterization of the legal necessity of distinguishing between de jure and de facto segregation as "unfortunate" was an admission that the condition of racial concentration itself, not the state acts alleged to have created it, was the true object of his concern.[6] It is hard to escape the conclusion that his inclusion of school violations was a reluctant concession to the requirements of legal precedent. Compared with the emphasis in his ruling on housing and demography, these acts of the school system are treated in almost cursory fashion: indeed, he devoted more space in the text of his ruling (see Appendix A to this volume) to praise for some of the pro-integration efforts of the Detroit system than he did to all categories of its school violations.[7]

In the Detroit case, as in others, the evidence of constitutional violations involved several types of offenses. In our analysis Evelyn Weissman and I have divided this material according to the categories used in the rulings, first of the district court, and then of the Court of

Appeals for the Sixth Circuit. There are four: (1) selection of sites for the construction of new schools; (2) racial discrimination in student transportation to relieve overcrowding; (3) the use of optional zones to permit whites to avoid going to school with blacks; and (4) manipulation of boundary lines and feeder patterns to create school zones that perpetuate or increase racial separation.

The contrast between the rulings of the two courts, not only in what was dropped but in what was expanded, is striking. Judge Roth devoted five sentences to the transportation violations, and gave no specific examples.[8] These five sentences became almost five pages in the appeals court ruling, which included excerpts from the trial record.[9] Zone and feeder pattern violations were dealt with by Judge Roth in a single long paragraph, with no examples given.[10] The appeals court devoted roughly four pages to this subject.[11] Judge Roth devoted less than a page to optional areas;[12] the appeals court ruling gave about three pages to the subject.[13]

Fiss in his analysis said only that the causal attribution of school segregation to the actions of school authorities "seems contrived." What about the evidence? My original intention, in studying the school violations testimony, was to see how a judge went about the task of evaluating the validity and assessing the significance of great masses of data on subjects unfamiliar to him. I approached the testimony on recent school violations with skepticism, for three reasons. First, from a sociologist's perspective, if schools are already segregated as a consequence of residential patterns, the principle of parsimony argues against further explanations for this condition. Second, my own research in changing neighborhoods in Detroit suggested that the school system had been trying to maintain integrated schools, albeit with inadequate and ineffective tools. Third, it did not seem likely that the strongly pro-integration leadership of the Detroit school system would countenance racial discrimination. If the court assessment of recent school violations had been accurate, it was important to see whether the testimony showed how supervision by these officials had been evaded, their orders disobeyed, and their aims frustrated.

The school violations testimony is voluminous and formidable. In addition to the transcript of almost twenty days of oral presentation, there are maps, charts, racial counts (since 1961), data on present and anticipated population movements and on school building and room capacity, consideration of local geography and traffic arteries, and discussion of the problems of changing parochial school enrollments—plus details on the whole matter of school organization, which was at times clearly confusing to the judge. Some of the testimony covered a period of almost twenty years. In the next chapters the accuracy of these materials is assessed and the extent to which the court rulings reflected the evidence is considered. Finally, we consider the difficult question of the extent to which, if at all, school policies and practices did cause or "augment" the racial separation of students.

CHAPTER 12
School Site Selection

The racially separated nature of residential areas in Detroit was well documented in the testimony on housing and population movements at the start of the trial. It showed beyond a doubt what had never been disputed and was obvious to anyone: almost all of Detroit's neighborhoods, like those of most other cities, were either predominantly white, predominantly black, or in the process of racial change (see T, pp. 366–69, for examples). Thus a school or any other facility—library, grocery store, community center, or laundromat—built to serve those who live nearby will reflect the area's racial composition. The clientele of such facilities, whether children or adults, in most instances will be either mostly black or mostly white. This simple fact of life was—surprisingly enough—a major basis for the finding of the courts that the Detroit schools were segregated de jure, i.e., as a consequence of official actions of the school system acting under state authority.

The appeals court, having rejected the material on housing and demography on which Judge Roth relied so heavily in his ruling, devoted considerable attention to school site and construction violations. Two pages were devoted to excerpts from the trial testimony intended to prove what nobody had questioned: that, neighborhoods being what they were, there was virtually no neighborhood in which a school could be built within walking distance of children without its being a predominantly one-race school. It is hard to understand why the Sixth Circuit Court felt obliged to belabor this uncontested fact of demography, yet its ruling quotes from the trial record at some length to document the charge. For example:

Q: Could you locate the Stark School, Doctor [Foster]?

A: The Stark School is in the Southeastern zone.

Q: And what was its enrollment?

A: The enrollment was 822 when it opened in 1969.

Q: And the percent black?

A: 98.4% black.

. . . .

Q: Can you locate the Field School Annex, Doctor?

A: Just to the northeast of King [Martin Luther King High School].

Q: And what was its enrollment?

A: 461.

Q: Its percent black?

A: 90.5 percent black.[1]

Such questions went on and on. They were followed by a list of additional schools which were predominantly of one race or the other when they opened. Twenty-eight of these were located in predominantly black areas, nine in white. As long as a geographic system of school assignment is permissible, how can this be defined by the courts as de jure segregation? This appears to be a classic "Catch–22" situation: if the new schools had not been built, a disproportionate number of buildings used by black children would have been old—some firetraps, some dangerously dilapidated. In its 1962 report, the Citizens Advisory Committee on Equal Educational Opportunities praised the Detroit School Board program of replacing old school buildings in the poor black center city, saying that "the most visible symbol of inequality . . . [is] the old school." It noted approvingly that the board had earmarked 50 percent of its construction funds for the inner city.[2] Superintendent Samuel Brownell (Drachler's predecessor), who had firmly declared a policy of racial disregard, stood off the protests of parents in white outlying districts whose schools were crowded in the mid-1950s and stated that he would urge the board to build where the needs were greatest—and the needs were obviously greatest in the older parts of the city.

Of the new schools listed by the Sixth Circuit to illustrate the board's segregatory construction practices, two-thirds were elementary schools. As noted above, it was inevitable that most new elementary schools, serving, as they did, children living within walking distance, would be one-race schools. It was somewhat less inevitable for junior high schools, as they draw their students from wider (but still surrounding) areas. Efforts by the board to site several new junior high schools in such a way as to maximize racial mix, yet adhere to its policy of pupil assignment to the nearest school, were described by the expert witness for the defense, Merle Henrickson (T, pp. 3018–23). Most such efforts were either unsuccessful or successful only briefly: Drew Junior High was in a mixed, but predominantly white, area when construction started but opened with a student body 95 percent black; Beaubien Junior High, planned as an integrated school, opened at 62 percent black and was over 90 percent black two years later. The rapidity of racial transition, which doomed many of the board's plans for new integrated intermediate schools, is illustrated here in a table showing the racial proportions of elementary schools in changing Detroit neighborhoods over the decade.

School	Percentage of Black Students		
	1960	1965	1970
Bagley	0	67	98
Clinton	12	54	97
Fitzgerald	20	79	99
Guest	17	15	94
Hamilton	5	42	71
Hampton	0	26	75
Herman	4	31	59
A. L. Holmes	36	47	93
King	0	11	92
Lillibridge	40	69	93
Lingemann	15	37	60
MacDowell	35	83	98
Marshall	0.1	22	65
Mason	0	27	53
McFarlane	1	38	82
Monnier	10	20	88
Noble	20	70	97
Parker	0	9	79
Pasteur	24	76	92
Schulze	9	52	97
Vandenberg	0	15	94
VanZile	0	12	52
Vernor	0	16	97
Winship	0	2	70

Despite these data, Dr. Gordon Foster, the plaintiffs' expert witness on desegregation, when asked if the schools' racial characteristics "can change dramatically in the course of a small number of years," replied, "Ordinarily, not that much" (T, p. 2462).

If most neighborhoods were either predominantly black or white, and if integrated neighborhoods did not remain integrated for long, it is difficult to see where the board could have built new schools that were not to be, or not to become, predominantly one-race schools.

In addition to the construction of new schools in predominantly black neighborhoods, the size of those schools was offered by the judge as a reason for his ruling of segregation de jure. As he noted: "Since 1959 the Board has constructed at least 13 small primary schools with capacities of from 300 to 400 pupils. This practice negates opportunities to integrate, contains the black population and perpetuates and compounds school segregation."[3] The small size of the new elementary schools reflected many citizens' and professional educators' belief that plant efficiency, once highly regarded in Detroit (prime user of the "platoon system"), was less important than the creation of smaller, more human and personal settings for young children.[4] Even if the board had built large elementary schools, it would still have been open to charges of segregatory intent and/or effects, for not only had Foster declared that elementary schools which are small and furnish "a close, walk-in type neighborhood school pattern" tend to increase segregation, but also that schools which are too big "contain or isolate minority students" (T, pp. 1405–6). There is no evidence that the variations in school size which he mentioned have any effect: even scholars who place a very high value on school racial mixture dismiss as inconsequential the impact of these manipulations, which are more fully discussed in Chapter 15 below.

The use of "sociological" and "social-psychological" concepts to strengthen the evidence on site selection and school construction was a sorry misuse of the language of these disciplines. For example (T, p. 1698):

Q: What effect in terms of perception of the community does it have when a school is opened with an overwhelming enrollment of one race or the other?

A: Generally, the community perceives, in my opinion, that the school has been thought of as being, going to be an all-white school, or an all-black school and in either case that it is racially isolated.

A spurious air of "social science" surrounds this reply. An elementary school in a neighborhood where all the children are black is not "perceived" by someone as racially concentrated; it simply is, "generally" or not so generally.

Another example of the abuse of the language is the following colloquy, also quoted in the Sixth Circuit ruling, between the plaintiffs' counsel and this same witness (T, pp. 1696–97):

Q: Dr. Foster, from your examination of the pattern of construction in this school system, 1960–1970, do you have an opinion of the effect of that pattern of construction on segregation in the Detroit School System?

A: My opinion is that construction practices were followed in such a way as to increase segregation. I say this because of the large number of schools that were opened that were all white or all black or with a disproportionate number of one race or the other upon opening.

This solemn pronouncement brings to mind that famous explanation of high rates of unemployment: unemployment rates are high because large numbers of people are out of work. As for the opinion that opening these schools increased racial separation, no supporting evidence was presented, nor do the writers know of any. It does not even appear to be a suitable question for research: how could one design a study to verify Foster's assertion?

It was the school system itself, at both the local and state levels, that provided the courts with support for the charge that the building program represented intentional segregation. Both had issued policy statements declaring that each time a site was selected for a new school or expansion of existing facilities was considered, there was an opportunity for integration if the right location were selected.[5] The state Board of Education had specified that "care in site location must be taken . . . if housing patterns in an area would result in a school largely segregated on racial, ethnic, or socioeconomic lines."[6] Thus the defendants were hoist by their own petard. This pious intention was clearly impossible to fulfill unless the geographic system of school assignment were to be abandoned, and this was not attempted until the ill-fated plan of April 7, 1970. While proclaiming the aim of integration via careful site selection for new schools, the Detroit Board had also declared, incongruously, that students were to be drawn from "as compact an area surrounding a school" as was practical.

Yet had the state and city school boards *not* adopted such policy statements, this fact too might have been used as grounds to establish their intent to perpetuate segregation. Superintendent Harold H. Spears of San Francisco incurred intense criticism from civil rights groups in that city for saying that, short of busing to redistribute children on a basis of race (which he opposed and did not believe was legally required), "I have no educationally sound program to suggest to the Board to eliminate the schools in which the children are predominantly of one race."[7] Detroit's former superintendent, Samuel Brownell, a proponent of racial disregard, might have made a similar statement; his successor, Norman Drachler, would not have done so. For the Detroit school leadership in the late 1960s, public statements that integration was a worthwhile goal irresistibly suggested the further declaration that the goal could be achieved by proper location of schools or some other means short of busing. Once having made these statements, the state and local board were vulnerable to attack on the grounds that if it were possible to achieve integration, why had they not done so?

Thus it would appear that the Detroit system would have been found guilty of segregation de jure regardless of which course it pursued. If it declined to support a policy of integration through careful school site selection, this would have been seen as evidence of intent to segregate. If it adopted (as it did) such a policy as both desirable and possible, but made no progress toward implementing it, how could this failure be justified or explained away? If it proceeded with a building program to replace old schools in the black center city with new ones, it would be judged guilty of perpetuating segregation. Had it failed to do so (as Owen Fiss and others have pointed out), it would be open to the charge that where it is possible to identify a black school or a white school by the quality of the school building (among other indexes), then "a *prima facie* case of violation of substantive constitutional rights . . . has been shown,"[8] regardless of the pattern of student assignment. The Detroit School Board was going to be found guilty whatever actions it took.

CHAPTER 13
Transportation Practices

The courts referred to three kinds of constitutional violations involving transportation to relieve school overcrowding: the practice of intact busing; the busing of black children to predominantly black schools, bypassing predominantly white schools with capacity to receive them; and the one-way busing of black children.

The practice of relieving overcrowding by taking an entire classroom of children (black, white, or both) out of a school, a practice later designated "intact busing," was common prior to 1962.[1] In his deposition (T, p. 47) Superintendent Drachler described how his own children had been bused in this fashion, along with their teacher. The alternative method that became policy and practice thereafter was to designate certain blocks, i.e., streets within the catchment area of a crowded school closest to the "receiving school," to which the children who lived on those blocks would be bused. Since children do not arrange themselves neatly by grade levels, these uneven additions to classrooms create administrative problems, especially for a school system attempting to keep class size down. But neither side alluded to the difficulties created by non-intact busing. They were in agreement that the segregative effect of intact busing made it impermissible. Since the practice had been discarded at least nine years earlier, no more was said about it during the trial, and Judge Roth did not even mention it in his ruling. The Sixth Circuit Court of Appeals ruling, however, referred to the matter at some length, in line with this court's reliance upon school violations as the sole basis for upholding the ruling of the district court.[2]

Judge Roth made the following statement on the matter of discriminatory busing: "The Board, in the operation of its transportation to relieve overcrowding policy, has admittedly bused black pupils past or away from closer white schools with available space to black schools. This practice has continued in several instances in recent years despite the Board's avowed policy, adopted in 1967, to utilize transportation to increase integration."[3] This reference aroused considerable speculation. The district court ruling did not mention the names of the schools involved, few people had been in the courtroom, and the press did not carry this testimony during the course of the lengthy trial. How could there have been "several instances" since 1967 of such flagrant violations of board policy? The responsibility for approving all busing orders was in the hands of Deputy Superintendent Arthur Johnson, the former director of the Detroit NAACP. Why had Johnson approved such orders, and why had Drachler concurred?

This category of violations poses three questions for study. First, had the courtroom procedures elicited full and accurate information? Second, if they had, did the judge understand the information and evaluate it correctly? Third, if both these conditions were satisfied, did the record suggest something about the nature of the bureaucracy of the school system which would enable "it" or "someone" (the principals, the regional boards, or the superintendents?) to frustrate board policy?

The Sixth Circuit Court of Appeals, in its ruling upholding that of the district court, described these violations as "a substantial number of instances of transporting black children past white schools with available school space,"[4] named the schools involved, and quoted extensively from the trial record.[5] With names of schools and years indicated, the trial record could be examined and other sources checked.

Because the transportation cases cited were, if true, violations of either the board's earlier color-blind policy of busing to relieve overcrowding or of the modified pro-integration policy of Superintendent Drachler,[6] we studied all of the violations which took place within the previous decade (1961–1971) along with the one that occurred a year earlier. Five such cases fell within that time period; each will be considered separately.

Case 1. Busing from Angell Elementary to Higginbotham, 1960

The witness for the plaintiffs, Gordon Foster, alleged that in 1960, 118 students from all-black Angell Elementary were bused to all-black Higginbotham, bypassing predominantly white schools with available space (T, pp. 1523–24). The charge was confirmed by the defendants' witness, who admitted that Fitzgerald (20 percent black) and Clinton (12 percent black) were closer to Angell and had spaces available (T, pp. 3203, 3405–6). This, then, was a clear instance of discriminatory busing.

However, both witnesses also mentioned the simultaneous busing of 186 black Angell students to the Greenfield Park school (T, pp. 1524, 3204), located in an all-white area, with a student body 12 percent black (including the bused-in children). Both the busing to Higginbotham and to Greenfield Park were apparently continuations of earlier established transportation routes, but exactly when or why they began remains unknown. There is nothing in the record to indicate why some Angell students were bused into a white school while others were bused past white schools. This action casts some doubt upon both the segregatory intent and the overall effects of the Angell busing—60 percent of all those bused ended up in a white school. However, the busing to Higginbotham did violate the board's 1960 policy of racial disregard and was clearly segregatory. It was discontinued in 1961, when the new Jamieson school opened (itself cited as a violation), relieving the overcrowded situation at Angell (T, pp. 3204, 3406–7).

Case 2. Busing from Ruthruff Elementary, 1969

The court's citation of this case reflected the judgment that the testimony of the plaintiffs was accurate. Foster testified that in 1969 143 pupils were bused from nearly all-black Ruthruff to Herman, then 55 percent black, past 13 percent black Parkman (actually 8 percent black in 1969), which had 136 spaces available for their use (T, pp. 1629, 1633). Defense witness Merle Henrickson, responding to these charges a month later, said only that there had been busing from Ruthruff to Herman in 1965 (when Herman was predominantly white) and that other Ruthruff children were also being bused to all-white Dossin (T, pp. 2867–68). Nothing in his testimony bore on bypassing Parkman, and he was not asked about it.

Our investigation of the case revealed some additional facts. Busing to relieve overcrowding at Ruthruff began in September of 1962, when the school was 80 percent black. Ruthruff children were sent to two white schools, Herman and Dossin. (The program was strongly opposed by Ruthruff parents.[7]) Busing to those schools continued until the overcrowding at Ruthruff ended in 1970 as a result of a shrinking school population and the completion of a long-promised school addition. Although Herman gradually became more and more black (by 1965 it was 31 percent black, partly as the result of another busing program; see Case 3 below), as late as 1968 Ruthruff children were still going to Dossin, which remained all white except for the bused-in children.

Foster, as noted, stated that 143 Ruthruff students were being bused to Herman in 1969, but this figure was not correct. Ruthruff school records show that in the first part of 1969, 240 children went from there to Herman; later in 1969, 210 children were bused to Herman. Thus the 136 spaces (if correctly estimated) available at Parkman were not nearly adequate.

The Ruthruff case, then, which seemed at first glance to be a flagrant violation of either the older color-blind or the later pro-integration (where feasible) policy, was surely not a violation of the former. Was it a violation of the latter? The children being bused to Herman were clearly going to a much "whiter" school—from the virtually all-black Ruthruff to a school only 55 percent black. However, some of the 210 to 240 children being bused there during 1969 might have been shifted to Parkman, 8 percent black, until Ruthruff was able to accommodate them. For some of these children, Parkman would have been their third elementary school. Henrickson testified that it was the school system's policy to provide young children with as much stability of assignment as possible rather than subjecting them to "constant reorganization and shifting about" (T, p. 2858). But Foster testified that "stability in pupil assignment is becoming less well thought of. . . . it may actually be good for children to have a little instability in assignment" (T, p. 2525). A value choice involving some cost-benefit calculations with respect to the 136 children who, according to Foster, could have been accommodated at Parkman is at issue here.

Case 3. Busing from Parker Elementary, 1970

Foster testified that 61 children from Parker (79 percent black) were bused to Herman (then 59 percent black), bypassing Parkman (13 percent black), which, he said, had 121 available spaces (T, p. 1634). He said nothing more about busing from Parker, and this case, too, appeared from his testimony to be a clear example of racial discrimination. Henrickson, when he testified on this matter one month later, gave more details. Children from overcrowded Parker were being bused that year to three schools, two of which were in entirely white areas; the only black children at Carver (9 percent black) and Ann Arbor Trail (12 percent black) were those being bused in (T, p. 2919). Parker school records show that of a total of 232 pupils bused to relieve overcrowding in 1970, three-fourths (173) were sent to all-white schools, but there was no mention of this in any of the court decisions.

No explanation of the bypassing of Parkman appears in the trial record in either the Parker or the Ruthruff cases. Our investigation, however, revealed the following. School capacity was calculated by a statistical report in which all rooms ever used for pupils were counted as having a capacity of 32 except for the gymnasium and auditorium, which were counted as having a capacity of 64. At Parkman during the years of the alleged violations the auditorium was used only for rehearsals, performances, glee club, and the like (seats in school auditoriums are of the type used in theaters). The gymnasium was used for a single class of children, although in some schools following the platoon system (once used throughout Detroit and still used in some schools) two sections of children have been simultaneously accommodated. By the official school capacity count, then, there were 64 available spaces for "classroom use" in the auditorium and 32 in the gymnasium. Still, the total is only 96 spaces. Where did the other 40 spaces (Foster had mentioned 136 available spaces at Parkman in 1969) come from?

The answer was as follows. There were about 40 children in Special Education classes being accomodated at Parkman during this period. The classes were very small, and the program took about twice as much classroom space as the conventional elementary school program. This accounts for the official statistic of 136 available spaces in 1969. In actuality, as one can see, Parkman did not have 136 spaces available.

Case 4. Busing from A. L. Holmes, 1970

The A. L. Holmes case, unlike the others, was presented largely by non-expert witnesses: three mothers of students who were to have been bused, plus a non-parent (a volunteer worker in a community agency) who had helped organize protests over transportation changes in the area (T, pp. 1136–46, 1151–61, 1176–79, 1188–1201). These witnesses testified that some students from A. L. Holmes, 93 percent black at the time, had been informed in June of 1970 that they would be bused to three predominantly white schools in the fall; shortly before the opening of school in September, they were notified that the children would be bused instead to the newly built McGraw, 95 percent black. Most of these witnesses objected to the distance involved in the Holmes–McGraw transportation. None knew why the change had been made; all but one suspected that the reassignment was based on race. Two of the mothers further testified that busing to McGraw lasted but one semester, and that the A. L. Holmes children were then bused to virtually all-white schools closer to Holmes.

The women also described their efforts to protest the reassignment of students to McGraw, among them a sit-in at the State Board of Education in Lansing and meeting with State Superintendent of Education John Porter. Porter testified about this meeting but contradicted the women's account of the protests they had lodged. Porter said that the group did not complain of the racial implications of the change: "They did not want their children bused, period—out of the elementary school district they were in. That was the complaint they had to us" (T, p. 2079). Judge Roth queried Porter further on this point: "Are you saying that their complaint was that they did not want their children to be taken out of the Holmes School?" Porter replied: "That was the only complaint they voiced to our office" (T, pp. 2079–80).

Of course, the responses and suspicions of a few parents have no bearing on the issue of whether or not a constitutional violation has been committed. Foster made no further allegations but merely mentioned that A. L. Holmes students were bused to McGraw (T, p. 1636). Henrickson did not deny that the busing had occurred; he confirmed that some students from A. L. Holmes originally scheduled to be sent to three white schools were indeed bused to McGraw. He stated that 300 students were bused out of A. L. Holmes (T, p. 3860), but it is unclear from the record whether all 300 were transported to McGraw (T, pp. 2912; 3857 and 3860 are inconsistent). Whatever the number of students bused to McGraw, this transportation was, according to Henrickson, an unanticipated and temporary expedient (lasting one semester) to meet an emergency situation which had developed during the summer (T, pp. 2911–16, 2927). The original plan was to have the A. L. Holmes children go to three predominantly white schools which, up to then, had been receiving 600 black children from Carstens Elementary. A building was to have been leased to increase Carstens' capacity, thus freeing the three predominantly white schools for use by the A. L. Holmes children. Shortly before school opened, however, it was learned that the building was not available, and the Carstens children had to continue their existing busing arrangements (T, pp. 2889–99, 3856–61), an example of the "ripple" or "domino" effect: one change produced another. The problem was compounded by the fact that an influx of students was expected because of parochial school closings and significant increases in tuition within the parochial school system. School officials were not sure how many would transfer to the area's public schools but decided that they had to be certain of places for the children to be bused out of A. L. Holmes. The board was aware that this abrupt reassignment was not in line with its pro-integration busing policy but saw no alternative. Deputy Superintendent Arthur Johnson explained: "We were convinced there wasn't another school that would satisfactorily accommodate the transfer need and we were fully aware of the fact that it wasn't meeting the conditions of the transportation policy. We invoke some . . . criteria, judgment of reasonableness about any of these measures at any given time, and that's what happened in this case" (T, Deposition of November 23, 1970, p. 65). The A. L. Holmes students were therefore assigned to McGraw for one semester, after which they were bused to the virtually all-white Williams, Pulaski, and Law elementary schools.

Case 5. Busing from Post Junior High and Hally and Clinton Elementary, 1970

The Detroit Board's transportation-to-relieve-overcrowding policy was not voluntary and was often opposed by both black and white parents. Children living on certain blocks or streets (those closest to the receiving school) were temporarily assigned elsewhere until space became available for their return to the sending school. For this reason, it was a surprise to discover that the busing in this case, while listed in the court decisions along with the others, was entirely voluntary. Henrickson testified that, in response to complaints about conditions at all-black Post Junior High, parents had been allowed to enroll children for busing to the predominantly white Lessenger Junior High. Parents at Clinton and at Hally Elementary, both all black, could also apply for this program instead of sending their children to nearby Post. About 80 children were bused to Lessenger under this program. Parents were also offered the option of sending their children to Jefferson Junior High, which was underused but was 88 percent black (this figure includes 54 children from Post and Clinton, whose parents chose to send them there) (T, pp. 2922–23, 3413–15). In his testimony Foster did not mention that the Jefferson program was voluntary. He stated only that Post Junior High and Clinton transported 54 students to Jefferson Junior High and that the children could have been sent instead to Vetal (virtually all-white) or Coffey (29 percent black) (T, pp. 1627–38).

Both Vetal and Coffey were, of course, open to black parents on an individual basis under the Drachler policy of permitting individual transfers if racial mixture were thereby improved, but under this program families had to arrange their own transportation. Vetal was probably not offered in the program described by Henrickson because it was a K–8 elementary school, an option usually disliked by children eager to go to junior high school, and one which left them without a ninth grade placement. But this is conjecture; the testimony does not explain the reasons for excluding Vetal and Coffey Junior High from the busing program.

The overall racial pattern of pupil transportation in the decade preceding the trial emerges not from the text of the court decisions but from considerable study of the testimony, school records, and school locations. From a legal perspective this may be entirely proper: a person may be found guilty of a crime despite the fact that this act was a unique event in an otherwise law-abiding life. But if one's purpose is to learn whether the Detroit School Board's overall pattern of pupil transportation to relieve overcrowding caused or augmented segregation, it would not be served by examination of the evidence cited in the decisions of the district court or the Sixth Circuit Court of Appeals.

Consider, for example, the case of the Carstens School transportation, a case not mentioned in the court decisions. Foster used the Carstens case as another example of discriminatory busing practices. He testified that in 1970 students from Carstens (48 percent black) were bused to three schools, all predominantly white, bypassing three closer schools which were virtually all-black (T, pp. 1641–42).

The implication was that white students were being bused past black schools to other white schools. In fact, 600 students, all black, were bused from Carstens to three schools, two of them only 18 percent black, one 24 percent black (the figures include the bused-in children) (T, pp. 2898–99, 3856–61). This was a consequence of the practice in use since intact busing was discontinued: children from the area closest to the receiving school were the ones chosen to be bused. Foster's inclusion of the Carstens case, a clear illustration of Detroit School Board pro-integration efforts, in his testimony on segregatory busing is puzzling. He apparently assumed (incorrectly) that since Carstens had a majority of white students (by a few percentage paints), it was white students who were being bused. NAACP Counsel Lucas apparently shared this erroneous assumption. He referred to the Carstens situation as displaying "a line of racial containment" (T, pp. 1642–43), a comment which made no sense in view of the fact that black pupils from Carstens were being bused into virtually all-white neighborhoods.

The Carstens case went unmentioned in the rulings, one reason why it is not possible to evaluate the transportation pattern from reading only the decisions of the district court or of the appeals court. The number of students involved in this single instance of black-to-white busing was almost as great as the total of all the black students cited by the plaintiffs (accurately or not) in Cases 1, 2, 3, 4, and 5 as having bypassed schools with larger white percentages than those to which they were bused.

There had been a large amount of busing to relieve overcrowding in both black and white schools during the early years of the decade before the trial (T, p. 3166) (in the testimony on transportation over fifty schools were mentioned as busing students out, and since the defense supplied data for only three years [1960, 1967, and 1970], the list of schools was far from complete). The cases just described involve the only instances between 1960 and 1971 in which the plaintiffs alleged discriminatory busing, i.e., busing black children past white schools that could have housed them.[8] In the case of Ruthruff and Parker busing, the "black" school to which some children were bused was a school that was 56 percent black (the figure includes all of the bused-in children), and this in a school system then almost two-thirds black over all. In our opinion the only valid instances of system-imposed busing of black students past white schools with capacity were the Angell-to-Higginbotham transportation, which was discontinued ten years before the trial began, and the busing from A. L. Holmes, which lasted five months.

The decision in *Bradley v. Milliken* stated: "With one exception . . . defendant Board has never bused white children to predominantly black schools . . . despite the enormous amount of space available in inner-city schools."[9] There is no doubt about the factual accuracy of this finding. The Detroit School Board transported students only to relieve overcrowding and only until they could be accommodated at the school closest to their residence. In 1960, following protests by black parents over busing to an inner-city school, the board adopted a color-blind policy of student transportation (T, p. 3399; Drachler deposition p. 33): "The emphasis was on relieving overcrowding . . . in a way that did not discriminate against any citizens in the direction or character of the transportation and this is the basis for the language about being transported to the nearest school . . . on a geographic basis" (T, p. 2863).

Most overcrowding, and, therefore, most busing, occurred in the early 1960s, and most busing of white students took place then. Invariably, white students were bused to other white schools since these were the nearest ones with unused capacity. The trial record noted five instances of white-to-white busing in 1960. At the same time 26 overcrowded black schools were busing children out; in 21 of these, black students were sent to schools which were all or predominantly white (T, pp. 2854–72)—not because of a pro-integration policy but because these were the closest schools with available space.

The school overcrowding of the 1960s was a consequence of the rapid demographic change taking place within the city. A typical pattern was the replacement in city neighborhoods of middle-aged white families by young black families with school-age children. As the white population decreased, overcrowding decreased in predominantly white schools. (As a result of a large building program—later cited as a constitutional violation—the number of overcrowded schools in predominantly black neighborhoods also decreased.) By 1965 no predominantly white elementary school was classified as over capacity (T, p. 2876). Thus the revised pro-integration transportation policy of 1967, which permitted the bypassing of the nearest school if racial mix therein would not be enhanced, affected only black youngsters; according to the trial record it was only black students who were being bused from overcrowded schools at that time and thereafter. Mention was made of 20 schools which were busing to relieve overcrowding in 1967 and 8 such schools in 1970; all were predominantly black, and the vast majority of them were sending children to schools with a predominantly white student body (and generally one of higher socioeconomic status) (T, pp. 2881–91, 2897–2923). (The exceptions were cited as violations and have been discussed.) Neither plaintiffs' or defendants' witnesses mentioned the busing of any white students after 1960, nor did anyone claim that the 1960 white-to-white busing incidents violated the School Board policy of racial disregard.

The testimony confirms Judge Roth's statement that white students were never bused to predominantly black schools; apparently, after the early 1960s they were not bused to other white schools either. These students were in areas of dwindling child population and, in line with the system's policy of busing only to relieve overcrowding, were not involved in any transportation program.

CHAPTER 14
The Optional Zones

During the decade beginning in 1950 the Board created and maintained optional attendance zones in neighborhoods undergoing racial transition between high school attendance areas of opposite predominant racial compositions. . . . All of the high school optional areas, except two, were in neighborhoods undergoing racial transition [from white to black] during the 1950's. . . . With the exception of the Denby–Southeastern option . . . all of the options were between high schools of opposite predominant racial compositions. . . . The natural, probable, foreseeable and actual effect of these optional zones was to allow white youngsters to escape identifiably "black" schools. . . . Although many of these optional areas had served their purpose by 1960 due to the fact that most of the areas had become predominantly black, one optional area . . . continued until the present school year.[1]

The record demonstrates that in many instances when neighborhoods in Detroit began to experience some immigration of black families, it was Board of Education policy to create optional attendance zones, thereby allowing white students to change schools to all white or predominantly white schools, generally located farther toward the city limits. For many years the record indicates this practice to have been pervasive.[2]

These findings concerning optional zones (the first from the District Court ruling, the second from that of the Sixth Circuit) were an important basis for the finding of de jure segregation. Both the factual accuracy and the general interpretation of the evidence that was presented are open to many serious questions.

An "optional zone" or area refers to a number of city blocks which sometimes, but not always, coincide with the catchment area of an elementary school. Families on these blocks could choose which of

180

two roughly equidistant high schools, or junior high schools, they wanted their children to attend. Although both decisions asserted that optional zones were created when neighborhoods began to change (and the Sixth Circuit asserted that it was Detroit School Board policy to do so), there was no testimony during the trial itself to support this. The defendants emphasized the absence of this information, and the plaintiffs' witness on the subject, Dr. Foster, acknowledged it at many points. When asked when the Central–Mackenzie option was first made available, Foster replied: "The data . . . on boundaries goes back only to 1959, and it [the optional zone] did exist [then]" (T, p. 2391). Similar statements from Foster can be found elsewhere with respect to other zones (e.g., T, p. 2405) or to the optional zones in general. "No exact date has been established" (T, p. 1413), he said at one point; "I only know it [another option] existed in 1959" (T, p. 2402), at another; and "it is unclear when the optional area was created" (T, p. 2408), a bit later. Elsewhere Foster conceded that optional areas could have existed when both schools involved were all white (T, p. 2403). The defendants elaborated: "there is no indication of how long . . . any of these [optional zones] existed prior to 1959. It could have been one year, it could have been twenty years, but the record is absolutely silent . . . as to that" (T, p. 1422). This contention was nowhere disputed, and the court, to judge from the trial record, appeared to be well aware of this. When Judge Roth asked NAACP attorney Lucas whether he had any information about the attendance areas or zones in 1950, Lucas answered that he did not. The judge asked him whether there were no records, or whether they were simply not available. Lucas replied: "My understanding . . . is that there were no [records of] high school zones available to the central record office at that time" (T, p. 1549).

At one point an intervenor-counsel objected to a question about the purpose of optional zones. He pointed out that if an optional attendance area had been in effect for some time, as Foster had testified, and "if that . . . time was sufficiently far back, then evidently it was an all-white area in either situation and would not remotely support the apparent conclusions of the witness that it was promulgated for some racially discriminatory purpose. If we do not know the time span under which the optional area existed, we can hardly conclude the purpose" (T, p. 1425). Judge Roth sustained the objection, adding: "I don't think he is qualified to tell us the purpose for which . . . the optional area was created. If we project the creation of the optional area back to the time we know little about, I wouldn't want . . . to guess as to why the optional area was created. . . . I am going to limit your witness to what he considers the effect of the creation of the optional area and not the purpose for which it was established" (T, pp. 1426–27). This limitation, however, is not reflected in the language of the court rulings, especially that of the Sixth Circuit.

Since the trial record was silent as to when and why optional attendance areas originated, and since no school records existed which could shed light on the subject, we utilized the reports of informants. The comments that follow are based on reports of persons who have been staff members (some of whom have been in bitter adversary relations with the Detroit School Board), or students, or both in the Detroit schools at some time during the past fifty years.

Many white adults between the ages of forty-five and sixty with whom we spoke can recall that either they or someone they knew had a choice between schools at some time during their school careers. The choices were not between one predominantly white and one predominantly black school. Blacks were only a small proportion of the population during the period being recalled by these informants: even in 1940 Detroit was but 9 percent black, and the black population was highly concentrated within the city. Thus most of the optional areas involved no racial lines or considerations.

It seems that the date of "establishment" of each high school optional area could not be ascertained because these areas emerged at different times, as holdovers from a period when attendance boundaries were more vaguely defined and depended to some extent upon the virtually unrestricted power of school principals, especially in the high schools (T, p. 3384). There was a brief allusion during the trial to this once indefinite nature of school attendance zones. Merle Henrickson, having testified that he had no way of knowing when one of the options mentioned had been created, added: "The high school boundaries were a matter of practice as between principals and the assistant superintendent and they were fixed only to the extent that high school principals got into an argument over a basketball player and they called the assistant superintendent and they would say, 'The east side of so-and-so goes here and the west side goes there' " (T, Henrickson Deposition, April 23, 1971, p. 20).

Before strong centralized authority developed in the Detroit school system, there was a period when, as resentful teachers and aggrieved parents put it, "the principal was king." In this period Detroit high schools differed markedly in educational philosophy, emphasis on subject matter, personal freedom accorded students, and extracurricular activities. These differences, as well as preexisting friendship patterns, often reflected, then as now, ethnic and social class divisions and guided the choices of some families when such choices were permitted. There is no doubt that when city neighborhoods began to change, some students used preexisting optional attendance areas to avoid attending predominantly black schools. However, by this time there had been a gradual tightening up of attendance policies and curtailment of principals' authority to recruit athletes, entice talent, and discourage or refuse students whom they did not want in their school. This movement toward formulation of policy at a central source was given impetus after World War II, as the Detroit NAACP pressed for adherence to strict school boundaries and conformity with the principle that a child must go to school in the district where he lives. Its demand grew out of the color-blind emphasis of the organization, which extended even to the demand that no school records indicating the race of pupils or staff be kept,[3] and out of the fact, well known to local civil rights activists, that some principals—either out of personal bigotry or timidity about anticipated objections from white parents—sometimes discriminated against blacks seeking to enroll at the school closest to their home. The trial record reveals very little of this history, and understandably so, for considerable research would have been needed to present a valid study of these events. For the purpose of the trial, such data were probably not necessary, although they would have placed the whole issue in better historical perspective.

Merle Henrickson, the board witness on this subject, testified that he reported the existence of nine optional areas to Superintendent Samuel Brownell in the course of a boundary study he began in 1959; when he did so, he was instructed to eliminate the areas as soon as was feasible (T, pp. 3165–66). These nine areas were the subject of the trial testimony and there was no dispute about the fact that nine years before the trial began—i.e., by 1962—all but three had been eliminated. After 1965 only one optional area remained,[4] the Western–Southwestern option, which gave students who lived in one portion of the Wilson Junior High district a choice between Western High School, 37 percent black in 1970, or Southwestern, 74 percent black in 1970.

The nine optional zones discussed at length during the trial included one junior high option; the remainder were high school options. The reference in the court ruling to the fact that, with but one exception, "all of the options were between high schools of opposite predominant racial composition" is puzzling. Foster presented the data on racial composition of the high schools involved in the optional zones using the earliest figures which were available, although, as noted earlier, everyone conceded that the optional zones were in existence before that count. These figures, however, show that only half of the high schools involved were, in fact, of opposite predominant racial composition:[5]

Optional High School Zones and Percentage Black, as of 1960

Same Racial Predominance

1. Northwestern (99%) and Northern (97%)
2. Chadsey (41%) and Mackenzie (12%)
3. Central (97%) and Northern (97%)
4. Denby (0%) and Southeastern (31%)

Opposite Racial Predominance

1. Northwestern (99%) and Chadsey (41%)
2. Central (97%) and Mackenzie (12%)
3. Northwestern (99%) and Western (15%)
4. Southwestern (62%) and Western (15%)

We have noted that, in the absence of testimony on *when* these optional areas were created, there was no way to know the purpose for which they had been created. Although Judge Roth so ruled, he did permit testimony on the effects of the zones. From a sociological standpoint, such testimony is as dubious as speculations as to their purpose. The concept of "effects" or consequences is either a temporal one, which of necessity involves a "before-and-after" component, or a "with-and-without" comparison. If we do not know when a practice began, we do not know the state of affairs which existed at that time. Lacking information on conditions which antedate a practice, how can we possibly evaluate its effects except in the most speculative terms? This difficulty was compounded by the absence of data on the racial composition of schools antedating the first racial count in February of 1961 (officially listed as 1960 data).

Furthermore, the testimony presented to show effects was sometimes inconsistent. For example, with respect to the Northern–

Northwestern option, Foster first testified that it "allowed the whites to attend Northwestern for as long . . . as this zone existed . . . until 1962, when it was discontinued" (T, p. 1430). He later testified, however, that Northwestern was 99 percent black in 1960 (T, p. 1432), at a time when Northern was 97 percent black. Clearly, North-western was not a white "escape hatch" between 1960 and 1962, nor, given our knowledge of racial change in that area, was it likely that it could have functioned as such for very many years prior to 1960. Some of the assessments on the effects of optional zones flatly contra-dicted each other. Foster, for example, asserted that the Southwest-ern–Western option allowed whites to go to Western and blacks to Southwestern, the result being increased segregation in both schools (T, p. 1445). Henrickson alleged that most students in the predomi-nantly black optional area who exercised the option went to Western (T, p. 3142). Neither witness offered evidence for these statements.

Despite the fact that there was no testimony on when the optional areas were created, and no school racial count prior to 1961, general-izations were made. Lucas asked his expert witness, Foster, whether he thought that new optional areas occurred between schools of dif-ferent or the same racial composition. Foster replied that such schools were usually of different racial composition (T, p. 1433). (If this observation was meant to apply to the country as a whole rather than only to Detroit, this point was not made clear.) During crossex-amination Dr. Foster conceded that options were available to both black and white students and that he had no knowledge of how many students of either race had elected one or the other of the optional schools, but he contended that black students were generally reluc-tant to exercise a preference for a predominantly white school (T, pp. 2403, 2411–12). There is simply no way to ascertain the extent to which this statement is accurate.[6] Throughout his testimony he em-phasized that options were used by whites to escape predominantly black schools and used, as an example, the Central–Mackenzie option (T, p. 1418). Yet another witness for the plaintiffs, Charles Wells (who in 1960 headed a citizens' organization [T, pp. 2232–33] concerned with school policy), testified that some black students in this optional area were attending the predominantly white Mackenzie, as were black students in the Chadsey–Mackenzie optional zone (T, pp. 2256–57).

The effect of allowing a choice between two high schools of differ-ing racial composition would be extremely difficult to evaluate even if there were complete information about the racial composition of the area and the schools involved when the option was instituted. Since only three optional areas remained after the practice of taking school racial counts began, there are no data available for most of the period in which they were in existence, and even if there had been, how could the effects of the options be assessed? One would have to know the age distribution of the black and white population, the rates of residential turnover and mobility and the reasons for such changes, the fluctuations in parochial school enrollments, etc. It seems virtually impossible to separate the "effects" of the school choices of small numbers of students of each race from the overall demographic trends and other influences in the Detroit metropolitan area.

In the absence of such data, Foster frequently cited the notion of "perception of segregation" to support his assertions about the effects of the school options. For example, despite the fact that in 1960 Southeastern was only 31 percent black and thus, to use Foster's own definition (T, p. 1382), "racially unidentifiable," he said that "in my opinion the creation of such an optional zone . . . would lead the general population of Southeastern to perceive their school as an isolated school, as a contained school, and therefore of less worth as a high school" (T, p. 1462). Earlier, he said: "Community people and residents in such a situation as this generally have a perception that there is something wrong with their school. . . . this increases their perception of racial isolation and . . . physical containment" (T, pp. 1418–19).

No evidence to support these assessments of the effects of optional zones was offered, nor was any research cited to make such judgments appear reasonable. Why would permitting students who lived on some streets a choice between two high schools make "residents" and "community people" (who? blacks only?) and the "general population of Southeastern" (the 31 percent of blacks in the student body or the 69 percent of whites?) feel "isolated" and physically contained? In view of the vagueness of the language, it is difficult to imagine even how one might devise tests for these generalizations. But Foster's testimony went far beyond the confines of the alleged impact on the two schools involved (T, pp. 1480–81):

I think there are some serious . . . side effects in terms of perceptions . . . not only of the schools affected but of the total system. If, in fact, the scuttlebutt is that there are optional zones, there are opportunities for both whites and blacks to option out of zone assignments in the way in which segregation is increased, then it appears to me . . . that school authorities are not interested in desegregating the system, because the decisions they make tend to further segregate it. I think this leads to a feeling of frustration.

Here is conjecture piled upon assumption and conclusions drawn for which there is no evidence whatever. How can anyone know what the resident population's "perception" was? How can anyone know that the net effect of unknown choices of unknown numbers of students was to "further segregate" the system?

We may use an instance in which Foster and Henrickson were in partial agreement on the effects of optional zones as an example of the impossibility of demonstrating causation. Foster asserted that both the Central–Mackenzie option and the Chadsey–Mackenzie option were used to keep Mackenzie predominantly white (T, pp. 1418, 1454). Henrickson conceded that eliminating these options was in part responsible for "integrating" Mackenzie, but added that population movements also played a part (T, pp. 3122, 3151). The following table shows the racial change at Mackenzie High.[7]

Year	Percentage Black
1960	12
1962	29
1963	35
1965	57
1967	75
1969	92
1970	97

NOTE: in 1962 the Central High option was eliminated; in 1963 the Chadsey High option was eliminated.

It is hard to know how the net effect of the elimination of the optional zones on a school's racial composition over the long run could be assessed: it seems to be a minor factor. But Foster continued (T, pp. 1482–83):

I think the perception is not only of rank-and-file community residents, but people of considerable influence in the community along with School Board members, . . . administration people. In many cases they have substantiated this perception that I have recounted: that the optional zones did lead to greater pupil segregation and a feeling of frustration that the school authorities were not doing what was called for in terms of desegregation, and it had a generally debilitating effect on the image of the schools as far as all of these groups were concerned.

All this testimony was drawn from data based on three small attendance areas after 1962. It was never learned on what basis the expert witness, who was from Miami, drew his conclusions about the opinions and views of community members, leaders, and school staff in Detroit.

Foster also alleged throughout his testimony that optional zones affected residential patterns by increasing white flight (T, p. 1420). But if optional zones were used by some whites as an "escape hatch," then the research which exists on the subject suggests that the opposite conclusion would be more likely. White families without school-age children or those who can "escape" from the public school system are somewhat more likely to remain for a longer time in mixed areas than others, and are even somewhat more likely to enter such neighborhoods.[8] The fact that students in the only optional area which existed after 1965 could choose Western (approximately 40 percent black and 20 percent Hispanic) instead of Southwestern (74 percent black) may have contributed to the stability of the "integrated" and much-praised Western.[9]

In addition to citing the nine allegedly racially segregative optional zones, both courts made mention of an earlier non-racial option: "There had also been an optional zone [eliminated between 1956 and 1959] created in 'an attempt . . . to separate Jews and Gentiles within the system,' the effect of which was that Jewish youngsters went to Mumford High School and Gentile youngsters went to Cooley."[10] The basis (and the language) for this charge came not from any witness but from the defendants' own counsel, George Bushnell, who asked: "at that point in history in this town of ours there was an attempt acted out, . . . was there not, to separate Jews and Gentiles within the system?" Henrickson replied: "Well, yes. There was also such a separatist tendency" (T, p. 2822). However, two days later, when plaintiffs' counsel repeated this charge in essentially the same language, the School Board attorney made a formal objection to the wording (T, p. 3384).

In his deposition Superintendent Drachler spoke freely of the Mumford–Cooley optional zone, describing it as reflecting the self-segregatory tendencies of some students, both Jewish and non-Jewish

(T, Drachler Deposition, p. 36). He stated that this zone had existed prior to former Superintendent Brownell's tenure and gave not the slightest indication that it represented any official attempt to create segregation. Our own investigation confirms the self-selecting nature of the Jewish-Gentile sorting out in the Mumford and Cooley areas. The self-segregation of Jewish students in Detroit was widely known and closely reflected residential choices. Even without the option, Mumford would have been heavily Jewish and Cooley would have been largely non-Jewish, given the residential concentration of Jews within northwest Detroit. If Jewish children living on certain blocks opted for Mumford, it was because of own-group preference plus their desire to attend a competitive and academically excellent high school, not because of any attempt at segregation on the part of the school system. A person who had been an administrator at both Mumford and Cooley, when told of this assertion, was incredulous. She recounted the rivalry between the principals of the two schools to entice academically talented youngsters: the principal of Cooley would phone the principal of Mumford and say, "Stop skimming the cream; there's no need for you to take more and more National Merit Award winners."

To focus for a moment only on the relative contribution which these optional areas could have made to the overall racial patterns in Detroit's schools, one is struck by how small a proportion of students were involved. The plaintiffs' testimony mentioned fifteen elementary school districts and portions of five others where there was evidence that a choice between schools had been available at some time. If these are counted as twenty simultaneous instances (they were not), they represent fewer than 10 percent of the Detroit school districts. After 1965 only four schools, representing about 1 percent of the school population, were involved, and students from these schools were "escaping" to a high school whose student population was 40 percent black, on the average, in the period 1965–1970.

[The testimony on optional areas did not support the conclusions drawn from it by the courts. It is troubling to discover how slight the foundation can be for assertions which eventually are enshrined in decisions all the way to the Supreme Court; as an example, Justice Marshall, dissenting, wrote: "Optional attendance zones were created for neighborhoods undergoing racial transition so as to allow whites in these areas to escape integration."[11]

In addition to the paucity of factual data offered in testimony, concepts and language adopted from the social sciences lent a spurious aura of expertise to highly dubious generalizations. The impact of these zones on distribution of students in the school system was highly exaggerated (considering the numbers involved and the period of time covered), perhaps because the evidence of constitutional violations by the Detroit School Board in recent years was so scanty.

The NAACP opposition to the exercise of student choice in situations such as that presented by optional zones undoubtedly grew out of increasing evidence that free choice often reflects own-group preferences. Many people had assumed that because external constraints *had* been imposed on blacks, lifting them would result in far more dispersion than has been the case—not only in the schools but in other areas of life as well. The persistence of own-group clustering, whether in residence or schools, regardless of how it comes into being, is considered by some civil rights leaders to be highly undesirable. NAACP opposition to the exercise of choice appears grounded to a considerable degree in the realization that it often results in some degree of ethnic separation.

Chapter 15
Boundary Changes

Zone changes by school authorities were still another category of violations found by the courts: "The Board has created and altered attendance zones . . . and . . . feeder school patterns in a manner which has had the natural, probable and actual effect of continuing black and white pupils in racially segregated schools."[1] Obviously, if school attendance zones are to be based on where children live and children live in racially concentrated neighborhoods, there is no disputing the influence of racial composition in their creation. But beyond this, had there been manipulations to increase racial concentration or to prevent school mixture occurring from residential changes? While Judge Roth devoted but a single paragraph to the rezoning violations (in accordance with his inclination to attribute school segregation to residential and demographic factors), the appeals court devoted nearly four pages to the subject.[2]

Boundary and feeder pattern changes involve intricate interrelationships. To describe such changes one must first set forth an existing linkage of various schools and then propose a new linkage. When alternatives to a given change are suggested, as was frequently done in the plaintiffs' testimony, a multiplicity of hypothetical linkages involving still more schools must be considered. Dr. Foster, for example, in the course of his testimony on rezoning (in which about a dozen allegations of discriminatory acts were set forth), made reference to almost fifty schools; by the time the rebuttal witness had answered the charges, approximately ninety schools had been mentioned.

In order to grasp the nature of a feeder pattern change, it is necessary, first of all, to know the entire articulation pattern, i.e., the

191

elementary, junior, and senior high schools involved. In some instances Foster neglected to mention the junior high school (see, e.g., T, pp. 1603–7), which was often a crucial explanatory factor. In addition, it is important to know not only the capacities, enrollments, and racial proportions of the schools but also the variations and/or changes in grade structures within them, locational factors, distances, and (often) new schools opening in the area. Frequently many of these factors went unmentioned in the testimony.

Excerpts from the trial record were cited at length by the appeals court in order to substantiate the violative nature of certain rezonings. Some of these "proofs" are puzzling. For example, most of the nearly four pages of documentation on zone changes were from the testimony of Assistant Superintendent Charles Wells, testifying as the plaintiffs' witness.[3] Eleven years earlier Wells had headed a citizens' group critical of certain Detroit School Board practices. Among its targets was a School Board proposal to eliminate two optional zones and to reassign the predominantly black schools in the optional areas to the "blacker" of the high schools involved.[4] These proposed changes were cited by the Sixth Circuit as instances where "attendance boundaries were shaped in a gerrymandered fashion to conform to the racial residential pattern."[5] The evidence cited, however, related to community concern over the expected effects if the two options were eliminated: the children "would have been pulled back into the Central area"; they "would have been returned" to the inner-city district (T, pp. 2256–57). The conditional tense of the witnesses' language must have been overlooked by the appeals court, as was Wells' subsequent comment: "we were talking about a condition which would have gone into effect at the beginning of the following school year. The fact was that it did not go into effect" (T, p. 2268).

In 1960 the Detroit Board, evidently in response to community pressure, reconsidered and then rescinded its proposal to eliminate these options. Elsewhere in the trial record it was established that the two options continued until 1962 and 1963, when the predominantly black students affected were assigned not to the predominantly black high schools, but to the predominantly white ones (T, pp. 1418, 3121–22, 3151), a fact not mentioned by the appeals court. In short, the Sixth Circuit made a finding of racial gerrymandering on the basis of School Board proposals which were never enacted. (It is interesting to note that Judge Roth's ruling made no reference to this material.) And while citing (erroneously) elimination of the two options as violations, the court also found the existence of optional zones to be unconstitutional.

Also puzzling was the appeals court listing of Courville Elementary School as an example of the segregatory alteration of feeder patterns.[6] Only the name of the school was included in the ruling. In the extensive testimony on Courville only one alteration had been mentioned; this was the 1962 rezoning of Courville (95 percent black) into the predominantly white Nolan Junior High (31 percent black). Prior to this change there had been a split in the Courville feeder pattern; half the students were assigned to the predominantly black Cleveland Junior High, half to Nolan. It is indeed possible, as Foster contended, that this peculiar feeder bifurcation was at some earlier time a racial dividing line. However, the trial record indicates only that this split existed in 1960, and that in 1962 the board did do precisely what Foster suggested could have been done: it zoned the entire Courville student body into the predominantly white Nolan Junior High (T, pp. 1547–48, 3222–26).

Higginbotham Elementary was another school listed by the Sixth Circuit as involved in segregatory feeder changes.[7] Obviously, Judge Roth was referring to this school when he said that the Detroit School Board "admits at least one instance where it purposefully and intentionally built and maintained a school and its attendance zone to contain black students."[8] This statement was accurate as far as it went; defense expert Henrickson had volunteered that Higginbotham "was built in the center of a black settlement for the precise purpose of serving just that black settlement. We shouldn't hide these things" (T, p. 3926), but he neglected to mention that the school was constructed in 1925. He did describe later efforts to integrate the Higginbotham students at the junior high level, the only feeder changes mentioned in the record (T, pp. 3204–5).

What of the remaining ten feeder pattern changes (six took place during the previous school administration, i.e., prior to 1967) cited by the appeals court?[9] The one factor common to all, according to the evidence presented by the defense, was overcrowding in certain schools.[10] In many cases the plaintiffs' witness did not dispute that point but contended that other schools could have been rezoned in order to alleviate the crowding and improve racial balance. In one case in which capacity figures and trends were crucial for determining the need for a feeder change, the two opposing witnesses gave contradictory information (the capacities of Pershing and Osborn high

schools were in dispute) (T, pp. 1593–95, 3226–27). Why the witnesses' testimony differed, in view of the fact that all of Foster's data
were supplied by Henrickson on behalf of the board, and which
witness was correct was not determined. Thus a critical contradiction
was left unresolved (an illustration of the problems inherent in the
method of ascertainment of facts in adversary proceedings). In two
separate instances, both involving reassignments from racially mixed
Chadsey High to all-black Northwestern, Foster maintained that
crowding was much more severe at Northwestern, and the implication was that the changes were, therefore, racially motivated (T, pp.
1605–6, 1609–10). The defense revealed, however, that the official
capacity figures used by Foster were misleading. A junior high school
next to Chadsey was joined to it under a single administration, and
data for both schools were grouped and listed under the name of
Chadsey; actually, Chadsey had less than half of the designated capacity (T, pp. 3133–34, 3247–49), a fact that Foster could not have been
expected to know. Despite this explanation, the Sixth Circuit listed
both instances as constitutional violations.

The complexities of feeder pattern changes and the difficulty in
assessing their purpose and impact might best be illustrated by examining the case of the neighboring Vernor and Vandenberg elementary
schools. The changes involving these two schools were singled out in
the Sixth Circuit ruling as exemplifying how "school feeder patterns
were changed so as to make particular junior . . . or senior high
schools either generally white or generally black."[11] The Vernor-
Vandenberg example is atypical only in that it involves multiple
changes over time. In the ten years prior to the trial the feeder
pattern of Vernor and Vandenberg had been altered three times (T,
pp. 1514–18, 1610, 3197–3202). In 1962 both schools were all-white,
and their students were reassigned from Mumford High School (30
percent black) to the all-white Ford High School; in 1967 both schools
were about two-thirds black, and their students were returned to
Mumford (78 percent black) from Ford (4 percent black); in 1970 the
students in both schools, now over 90 percent black, were switched
back from the all-black Mumford to the predominantly white (20
percent black) Ford.

Why were Vernor and Vandenberg students moved back and forth
between Mumford and Ford? It is important to note (though it was
not so noted during the trial) that unlike most elementary schools in
the city Vandenberg in the early 1960s went through the eighth grade

and Vernor through the ninth; both then fed directly into Mumford. There was no junior high nearby. The 1962 and 1967 changes were made, according to the defense, because of the shifting pattern of overcrowding in the two high schools. Mumford was extremely crowded during the early years of the decade (it was 1,220 students over capacity in 1960 and 643 students over capacity even after the removal of Vernor and Vandenberg students), while Ford was under capacity. To relieve the situation at Mumford, the most distant of its feeder schools, Vernor and Vandenberg, were reassigned to Ford.

Foster acknowledged the crowding problem at Mumford but suggested that students from MacDowell (48 percent black) and Higginbotham (99 percent black) could have been removed from Mumford and reassigned to Ford. Assuming the comparability of the two pairs of schools in terms of grade structure and student enrollment (Foster provided no data other than those on racial proportions), such a switch might have better balanced the racial proportions of the two high schools. From the perspective of the 1970s, this alternative may seem preferable, but in 1962 it would have been a clear violation of the School Board policy of geographic assignment without regard to race—a policy first urged and later supported by civil rights groups. In accordance with this policy, Vernor and Vandenberg students were reassigned because they were farthest from Mumford and closest to Ford.

Permanent relief for the overtaxed Mumford awaited the construction of Beaubien Junior High. When completed, Beaubien was to house the ninth-graders assigned to Mumford, easing its overcrowding and at the same time providing a uniform grade structure throughout the area schools. When Vernor and Vandenberg students were transferred to Ford in 1962, it was made clear that this was a temporary arrangement; they would be sent into Beaubien when it was opened and would go from there into Mumford. Ex-residents of the area told us of pressures exerted on the board to make the Vernor and Vandenberg assignment to Ford permanent. It was known that Beaubien would receive low-income black students as well as middle-income whites. The parents feared and forecast white exodus from the area should their children be fed into Beaubien and then back to the increasingly troubled Mumford. However, the board stood firm in its insistence that Vernor and Vandenberg students be returned to the Mumford district on the completion of Beaubien.

By 1967, when the planned shift became a reality, the available spaces at the two high schools had been reversed, as had the racial proportions at the two elementary schools. Ford High, rather than Mumford, was now overcrowded, and black students, rather than white, were now a majority at Vernor and Vandenberg. Four years later the board was charged with a double-barreled violation: constructing a new junior high school in a predominantly black neighborhood and rezoning mostly black elementary students into that school and then on to a black high school. Despite the fact that Beaubien Junior High was planned as an integrated school, it opened in 1966 with a student body 62 percent black; the proportion increased to 95 percent in two years. Despite the fact that the original plan to return Vernor and Vandenberg to Mumford had envisioned the return of white students to the area, both grade schools had become over 50 percent black by the time the switch was made. Efforts to equalize the racial proportions of the two high schools followed in 1970: Vernor and Vandenberg students were returned to the still largely white Ford, a "good" move, according to Foster, and one unmentioned by the courts.

It is unlikely that the Vernor and Vandenberg changes made Beaubien and Mumford "generally black" and Ford "generally white," as the appeals court charged. Even if there had been no rezoning of the two schools, Beaubien and Mumford would still have been mostly black and Ford mostly white. Vernor and Vandenberg were but two of a number of elementary schools involved in these feeder patterns. Every school untouched by zoning changes which fed into Mumford became overwhelmingly black in short order because of the movement of young black families into the area, "making" Mumford black. The removal of Vernor and Vandenberg students from Mumford in 1970 still left it 98 percent black. Similarly, Ford was not "made" white because of the transfer out of Vernor and Vandenberg students in 1967: it was predominantly white because it was located in a white area. The Vernor and Vandenberg students certainly added to the black proportion at Ford, but their removal did not make Ford predominantly white; when they were returned to Ford in 1970 the black proportion was increased, but Ford was still 80 percent white.

The Vernor–Vandenberg case has much in common with the other school zoning changes cited. All of them stemmed from the need to relieve overcrowding in certain schools. School board records confirm this overcrowding, and in most cases the point was not challenged by the plaintiffs. Some of the changes involved the opening of a new school designed to cope with the basic problem of overcrowding; in these cases dual violations were found (in site selection and in rezoning). All of the changes made after the board's 1967 pro-integration policy was begun were followed by plans for further changes to bring about better racial balance in these schools, as in the case of Vernor–Vandenberg reassignment to Ford High School in 1970. Vernor–Vandenberg was the only such proposal which was in effect by the time of the trial. Two others were incorporated in the ill-fated April 7 Plan (T, pp. 3240–43, 3439), and one was scheduled to go into effect on completion of a new middle school (T, p. 3221).

School authorities attempt to deal with the problems of overcrowded schools in various ways: busing children to other schools with capacity (always described as a temporary measure in Detroit), adding portable classrooms, building additions onto existing buildings, building new schools, and changing zone and feeder patterns. Each solution carries the risk of accusations of segregatory intent when a city's schools reflect, as they do in Detroit and most large cities, the non-random racial distributions of neighborhoods.

The question of how attempts at handling overcrowding via zone and feeder alterations are to be distinguished from racial gerrymandering is a troublesome one. If a school system rezones on the basis of geographic proximity without regard to the racial characteristics of the schools involved, should this be defined as racial gerrymandering? In the half-dozen rezoning actions that occurred prior to 1967, did the Detroit School Board violate its policy of racial disregard? Did the four post-1967 changes violate its policy of integration where feasible? Were all of the cited rezonings necessary, and, if so, could other changes have been made which would have enhanced the racial mix of the schools involved? In many instances, the answers to these questions could not be determined from the evidence offered. Some allegations and findings seemed entirely without substance. Others, such as the charges pertaining to the 1962 Vernor–Vandenberg reassignment to Ford High School, indicated that although the Detroit School Board was acting in compliance with its color-blind geographic assignment policy, it could still be cited for a constitutional violation—again we have the puzzle of how school policies can simultaneously be defined as legally permissible and as acts of de jure segregation. But in most of the rezonings cited as violations we found it impossible to arrive at any definitive assessment of their overall impact on school racial concentration over time.

Nowhere were the shortcomings of the adversary system in eliciting accurate and complete data more clearly illustrated than in the body of evidence here on zoning and feeder pattern changes. Judges must rule on the basis of what is offered in the trial record. When what is offered in the record is ambiguous, contradictory, and insufficient, a satisfactory judgment cannot be rendered. Unlike the courts, we as social scientists found it impossible to assess the legitimacy of many of the claims and counter-claims involving the specific zoning and feeder changes, yet we are skeptical of the finding that the effect of the attendance zone alterations was to "create and perpetuate" school segregation, as the court stated.[12] School segregation was "created" by geographic assignment, which reflects residential divisions, and no rezoning was necessary to perpetuate it. Given racially divided neighborhoods and a neighborhood school assignment policy, boundary and feeder manipulations to perpetuate segregation are unnecessary. If the changing of attendance patterns did indeed "create" or increase school segregation, we would expect the schools to be more segregated than would be predicted from residential segregation, but such was not the case in Detroit. Under a strict policy of geographic, color-blind school assignment, we would expect the student population to be much more segregated than the general population, given the large proportion of older white families without school-age children and the disproportionate use of non-public schools by whites. In 1970 the index of residential segregation in Detroit was 81;[13] the segregation index of the city schools was approximately the same.[14]

The courts' findings of constitutional violations, however, were based not only on actions taken by the Detroit School Board but also on its "inaction,"[15] its "failure to act,"[16] and its "omissions."[17] It was found guilty of segregation de jure not only because of changes it made which it should not have made but also because of changes it could have made but did not make. Such failures were heavily stressed in Foster's allegations of zoning violations. His testimony on feeder changes, as noted above, was liberally sprinkled with "could haves," alternatives that, in his opinion, would have provided relief from overcrowding while promoting desegregation. In addition, he discussed a number of schools uninvolved in any such changes that, he claimed, could have been rezoned or paired with contiguous or nearby schools to further the goal of racial mixture (T, pp. 1700–1705).

Many of the schools Foster suggested pairing are located in the heavily industrialized southwest section of the city, an area of huge manufacturing plants, railroad sidings, and railroad and expressway intersections. There are some stable, almost all-white neighborhoods (and schools) located near largely black neighborhoods (and schools) in this section, but these white and black areas are separated by physical barriers (this, along with their generally low socioeconomic status, may explain the stability of the white neighborhoods), which are formidable obstacles to the school pairings suggested by Foster. For example, two schools he mentioned, although only about a mile and a half apart, are separated by a major traffic artery, railroad tracks, an expressway, a cemetery, a salt mine, and a river. The board witness commented that Foster would not have made the pairing recommendations if he had himself visited the sites of the schools in this sector (T, p. 3255). (The schools in this area *could* have been paired, but only if transportation were provided, a practice that would have been contrary to the stated policy of busing only to relieve overcrowding.)

Of the pairings suggested by Foster in other areas, defense witness Merle Henrickson said (T, p. 3251):

These . . . all involve schools where transition is occurring. There are black families moving into this belt and the chief difference between the two schools that he [Foster] paired in most cases is that the school with more black students is about three years in advance of the school with less black students in the amount of change that has occurred. . . . There is every reason to expect that the change will continue at approximately the rate it has been occurring and that both schools in these pairs will be predominantly black schools in a period of three to five years. . . . Under these circumstances, I would very much question the wisdom of tampering with the situation.

This assessment was no doubt based on the School Board's experiences with changing neighborhoods. The number of all-black schools which were once all-white in the areas involved points to the fleeting gains that would accrue from the manipulation of school boundaries. Such efforts might result in racial equalization between two schools in a given year, but the next year—or the next—further boundary changes would be required, and these, too, would soon be inadequate. There simply were not enough white children to go around, and the proportion of black children in the schools was increasing each year. Only seven months after the April 7 Plan had been rescinded, Deputy Superintendent Arthur Johnson was asked whether there had been demographic changes which would have affected the results had that plan been carried out. He replied: "There has been some population movement . . . which would cause us to want to update that plan. And any such plan . . . , you would have to, I think, after six months, certainly after a year, . . . take a fresh look at the data on which the plan was based, and chances are, the way we see mobility in this community, you would want to update it" (T, Johnson Deposition, p. 11). Clearly, any plan to improve racial balance would require continuous reassignment—in short, a permanent system of racial quotas. Even if every white family in the city stayed where it was, and even if its children remained in the public schools, age and family size differentials between the white and black population would soon change the racial balance, and the system would move inexorably toward a larger and larger number of predominantly black schools. Reviewing the evidence for New York City in 1965, Eleanor Sheldon and Raymond Glazier concluded: "It is apparent from the materials presented . . . that the constant changes in attendance lines, whether traditionally or imaginatively conceived, are ineffective in promoting large-scale ethnic balance. . . . With increasing proportions of Negro and Puerto Rican children attending the city's public schools and a spread in the size and geographic extensiveness of ethnic 'ghettoes,' no amount of boundary changes will effectuate integrated schools."[18]

CHAPTER 16
Effects of School Violations

The legal basis for the rulings in the Northern school cases now deemphasizes or completely avoids the treacherous and shifting issues of the educational or attitudinal benefits of integration or the harm of segregation. Attempts to challenge these harm-benefit assessments are ordinarily set aside as irrelevant, or as already established. But as a substitute for this kind of sociological underpinning a new type of empirical analysis has been introduced: since the condition of racial separation is illegal only if it can be shown to have been produced to a substantial degree by actions of school authorities—and thus de jure—evidence of this causal relationship is required. The plaintiffs provided such material in the Detroit case, but in our view their evidence was unconvincing, a hodgepodge of inaccurate information, illogical propositions, inconsistent declarations, and unsupported assertions, couched in the language of social science.

As noted at the start of Part III, there is considerable evidence that Judge Roth did not take this testimony very seriously. He was deeply concerned with the condition of racial separation, and regretted in his ruling that the law required him to attribute the responsibility for it to school authorities.[1] When the appeals court removed residential segregation as an empirical foundation for the case, the burden of causation was left on school system acts, a logical fallacy not corrected by the higher court's elaboration and lengthy citation from trial testimony.

More specifically, our study of this testimony leads us to four conclusions.

1. On *site selection*, the evidence approached the absurd. There was no basis for concluding that the selection of sites other than those

chosen, assuming the continuance of the still-lawful geographic assignment policy, would have made any difference in the degree of
racial concentration throughout the city schools.

2. On *transportation violations*, the evidence was in some cases
inaccurate and in most cases trivial in nature.

3. On *optional zones*, the evidence was not sufficient to warrant
the conclusions drawn by the courts as to extent or effect.

4. On *boundary and feeder pattern changes*, the material was inadequate to answer the question as to whether these alterations over
the years increased or decreased racial concentration. The most plausible interpretation is that, overall, they made no difference.

Our analysis involved both the question of factual accuracy and
the question of the validity of the causal analysis. There are so many
specific errors and omissions in the testimony or in conclusions
drawn from it that there is a risk to which we have sometimes
succumbed of becoming so absorbed in exploring this material that
the central problem of causal validity is obscured: a high degree of
racial separation in residence, developed in the previous century,
means that any system of pupil assignment based on where children
live would of necessity reflect this separation even if no instance of
cheating or discrimination by school authorities had ever occurred.
This fundamental fact makes Supreme Court Justice Byron White's
conclusion about the impact of school violations—"had the Detroit
school system not followed an official policy of segregation throughout the 1950's and 60's Negroes and Whites would have been going
to school together"[2]—quite incomprehensible.

Since Justice White does not simultaneously assert that a geographic assignment system is impermissible, one must assume that he
believes that violations of this system (assignment to the nearest
school) during the 1950s, and the Drachler integration-where-possi-
ble policy within this system during the later 60's, were the cause of
racially concentrated schools. But since school segregation in Detroit
was not as intense as residential segregation, when the location of
households with children in the public schools is considered, his
assessment is without foundation. Even the appeals court did not
actually state that in the absence of school system discrimination
more Detroit schools would have been racially mixed. It did say that
official acts of the system were "causally related" to racial segregation
in the schools, and, later, that "however rooted in private residential
segregation," school racial concentration was "validated and aug-

mented" by acts of the Detroit School Board and the State of Michigan.[3] Any system of school assignment based on residence "validates" existing residential patterns, but it cannot be said to "augment" them—that is, to increase racial concentration when public school children are somewhat more separated by race in their homes than in their schools.

It is of interest to note that while racially concentrated schools have been the subject of discussion and concern in England of recent years, in the absence of any need to find judicial grounds for mandatory dispersion no social scientist, to our knowledge, has suggested that this concentration is the result of machinations by school authorities. How can it be that this odd theory to explain what requires no explanation (as long as school assignment is based on residence) has been so infrequently challenged by American sociologists? One must conclude that the few who know that this has become the legal basis for the Northern school decisions accept it as a justifiable means of achieving a goal that many find desirable and unattainable by other methods.

None of these comments should be taken to mean that we are blind to acts of discrimination in the public schools in this city, as in others, especially in earlier years. But an illegal act is not necessarily a cause of a social condition. The contention that these acts of discrimination "caused" racially concentrated schools, given the existence of racially concentrated neighborhoods, seems to us as far-fetched and implausible now as when we first encountered it.

The courts have tried to support their illogical theory of causation by a judicial doctrine of interactive, corresponding, or reciprocal effect between school and neighborhood. The Supreme Court first referred to this relationship in *Swann*[4] and Judge Roth reasserted it in his ruling: "just as there is an interaction between residential patterns and the racial composition of schools, so there is a corresponding effect on the residential patterns by the racial composition of schools."[5] This often-quoted sentence is one of those axioms which may at first glance seem sensible but which proves upon reflection to be meaningless. If a school system uses an honest geographic system of proceeding outward in all directions (as physical barriers permit) until the capacity of a school building has been reached, the racial composition of the school will be determined by the race of the public school pupils living on the surrounding blocks: no "interaction" is involved. The only possible meaning of the second half of the sentence is that when a school is thus composed, its racial composition will affect the future locational decisions of those present and prospective residents who are able to exercise choice in residential location. This is simply another way of saying that the present population of a neighborhood affects the future population. Those who encounter this population less frequently or in less important ways will be less affected. Thus childless households, or households who use private schools, will have their residential preferences less influenced by the class-racial composition of the area's children collected in a public school building.

A number of empirical studies support these deductions. There are some prosperous families who live in areas where most children are poor and black; they do not use the nearby public schools but use private facilities instead. Parochial school users often remain longer in (a few even enter) racially changing neighborhoods because they use schools that are not composed of all the area children. There are similar findings for childless households.[6] But the effect of this avoidance of public schools in such neighborhoods should not be exaggerated: areas where only a small minority of households used the public schools—about 15 percent in the South Shore in Chicago, about 30 percent in the Bagley area in northwest Detroit, for example—did not look much different, ten years after black entrance, than similar areas with much higher proportions of public school users.[7] While the ability of white households to avoid schools attended by area children makes residential proximity acceptable in some Northern situations, it made "integrated" neighborhoods possible in some areas in the old South. If all facilities are segregated and social interaction of other types is firmly under white control, residential proximity is of less consequence to whites and may even be convenient.[8] The end of mandatory dual systems in the South caused an increase in residential segregation and the end of these few old stable mixed areas.

There is much other evidence to show that the racial composition of a school does not generate what has been called a "corresponding effect" upon the neighborhood. Small towns with only one secondary school are not residentially integrated. In years when the black population in Detroit was so small that some schools (especially junior and senior high schools) had but small proportions of black students, these mixed schools did not produce residential racial dispersion. There are a few instances where poor white families lived close enough to black neighborhoods to produce some mixed schools for a considerable time, but this situation has not had an integrative effect on housing.

Gerald Suttles' study, for example, showed how blacks, Italians, Puerto Ricans, and Mexicans maintained compact residential enclaves, despite the fact, as Suttles points out, that "many of the schools depart sharply from the ethnic divisions in the area."[9]

Studies of suburbs, towns, and cities where residence has been deliberately divorced from school assignment (through court order or voluntary action) show clearly the absence of a corresponding effect. A study of black neighborhoods in a number of predominantly white suburbs of Philadelphia concluded: "While suburban residential segregation continues, segregation by race has largely disappeared from the schools. . . . even at the grammar school level de facto school segregation is relatively rare because of the extensive use of school buses."[10] Although these black areas were of long standing (almost 70 percent of the families had lived in these locations for ten or more years) and were a "composite of 'black bourgeoisie' and 'respectable' families," racial mixture within the schools did not produce any discernible effect upon residential patterns. We have as yet seen no evidence that system-wide school dispersion in Princeton, Pasadena, or Evanston has had a significant corresponding effect on residential mixture, although these efforts have been in existence for many years.[11] Indeed, it is ironic that some proponents of school racial dispersion argue in court that very minor changes in student assignment such as we describe in the chapters on these violations have intensified school segregation through their effects on residential patterns. However, they often insist, in discussing the effects of large-scale busing, that these major changes in school assignment will have only negligible effects on residential decisions.[12] Thus the NAACP expert witness on school violations in the Detroit case as well as in several others, Gordon Foster, responded to a question from the NAACP counsel, Louis Lucas, on demographic trends over a ten-year period (T, pp. 1418–20): "Dr. Foster, from your examination of the 1950 . . . and 1960 census exhibits . . . do you have an opinion as to the effects of . . . an optional zone on the residence pattern in the community?" Foster replied: "This tends to increase the instability of the community because they generally feel this is an ad hoc temporary interim situation and it increases white flight."[13]

Foster also declared repeatedly that if certain high school boundaries had been altered or specific feeder patterns adjusted, these changes would have "stabilized the racial situation" or "held the integration status" of various schools (T, pp. 1523, 1433). He can only mean that such actions would produce significant changes in residential behavior. The notion that demographic trends of the magnitude seen in metropolitan areas throughout the nation during these years were affected by miniscule numbers of children in an optional zone or that they could have been reversed or arrested by changes of the type proposed is without foundation. In 1967 the U.S. Commission on Civil Rights concluded: "In some cities Negro students already constitute a majority of the public school enrollment. In these cities solutions not involving suburban participation no longer are possible."[14] To support this assessment the commission cited John Fischer's review of data on these attempts:

Twelve years of effort, some ingeniously pro forma and some laboriously genuine have proved that desegregating schools . . . is much more difficult than it first appeared. Attendance boundaries have been redrawn; new schools have been built in border areas; parents have been permitted, even encouraged to choose more desirable schools for their children; pupils from crowded slum schools have been bused to outlying schools; "Negro" and "White" schools have been paired and their student bodies merged . . . Despite some initial successes and a few stable solutions the consequences for the most part have proved disappointing. Steady increases in urban Negro population, continuing shifts in the racial character of neighborhoods . . . produce new problems faster than old ones could be solved.[15]

This description is most appropriate for Detroit, where the school leadership was generally conceded to be strongly pro-integration. Years of voluntary efforts by citizens' community councils to achieve racial stabilization in various neighborhoods were marred, in the period preceding the trial, by bitter disputes over how to divide up the rapidly dwindling asset they agreed was so precious: Detroit's white middle-class students.[16] Thomas Pettigrew concluded that in cities with large and growing black pupil populations such attempts were "mere Band-aids."[17] Their ineffectuality had been asserted earlier by the same demographer who was the principal witness for the NAACP on residential segregation (but Taeuber did not make this point during the trial):

The racial composition of city schools is becoming more homogeneously Negro. This occurs whether or not the pattern of segregated public schools changes. As black children replace white children in a public school system, administrators, even if they attempt to utilize the available repertoire of desegregation techniques, are likely to find the number of blacks in predominantly black schools increasing. In other words, even if the all-white schools are integrated, the other schools will become more predominantly Negro.[18]

This assessment, which was well supported by data from Taeuber's own and other sources, is at variance with his oral statement to the Mondale committee that "residential segregation causes school segregation, but the reverse process is just as much in force. School segregation operates to recreate residential segregation."[19] There is simply no evidence to support this version of the "corresponding effect," and, as noted earlier, the weight of the evidence suggests that parents whose neighborhoods have become mixed tend to remain in them somewhat longer if they can avoid schools composed of the children in the area.[20] Elsewhere Taeuber suggests that what he means is that, historically, "segregated" schools and "segregated patterns of residence" developed simultaneously.[21] If student assignment is based on residence, this is a truism. The clientele in the children's room of the local branch library will also be "segregated" if residences are racially separated—the more so if library attendance is compulsory—but the generalization lacks any sociological substance. Perhaps Taeuber means to say that had another system of pupil assignment been used, i.e., had the Detroit schools in 1900 or 1910 dispersed their tiny black population (85 percent of it lived in one small area at the time[22]) by a horse-and-buggy "busing" program, residential segregation would have been diminished or abolished in Detroit. Maybe so. It would have been a different country, with a totally different history, and a different Constitution.[23] What did happen was that almost all children went to the school closest to their homes, and in a big city most children who live near each other are of the same race. Efforts to modify the rule of attending the nearest school in Detroit were limited by demographic factors, were very difficult to implement because of public opposition, and produced only fleeting results. If the experts quoted above were correct, these efforts were doomed to failure. The courts generally agreed, for it was on this basis that Judge Roth and the judges of the Sixth Circuit imposed a metropolitan desegregation plan. The Detroit public schools, which, the reader is reminded, had a black majority eight years before the trial began, could not be desegregated, said these experts, unless white children were brought in from the suburbs. The testimony to suggest that Detroit could have "desegregated" its schools on its own served only as a legal rationale to justify the use of judicial power.

PART IV: THE REMEDY HEARINGS

CHAPTER 17
The Desegregation Remedy

In the spring of 1972 Judge Roth began to conduct hearings on how Detroit's schools should be desegregated. In a conference with attorneys shortly after he ruled that the city's schools were segregated de jure, he declared that he had no preconceptions about the nature or scope of the remedy: "The options are completely open."[1] This was not quite the case. He could not foresee, of course, that two years later the Supreme Court was to interpret rather strictly the doctrine articulated in *Swann* that "the nature and scope of the remedy is determined by the nature and scope of the violation." Only Detroit had been found guilty of de jure segregation; therefore the only option available to Detroit was to confine desegregation to the city.

The judge's "preconceptions" concerning the remedy needed were clearly evident from the record and the ruling, with its stress on the history and future of Detroit's demography. From the fourth day of the trial his questions had shown his preoccupation with the problem of how to desegregate a school system already two-thirds black and his awareness of the danger of accelerating white attrition by imposing involuntary student reassignment under such circumstances. The record must show that the Detroit-only alternative got a fair hearing, but there is little to suggest that this would be more than pro forma.

As in most other large cities, in Detroit the Board of Education was faced with a dwindling supply of white children and a chronic financial crisis. Before the remedy hearings began, the board majority voted not to contest the district court findings of de jure segregation but to press for metropolitan busing instead of a plan confined to the city. The NAACP position was much more cautious and reflected a concern for precedent and the effect of the decision on national developments. Having won a stunning victory in a landmark case against a Northern school system noted for its pro-integration leadership, the plaintiffs appeared reluctant to jeopardize this victory by pressing for a remedy of unprecedented size and scope.[2] It is clear that the NAACP considered the essential element in any remedy the institutionalization of the principle of racial "unidentifiability": the definition of desegregation as the creation of schools of approximately similar racial composition must receive the sanction of law in the North as it had in the South. But after a lengthy trial in which so much had been said by expert witnesses on the benefits of racial mixture, explicitly or implicitly defined as majority white, they were not in a good position to make a strong case for the educational advantages of schools which were 65 to 70 percent black. And on what basis could anyone claim that such a desegregation remedy offered any reasonable prospect for stability?

Hearings began in March of 1972, with both counsel and the expert witness for the NAACP, Gordon Foster, treading warily. When pressed, Foster conceded the desirability of a metropolitan remedy but was always careful to leave the door open for a Detroit-only plan if the higher courts declined to open the door marked "suburbs, too." Foster warned that a metropolitan plan might be "pie in the sky" and that Detroit's black children needed "immediate relief" (T, DR, pp. 300–301). A bird in the hand, he declared, "is always worth more than a bird in the bush" (T, DR, pp. 350–51). He offered rather bizarre testimony to support the contention that a busing program to make every Detroit school two-thirds black would be helpful to black children, declaring that uniform racial proportions in the schools regardless of the proportion of black students improved both self-image and academic achievement. These benefits were such that even kindergartners should be included in such a program, he advised (T, DR, p. 334). When asked how black children would benefit psychologically from schools two-thirds black, he declared: "in a variety of ways. One certainly would be in his own self-concept in knowing that the city . . . and the school system was offering him the same opportunities that it offered all the other children. . . . [He] would not feel that he was . . . racially isolated or contained in a segregated situation." A black child, he continued, would be better served in a school of uniform racial composition, even though it was 65 percent or more black, than in one 50 percent black if the half-black school were different from the others.

He was then asked by an attorney for the Detroit Board whether he was suggesting that "if in . . . a magnet . . . school . . . 50% black, a child is moved to a school . . . 70% black . . . having his association with whites virtually halved [would] be overcome by his awareness of the fact that other children in the city were being treated in the same way." Yes, said Foster, "if he perceives other schools in the same situation." Uniform racial composition would tend to improve academic achievement, he said, because of "the expectations that were made for him by . . . teachers in terms of such things as a self-fulfilling prophecy and also parents and others whose expectations for children in ghetto schools or racially isolated schools seem to be considerably different from those in suburban-type schools." Further, he said, having all schools 65 to 70 percent [or whatever] proportion black would aid learning because "the chances in a city like Detroit of his [the black student's] obtaining . . . services would be greatly enhanced by this . . . process because there seems to be a tendency for desegregation to more equally balance such delivery of services" (excerpted from T, DR, pp. 363–70).

Foster, a widely experienced expert witness in school segregation cases, knew that plaintiffs do not have to show any educational benefits from desegregation following a ruling that de jure segregation exists and perhaps, as was noted above, not even prior to such a finding. Although educational benefits "cannot be guaranteed in all cases, we go on the assumption that is what we are doing it for in the first place and if . . . carried out with propriety and respect it will be educationally beneficial" (T, DR, p. 358). However, asked directly whether a Detroit-only plan would improve test scores, then among the lowest in the state, he said: "if accompanied by sound implementation, yes" (T, DR, p. 398). How was it, he was asked at one point, that in schools of the very racial proportions he was proposing (65 to 70 percent black) achievement was so low? Foster advanced a novel explanation: "it is generally agreed that . . . what we call an unstable desegregated school is not conducive to increased achievement" (T, DR, p. 371).

This non-explanation went unchallenged. Later, perhaps to offset the information about substandard learning in schools which were between 55 and 75 percent black, the NAACP counsel inquired about achievement levels in schools 80 percent or more black. Here scores were even lower. It seems incredible that in this testimony, as during the trial, the inference that performance was a function of the classroom mix was not questioned—although since student scores were not classified by race no one could say to what extent black achievement differed in schools of varying racial proportions.

Foster also declared that making all Detroit schools two-thirds black would "promote [residential] stability" and later expressed surprise when school board counsel confronted him with reports of very substantial white attrition following implementation of a busing plan Foster had developed elsewhere (T, DR, pp. 357, 372–74, 378). The obvious fact that schools 65 to 70 percent black will have larger proportions of poor black children than schools in many transition neighborhoods, and would thus contribute to the wish of whites to leave or avoid them, went unnoticed here, as it did throughout these proceedings.

Foster's claims concerning residential behavior, like those concerning educational benefits, reveal that despite the absence of any legal obligation to show the benefits of desegregation the pressure to offer some semblance of plausible evidence to justify it remains. Unfortunately, Foster's wholly unsupported statements were not met by firm demands for empirical evidence, nor would defendants' counsel have been able to evaluate such evidence had it been given.

The defendants' experts in their turn strongly disputed Foster's claim that making each school in Detroit approximately 65 percent black would cause black children to "perceive" them as "unsegregated," but, like Foster, they offered no evidence in support. According to Rankin: "After ten percent [black] the school is seen as desegregated . . . and that condition of absence of racial identifiability, continues to exist until . . . somewhere between 35 and 65% black. I'm not sure when it happens" (T, DR, pp. 564, 618). James Guthrie, the chief education expert for the defendants, insisted that schools two-thirds black would be seen as segregated because of their contrast with the national proportion—or perhaps the proportion in the metropolitan area. The black child would be "torn" by "the tension of knowing that [he is in a school] which is majority black and the society, or the surrounding area isn't." The child would ask himself, said Guthrie, "What has society done that has placed me in this situation? What is there about me that I should be with so many other black children in such a low proportion relatively of white children? . . . Anytime one begins to move beyond the proportion of blacks in society . . . the black child must begin to wonder what kind of factors are in operation which are aggregating him there in a . . . disproportionate way" (T, DR, p. 457). The black child, he said, develops the perception of isolation by having "two opposing pieces of information constantly or sometimes crossing his mind. One set . . . is that he goes to school with children who are primarily black, or lives in a neighborhood which is primarily black, yet his picture of the world which is presented to him by the newspapers, television . . . is . . . primarily a white world" (T, DR, pp. 458–59). He did not attempt to explain how living in a black neighborhood would be affected by school reassignment, and reconciling school area and national racial proportions presented a sticky problem.

Guthrie continued his testimony with the observation that his own children, accustomed to schools in Berkeley that were 40 percent black, had concluded that there must be something wrong with a school shown on a television program because it had only 10 to 20 percent black students in it (T, DR, p. 460). Evidently schools reflecting the national proportions were not, after all, the answer, at least for white children, but no one was disposed to explore this difficulty. During crossexamination NAACP counsel J. Harold Flannery, in an apparent effort to cast a shadow on Guthrie's opposition to schools two-thirds black, suggested that a white man's assessment of black children's perceptions might be open to question. Guthrie effectively refuted this criticism (T, DR, p. 482). Their lengthy colloquy included this memorable concept: "the two levels of perception of discriminatory racial identifiability" (T, DR, p. 487).

The defendants relied upon social science "evidence" as a basis for their educational objections to a Detroit-only remedy, although this required some shift in emphasis from the testimony of the same experts during portions of the trial. Rankin's earlier references to the contribution made to student achievement by parent and student participation and the need for "greater autonomy within an individual school . . . so we can have programs . . . designed by the people who are there" was conspicuously absent (T, pp. 3811–14, 4226–29). Not only had there been some decline in black militant protest on behalf of "community control," but, more important, once busing was mandated, these demands had to be soft-pedaled. Gone, too, was Guthrie's previous emphasis on the contribution made by programs of compensatory education for disadvantaged children. He had strongly disputed the Coleman Report finding that resource variation did not account for achievement variation: now he not only warned that somehow poor children never get the additional dollars allocated for them but insisted that, even if they did, this aid would be ineffective without a change in classroom composition (T, DR, p. 524). The defendants' expert witnesses now stressed above all the overriding necessity of including the suburbs in any remedy so as to secure a middle-class majority in the classrom. (The assumption that there was such a majority available was only feebly challenged; this matter will be discussed below in the discussion of metropolitan plans.) Asked what he would recommend were the City of Detroit wholly surrounded by water, Rankin replied: "Build a long bridge. . . . the solution of the problem no matter how large the body of water, is to cross that body of water" regardless of the distance (T, DR, p. 643). Counsel for the state, crossexamining, pursued the point, asking whether he meant that "if it were necessary to bus children fifty or sixty miles you would do that in order to achieve something of a racial balance?" Rankin's response was: "if . . . that was the only way we could deal with it, then, yes, sir, I would" (T, DR, p. 644).

Guthrie insisted that "a higher-status majority" in the classroom would produce educational improvement for all (T, DR, p. 470), although how the achievement of the higher-status majority would be improved by mixture with lower-achieving classmates was never explained. In an interesting exchange at the close of Rankin's testimony, NAACP counsel Flannery pointed out—and this was the first and only time in these proceedings that anyone did so—that social class integration would almost certainly have a leveling effect: poorer students would presumably be placed in a more stimulating setting, but students of higher socioeconomic status would be moved to one less enhancing. Rankin replied that his concern was for the disadvantaged learner (T, DR, pp. 620–23).

Guthrie continued to stress that the average socioeconomic level of the class is a "critical factor" in a student's learning; a low average level was "a major effort in the direction of educational deprivation" (T, DR, pp. 573–74). As he had during the trial, Guthrie supported his assertion that poor children's learning improved when they were placed in a classroom with a middle-class majority by emphasizing the cultural differences between such groups (T, DR, pp. 449–54). But his single reference, during the trial, to the possibility that this relationship, found in a crosssectional study, might be spurious was not repeated. The aspirations and values and attitudes of middle-class children were transmitted to poor children in classrooms where the more advantaged predominated. This was the mechanism accounting for the higher achievement of children in such settings: "the tone of [the school] is determined by the SES of the majority of its students. The higher that goes the higher the achievement of the student or the classroom will be" (T, DR, p. 452). Thus, as in the trial, the distinction between the strong impact of a student's own social background and the weak (or doubtful) impact of the background of his peers upon his learning was ignored. Both experts stressed that the peer effects were associated with social class, not race. As evidence, Rankin offered (T, DR, pp. 575–77) the statement that achievement scores were lower among the poor white children of Burton school than among black middle-class children at Bagley: in fact, 1972 Board of Education records showed 51 percent of Burton fourth-graders but only 34 percent of Bagley's fourth-graders reading at or above grade level.

No one appeared to find it incongruous that after lengthy and repetitious testimony stressing that Detroit students had to be mixed with suburban children because such a large proportion of the city's children were very poor (statistics were offered [T, DR, p. 638] to show that in 1971 only 4 percent of Detroit's elementary school districts had average household income of over twelve thousand dollars), it was also contended that Detroit-only busing deprived white suburbanites of the contact necessary to overcome "racism," a grave shortcoming (T, DR, p. 584).

The only uneasiness concerning the validity of research proving the benefits of integration expressed during the Detroit-only remedy hearings came from Judge Roth himself. Referring to the just published reanalyses of the Coleman Report data, edited by Frederick Mosteller and Daniel P. Moynihan, he asked whether "it in any way shake[s] the general conclusions reached by the so-called Coleman Commission." Guthrie's reply was far from accurate (T, DR, pp. 500–521):

It shakes one conclusion greatly and I believe that it does not reaffirm another one at all, even though it claims to. . . . One of the Coleman Report findings is that the quality of school services . . . does not influence the performance of the child, independent of social class. The criticisms of that finding . . . still hold even after these reanalyses, despite what . . . Mosteller and Moynihan say. . . . I do not believe that finding has been reaffirmed.

The . . . finding that has been exploded by their re-analysis—the Coleman Report held that the racial composition of a child's classroom had a strong

effect on a child's achievement, and they published tables to try to demonstrate that. Subsequently, it has become more evident . . . that it is a social
class, not a racial effect.

It was true that the papers in the volume tended to support the
Coleman finding that resource variation did not account for achievement variation.[3] But as for the finding that had been "exploded," it
never existed. The Coleman Report authors had gone to some pains
to make that clear:

> The apparent beneficial effect of a student body with a high proportion of
> white students comes not from racial composition per se but from the better
> educational background . . . found among white students. The effects of the
> student body environment upon a student's achievement appear to lie in the
> educational proficiency possessed by that student body whatever its racial or
> ethnic composition.[4]

Experts for the defendants repeatedly stressed the danger of white
flight if a city-only busing plan were imposed. There were many
references to a tipping point, placed by Rankin as probably between
25 and 40 percent black (T, DR, p. 569) and by Guthrie as between
"35 and 50 percent black," after which whites begin to leave (T, DR,
pp. 458, 493, 510). Since the interests of no party present were
served by challenging these assessments, none did so. No studies or
research data were cited; Guthrie offered as evidence only the apparent stability in racial proportions in the 40 percent black Berkeley
schools (T, DR, p. 481).

With Detroit-only busing, Guthrie said, the more prosperous white
families, who are also those with the most concern for their children's
education, would leave; poorer white households, "typically the most
prejudiced and intolerant . . . according to social science findings,"
would remain, leaving a potential for serious violence. The presence
of students of high socioeconomic status would lessen the probability
of conflict, he declared, citing in support the high school study of
1970 directed by Stephen Bailey (T, DR, pp. 465–68, 507–8). (Since
it appeared that no one else had read this work, its finding that some
kinds of serious disruptions "occur most frequently in . . . middle-
class schools into which are bused significant numbers of low-income
students"—precisely what was being recommended—was not
mentioned.)[5]

The theme of the testimony on residential behavior was that the tipping point could be avoided if the proportion black were kept to between 25 and 30 percent, the proportion that a metropolitan remedy would provide. Counsel from the state attorney's office questioned Guthrie on the expert's assertions that high-status families were the least prejudiced, yet would be the first to leave Detroit if a busing remedy were imposed on the city. Guthrie offered a novel explanation: "I do not lay that completely at the feet of racial intolerance [but attribute it to] the tendency in the neighborhood for racial discrimination to take place in consonance with racial segregation" (T, DR, pp. 508–9). Higher-income white families, he explained, often leave predominantly black areas either because the schools in such neighborhoods tend to be discriminated against with respect to the allocation of school resources or because of fear that this might happen. He offered no evidence for this assertion. Altogether, the chief expert witness for the defendants concluded, a metropolitan remedy would offer the greatest possibility for maximizing desegregation over time: "the number of individuals who have such mobility that they can switch their jobs . . . uproot their family . . . from one section of the country to the other [is very limited]. The number of people who are willing to take the psychological risk in moving such distances over such a matter . . . is small" (T, DR, pp. 516–17).

Guthrie warned that a Detroit remedy would fail, and that imposing a metropolitan plan now, while it would cost no more, would "avoid the excessive dislocation of relationships between parents and school . . . students and schools [and] students and students" which would be required if a city plan were later changed to a metropolitan one (T, DR, p. 472). This was one of the rare instances in these proceedings when anyone acknowledged this burden upon children.

The plaintiffs, having established their position that substantial benefits were available from Detroit-only desegregation, had no interest in challenging the additional gains for a far more inclusive remedy which the defendants claimed. The position of the state attorney general's office was that the problem was essentially between the plaintiffs and the school board. Their interest was limited to having the record show that a noted author of desegregation plans, Gordon Foster, believed both stability and educational improvement could be had from a desegregation plan limited to Detroit (T, DR, pp. 370–71). Thus during the hearings on a Detroit remedy there was virtually no challenge to a large number of unsupported claims for the effectiveness and feasibility of metropolitan busing.

Shortly after the Detroit-only remedy hearings ended, Judge Roth ruled that the city schools could not be desegregated without the suburbs and at once commenced hearings on metropolitan plans. If the judge saw any logical contradiction between this conclusion and his finding of the previous September that the Detroit system was guilty of failing to achieve what he now said was an impossibility, he did not refer to it. It had been clear from his questions and comments throughout the trial that Judge Roth did not consider an overwhelmingly black school system to be "integrated"—no matter how children are distributed therein—but there is no clear legal basis for such a definition. The social science evidence that had been offered during the city-only hearings supported his view that a predominantly black system, with so large a proportion of students from poor families, was educationally ineffective and would soon lose its white students in any case. Although Gordon Foster had testified that making each school in Detroit approximately 70 percent black would confer academic and psychological benefits upon black children and would also contribute to residential stability, he produced no evidence to support this bizarre theory, and the court was not persuaded. It also seemed obvious (although no one referred to it) that given the city's existing age composition, even if every household were frozen into place, the supply of white children in the schools would soon be exhausted.

This second set of hearings was marked by the appearance, for the first time in these proceedings, of parties who were strongly adversary in every sense of the word—the suburban communities. They had been hastily added at the last minute and were ill-prepared and in disarray.[6] The lawyers were unfamiliar with the subject matter and the professional literature; they had no expert witnesses to assist them. But even if they had been superbly competent, experienced, and knowledgeable, it is doubtful whether they could have functioned to any purpose within the legal restraints that operate at the remedy stage in school segregation cases.

A serious consideration of the advantages and disadvantages of busing plans is, like any other discussion of social policy, a process of weighing alleged benefits against estimated costs, material and social. If such a discussion is honest, it cannot begin with a conclusion but must permit the introduction of evidence asserting that costs outweigh benefits, or perhaps that no benefits can be demonstrated to exist. But remedy hearings, as the lawyers for the suburbs were so frequently reminded, are held to formulate the broad outlines of a desegregation plan, not to decide whether or not desegregation can achieve certain policy aims. It is true that the precise legal meaning of the term "desegregation" was (and still is) somewhat unclear, but the court was obviously inclined to follow the ruling just issued in *Swann* to the effect that the creation of roughly similar racial proportions in all schools was a "useful starting point." Since a Detroit-only remedy had been rejected on the grounds that it was ineffective and unstable, proponents of metropolitan busing relied heavily upon social science evidence to show the educational benefits and residential stability to be had from creating classrooms more than two-thirds white.[7]

If expert testimony questioning the assertions concerning both educational benefits and residential behavior had been offered during the trial, Judge Roth might not have ruled as he did, but by the time the remedy stage is reached it is too late, for in the world of law, if not in life, there can be no problem without a solution. A legal Rubicon had been reached from which no turning back was possible, and if you must cross the river, what is the point of hearing evidence to show that the journey is of doubtful value? Thus voluminous social science materials of doubtful quality were offered as a rationale for various busing plans, but attempts by the suburbs to challenge this material and, in one instance, to offer opposing testimony (David Armor's deposition) were rejected (this matter is discussed in Chapter 19 below). Despite extended discussion of residential behavior and predictions about its future course, no experts on this topic were called during the remedy hearings. An area of great public concern, school crime and disorder, was taboo. As it turned out, however, none of these defects made any difference. The nature and scope of the remedy was to be determined by the scope of the violation, not by considerations of educational effectiveness, feasibility, residential stability, or cost-benefit tradeoffs. But this legal doctrine was not fully crystallized until the Supreme Court ruled on *Milliken* two years later. All of those involved in the metropolitan remedy hearings, therefore, proceeded as though the basic guidelines for a busing plan would be derived from the testimony offered during these hearings.

Various plans for metropolitan busing were presented. The Michigan Department of Education, with its board unable to reach agreement, submitted, without recommendation, one of several alternatives. The Citizens Committee for Better Education (C.C.B.E.) an intervenor-party during the trial, as often happens with city-based groups in these cases after a finding of de jure segregation is made against a city school system, now bent its efforts toward making the encompassed area as large as possible. The NAACP, on the other hand, was much concerned about the precedent that would be established for other lawsuits in which it was involved: the essential component in a remedy was the principle of racial "un-identifiability," i.e., rough uniformity of racial composition in each school. It was wary of a busing plan that might strike the appellate courts as too large or expensive or administratively clumsy; its plan favored a rather compact area. Emphasis on these concerns also avoided the awkwardness of any posture that might be described as imputing inferiority to schools that had "too many blacks."

Both the Detroit School board and the C.C.B.E., in presenting and defending their plans, utilized assumptions that they reported as derived from social science research. They claimed that their plans would furnish a substantial (white) middle-class majority in the classrooms of the region. This proportion would markedly enhance black academic achievement, yet protect high achievers (mainly white) from adverse effects. Simultaneously, these proportions would improve race relations and avoid the conflict engendered by a Detroit-only mix of poorer whites and very poor blacks. The one-third black–two-thirds white proportion was high enough to protect "black identity," yet low enough to avoid the tipping point at which, they said, white parents would tend to withdraw their children. Even if such parents wanted to leave, they said, the area covered was so large that flight would not be practical. (It appeared that no one really believed that the so-called corresponding effect would operate to create integrated neighborhoods as a result of integrated schools.) However, if whites did try to escape, provision was made to reallocate students to maintain the desired racial proportions.

Virtually all of the expert testimony (with the important exception of that offered by the NAACP) was based on the notion that a metropolitan plan would furnish a substantial majority of middle-class children in the classrooms of the area encompassed. Much of the expert testimony went well beyond this, and referred to this majority as "high income." Some of this material was offered during the trial, where it played, I think, a crucial role in persuading Judge Roth that if the remedy were imposed on a metropolitan basis educational achievement would be enhanced. As Dr. Rankin put it, "if it is possible to place low-income students with a majority of high-income students . . . the low-income students are likely to achieve better [and] . . . the high-income students are likely to stay at least where they are. . . . I would like to shoot for at least 60% high-income students and maybe higher. . . . how are we going to do that without going beyond the bounds of the city?" (T, p. 4229). Testimony from others also frequently described the social class distribution in these categories. When the question of whether it was true that the "fortunate child . . . the rich child, does not need as much educational tender loving care as the poverty child" was asked, the response was that "this child from a wealthy household is going to achieve with much less attention" (T, p. 4108). A later comment was that "wealthy children have waiting for them good schools and poor children have waiting for them bad schools" (T, p. 4117). The terms "wealthy" and "rich" appear to have been used deliberately: "you have talked about [needing] a majority of high socio-economic status kids. . . . Is there a significance to your use of the word majority?" The answer was "Yes. . . . if there were only, let's say, 20% upper socio-economic status children . . . the tone of the class and of the teacher's expectations for it tends to be established by the remaining 80% low socio-economic status students. So you take some . . . middle or upper-SES students to tip this perceptual value of the teacher" (T, pp. 4125–26).

The assumption that a majority of high-income children would be furnished by adding suburban districts to Detroit went unchallenged during the trial. During the city-only remedy hearings, Guthrie, the defendants' expert, was pressed for a definition of "high-SES children" by counsel from the state attorney general's office. He explained: "We are talking about one on the average, modally. This is a child whose parents have enjoyed a college education or above" (T, DR, p. 501). Was he suggesting that such a majority would be created by including the Detroit suburbs? (Fewer than 10 percent of metro area adults were college graduates.[8]) Shortly thereafter he estimated that between 10 and 20 percent of the metropolitan population was "high SES," while between 20 and 30 percent were "low SES" (T, DR, p. 505). It was not clear whether the second estimate included the proportion of 20 to 30 percent black that a metropolitan mix was calculated to produce. If it did, no white children were being counted as of "low SES." Rankin (T, DR, p. 642) had noted that families of high socioeconomic status were a small minority.

The author of the most inclusive of the busing plans (that of the C.C.B.E.) explained that in preparing it his team, lacking socioeconomic data on the student population, had assumed "an almost one-to-one relationship" between race and class (T, MR, pp. 41–45, 55). Although Guthrie had observed during the trial that most of the nation's poor were white, what proportion of whites in the metropolitan area were in the poor category was not made clear by those participating, and at many points the terms "white" and "high SES" were used interchangeably. (There was a particular irony to this usage because some of the same speakers had declared at other points that the assumption that blacks were poor and whites well off revealed the prejudices of teachers or parents.)

One of the most astonishing features of both the trial and the remedy hearings was that the presence of blue-collar or working-class families in one of the world's great industrial centers was never mentioned. The failure to refer to them is especially puzzling in view of the great emphasis placed by most of the expert witnesses upon the social class proportions of the pupil population. The testimony stressed the nature of the social class mix as the basis for claims of educational effectiveness, improved race relations, parent satisfaction, and residential stability, yet the factual basis for the calculations of social class proportions was sometimes mistaken and generally unclear. Suburban counsel attempted to challenge some of the computations, but these attempts either were rather feeble or took the form of random sniping. If demographic experts had been called, the inadequacy of the evidence for claims that metropolitan busing would yield a "substantial middle-class majority" in the classroom would have been clear. The NAACP remained aloof from these controversies, in conformity with its position that regardless of other benefits that might be forthcoming the constitutional requirement for desegregation was the creation of racially unidentifiable schools. This "racial unidentifiability," both their counsel and their expert witness Gordon Foster repeatedly insisted, was not racial balance but was intended to "minimize disproportion from a normative figure" or to prevent straying "too far from the norm" (e.g., T, MR, pp. 1240–41). If the judge recognized that this was double talk, he did not say so. The comment which follows is typical of the expert testimony offered by Detroit School Board witnesses (T, MR, pp. 1397–98):

I calculated a . . . weighted mean for the fifteen clusters [of schools] and . . . found it to be 26.8 minority . . . but . . . there were three clusters below 46 [on the SES scale] and . . . that's getting pretty low to expect the values from the socio-economic mix to pay off. . . . the slight saving in distance traveled . . . resulted in lopping off a number of districts with a fairly high socio-economic level . . . a very serious deficiency.

Rankin insisted that inclusion of suburbs of high socioeconomic status but distant was critical to achieve "educational quality." Distances would be increased, but it was "worth it" to bring "those values and . . . expectations" which were "known to be helpful" to the learning situation. This lengthy testimony (T, MR, pp. 1398–1415) was presented in terms of cost-benefit calculations ("we have to balance the SES difference against the difference in distances"). As I have pointed out, however, this "weighing" was spurious since no challenge to the measurement of the benefits of integration was permitted, but the mathematical calculations gave a show of scientific precision.

At various points Rankin expounded on the meaning of the normal curve, discussed the conversion of scales into standard scores, explained the meaning of the standard deviation, and considered the implications of too low a socioeconomic status average (T, MR, pp. 1411–12):

Cluster No. 3 [in the NAACP plan] is 44.7. . . . Now if we were able to move that distribution further this way . . . even a couple of points we would begin to include more and more students on the right edge of this [distribution]. . . . I admit this is a matter of degree. . . . it would be hard . . . to postulate that there is a certain point at which you have achieved the ideal socio-economic mix. . . . But . . . if it is possible to create a plan where the lowest one is 46.3 it would be better to do that than to create one where the lowest point is 44.9 and we have to balance that difference against the difference in distance. . . . I just feel that the difference is substantial and should receive greater weight than another five minutes on the bus.

NAACP argued for a more compact busing area. Mindful of the constitutional grounds for a busing remedy, its counsel declared: "I don't think the 14th Amendment has been read to speak to SES. . . . we have no particular quarrel with SES considerations to the extent they don't interfere with the desegregation process [but] I don't think they are relevant. . . . If the districts were all poor or all rich the 14th amendment desegregation requirements would be precisely the same" (T, MR, p. 1399).

During the trial and Detroit-only hearings there had been no challenge to the frequent assertions that race-class mixture had beneficial effects upon achievement and attitudes because both sides were generally in accord on these matters. We do not know whether the court would have permitted opposing evidence; such material is frequently characterized as an attempt to re-litigate the *Brown* case. During the metropolitan remedy hearings suburban counsel seized upon a statement Judge Roth had made before these proceedings began to the effect that his purpose was to achieve "quality education for all children" and that he was "not concerned with parties litigant here" (T, MR, p. 974, quoting from T, October, 1971, conference, p. 10). But at many points when suburban counsel asked for evidence that such and such a racial mix did in fact produce "quality education for all children," the NAACP objected to the inquiry, and Judge Roth usually sustained the objection. For example, when suburban attorneys cited research (published after the trial) that cast doubt on claims for the impact of racial mixture upon academic achievement,[9] NAACP counsel said: "This is the separate but equal argument again and I object. This is a desegregation case, not an SES trial, not a retrial of *Brown v. Board of Education*" (T, MR, p. 585). The judge agreed, adding a warning which was to be heard many times (T, MR, p. 587):

Your inquiries into such matters as broad educational policies or philosophies may be interesting and you may at your leisure question whether the policies actually educate children or not. . . . These are all intriguing matters. I am not an educational expert. . . . right now I'm interested in what we can do about our assignment and this is to desegregate the Detroit public school system.

Evidently the issue of whether, or to what extent, racial mixture would contribute to "quality education" was not really open to question, for as Judge Roth explained later: "I can take no position except that commended . . . by . . . the higher courts. . . . They say when you find segregation you have to go about desegregating. . . . As I see it under the law and the evidence in this case I have to go to a metropolitan plan to achieve that desegregation" (T, MR, p. 994). The effect of this position was to prevent challenges or demands for proof of integration's benefits while permitting introduction of all materials that supported such claims when they were offered as a rationale for various busing plans. This gave these hearings something of the quality of the trial in *Alice in Wonderland*.

The testimony offered in support of mixture was, like that given during the trial, sometimes inaccurate or exaggerated, often garbled or confused. It was during these hearings that wholly unsupported claims were made for the improved achievement of black children bused to white schools to relieve overcrowding in Detroit over the years (T, MR, pp. 984–86). It was also asserted that a "substantial jump" in academic performance generally took place when black children were placed in classrooms where the "middle-class majority went beyond half to 65 or 70%," an "acceleration of impact" described as a "logarithmic curve" and other such nonsense (T, MR, pp. 675, 1419).

The following colloquy illustrates the generally poor quality of the testimony, the inability of suburban counsel to detect and expose its defects, and the failure of the proceedings to educate the judge in the fundamentals of the topic he was dealing with (the expert witness testifying is Dr. R. W. Morshead, a professor of education at the University of Michigan, Dearborn):

Q: You do recognize that children start . . . school on unequal terms, that some . . . bring varying degrees of capabilities . . . that are either due to genetic reasons . . . or . . . socio-economic status . . . ?

Morshead: . . . That's correct.

Q: And education, to be truly equal . . . would have to provide . . . treatment [which takes into account those differences]?

Morshead: That is correct.

Q: Now how would that be accomplished by mixing . . . low socio-economic status groups where they would only represent 20 to 30% of a school district, where the rest . . . 70%, is composed of . . . higher socio-economic status . . . since the school system is geared to those people, how would it take care of . . . this low SES group?

Morshead: The same way we do in Detroit. . . . Title I funds and various state funds . . . were channeled to these . . . schools . . . for special training.

It should be noted that the attorney began by asking how compensatory education would be implemented within a system geared to higher-achieving students; the response was that funds in Detroit are channeled to predominantly low-SES schools, not students, but counsel appeared not to notice this and proceeded to another point. He asked Morshead whether he was familiar with the results of the use of Title I funds in Detroit. The witness replied that he was, but did not say what those results were. Counsel then moved to another subject, leaving the issue of compensatory programs under busing up in the air (T, MR, pp. 111–16):

Q: Would you agree or disagree with . . . Dr. Armor [the reference is to Armor, in Mosteller and Moynihan (1972), p. 226] . . . that programs which stress financial aid to disadvantaged black families may be just as important if not more so than programs aimed at integrating blacks in white neighborhoods and schools . . . ?

Morshead: I agree . . . up until the "if not more important." I have no evidence to support that claim.

Q: I take it then that what you are saying is that equality of education is not measured by what we would call input, but rather by . . . measuring . . . output. Is that correct?

Morshead: . . . I am not agreeing with that. I think input is significant.

Q: Do you think input is more important than socio-economic status?

Judge Roth (interjecting): Well, isn't that input?

Counsel: No, sir. Socio-economic status is unrelated to the direct school environment.

Judge Roth (to expert): Do you consider it as input?

Morshead: We are using a sort of jargonese that has grown up in the educational area. Input usually . . . [refers] to measurable hardware, materials. . . .

Judge Roth: You mean it is limited to dollars?

Counsel: Dollars or the things dollars will buy, such as staff, facilities, curriculum, programs, textbooks, special courses, special education.

Judge Roth: Well, I assumed that input encompassed everything you put into the system, including your socio-economic components. Apparently I am in error. . . .

Morshead: You are asking which . . . is more important, the . . . input or the socio-economics of the youngsters?

Counsel: Yes.

Morshead: I would have to agree with the court that socio-economics isn't input [note that the court had just said the opposite]. . . . I have no way of concluding that the . . . input is more important than is the socio-economic mix.

Counsel then went on to another line of inquiry.

It is startling to learn that the judge, after a lengthy trial during which there were so many references to school resources as input, in contrast with student's socioeconomic background, still did not distinguish between these two categories. Apparently the central finding of the Coleman Report, cited so frequently, was not clear to him, and one wonders what he made of the lengthy testimony in the trial concerning the relative contribution of in-school and out-of-school variables. Cross-examining counsel failed here to distinguish between financial aid to poor families and enriched school offerings, yet Armor's whole point was that income-additive strategies might be more effective social policies than any school programs. Finally, the expert witness altered the entire meaning of the last question in the cited excerpt by transforming an inquiry about the effect of a child's socioeconomic status into an inquiry about the effect of the socioeconomic mix of the classroom, a common error in these proceedings which, as usual, went unnoticed and uncorrected.

Elsewhere in these hearings an expert witness defined equality of educational opportunity as equal educational results for black and white students, with no reference to the fact that such an outcome was unlikely as long as disproportionate numbers of the black population were of low income (T, MR, pp. 410, 564–65). Generally, the defendants' experts relied to some extent on socioeconomic factors as an explanation of the low achievement of black children when questioned about this during the trial, but during the remedy hearings the impression was conveyed that a metropolitan busing program would overcome this disadvantage. This shifting emphasis, together with the definition of "opportunity" as "outcome," probably contributed to the judge's confusion.

In addition to testimony concerning academic achievement, there were many references in these hearings to the proportion of black children needed to protect "black identity," sometimes called "self-identity." One expert put the required percentage at "not less than 20% to secure social and self-identity . . . so they are not lost in the woodwork as it were" (T, MR, pp. 60, 118). Rankin, on the other hand, believed that "a person can retain identity at 10%" (T, MR, p. 506). Three black children in a class of thirty did not seem sufficient to Dr. Freeman Flynn, expert witness for the Detroit School Board, who agreed with Morshead that 20 percent was the minimum "to protect . . . feelings of self-identity and belonging necessary to a group which has dignity" (T, MR, pp. 904, 919). Dr. William Pierce of the State Board of Education said that 25 percent was the proportion needed to "maintain identity" (T, MR, p. 279).

It has been noted earlier that one of the disadvantages cited for any Detroit-only plan was that it combined lower-income whites with blacks. Metropolitan busing, because it kept the proportion black under 30 percent and included large numbers of well-off whites, was presented as a solution that not only would avoid interracial conflict but also would make a positive contribution to race relations by helping to overcome the stereotyped conceptions of black students held by suburban whites. Asked why this happy outcome had not taken place in Detroit schools at the time when they had a black population of under 30 percent, an expert witness said it was because this mix had come about as a result of "rapid and radical neighborhood change" (T, MR, pp. 1016–17). The crossexamining counsel did not seem to understand that a busing program would be far more "radical" because school composition would change overnight and would not involve the economic screening that occurs, to some degree, when households must be able to buy or rent homes in an area. The explanation went unchallenged, as did the general proposition that contact with a black population which the experts themselves characterized as generally of low socioeconomic status would improve racial attitudes and correct inaccurate stereotypes.

Some evidence questioning the effects of racial mixture on achievement and attitudes was suppressed by defining such material as an attempt to relitigate *Brown*. Other negative effects, well known in the literature, were not mentioned because the suburban attorneys appeared unaware of them. There was, for example, no reference to findings that lowered self-esteem tends to occur when children who are not doing well in school are placed in classrooms with children working at a considerably higher level (these findings are noted in Chapter 10). There was no mention of the possibly adverse impact of classrooms with lower achievement averages upon higher-achieving (mostly white) students; on the contrary, experts declared that research shows that middle-class children do well regardless of their school situation (T, MR, pp. 221, 618). Despite some references to the work of Alan Wilson, his 1959 findings that middle-class children in predominantly working-class schools were doing less well than those in middle-class schools was ignored.

There was no testimony on the effects of frequent school transfers, a feature of those plans which called for sharing the burden of busing, as it was called, by having children alternate attendance at their neighborhood school with attendance at more distant schools. The departing superintendent, Norman Drachler, had identified frequent school changes as an important cause of poor scholastic performance, but the adversary parties may not have seen his deposition.[10] Since the suburban attorneys were not familiar with recent studies on the uncertain effects of interracial contact (see Chapter 10 above), they did not attempt to call attention to these findings. Experts therefore persuaded the court that these uncertain benefits were worth an hour and a half or even two hours of travel time for a kindergartner's three-hour school day. Five-year-olds were included in Judge Roth's final set of guidelines for a metropolitan busing plan.

The testimony on school resources was a prime example of courtroom sociology. During the trial much testimony stressed the importance of school resources, but during the remedy hearings some of the same experts who had testified to this effect now minimized their importance. For example, suburban counsel tried to use earlier statements from Detroit School Board experts attributing the poor performance of Detroit's children to inadequate school resources: "you point out that Detroit schools are 'laden with burdens.' . . . you say that the 'burden of inadequate education will continue to be borne by our students.' . . . you are stating a deficiency in the quality of education in Detroit . . . [implying] that in certain suburban school districts there is not such deficiency" (T, MR, pp. 614–15). Dr. Rankin interrupted to dispute this statement, saying that despite high levels of achievement in the suburb of Southfield its schools were deficient in quality education because they lacked a "substantial" black presence. Suburban counsel continued: "the deficiency in the quality of education you have mentioned in the Detroit schools . . . such things as staff, class size, teaching materials . . . the deficiencies had to do with input . . . correct?" Rankin said yes. The counsel continued: "If we bring a student who is in a class of acceptable size . . . faculty . . . teaching materials . . . into a system that does not have these items, you are not suggesting that there will be no effect, are you?" Rankin's answer was that "class size is not a critical variable in achievement. I would be glad to match the quality of the teaching staff in Detroit against . . . Southfield. . . . I would argue that Detroit's instructional materials are superior. . . . based on those criteria you would be moving [the student] from a system of lower quality to one of higher quality." The counsel asked: "Doing him a favor, then?" (T, MR, pp. 616–19).

Crime and violence in the schools were much on the public mind in 1972, but references to this topic were not permitted. An attempt by suburban counsel to offer statistical data on the volume of such incidents in and near schools in Detroit failed. Judge Roth sustained the combined objections of the NAACP and the Detroit School Board, despite suburban counsel's assurance that they sought neither names nor racial identification of those involved (T, MR, pp. 1140–41). Opposing counsel declared that such material would "violate confidentiality," incite racial fears, and "propagandize racial hatreds"; it was an "attempt to inflame . . . the community" (T, MR, p. 1139). The School Board counsel made light of reports of school crime, suggesting that these events were "the usual scuffle between youngsters . . . that we have all experienced. I have sat under the teacher's desk a couple of times myself when I was young. . . . I don't think this is relevant or material. . . . I think it is oppressive" (T, MR, p. 1138).

In view of what was taking place at this time, this assessment was grotesquely inappropriate. Following the trial (but unrelated to it) a Citizens Commission on Unrest and Disorder in the Schools, after completing its study, reported to the Detroit School Board that school disruptions and violence were so serious that they were "beyond the power of the Board . . . to solve." They urged immediate measures of surveillance and security to diminish their impact and referred to reforms that might be helpful.[11] No mention was made of this report during these proceedings. Expert testimony during the metropolitan remedy hearings minimized both the amount and the gravity of school-related crime and disorder. Challenges to this assessment were not permitted: "rumor and mythology about incidents and difficulties in the schools is exaggerated and exacerbated by all kinds of fears which are irrational and which come from stereotypes." Asked at one point if there were no truth whatever in charges of safety problems in some schools, Dr. Flynn replied that there were such problems, but went on to say that "drugs and other matters" caused problems in suburban schools as well (T, MR, p. 1009). By 1975 a changed social climate allowed the discussion of these matters. In retrospect, the amount of concealment and dishonesty in the appraisals of 1972 is dismaying. The conditions that later were discussed so freely were obviously of long standing.

In view of the fact that the movement for community control of schools was at its height during the trial, the success of the parties in virtually excluding representatives of the movement from the remedy hearings is surprising. Malcolm Dade, Jr., and Lawrence Doss had offered some support for a rather moderate version of the movement's aims (see Chapter 11 above). In a deposition taken after the Detroit-only remedy hearings, the state superintendent of instruction expressed doubt that many parents would regularly travel many additional miles to attend P.T.A. meetings; by implication, this was a disadvantage of metropolitan busing. In one of the rare instances where hard evidence was demanded to support such generalizations, Paul Dimond, the NAACP co-counsel, asked Porter for data on parent participation before and after the implementation of busing in Charlotte-Mecklenburg. He wanted to know whether Porter had figures on parent participation, whether he had any basis for saying that parents who have to go ten to twenty miles to P.T.A. meetings do not attend them, and whether he had any data for the nation as a whole on parent participation after desegregation (T, Porter Deposition, p. 100). During the metropolitan remedy hearings the obstacles to parent involvement created by increasing the distance between home and school were sometimes minimized but were generally ignored. One of the sorriest examples of the way in which a topic of legitimate concern was handled was the testimony from two students who attended a very expensive private school for gifted children. The Detroit School Board brought them as witnesses to show that there was no conflict between long-distance busing and participation by both students and their parents in extracurricular activities (T, MR, pp. 379–98). The suburban communities had no experts of their own during these proceedings, and no other participant was inclined to challenge the assertion that travel times as long as an hour each way would be no bar to parent involvement and participation in school affairs.

In all of the plans presented during the metropolitan remedy hearings, the proportion of black students was much smaller and the encompassed area was much larger than was proposed by any city-only busing remedy. White parents would be so satisfied with the schools that they would not want to flee, it was claimed; the 25 percent black proportion, the judge was told, was well below the famous tipping point (T, MR, pp. 502–3). The extent to which the danger of white exodus dominated these hearings is suggested by the fact that on a single day (March 28, 1972) there were twenty references to the problem of "white flight."

It appeared that confidence in parental satisfaction to a degree sufficient to stabilize racial proportions in the schools was not very great. A theme given almost equal emphasis was that metropolitan-wide busing would make it very difficult for white households to escape these school assignments. As one expert put it early in the proceedings, "White flight will be minimized to the point that . . . it will be insignificant . . . . there comes a time when one can no longer commute to one's work from massive distances . . . . it becomes economically overburdening to continue to move further and further away" (T, MR, pp. 72-73). This line of argument, repeated throughout the hearings, was never challenged. There were no experts to raise the question: farther and farther away from what? Rapid and continuing economic decentralization means that a dwindling proportion of people living in the suburbs work in the central city; in many areas more than 70 percent work in other suburbs.[12] Suburban dwellers generally spend less time reaching wanted facilities than do city households.[13] The length and cost of the journey to work has usually been given much lower priority by parents than the socioeconomic characteristics of their children's contacts.[14] Wherever the outer perimeter of the busing area was drawn, those living near it would not have to go far to avoid inclusion. Opposing counsel, if forbidden to demand evidence of the educational or attitudinal benefits of race mixture, might have been permitted to question proponents concerning the destabilizing consequences of the racial differential in the birth rate, but the issue was not raised.[15] They might have called attention to the emerging national migration trends (perhaps not fully recognized in 1972) showing white middle-class migration away from, avoidance of, or attrition in, metropolitan areas of the East and Midwest.[16]

Suburban counsel did not refer, either, to the substantial growth

in attendance at non-public schools already apparent in many districts in the south under busing orders.[17] No mention was made of
the fact that approximately 10 percent of children (mostly from
higher-income white households) in the Detroit metropolitan area
were already using non-public schools.[18] Most important, no one
seemed to understand that unless existing population trends and
established residential patterns were altered, pupil racial imbalance
would soon be re-created.

There was considerable attention to measures designed to recapture white households attempting to flee, for despite repeated claims
that parental satisfaction would be high, no one was inclined to depend upon it. Even the assurances that the "massive distances" would
prevent flight were not deemed a sufficient barrier. The busing plans
provided for a continuous series of boundary changes. One proposal
suggested that these changes would operate "much like a rubber
band in connection with white flight. As parents move out, the bor-
ough extends and snaps the students back into the district from which
they fled" (T, MR, pp. 99, 126).

Another expert witness reported a recommendation that children of
each race be selected on an alphabetical basis to make it easier to
locate households attempting to escape by shifting residence within
the desegregation area (T, MR, p. 260). Nor did the NAACP seem to
have much confidence in the stability of a metropolitan remedy; at
several points during these hearings reference was made to their
intention to seek a court order restricting school construction in the
outlying suburbs beyond the metro busing area (T, MR, pp. 840,
1023, 1197, 1436, 1454). Whether this interference with residential
mobility would have been granted or how it would have been possible to distinguish between the (legitimate) school needs of an exurban
community and those generated by flight from a busing program we
cannot say.

The judge who began the consideration of the Detroit case so
strongly opposed to what he described as "integration by the numbers" concluded the case with remedy proposals completely guided
by them. "Desegregation" turned out to mean the creation of schools
where the proportions of black and white children were roughly uniform throughout the area. The NAACP contended that if these proportions were approximately the same in each school—regardless of
what these percentages were—the "perception of segregation" would
tend to vanish. Others said the racial proportions had to reflect those

of the overall society, or perhaps those of the surrounding area. Most who testified told him that the educational benefits of integration would accrue only if the advantaged (nearly all white) were twice as numerous as the disadvantaged (nearly all black). This proportion of blacks was also, he was told, the optimum, or perhaps the required, percentage of blacks needed to protect their "identity."

If you extended the catchment area a sufficiently large number of miles you would inhibit white flight, which, the judge was told, occurs when the proportion of blacks goes beyond 30 or 40 percent. However, you could not go out too far, or the travel time would be too great and the supply of blacks would become too small to afford whites the benefits of integration and would jeopardize blacks' identity needs as well (T, MR, p. 1216). But there were also references to the danger of including some of the far northern suburbs because in the future they might be needed to provide more whites for metropolitan desegregation of Pontiac schools (T, MR, pp. 29–30).

If you could fashion a plan based upon the proper numerical formula, you would discourage flight, avoid the tipping point and segregation (defined as actual or "perceived" concentration, or both), provide enough blacks so that they would feel secure, and enough advantaged students so that everyone could learn. But no evidence was offered to show how this precarious equilibrium, involving so many factors, could be maintained.

Even if a metropolitan busing plan had been imposed and the curb on school construction sought by the NAACP granted, there is little reason to believe that racial imbalance would not have been regenerated. In order for this not to happen, white and black families would have to be continuously replenished, in about the same proportions as existed at the outset; that is, a steady recruitment of 75 percent new white public school children in the Detroit metropolitan area would have been required to replace those graduating or leaving for other reasons. A permanent system of racial quotas in student assignment would be required, and the power of such periodic redistribution to make the area sufficiently attractive to those white households which have a fair degree of choice in residential location is very doubtful. But in all of the hundreds of pages in the two sets of remedy hearings the problem of enticing new white households to enter an area under a busing order was never mentioned.

In his final ruling ordering a metropolitan remedy, Judge Roth included fifty-three districts, containing 780,000 children, 25 percent of them black.[19] The schools were to be divided into fifteen clusters, ranging from 20 to 31 percent black, within which transportation (not to exceed approximately one and a half hours of total travel time) was to take place. About 40 percent of the students would be transported by bus; all grade levels including kindergarten were to be included, and there were provisions for some staff integration: no school could have a faculty less that 10 percent black.

In August of 1974 the Supreme Court by a single vote rejected the metropolitan remedy.[20] The majority held that the constitutional basis for ordering student reassignment by race requires, as it did in the South, a prior finding of de jure segregation, and only Detroit had been found guilty of this offense, nor had it been established, said the Court, that official acts of suburban school boards had been involved in creating Detroit's segregated schools. At a meeting held shortly after the ruling, an attorney explaining it to the public remarked that "if Stephen Roth knew what Detroit's schools were being ordered to do he would turn over in his grave." (The judge died two weeks before the ruling was rendered.) The record supports my belief that, if Roth had been certain that the final outcome of *Milliken* was to be a city-only busing plan, he never would have "found" (the verb is singularly appropriate) de jure school segregation. No party had appealed the finding of segregation within the Detroit system, and the unchallenged ruling was accepted by the high court.

The problem of fashioning a city-only remedy was thrust upon another district judge, Robert DeMascio. He appointed three experts (John Finger, Francis Keppel, and Wilbur Cohen) to help formulate guidelines for a plan to desegregate Detroit's schools, which, by the summer of 1975, were almost 75 percent black. The final plan included a substantial number of educational components whose cost was to be shared by the state, a provision later upheld by a unanimous ruling of the Supreme Court. But DeMascio refrained from redistributing all of the white minority, as the NAACP demanded, and concentrated mainly on adding black children to the predominantly white schools near the city's periphery.[21] Only about 10 percent of the students were to be bused to alter racial proportions; in addition, some magnet schools were to operate on a 50:50 racial quota.

The plan was met with outraged protest by the NAACP. Their spokesman attacked Judge DeMascio's remedy order in the strongest language. It was "racist," "Jim Crow," "a return to Dred Scott," "lawless," "an abomination." The order was appealed to the Sixth Circuit.[22] Nathaniel Jones, the NAACP general counsel, explained the fundamental reason for the objections: "The basic question here is a Constitutional one. The fact that Detroit's schools are 70 percent black and 30 percent white doesn't make any more difference than if they were 70 percent white and 30 percent black. The basic question is this: Are the Constitutional provisions for integrating schools that are mostly black the same as for those that are mostly white? The Detroit decision would seem to say they are not.[23] In a confusing opinion, the Sixth Circuit Court of Appeals agreed that the order was improper in its failure to desegregate—but simultaneously admitted that it did not know what Judge DeMascio could do about it in view of the city's demography.[24] This admission suggested that the appeals court, unlike the plaintiffs, defined desegregation as requiring a white presence, but this point was not spelled out. At the time of this ruling, the Detroit schools were almost 80 percent black; in the fall of 1977 only about 15 percent of public school students in Detroit were "non-minority." This did not deter NAACP attorney Louis Lucas from demanding in hearings conducted by Judge DeMascio that the busing program be expanded.[25] This insistence, which has continued up to the present and has been so puzzling to the public, underlined the importance that the NAACP gives to the institutionalization of "reasonably uniform" racial proportions in schools as the definition of desegregation. Detroit was widely cited by busing proponents as an example of "harmonious" or "peaceful" integration, a reminder of those heroic surgical procedures of which it is sometimes said: the operation was successful but the patient died.

PART V: ISSUES RAISED BY THE SCHOOL SEGREGATION CASES

CHAPTER 18
Legal Puzzles: A Layman Looks at the Law

What Is Segregation?

One searches the several thousand pages of this trial record in vain for some passage where the court imposed, or litigants agreed upon, a common use of the term "segregation" that so dominated these proceedings. Sometimes it was defined as the degree of departure from a condition of random distribution of students (T, pp. 342–43, 1029). Sometimes it was the concentration that resulted from discrimination or "containment," or even the failure to correct imbalance (T, pp. 919, 998–99, 2377; DR, p. 486). Sometimes it was the condition of "racial identifiability" (T, pp. 865, 997–98, 1028, 1380–82; DR, p. 474; MR, p. 1351). Sometimes "segregation" was declared to be dependent on the perceptions of observers; if they see segregation, it exists; otherwise, not (T, pp. 882–86, 920, 1025, 1379–82, 2380). However, the problem of "anticipatory segregation" complicates the matter; observers may not perceive segregation now but think that they will in the future (T, DR, p. 565). Sometimes "segregation" existed when racial proportions differed substantially from those of the system as a whole (T, pp. 1382, 2377; DR, p. 359) (back to statistical randomness again). But what system? The city, the metropolitan area, or the nation as a whole? This problem gave rise to still another refinement: "perception of discriminatory racial identification" (T, DR, p. 486). A lone suburban attorney during the remedy hearings offered as a legal definition "the use of race to exclude," but at that stage only the suburbs could have used such a definition, and the attempt was ignored.

241

Since the legal meaning of a term emerges and is crystallized through judicial decisions, one would expect to find both plaintiffs and defendants offering a reasonably clear, although differing, definition. But neither side did so, and a series of Northern school cases has not clarified the concept.[1] The confused and inconsistent language in *Milliken* and other litigation reflects the state of the law. It is indisputable that *Brown* made unconstitutional the exclusion of black children from the public schools. But the extent to which specific or isolated acts of racial discrimination (or even the failure to dissipate the putative consequences of such acts in the rather distant past) might be considered the equivalent of a dual system is not at all clear. Further, the reference within *Brown* to the inequality of "separate" education suggests the possible, although not widely accepted, interpretation that separateness, regardless of cause, might also be defined as a denial of equal protection. The judicial exegesis on this topic is complex and voluminous; it would be foolhardy for a layman to do more than indicate a few of these contributions.[2] An interpretation that separateness, regardless of cause, is unconstitutional is fraught with obvious perils. What about voluntary congregation? What is separateness? Once the test of exclusion is rejected, numbers take over. Does this interpretation apply to all ethnic groups? What about those geographic areas where blacks are, or may become, predominant? If the harm resides in concentration, regardless of cause, is a constitutional wrong without a remedy not created? Why is predominance a constitutional violation? How can we avoid the interpretation that "too many blacks" is bad? Is it reasonable to insist that assertions of "harm" from black predominance in a school be empirically supported? If societal conditions and research findings change, might racial isolation (not exclusion) move from being constitutionally proscribed to being permitted?

The courts and those seeking redress in them have gradually moved away from the path of finding a constitutional violation in the harm resulting from racial concentration, perhaps because such assertions invite empirical tests and the introduction of opposing evidence, which is ample. Instead, the path chosen is the one discussed earlier: racial predominance in schools is unconstitutional if it can be shown to have been caused or augmented by the acts of school authorities. It is then segregation de jure and, after *Brown*, is forbidden. No further proof of its educational, psychological, or societal harm is required. I am not alone in believing that this theory—that school segregation is caused by school authorities—is deceptive and harmful to judicial credibility. Furthermore, the use of this unsubstantiated causal theory generates its own confusions. I will comment on some of them below.

What Is the Remedy?

Because there is no clear definition of what segregation is, there can be no clear definition of what constitutes desegregation. This problem is seen most clearly in the recurring controversy over the extent to which desegregation requires the presence of white children.

A remedy order is not a legal penalty or punishment; those affected did not commit the unlawful acts. Chief Justice Warren Burger has described the school desegregation remedy as an effort "to restore to the victims of discriminatory conduct the position they would have occupied in the absence of such conduct."[3] Even if we ignore the assumption that a court can unravel history, this explanation is based on two false premises: first, that in the absence of discrimination an ethnic group distributes itself randomly, and second, that the conduct that created the racial concentration was that of school authorities.

The use of the legal fiction that racial predominance in schools is caused by manipulations by school systems will increasingly be called into question as it becomes clear that school desegregation or "busing" remedies leave residential trends and demographic processes more or less intact. For this reason the NAACP has continued to press for a definition of the condition of segregation as disproportion ("racially identifiable schools") and of desegregation as racial proportionality, or balance. The NAACP contends that the effects of past conduct, i.e., discrimination, have so strong a continuing effect as to require a seemingly unending series of remedy orders to reassign children in order to maintain racial balance or proportionality. But the courts show varying degrees of reluctance and uncertainty on the question of remedy. One of their most serious problems in fashioning desegregation plans is that they are caught in their own legal trap concerning the causal role of school system actions as the constitutional basis for imposing a remedy order. On what basis then, can courts compel the inclusion of white suburbs, which did not commit such acts? As so many city school systems become predominantly black, remedy orders confined to them are ineffective.

The Logic of the Violation v. the Logic of the Remedy

An inevitable and immediate consequence of the use of the legal fiction that school racial concentrations are substantially caused by school authorities is the sacrifice of logical consistency between findings of violation and the orders to correct the condition of racial concentration. This is exemplified by Judge Roth's conclusion after he reviewed the plans submitted to him for desegregation of the schools in Detroit: "none of the plans would result in . . . desegregation of the public schools of the Detroit school district. . . . Relief of segregation . . . cannot be accomplished within the corporate geographical limits of the city."[4] The Sixth Circuit Court of Appeals concurred, yet this same court had declared that if school authorities had not done what they had done but had done something else (all the actions mentioned were of a minor nature compared with the student reassignment within the power of the judiciary to impose in Detroit), segregation would not have existed. One may fairly ask whether Judge Roth and the Sixth Circuit meant that school segregation could not be abolished within the city at the time—but that it could have been achieved earlier. They did not so state; if they had, it is hard to imagine what date they would have set for the abolition of segregation. At what point could a system which had a black majority many years before the trial began have desegregated itself successfully? If a school system with a smaller proportion black can correct or prevent racial concentration by site selection, boundary changes, and the like, why have these remedies in such situations not been ordered instead of large-scale busing programs? In systems like Denver and Boston, the courts have declared that violations in one place "infect" the entire system, making a system-wide remedy necessary. But if this is true for the courts (armed as they are by the power to compel), how could it not apply with much greater force to school authorities?

In Detroit the Sixth Circuit Court stated that no Detroit plan could desegregate. Any plan confined to the city "would change a school system which is now Black and White to one that would be perceived as Black, thereby increasing the flight of Whites from the city and the system, thereby increasing the Black student population. It would subject the students and parents, faculty and administration to the trauma of reassignments, with little likelihood that such reassignments would continue for any appreciable time."[5]

There can be no disagreement with the last sentence. But the same was true of the April 7 Plan and any other actions that the school system was faulted for not having carried out. The logic of these pronouncements concerning the futility of even a total desegregation plan which would be confined to Detroit destroys the logic of the contention that anything the system itself could have done would have made any substantial difference.

What Testimony Is Relevant?

The doctrine that racial predominance violates the constitution only if it can be shown that acts of school authorities played a substantial causal role immediately suggests this question: is an identical degree of racial predominance no violation if it is caused by other factors? Testimony on the harm, educational and psychological, of segregation and the benefits of racial mixture in the Northern school cases does not reflect the distinction that harm comes only from racial concentration when school authorities' actions are, or were, involved. Such testimony, which in some cases has been copious, has dealt with the alleged effects of the condition without regard to its causation.

The legal justification for permitting such testimony is unclear. If actions are illegal, why offer elaborate proof of their educational and attitudinal impact? It would appear that this practice became customary during the earlier phase of the attack on Northern school segregation, when the doctrine that imbalance is inequality regardless of cause was mingled with the approach showing that it had been caused by state action. The *Milliken* rulings contained no references to educational issues, but I am convinced, although I cannot prove the point, that in Detroit, as in some other cases, the proofs of the harm of segregation and the benefits of integration were crucial in motivating the judge to "find" that Detroit School Board actions caused racially segregated schools, despite the murky and illogical nature of this evidence. Testimony on educational effects may influence a judge to use his power to create racially mixed schools without serving as legal grounds for such rulings.

Altogether, the judicial view on the use of educational testimony appears, at least to a layman, confused and inconsistent. Mark Yudof states that "with rare exceptions courts have not allowed school boards or white intervenors to introduce social science data and testimony to contradict the *Brown* result."[6] Empirical studies, research findings, and citations from authorities can be presented to show the courts the harmful impact of racial concentration on achievement and attitudes and the benefits of integration, but apparently these claims cannot be disputed or challenged. Judge Roth's ruling declaring David Armor's testimony inadmissible (see Chapter 19 below) was based not only on the grounds that by the time it was offered (during the metropolitan remedy hearings) the topic was irrelevant, but also on the grounds that it had become irrelevant after *Brown*—and, finally, that a previous court decision in the Sixth Circuit had determined that disparity in achievement is corrected by more rather than less integration.

Precedent cases have been influenced, perhaps crucially, by poor or inadequate evidence which has since been much revised, but the courts are now bound by precedent rulings and are insulated from hearing conflicting evidence. To compound this absurdity, judges may permit copious testimony to support the earlier evaluation, now rejected by many scholars, but will not hear contrary evidence because the issue, they say, is settled.

Past Actions

There are two somewhat different aspects of this problem. First is the matter of culpability for actions which, when they were carried out, were legal, as well as the responsibility for having failed to take certain steps which were then defined as illegal. An example is the role played by two prominent black attorneys, now federal judges, in the planning of new schools described in *Milliken* as instances of de jure segregation. Judge Wade McCree (later on the Sixth Circuit Court of Appeals) had been chairman of an important subcommittee (T, Drachler Deposition, p. 27) on the rebuilding of Eastern (now Martin Luther King) High School. Judge Damon Keith, author of *Davis* (the Pontiac schools case), as a civil rights leader had led citizen demands for the rebuilding and restoration of schools in the central city, stating that their age and condition made them visible symbols of second-class citizenship. Both these judges were thus in effect declaring that their actions of a few years earlier amounted to complicity in segregation de jure, a conclusion that is an offense against common sense. Similarly, the only action that could possibly have stabilized the racial mix in Detroit schools—and even then only temporarily—was the use of racial quota assignments, but by the time that such mandatory assignment to promote integration was clearly legal, Detroit schools were approximately 60 percent black.[7]

This problem surfaced early in the trial. Responding to objections to the testimony on policies of the Detroit Real Estate Board from 1925 and 1930, Judge Roth asked plaintiffs' counsel if these actions were not consistent with the law of that time: "Are you taking the position that the Detroit Real Estate Board should have anticipated forty years before that the Supreme Court would in time see the light?" NAACP counsel Pressman replied: "Our position is . . . that . . . conduct lawful at the time it was undertaken which has a continuing impact beyond the point where the law changes . . . that conduct, even though lawful at the time, can be shown to bring into play the legal rules in effect at the time a case occurs" (T, p. 656). Roth restricted some material introduced into the court record to the period after 1948, the date of the Supreme Court ruling barring judicial enforcement of restrictive convenants. However, he did not invoke a similar prohibition on school system actions or inactions not defined as illegal by the Supreme Court at the time they were executed.

Pressman's reference to "continuing impact" illustrates the second aspect of the problem of past actions. This doctrine has been much used in employment discrimination cases and has been criticized because the evidence to support such contentions has been dubious. All social phenomena, one may assume, are the product or outcome of past conditions, but the questions of which condition caused which outcome and of how far back one traces such linkages are shrouded in uncertainty. Robert Tucker, asked during the trial for the cause of residential segregation, began by suggesting that the basic cause was slavery, but the infinite regress approach is not very helpful.

It is difficult to ascertain the extent to which even current busing orders, i.e., large student reassignment programs, create more white attrition than would have taken place without them. One cannot peer back into the past and estimate what fraction of residential decisions was affected, and in what way, by tiny shifts in student assignment following this or that zone change or placement of a building. This problem is not solved by lumping some incidents together and saying that they constitute a "pattern": to multiply a question by several other questions does not produce an answer. Yet this shaky doctrine of the continuing impact of past effects seems to constitute much of the legal ground for decisions in the Northern school cases.

Recision—The Backward Step

Once a governmental body moves toward integration, it is not permitted to reverse its direction.[8] But if a school board voluntarily institutes a busing program and then finds it ineffective, how can abandoning the useless program be a constitutional violation? The law seems to be that revocation of a busing program for non-educational reasons is the forbidden step, but if the program was begun to improve race relations or promote other general educational aims it would seem impossible to put opposition or disillusionment into compartments labeled "legitimate" and "non-legitimate." There would always be some segment of opinion that could fairly be described as opposed to busing on non-educational grounds. What if educational outcomes are doubtful and costs great, or if educational outcomes are uncertain and white attrition is increased? When Judge Roth selected the voluntary magnet school plan instead of the involuntary April 7 reassignment plan before the trial in Detroit began, was he practicing de jure segregation? He refused to reinstate the integration plan, as the plaintiffs requested, and instead took the forbidden backward step.

"Foreseeing" the Future

The Northern school cases now impose a curious standard of permissibility concerning the future. Sometimes forseeing the course of future events is required, but sometimes it is forbidden. Permission to look ahead depends on who is looking—and what they see. Thus it is contended that a school board should have foreseen that building a school in a heavily black area would mean that the school would be mostly black when it opened. Not to have foreseen this and, therefore, to have refrained from building there is a constitutional violation. But it is also a constitutional violation for the school board to foresee that choosing a site in a presently mixed area will mean, based on the best available data on residential trends and demographic composition, that it too will be virtually all-black by the time the roof of the building is on. It is easy to foresee that compulsory reassignment of a minority of white middle-class children to a slum area school will stimulate white withdrawal, or avoidance, but again, this glimpse of the future is forbidden. Failure to use available space in such schools to house white children from crowded schools in other areas is a commonly cited constitutional violation.

Thus the district court and the Court of Appeals for the Sixth

Circuit (and some of the dissenters on the Supreme Court) concluded that a Detroit-only plan was futile because of the city's growing black predominance, but it was not permissible for others to take note of this trend. During the trial, as Judge Roth pondered population data, he said: "I will be surprised if [the demographic projection] doesn't follow the course which history has shown since 1940. . . . then this occurs to me, how do you integrate a school district where the student population is 85%–90% black?" (T, p. 3537). School system experts had been looking at those same data for years, but apparently were not allowed to see into the future as the judge did. (By 1979 Detroit schools were indeed approximately 85 percent black.) Betsy Levin and Philip Moise, legal scholars, declare that by confining a remedy to Detroit the Supreme Court "has now ensured that white flight will proceed even more rapidly from Detroit than heretofore has been the case."[9] Whether this can be demonstrated empirically is a question for social scientists, but it seems quite illogical to fault a school system for reasoning in the same fashion as do legal scholars. (This reflection suggests a paradox: is the Supreme Court majority guilty of de jure segregation for not having foreseen the predictable consequences of *its* Detroit decision?)

This swamp of illogic and inconsistency is nowhere better illustrated than in those portions of the 1976 ruling of the Sixth Circuit Court of Appeals which respond to NAACP objections to Judge De-Mascio's remedy order. First, the justices cite their 1973 concurrence with Judge Roth's rejection of a Detroit-only remedy because, as he had said, it would only lead to an "overwhelmingly black" school system in Detroit.[10] Then the court rejects the explanation offered by Judge DeMascio for the failure of the present plan to desegregate the inner city. The reasoning that desegregation was impossible in a school system which was 75 percent black, and that its only result would be further white attrition, is unacceptable, said the Sixth Circuit, because the Supreme Court ruled that "apprehension of white flight . . . cannot be used to deny basic relief from de jure segregation."[11] Two pages later, however, the circuit court judges declare that the NAACP's more comprehensive desegregation proposal "would accelerate the trend toward rendering all or nearly all of Detroit's schools so identifiably black as to represent universal school segregation within the city limits."[12]

How does this differ from the forbidden concern for future white attrition? On the following page, the Sixth Circuit holds that "where unconstitutional segregation has been found," a plan that fails to deal with it where it is at its worst (in Detroit's inner city) cannot be permitted to stand.[13] But, the court added, it was unable to offer guidelines to solve the problem because, in the absence of a metropolitan remedy, a solution was not possible.[14] What is the source of this confusion and illogic? The source is the wish to preserve legal continuity with *Brown* and use its moral authority to achieve a goal completely different from that articulated by Thurgood Marshall before the Supreme Court: "the only thing that we ask for is that the state-imposed segregation be taken off, and leave the . . . school board . . . to work out their own solution of the problem, to assign children on any reasonable basis."[15]

In his discussion of the impact of Social Darwinism upon the United State judiciary at the end of the last century, Paul Rosen characterized the Supreme Court of that period as "a most willing victim of a well-coordinated ideological crusade." He quotes a study by Benjamin Twiss which concluded that "Social Darwinism and laissez-faire economics were deliberately foisted upon the Court primarily by a brilliant group of leading corporation lawyers."[16] Change a few words, and there is a provocative similarity to the present effort. The superior expertise of the lawyers who have been trying school segregation cases, aided by the overwhelming majority of the academic community (either by testimony, informal aid and consultation, or simply refusal to aid defendants), has surely been one of the reasons for the past success of the plaintiffs' efforts. But this is by no means the whole story. Behind the receptivity of the judiciary and the cooperation with NAACP efforts of so many persons of knowledge and goodwill, grave problems lie. They have proved much more difficult to overcome than we would have guessed at the time of *Brown*. "Poor schools" were not, it turned out, an entirely adequate explanation for poor schoolwork, and neither improvement in the economy nor the elimination of legal barriers produced the kind of residential dispersion that many of us assumed would take place. Efforts to achieve at least a moderate amount of school mixture within the normal geographic assignment system show only modest success, and some have questioned whether racial mixture per se is a reasonable aim or is better seen as a natural byproduct of other processes. To those alarmed over the continued separation of the races, especially of the nation's children, indefinite delay in achieving this goal seemed a dismal or even a dangerous prospect, and court action appeared to provide the only practical solution.

CHAPTER 19
Law and Social Science

One of the most controversial features of the school cases of 1954 ending state-imposed racial exclusion from public schools was the citation of research from the social sciences to strengthen the rationale for this break with legal precedent. Protests against so-called sociological jurisprudence from those who disagreed with the decision were predictable. But there were legal scholars who, while they fervently supported the outcome, regretted the introduction of this material as both unfortunate and unnecessary. One of the most eloquent of these was Edmond Cahn:

I would not have the constitutional rights of Negroes—or of some other Americans—rest on any such flimsy foundation as some of the scientific demonstrations in these records. . . . [S]ince the behavioral sciences are so very young, imprecise, and changeful their findings have an uncertain expectancy of life. Today's sanguine asseveration may be cancelled by tomorrow's new revelation. . . . It is one thing to use the current scientific findings, however ephemeral they may be, in order to ascertain whether the legislature has acted reasonably in adopting some scheme of social or economic regulation; deference here is not so much to the findings as to the legislature. It would be quite another thing to have our fundamental rights rise, fall or change along with the latest fashions of psychological literature.[1]

The distinction drawn between the sciences is perhaps unsupportable. All scientific work is an everlasting process of revision; the undertaking to tell the truth, the whole truth and nothing but the truth is in the strict sense impossible for the scientific expert offering testimony in court. But the distinction between ethical values and

251

ideals of justice, on the one hand, and current scientific evidence, on the other, seems to me entirely proper.

There is a rather substantial literature devoted to evaluation of the role played by social science evidence in *Brown* and the discussion of the desirability of having introduced it.[2] But the doubts and cavils came almost entirely from the men of law. Most academics from sociology and social psychology were enthusiastic about the use of contributions from the behavioral sciences. Chronically beset by status anxiety and uncertain self-esteem, these disciplines indulged in a fair amount of self-congratulation: the Supreme Court had taken notice of us, if only in a footnote.[3]

Within the past several years the situation has changed quite markedly. At present there is widespread dissatisfaction with the role of social science research in the school cases. As goals changed from ending state-imposed exclusion to creating racial mixture, the earlier moral and value consensus has been shattered. As research findings on the impact of racial dispersion upon achievement and attitudes proved disappointing, much of the earlier zeal for the use of such evidence (if not for the enterprise as a whole) evaporated. Kenneth Clark, for example, whose work figured prominently in the *Brown* litigation, moved from enthusiastic support—including the assertion that such research could provide a "verification of moral laws"[4]—to warning that only the constitutional protection of the federal courts is to be trusted. By 1972 this shift was reflected in a *New York Times* story under the headline "Lawyers Group Fears an Over-Reliance on Educational Studies."[5] Civil rights attorneys were clearly dismayed by a steady flow of negative findings on the impact of busing programs and attempted to minimize their influence by characterizing them as "flawed," "inconclusive," or "skimpy."[6] In fact, the works singled out for censure were considerably more substantial than most of the studies cited in the *Brown* footnote.[7] At present, proponents of busing programs have turned away from attempts to win public support on the basis of findings from the social sciences. This does not mean, however, that social science testimony has been removed from litigation concerning segregation in the public schools.

Is "social science" necessary in the school cases? Discussions of the use of social science in recent school segregation litigation often refer to the kind of testimony utilized in a case that was a striking example of the uncritical acceptance of such material, *Hobson v. Hansen*, in

1967.[8] The ruling is replete with ill-founded generalizations from behavioral sciences, e.g.:

actual integration of students and faculty . . . by setting the stage for meaningful and continuous exchanges . . . educates white and Negro students equally in the fundamentals of racial tolerance and understanding. . . . Negro and white children playing innocently together in the schoolyard are the primary liberating promise in a society imprisoned by racial consciousness. If stereotypic racial thinking does set in, it can best be overcome by the reciprocal racial exposure which school integration entails.[9]

These naive and unsupported observations concerning the effects of contact are followed by numerous generalizations (equally dubious) concerning the impact of other variables. Judge J. Skelly Wright cites James Coleman as the basis for his assertion that "Negro students' educational achievement improves when they *transfer* into white or integrated . . . institutions."[10] There is a lengthy discussion of the psychological and educational impact of testing, with references to self-images and the self-fulfilling prophecy.[11] Ability grouping, said Judge Wright, "tends to alienate the disadvantaged student who feels unequal to the task of competing in an ethnocentric school system dominated by middle-class values, and alienated students inevitably do not reveal their true abilities either in school or on tests."[12]

Among factors held responsible for increased juvenile crime are "inferior teachers" and "textbooks unrelated to the lives of disadvantaged children."[13] Many social science authorities are cited, in addition to Coleman, in the text of the ruling, including Thomas Pettigrew, Kenneth Clark, Robert Coles, Sidney Peck, Robert Rosenthal, and Martin Deutsch. Others are quoted as asserting that "a racially imbalanced school seriously affects a child's ability to learn."[14] The court concluded: "segregated Negro schools, however the segregation is caused, are demonstrably inferior in fact. This principle is unanimously attested to by reports from every quarter."[15]

This was not true in 1967, and it is hardly necessary to add that both this statement and the earlier declaration concerning the effects on learning of racial imbalance are much in dispute today. I have noted Paul Dimond's judgment: "I do not believe the evidence on the educational advantage of integration proves much of anything."[16] (Neither he nor anyone else said this during the trial, however.) As we have seen, the NAACP now claims that recent court rulings are based solely on clear violations of the Constitution. In fact, such violations are often not at all clear, but they do provide the legal grounds for holding northern school systems to be segregated de jure. Nevertheless, findings from the social sciences continue to play an important role in supporting and rationalizing decisions, as well as in motivating judges to issue them. The Richmond ruling, five years after *Hobson*, contains numerous references to social science and educational authorities in addition to the ubiquitous Gordon Foster; among them are Thomas Pettigrew, James Coleman, Robert Green, Calvin Gross, and Karl Taeuber.[17] The Denver ruling cites the work of Dan Dodson, Neil Sullivan, Robert O'Reilly, James Coleman, and others.[18] The Coney Island ruling of 1974 cites, among others, James Coleman, Dan Dodson, Robert Coles, Christopher Jencks, Charles Silberman, Jonathan Kozol, Nathan Glazer, and Frederick Mosteller and Daniel P. Moynihan. A few had apparently testified at the trial; others were only cited and (in some instances) misinterpreted. There are references to perceptions, self-images, motivation, the effects of contact on interracial attitudes, and the impact of a middle-class majority on academic achievement, as well as the causes of racial separation in residence.[19]

These illustrations are not exhaustive, but they cast doubt on the denial that social science plays no role in more recent school cases. But there are additional factors that further qualify the disclaimer. The content of the ruling made by a judge at the district court level may not reveal the extent and influence of social science testimony presented during the trial. Only a study of the transcript of the proceedings will reveal this. My comments concerning the Richmond and Coney Island school cases are based on a study of the rulings alone, and I have seen only a small portion of the trial record in the Denver case. Judge Roth's ruling in *Milliken* suggests the influence of the substantial social science testimony on residential movements and behavior but gives no hint of the voluminous evidence that he heard on educational topics, evidence that, as indicated in earlier chapters, deeply affected his views on the necessity of racially mixed classrooms. On the other hand, if one happened to have read only the Detroit ruling as it issued from the Sixth Circuit Court of Appeals, one would have no inkling of the crucial role played by the testimony on racial segregation in residence.

Even if school cases in the future were to exclude expert testimony on education (e.g., the harm of segregation, the benefits of mixture) entirely, the importance in law of precedent rulings gives a powerful and continuing influence to testimony given years ago—even when it is later seen to have been of poor quality. As noted in the previous chapter, testimony which puts in question the benefits of mixture has often been excluded on grounds that when de jure segregation is found it must be disestablished; the educational effects of integration are defined as either irrelevant or, almost by definition, beneficial. (This leaves unanswered the question of why lengthy testimony asserting the harm of segregation and the benefits of mixture is permitted, while challenges to such assertions are not.) But even if all such materials were excluded, these issues would tend to remain, albeit underground, a kind of hidden agenda during a trial. Whatever legal rationale is used, it is hardly conceivable that a judge would press the lever offered by a finding of a de jure segregation unless he thought there was a reasonable promise that court-ordered desegregation was both feasible and beneficial.

During the 1976 trial in Cleveland, the plaintiffs offered no testimony on integration effects.[20] Adherence to such a practice, however, will simply ensure that the judge's pre-existing opinions will not be clarified. Judicial views on both the harm of imbalance and the benefits of mixture will then be formed entirely from fragments of knowledge, snippets of popularized research reported in the media, and whatever other materials happen to come to a judge's attention. Thus, as Paul Rosen has noted, Justice Oliver Wendell Holmes' ruling upholding a state compulsory sterilization law was shaped by popular misrepresentations of Darwin and Spencer; Holmes seemed not to have read either writer, but the pseudoscientific notions of the eugenics movement were simply "in the air."[21] Holmes' scanty information, however, did not restrain him from writing an opinion of astonishing boldness, culminating in the famous sentence, "Three generations of imbeciles are enough."[22]

The rejection of educational effects as legal grounds for busing orders in the northern school cases has aroused considerable controversy among constitutional scholars, especially those who regard the school violations approach as unconvincing.[23] On the other hand, empirical demonstrations of the harm of segregation and the benefits of integration are not only uncertain but, like any other scientific demonstration, are always subject to revision. For this reason some other basis has been sought on which to justify defining racial concentration in schools, regardless of cause, as a deprivation of constitutional rights.

Mark Yudof's admirably expressed criticisms of both harm-benefit analysis and the constitutional violations approach as grounds for court-ordered racial dispersion leads him to consider the courts' use of a "universalist ethic" as an alternative.[24] He does not vouch for its constitutional adequacy, noting that it "may not serve" as legal grounds. The open declaration of assimilation ("a shared culture") as a goal for public education would have the merit of candor, for the conception of society underlying most of these decisions is indeed of this nature: in the final section of Judge Roth's ruling in Detroit, for example, all ethnic concentrations, past and present, voluntary or not, are cast in negative terms.

But on what basis does the judiciary impose its vision of the good society upon others? Legislative and administrative policy provisions to compel or persuade school systems to correct imbalanced schools have used language reflecting some version of a universalist ethic, but these measures require some degree of public support for enactment, to say nothing of later compliance. The need for empirical verification is not completely avoided because the case for mandatory integration is argued largely in instrumental terms: an integrated society is required, and a racially separated one is rejected, in terms of its effects. As Yudof describes the basic premise of this ethic: "a stable just society without violence, alienation and social discord must be an integrated society. Segregation of the races in public institutions, employment and housing will inevitably lead to conflict and the destruction of democratic values and institutions."[25] Segregation cannot here mean discrimination or racial exclusion, for these have long since been outlawed. The reference must be to a condition of racial concentration without regard to cause; integration, as used here, must mean dispersion, not open access. The grounds, then, would be that involuntary redistribution of students to achieve racially mixed schools is a societal necessity. It is asserted that racial concentration leads to conflict and the eventual destruction of democratic society; dispersion is a necessary, although, no doubt, an insufficient, condition in order to avoid violence, alienation, and social discord. These are empirical propositions, versions of the contact hypothesis in race relations, albeit on a considerably larger scale than those which we usually deal with. Further, the case for the school as the most effective arena for the work of societal unification rests upon empirical propositions related to both efficacy (e.g., schools reach people at an early age) and various feasibility considerations of cost, control, and scope.

None of these propositions is self-evident, and there is enough contrary evidence from both this and other societies to justify a considerable degree of skepticism about them. Stability and the absence of social discord do not necessarily coexist with "justice," and there are other social reforms that offer more promise of creating a just society than involuntary racial dispersion. Conflict avoidance is a goal with doubtful ethical claims, as well as empirical uncertainty, in a multigroup society. Once again "social science" has not been avoided; only the scope and the subject matter have changed. Instead of emphasis on peer effects on academic achievement, we have shifted to larger and more difficult areas while not avoiding empirical challenges to contact effects in the classroom.

Curiously, while the testimony on residential segregation is generally recognized to be "social science," a similar causal analysis of the effects of school system practices is not ordinarily so categorized. Whether the attempt is to show that racial concentration in schools is caused primarily by residential patterns in large part the result of state-supported discrimination or to show how acts of school authorities were an important cause of this concentration, or both, such an enterprise is wholly within the realm of social science. Plaintiffs have been generally successful in their efforts to equate the self-evident effect of racial exclusion in the pre-1954 Jim Crow South with the doubtful or inconsequential impact of the so-called cheating by systems using the "assign to nearest school" system. This theory of the causes of racial concentration in northern school systems is both illogical (in view of intense residential segregation) and lacking in empirical support. The attribution of school racial concentration to acts of school authorities has been only a matter of a series of declarations studded with sociological or psychological terms, but the plaintiffs' failure to establish (and the defendants' failure to rebut) these alleged causal linkages cannot conceal the fact that this is an attempt at a sociological-demographic analysis.[26]

Social science evidence on the harm of segregation, benefits of mixture, and perhaps even on residential behavior could be deliberately excluded from the trial stage in these school cases but the issues underlying such testimony will inevitably surface during remedy hearings. At this stage, however, the social science evidence has a spurious quality because all participants are required to accept the hypothesis that racial mixture is beneficial. This axiom—it is a travesty of a scientific statement—scarcely solves any remedy problems, however. Busing, like any other social policy, is based on hypotheses, implicit or explicit, concerning the relationships between certain variables. Their consideration within the judicial framework, however, thwarts and distorts an objective and systematic evaluation of the assumptions on which a busing plan is based. What range of racial proportions shall be defined as "desegregation"? How much does this racial reassignment plan help? Enough to justify a two-hour ride for a kindergartner whose school day is only three hours long? How can we balance the presumed benefits to be derived from securing certain race and social class proportions, which will require more reassignment and transportation, against their impact upon residential trends? I have noted, for example, that legal sanctions may be invoked against open consideration of the danger of white attrition due to busing, but an honest appraisal of the effects of a social policy cannot ignore a consequence that will determine the lifespan of the remedy itself.

A serious consideration by experts, at the remedy stage, of the costs versus the benefits of busing would run the risk of throwing these proceedings into confusion. There is no way, for example, to assimilate new research findings that might show negative effects from busing; such material must be ignored or excluded. Thus we have cost-benefit discussions that are not permitted to question benefits and decisions about the size and inclusiveness of the busing program that cannot be openly and explicitly guided by a consideration of the probable effects of the program on the supply of white households. Furthermore, all decisions are subject to rejection by the courts (as happened in Detroit), under the legal doctrine that it is the nature and scope of the violation that is to determine the dimensions of the remedy. We may liken it to the futile effort to combine law and social science findings in the sentencing of a convicted felon. If a judge asks for expert guidance as to what type of prison such a person should be sent to, and what length of time will have the greatest rehabilitative impact, he runs the risk of hearing that there is little evidence that any penal facility has any rehabilitative effects. At this point the court is obliged to tell the experts that the guilty person must go to prison, and the experts must accept the conclusion that the prison experience will be helpful to him.

I see only two alternatives to the intrusion of social science materials into remedy hearings in this deceptive manner, which prevents their honest consideration. One is the approach favored by the NAACP. Following a finding of de jure segregation, the desegregation remedy must be defined as a permanent system of racial quota assignments, stated as a permissible range of percentages. A plan can then be produced by a computer and by transportation technicians whose aim is to create schools of approximately similar racial composition. No "social science" is involved here. The other alternative is to abandon any attempt to unravel history in order to restore black students to the condition in which (according to this rationale) they would have been if there had never been constitutional violations by school authorities. Instead, the system would simply be ordered to cease its unlawful practices. But since most of these practices took place in the past and, in my opinion, had little or nothing to do with the creation of racially imbalanced schools, such a command would have no noticeable effects and thus, in the eyes of busing proponents, no purpose.

Neither of these alternatives is likely to be followed. The second would not create the condition of racial mixture for which busing proponents strive, while the first would remove from remedy hearings the social science findings that serve to legitimate and rationalize orders that, without them, would be seen as an arbitrary exercise of judicial power.

If I am correct in concluding that there is no way in which social science can be excised from the school segregation cases, it is necessary to consider some of the problems that arise as a consequence of the incorporation of these materials in the world of the law. There is a basic conflict or incompatibility between them that is revealed in a variety of ways. The courtroom setting and procedures are unsuitable for the communication of social science research to anyone, and especially to a layman. Fact-finding—the collection and verification of masses of raw data—is very difficult within the adversary framework. Most important of all, the comprehensiveness, quality, and integrity of scientific material is jeopardized by judicial norms and adversary procedures generally. I will discuss some aspects of these problems below.

The Courtroom as Classroom

Even if the testimony in *Milliken* had been of much higher quality and the experts had been the most competent in our disciplines, a novice at the trial would require a great deal of help in assimilating and evaluating such evidence. Instead, the problems of a layman confronting testimony on a wide array of social science topics are compounded by their mode of presentation. The logical order needed for a systematic consideration of findings on a specific topic is greatly hampered by being forced into the two-sided trial format. Imagine a seminar or symposium where highly selective presentations on a complex subject are elicited first by plaintiffs, often in disjointed segments (via direct examination); then follows a series of sniping questions by opposing counsel that often lurch from one aspect of the topic to another. The attorneys either do not know enough about the subject to ask the most important questions or find no advantage in so doing, and often are not well enough acquainted with the literature to know whether the findings offered are being reported with reasonable accuracy. Days or weeks devoted to other subjects intervene. The plaintiffs' experts depart. The defendants' experts then take the stand and revert to the topics considered weeks earlier. (The time for an opposing expert to cite research countering Robert Green's assertions concerning the absence of entry-level differences among children, for example, was when Green had testified, not two months later.) The experts never confront each other directly; discrepancies and contradictions in their testimony are "confronted," if at all, circuitously, via the lawyer intermediaries. Thus they cannot resolve differences readily reducible to facts, nor can they expose and elucidate stubborn disagreements over evaluation and interpretation of those facts. From the perspective of the logical ordering of subject matter, the scientific testimony as offered during a trial is an utter hodgepodge.

Presumably the judge is learning during this process, but there is no one in the courtroom who has an educational role. Part of my dismay upon reading the *Bradley v. Milliken* record was a response to testimony which was sometimes at so low a level as to be a caricature of social science. Some of my dismay, however, was the reaction of a teacher reading a verbatim account of a class discussion in which terms were not carefully defined nor consistently used; contradictions were not explored, resolved, not even acknowledged; errors were ignored; issues were muddled; and the judge's misinterpretations were often

uncorrected. The term "integration," for example, was used throughout the trial without ever being defined. Judge Roth's use of the term
offered many opportunities (all ignored) to direct his attention to a
variety of possible meanings. When he asked an expert witness near
the start of the trial whether "integration can be achieved simply by
the numbers" (T, p. 515), a teacher would want to ask whether he was
thinking about the effect of racial proportions on stability, or learning,
or intergroup relations, or what. And did "integration" no longer mean
ending racial exclusion? Near the end of the trial the judge, putting a
question to a witness, appeared to be as unaware of these complexities
as he had been at the beginning: "let's go to the point. Are you for
integration?" (T. p. 4400).

The aim in a lawsuit is not to improve the judge's grasp of a subject
but to propagandize and convert him. No one questions this learner
to see if he has understood an explanation, and unless he initiates a
question or interjects a comment there is no way of knowing whether
he has. Deference to courtroom etiquette or fear of offending the
powerful person who holds the outcome of the trial in his hands
appears to keep those present from correcting those misinterpretations which are sometimes clear from the judge's own remarks.

There is no one at a trial whose only interest is to clarify and
synthesize, in short, to "teach." For example: in some of the lengthy
exchanges when speakers hopelessly confused the distinction between the strong impact of the individual student's social background
and the slight impact of that of his peers, there was nobody to say
stop—which are you talking about? When testimony describing the
adverse effects of severe disadvantage upon intellectual development
was followed by the assertion that the reason for educational problems is that "teachers don't perceive that children in poverty learn
just as readily as others," there was no one to ask whether this was
merely a case of misperception or a report of reality. A participant
with a continuous educational mission throughout a trial would have
observed, for example, that no one had explained the term "input" to
the judge. I suspect this blunder occurred because everyone thought
someone else had already done it.

Clearly, a trial was never intended to be used for the consideration
of large bodies of scientific materials. The subject of residential behavior, for example, simply does not lend itself to a two-sided presentation. Its complex, multifaceted character cannot be understood in this
way. But the awkwardness created by forcing presentations into this

Procrustean bed is not the only problem created by adversary procedures and pressures.

Fact-Finding through Debate

To a social researcher the use of adversary procedures to gather data about factual matters such as dollar expenditures or whether a certain school did or did not have suitable space for 240 children in the winter term of 1969 is absurd. It is like staging a public debate on the topic: what is the population of Michigan? During the trial many hours were consumed in a pointless battle of wits on such subjects.[27] The alternating mode of presentation (first the plaintiffs' experts, then, after a long time lapse, the defendants' experts) makes these competing versions of factual data even more difficult to follow than is the case with substantive issues in social science.

There are not two sides to purely factual matters any more than there are two answers to a problem in arithmetic, nor is the answer somewhere in the middle. I see no reason why tasks of this nature cannot be turned over to fact-finders from each side who would bring in a report of agreed-upon data. But assuming that this were done, there are still problems remaining that are far more difficult to solve.

The Quality of the Testimony

Even if the social science testimony had been of high quality, the trial format makes it very difficult for a layman to understand and evaluate these materials. Much of the expert testimony in this case, however, was scarcely above the level of pop sociology. Important bodies of evidence went unmentioned. In preceding chapters I have pointed out that the court never heard, for example, that research on the effects of ability grouping is inconclusive; that the expectancy research findings cited have been seriously challenged; that no studies show a consistent relationship between racial "attitudes" and residential behavior; that peer group effects on achievement, if they exist, are slight (and that Coleman and others had warned of this in papers published well before the trial); that ethnic (i.e., subcultural) differences are often an important factor in academic achievement; that interracial contact when combined with extreme social class heterogeneity has doubtful or negative effects on attitudes—and so on.

In the course of these proceedings there were many references by expert witnesses on both sides to specific works of research. Most of these citations were inaccurate, and none of these errors was ever corrected. Gloria Powell's research (1973) does not show that poor black students' aspirations and self-conceptions were damaged by placement with *poor* white students (T, p. 4122). Research by Otto Klineberg and Robert Havighurst does not demonstrate that children enter school at about the same level of academic proficiency (T, pp. 874–75). Alan Wilson's research does not show that students of lower socioeconomic status, if transferred to classes with those of higher socioeconomic status early in their schooling, would have their performance improved, while children of higher socioeconomic status would not be adversely affected (T, DR, p. 1394). Stephen Bailey's high school study (1970) does not conclude that much school disorder could be avoided by making classrooms more heterogeneous (T, DR, p. 508). Rosenthal and Jacobson (1968) do not attribute the expectancy effects they found to the presence or absence of "strong teacher press," they do not describe one class as bright, the other as dull; they do not discover that the teachers "with the so-called bright youngsters spent more time with the class and presented them with more information, more educational data and [thus] did in fact cause the spurt" in I.Q. (T, pp. 891–93). William Drake's educational history (1955) does not attribute to public schools "great responsiveness to the needs of immigrant children such as the Irish" (T, pp. 963–64). I can find no research by "Nevitt and Sanford" that, as the trial testimony reads, "systematically documented that large numbers of white undergraduates and other college students, including many at the Ph.D. level, believe that black Americans are inferior, even those who have attained good training . . . at schools such as Harvard, Yale, Fordham and so forth" (T, p. 960).

The Coleman Report does not claim that the "effects of classroom heterogeneity came from race rather than social class mixture" (T, DR, p. 521); it does not claim to have demonstrated that teacher attitudes were a significant cause of pupil performance (T, p. 987); its findings do not prove that schooling has had a "dramatic effect" upon the degree of upward mobility of various ethnic groups (T, MR, pp. 97–98). It does not show that if students of low socioeconomic status are placed in classrooms with a majority of those of higher socioeconomic status, the former group's achievement would increase, while that of the latter would remain at least as high as before (T, p. 4228), nor does it assert that middle-class youngsters will prosper regardless of what is offered in school (T, MR, p. 221).

Many of the factual statements and substantive generalizations offered in expert testimony during the trial were, like many of the research citations, simply incorrect. The proportion of children attending school in 1900 was not 11 percent and in 1930 was not "35 or 40 percent" (T, p. 947). The first public school education law in the United States was not passed by "the black legislature of either North or South Carolina in 1887 or 1880" (T, p. 947). Scores on ability tests are not determined by school inputs (T, p. 894). The standard error of the mean does not correct for cultural bias in testing (T, p. 936). It is absurd to say that "black parents have never opposed busing as a concept" (T, p. 914). A pattern of racial segregation did not begin in 1920, in Detroit, but existed well before that time (T, p. 174). Nor is it true that in the 1950s there were no Detroit schools west of Woodward Avenue with significant proportions of black students (T, p. 886). It was misleading to state (in 1971, five years after the Coleman Report) that "the national pattern is unequal allocation of educational resources on a basis of race" (T, p. 972). Income is not, as asserted, "consistently a better predictor [of academic performance] than race" (T, p. 4215). There were not "eight black families west of Livernois in Detroit in 1962" but many hundred of times that number (T, p. 532). The peak years of European immigration to the United States were not 1914 to 1928 (T, pp. 963–64). There was no urban renewal legislation during the Great Depression (T, p. 154). It is not, as was stated at the trial, rare for a child who excels in one subject to excel in others, nor for the slow learner to be slow in many areas (T, p. 4206). Black-white differences on various tests at time of school entry are not "a function of geographic region" (T, pp. 877–88). The achievement gap between black and white students has not "closed in mixed schools" (T, p. 1008). There was no evidence to show that black children in Detroit bused to predominantly white schools (to relieve overcrowding) improved their academic performance as a consequence (T, MR, pp. 984–86). The busing program in Riverside, California, had not, on the whole, produced improvement in the academic achievement of black children (T, p. 939).

Some factual errors appeared in the ruling of the district court.[28] Blacks of childbearing age did not "equal or exceed" the total white population in 1970.[29] The typical residential movement of inner-city black residents is not of the "leap-frog" variety, nor is the typical white family moving to the suburban areas an "older white family without children of school age," and "steady out-migration" of Detroiters is not properly characterized as "since 1940."[30] (The factual errors contained in the rulings of both the district and the appeals court concerning school violations, as well as the weakness of evidence to show how they caused or augmented racial segregation in the school system, have been discussed in Part III.)

Spurious Precision

When I first began to read this trial record and saw the rather elaborate statistical presentations, technical explanations, the heavy use of terms from quantitative research, and the controversies concerning the propriety of using this or that technique of data analysis, it seemed quite unreasonable to expect any layman to be able to follow the testimony. Judge Wright, who presided over the trial of *Hobson v. Hansen*, observed: "The unfortunate if inevitable tendency has been to lose sight of the disadvantaged young students . . . in an overgrown garden of numbers and charts and jargon like 'standard deviation of the variable' . . . 'statistical significance' and 'Pearson product-moment correlations.' "[31]

In the course of the lengthy proceedings in Detroit there were disputes and explanations concerning the meaning of sampling error, the identification of variables as dependent or independent, the meaning of a scattergram, ascertainment of item-reliability in an index, the suitability of multiple-regression analysis, trend-extrapolation in demographic prediction, the use and meaning of chi square tests, the interpretation of scale differences, computation of various indexes of segregation, the meaning of the normal curve, problems in making inferences about public school populations from census data, the use of polar categories, and many more. An example (T, pp. 1818–19) of a question from an attorney: "you ran some statistical analyses on these data. . . . I take it you drew those conclusions from the regressions of whatever statistical—." The answer, from an expert witness, was as follows:

I certainly did not. Let me make clear that I'm an experienced data analyst. Thus, the thought of replacing the judgment that I can draw from the display of these data with a statistical index that, unlike the mean, reflects the degree of correctness to a hypothetically assumed mathematical relationship, that I should ever replace that with an ability to see the pattern of numbers in my own judgment would be just incontestable. It would be like a man who was looking at several hundred thousand dollar differences in, for example, his income and his neighbor's and who is then told by a statistical test that this difference could indeed come about in a widely various population—if you took a sample of size two, clearly his income is different because he is comparing the two actual incomes. Thus, if you mean what would I do, what would I use—for example, the experiment regarding correlations; that I would use that index in preference to simply seeing that I have 22,000 children here and then I have 500 children there and that I have 11,000 children there, just using my judgment, it's incredible.

Q: The basis of your testimony was the visual testimony rather than computing whatever numbers you computed?

A: One does that as a ritual necessity in my profession.

After further study, however, I decided that the problem to which Judge Wright refers need be no more than a minor obstacle to a judge's understanding. Given the crudeness and inadequacy of most of the data offered, the analytical techniques that were most appropriate were well within the capacity of experts to explain and of laymen to comprehend. For example, the distinction between the meaning of the word "significant" in everyday speech and its meaning in sample statistics was explained well and understood by Judge Roth with no difficulty. It is unfortunate that much of the statistical material presented in this and other school cases created a false impression of rigor and precision and inferred cause-effect relationships that in fact have not been shown to exist.[32] There were elaborate presentations of the allocation of educational resources, right down to school-site acreage; there was much controversy over how these inputs were measured, classified, and presented (the previous lengthy quotation is an example).

As noted above, however, during the remedy hearings it was revealed that Judge Roth did not clearly understand how the term "input" had been used throughout the trial and had assumed, he said, that it included the student's socioeconomic status (T, MR, pp. 111–16). Lengthy testimony and cross-examination about the significance of various degrees of variation on a socioeconomic scale used in calculating desirable proportions of students under various desegregation plans gave an appearance of scientific rigor until one recalls that the children (some from rather heterogeneous districts) were being assigned to schools on a basis of district averages. As also noted, in some plans "white" was used as a synonym for "middle income" and "black," for "poor."

More serious than factual errors, misquotations, omissions, the problems of an unfamiliar vocabulary, or even the deceptive impression of scientific precision was the failure of the testimony to confront in a clear, systematic, and logical fashion the central causal issues involved in the three main topics: residential segregation, racial concentration in schools, and social factors in learning. Nor was the court given an understanding of the fundamentals of the scientific method, by way of explaining why some of the most important questions could not yet be answered with reasonable certainty.

No expert-layman gap, no esoteric vocabulary, can explain why there were dozens of references throughout the testimony concerning the effect of various racial proportions upon the achievement of black children in Detroit: such comments could not be valid because the school system did not classify achievement scores by race. Nor was it ever explained to Judge Roth that in order to discover the impact of school inputs, entry-level data on students are needed.

The failure of the testimony to convey to the court a basic understanding of what is known about the causal relationships in the topics under discussion is, to judge from the content of other rulings, not unique to *Milliken*, nor is it confined to the social sciences. In a study of expert testimony from the physical sciences used in product liability litigation, Henry R. Piehler and his associates concluded: "the presentation of evidence was such that this most significant question of causation, pivotal to the litigation on any premise, was dispersed and never clearly and coherently addressed in the lengthy trial. Irrelevancies dominated, and the treatment of this major issue was sporadic and shallow. . . . The analogy to the blind leading the blind is not inappropriate."[33]

There was no single reason for this failure to "inform the judicial mind," nor was there a defect in the capacity of the judicial mind at work here: Judge Roth emerges from these pages as intelligent and deeply interested in the underlying issues. It was he, and only he, who raised the question of whether black Americans compose a cultural group. It was he who raised the question of whether re-analyses (published after his ruling) of the Coleman Report data altered its conclusions. He raised important questions about the residential behavior of white ethnic groups, persistently sought to learn whether community control and large-scale student dispersion were compatible, challenged the plaintiffs' expert witness concerning the absence of entry-level differences between black and white children, and introduced many questions that the expert witnesses had avoided, for example, was there not an advantage to a small elementary school, would frequent school transfers be harmful to children, and can early deprivation be overcome by compensatory programs? He asked more than once about race differentials in the birth rate and tried to project the effects of black and white demography upon any plans for creating stable racial mixture (e.g., T, pp. 3717–18).

But to these questions and many others—questions similar to those a thoughtful student would raise in a seminar on education and urban society—the judge got poor answers or none at all. One of the reasons for the dispersed presentation and the "sporadic and shallow" treatment so deplored by the research team studying product liability cases (see Piehler et al. [1974]) is, as we have suggested, inherent in the courtroom procedure itself. But the problem of format is but one manifestation of a deeper underlying difficulty. The adversary system as used in litigation is not a dependable method for insuring that adequate social science testimony and a sufficient grasp of the logic of causal inference in science will be made available to a presiding judge. In what follows I will try to show some of the reasons for this.

Unequal Adversaries

In courts of law decisions often depend on which side has the best legal battalions, a matter that may be entirely unrelated to the weight of scientific evidence. In the school segregation cases, especially in past years, the superiority of the plaintiffs' knowledge of and experience with this litigation and the help they get from the academic community have contributed to their repeated success. The plaintiffs have been, in effect, trying the same case for twenty years and work closely and continuously with friendly social scientists; they, in turn, supply judges as well as legal counsel with substantive background materials. Some judges who rule on school cases attend conferences where academics and civil rights attorneys discuss both legal strategy and key issues in the social sciences. Help from universities is not concealed; thus the chief NAACP counsel, referring to the testimony on residential segregation in the Detroit case: "As I'm sure the Court noted, the lawyers from the Harvard Center on Law and Education have done the primary work of presentation" (T, p. 684). Defendants in such cases received no comparable aid, and those few well-known academics who offered them assistance were sometimes the targets of severe criticism and informal sanctions. In one instance, there was an attempt to formally censure a scholar, some of whose research was described as "anti-busing."[34]

Defense counsel generally lack familiarity with the social science literature. Even if they were permitted to offer expert testimony challenging the benefits of integration, they would probably be unable to expose the flaws in the testimony offered by the plaintiffs' experts in support of it. (In the Detroit case NAACP counsel Flannery's relentless crossexamination of David Armor was an example of the plaintiffs' advantage in this regard (T, Armor deposition, May 24, 1972). The defense was generally unable to challenge scientific evidence on its own ground and never even tried to compel a witness to reconcile his testimony with the findings of other authorities or, upon occasion, with his own previously published work. The incorrect citations to the research literature were never questioned, probably because the defense experts did not know that they were erroneous. Instead, their attorneys tended to argue with the witness on what appeared to them logical grounds or to focus on trivia.

Defendants in such cases are further handicapped by their lack of intimate knowlege of the civil rights movement. Their counsel in Detroit appeared unaware, for example, of the earlier demand by the civil rights movement that no records of students' race be kept; this was made to appear at the trial as evidence of neglect or concealment by school authorities. Defense counsel also seemed not to know of the insistence by the NAACP up to about 1960 that children must attend schools in the neighborhood where they live and·that staff assignments should be color-blind.[35] The concept of racial balance was anathema at that time. The defense said virtually nothing about a state-supported effort to maintain racially mixed schools and said little about the reasons for the failure of this and other similar efforts by local citizens' groups which had been going on for almost twenty years in one racially mixed area after another. This general lack of sophistication and relative unfamiliarity with the civil rights field seems typical of law firms representing defendants in school cases throughout the nation, notwithstanding their general expertise in other matters. But this is not the only handicap they face in presenting their case in court.

Calculations of adversary advantage control the production of social science testimony of all parties during a trial. But in these cases there are some additional constraints on the testimony of school system witnesses that may limit and distort the testimony heard by the trial judge. In the Detroit case the defendants' expert-witnesses, in line with the prevailing policy in the Detroit school system, vied with each other in expressions of support for dispersion ("integration") and repeatedly stated that there could be no quality education without it. It is unclear whether or not administrators realized that the price of a court order to desegregate was to have their school system found guilty of de jure segregation. I think that at the start most did not, understand that this predicate was required. Those few who had some knowledge of the legal aspects of the case were apparently hoping for a break with precedent that would declare racial concentration regardless of cause to be a constitutional violation. If, as the trial proceeded, they became increasingly aware of the extent to which certain of their past actions were being interpreted as intentional segregation, they were in a poor position to dismiss them as inconsequential, for they were prisoners of the system's own foolish declarations and unrealistic commitment to the goal of achieving stable integration within the city. Neither the board nor the staff leadership had been willing to say publicly what many said privately: there was no way of achieving such "desegregation" within Detroit. Site selection as a means to integrate schools was nonsense, and other methods of student reassignment within city limits would have been, at best, so fleeting as to be futile, and at worst, counterproductive.

The constraining effects of past policy declarations were not the only obstacles to full and frank testimony by public officials and staff. A vigorous and rational response to the false or exaggerated assertions from the plaintiffs' experts would have required the school system witnesses to offer negative evidence which questioned the benefits of racial mixture on achievement, attitudes, and race relations. Such testimony would have placed them in a position of contradicting years of pro-integration declarations made to gather public support for this cherished goal, and while the norms (although not always the practice) of science may honor the scholar who changes his views when the evidence compels it, this is rarely the case in public life. What is more, expressions of doubt or skepticism concerning the benefits of integration, had they been permitted, would have cast suspicion on the system's effort to rebut accusations of constitutional violations, for a key element in its defense against these charges was its well-known commitment to the goal of integration. To question the value of that goal would have exposed the School Board to a charge of hypocrisy and the accusation that its vaunted efforts on behalf of integration had been ineffective and feeble because school officials had not been genuinely convinced of its benefits. As long as the question of intent retains any legal weight, this constraint may well inhibit the defense of any school system on trial.[36]

To counter the implications of some of the testimony on resource allocation, defense experts would have had to cite studies showing the lack of evidence for the impact of resource variation and would have had to stress that Detroit, about average in the state in dollar appropriations, was among the lowest of the state districts on achievement tests. We have seen (in Chapter 8) that the state superintendent avoided a clear statement on this matter. No school system which must appeal to the public for support by a millage vote and which rationalizes staff salaries and other expenditures on a basis of educational benefits can afford to make such public statements. No adequate defense testimony on black underachievement could be offered unless the information vacuum were filled, but to fill it would require testimony that was completely unacceptable from a political and public relations point of view. Entry-level disadvantage of black children and underachievement of large proportions of black students in mixed classrooms and of black pupils at average income levels—full consideration of these facts would clarify much that, because it was left unanswered, invited an interpretation of hidden discrimination, but such material would be political dynamite.[37] It would be immediately characterized as racism, elitism, defeatism—as leading to "low expectations" and thus, by the dreaded self-fulfilling prophecy, to the low levels of achievement for which the explanations had been offered. It is doubtful whether any school leadership could continue to function in a city with a large black population after being publicly identified with such views, especially when those who would voice them were then, for the most part, white.

School officials may not discuss cultural (ethnic) differences except to praise them; they may not show skepticism about the power of schooling to overcome societal inequality and a host of other ills. Such statements are usually dismissed as an attempt to "evade responsibility." Dr. Green, for example, so characterized explanations of low achievement that stressed societal inequality (T, pp. 938–39). The defense counsel appeared to join in, or accept without challenge, the plaintiffs' experts' exaggerations of the power of schooling as the cause of "all-white suburbs," of discrimination in private clubs, of the riots of 1967, of crime, etc. (T, pp. 969–70, 963–64; Drachler Deposition, p. 109). Perhaps the unanimity of these inflated estimates of the influence of schools contributed to Judge Roth's conversion to an activist role.

Throughout these proceedings the defense experts failed to exploit their superior knowledge of the public schools because of their steadfast adherence to the established pieties and avoidance of taboo subjects. For example, at a time (1970–1972) when many of the city's schools were racked by violent disorders and an increase in serious delinquency, there was little emphasis on such problems in the forty-one days of the trial, though there were repeated references to the problems of white withdrawal and attrition. On those infrequent instances when a School Board expert did allude to anti-white incidents, the extremely euphemistic language used served to conceal the witness's meaning. Merle Henrickson, asked what had happened to a high school that had been planned to remain racially mixed, replied that "after the summer of 1967 [the year of the Detroit riots], the school was promoted by the students in it as being a black school, and whites have been encouraged to leave by the other students" (T, p. 3044). Henrickson's responses to questions from an intervenor-counsel concerning the reasons why both black and white parents in the high-income Lafayette Park area refused to send their children to Miller Junior High (located in a poor black neighborhood) were similarly strained and evasive (T, pp. 3919–24). No social researcher seeking the views of school officials would expect to hear them candidly revealed in public but would instead assure respondents of complete anonymity even if scrambled identity clues were required. No investigator would expect a public official (who must continue to work harmoniously with various groups no matter how a court rules) to speak freely on explosive subjects in a tense and troubled city. In such cases the plaintiffs, accountable only to a small national constituency, have a great advantage, while school system experts, especially local school officials, have learned that it is best to speak in platitudes, to offer bland inoffensive observations and to be guarded and circumspect. Colleagues in such a hierarchy never contradict each other in public. Their safest strategy, oddly enough, is one of general self condemnation: "We have failed in our duty," and so on. To expose factual errors, poor logic, or insubstantial evidence, to say that an official policy was silly, evasive, or lacking in empirical support, would anger some group or other in the city school system and thus was never done.

Why Testimony Can Be Poor

Many academicians whose testimony would much enlighten the court are unwilling to have anything to do with litigation because of their dislike for adversary procedures.[38] The manner in which testimony is presented, i.e, though a series of questions put by counsel acting for the party on whose behalf the expert appears, encourages distortion and tends to push the witness into advocacy even if he would prefer to avoid this role. Adroitly phrased questions are designed so as to avoid eliciting any negative evidence, and summaries of testimony that overstate and exaggerate findings are frequently interjected by counsel under circumstances where cavils and qualifications are awkward. Barrington Moore's comment about lawyers during a trial also applies, unfortunately, to social scientists in the courtroom: "If a defense lawyer is suddenly surprised by a piece of evidence as an argument turned up by the prosecution he is never supposed to say: 'My, I had never thought of that! It's a good point and my client must be guilty.' On the other hand, that is exactly what an intellectually honest scholar is supposed to do under the circumstances."[39]

Some academics who have served as expert witnesses have expressed (generally in private) some misgivings about the experience. My late colleague, the historian Alfred Kelly, who worked on the preparation of the *Brown* cases, candidly described the conflicting pressures that he experienced: "I was trying to be both historian and advocate . . . and the combination . . . was not a very good one. . . . I was facing for the first time in my own career the deadly opposition between my professional integrity as a historian and my wishes and hopes with respect to a contemporary question of values, of ideals, of policy, of partisanship and of political objectives. I suppose if a man is without scruple this matter will not bother him but I am frank to say that it bothered me terribly."[40] And later, speaking of his role in the preparation of a brief, he wrote:

Never had there been . . . a more dramatic illustration of the difference in function, technique and outlook between lawyer and historian. It was not that we were engaged in formulating lies; there was nothing as crude and naive as that. But we were using facts, emphasizing facts, sliding off facts, quietly ignoring facts, and above all interpreting facts in a way to do what [Thurgood] Marshall said we had to do—"get by those boys down there."[41]

The problem of preventing one's biases or ideals from affecting the validity of one's work is an old and endlessly discussed issue in the social sciences. The community of science and scholarship relies upon some safeguards and restraints that help to minimize such distortions, but these are almost entirely absent when social scientists take part in a trial. Pressures for advocacy are of course not confined to the school cases nor to legal proceedings. Speaking of the exaggerated statements and inaccuracies of some physicists in policy debates a noted scientist writes: "Inside the scientific forum science has constructed an elaborate system of self-policing, to expose or ignore false science, to punish those who insist on promulgating falsehood. But outside the scientific forum (where there is no mechanism for monitoring the discussion) such sanctions hardly exist."[42]

The expert testimony given during a trial is virtually a secret as far as the "scientific forum" is concerned. Thus, while these legal proceedings lack the confidentiality and anonymity needed for free disclosure by vulnerable school system experts, the courtroom is too remote from scientific surveillance to insure the integrity of scientific evidence. Testimony is not published in the journals. The trial record can be read only with considerable difficulty, and a copy is too costly for most people.[43] No single reform would do more to improve the quality of social science testimony offered during the segregation cases than for these materials to be made easily available and for the learned societies to encourage critical evaluation of them.

Making this record readily accessible will do no good, of course, unless there is an end to the moratorium on criticism of testimony offered on behalf of plaintiffs as well as defendants. The participation by David Armor and the recent offerings by James Coleman have been criticized unsparingly, while material of much less scholarly merit, offered on behalf of plaintiffs, generally has escaped such harsh scrutiny. Strong expressions of support and encouragement from the learned societies for more even-handed review and evaluation would be a help.

Adversary-System Distortions

The production of entire bodies of evidence is controlled by litigants' considerations of adversary advantage. The inadequacy of the housing testimony in *Milliken* was in part due to the defendants' calculation of their best legal position and their confidence in the precedent set by *Deal*.[44] Yet to some degree the inadequacies in this testimony did give Judge Roth a defective understanding of residential behavior and in the process created invalid expectations of post-busing residential stability. In the same way, as I noted earlier, even if the courts permitted negative testimony on the effects of school integration it seems likely that defendants accused of constitutional violations would be reluctant to cast doubt upon their devotion to this goal. Thus a system that can work well to determine the guilt of an individual proves to be clumsy and undependable for producing adequate presentation of relevant bodies of knowledge in the social sciences. The courtroom is the best place to decide whether X committed a murder; it is a poor place to consider the causes of homicide.

Judicial norms allow bodies of evidence that are inconsistent with each other to remain unreconciled. In the courtroom serious discrepancies and contradictions can remain unresolved; they may even not be explicitly revealed. For example, the testimony on residential segregation greatly minimized the socioeconomic distribution of blacks as a causal factor. But later in the trial, during the testimony on education, other experts stressed social class disadvantages as a key factor in the underachievement of black children. Still later, during the remedy hearings, the correlation between being poor and being black was described as so high that race could be used as a dependable indicator of class in calculating proportional student assignments. Such disjunctions must be reconciled or at the very least openly confronted. Where were all those poor children and their families during the testimony on residential segregation? If their proportion is so great and their disadvantage has so powerful an impact on behavior, how could this fail to influence the residential behavior of whites? What are the implications of this social class distribution for the repeated assurances given to Judge Roth that contact between black and white students would help to correct stereotypes? If no one's legal advantage is served, glaring inconsistencies of this kind can be left unresolved—and unremarked—throughout an entire trial.

Litigants in judicial proceedings may offer a judge alternative

grounds for decision, leaving him to select the cause-and-effect relationship that he prefers to depend upon. In *Milliken*, the court was
first offered testimony on residential segregation, showing that the
city's neighborhoods had been almost totally separated by race for
more than thirty years. The following testimony, while it did not
challenge geographic assignment as a permissible method, attributed
school segregation to unconstitutional actions, i.e., "cheating"—and
this within a system of geographic assignment which, if honestly followed, would have resulted in a degree of racial separation in schools
at least as intense as that which then existed. The plaintiffs served up
these empirically incompatible explanations to the judge with no attempt to reconcile them except for the assertion—with no evidence
brought forward to support it—of a "corresponding effect."

Subsequent events revealed the reasons for offering alternative
grounds to the court. Judge Roth relied heavily on state complicity in
residential segregation as the basis for his ruling, but the appeals
court, as we have seen, repudiated these grounds, not, I think, because the evidence to support the conclusions was insufficient, but
because the housing approach appeared to the appeals court less
likely to be upheld by the Supreme Court and because rejection of it
was more consistent with its previous ruling in *Deal*. These considerations, of course, are wholly irrelevant to the question of the adequacy of the empirical evidence. Indeed, the decision on whether or
not a ruling will be exposed to further scrutiny in appeal proceedings
depends on political and public relations considerations and legal
costs rather than the weight of the evidence. The finding of de jure
segregation in Detroit was not appealed to the Supreme Court because the school board deemed support of a metropolitan remedy the
more prudent course. Thus a precedent-setting case of enormous
importance was allowed to stand on a basis that the trial judge himself
appeared to consider inadequate.[45]

Judicial standards of causal adequacy are those of a layman, not a
scientist. In the testimony and crossexamination on school violations,
for example, no distinction was maintained between an illegal act and
a cause of a social condition. Thus the defendants automatically responded to charges of legal wrongdoing (constitutional violations) by
offering a recital of extenuating circumstances rather than challenging
the causal power of these actions, while the plaintiffs merely asserted
that this or that act, or failure to act, had contributed to the condition
of racial concentration in the system.

Neither the assertion by one expert that white parents' departure from mixed schools arose from resource discrimination against such schools nor the contention of another expert that assigning some number of students to School A instead of School B would have "promoted residential stability" was met with a request for supporting evidence. Such claims either went unchallenged or met with lawyerly sniping, which often involved defensive alternative explanations for these actions. For example, the contention that a few instances of busing twenty years earlier had made a difference in the pattern of school racial proportions is simply not demonstrable by scientific standards. In the same way, the general line of argument on the effects of optional zones, given the fact that no one stated when they were instituted, is unacceptable in a scientific discussion. In addition, the courtroom setting encourages the focus of attention on the personal characteristics of the expert witness rather than on the causal adequacy of the evidence offered. Anecdotal material from a black educator-psychologist, for example, met with surprisingly little challenge. There seemed to be tacit agreement that considerable weight should be accorded testimony offered by someone who had attended the city schools. An intervenor-counsel objected, at one point, to the importance attributed to these personal reminiscences, but nobody asked the court to declare all such testimony immaterial or irrelevant as findings of social science, and it is not likely that Judge Roth would have agreed with such an evaluation.

These fundamental differences between the worlds of science and the law can hardly be resolved, but they were not even acknowledged. The entire question of who should bear the burden of proof, for example, illustrates the way in which considerations of justice (a matter of the hierarchy of values) are mingled with the evaluation of the weight of scientific evidence. No distinction was maintained between the value components of social policy and scientific knowledge concerning causal relationships. Speakers—laymen and experts alike—slid back and forth between the realms of value and science, seemingly unaware that declarations about human rights were of a different order from testimony about the findings of social scientists and were subject to different standards of evidence.

Scientific Truth and Judicial Authority

The exercise of judicial authority reveals the basic conflict between science and the law. When a judge declares a line of social science testimony irrelevant or a certain kind of expertise unnecessary in a proposed witness, a layman is ruling on whether or not certain variables are involved in causation. An example is Judge Roth's ruling (T, pp. 206–10) that a witness who had no training in sociology and (admittedly) no knowledge concerning the residential behavior of white ethnic groups was qualified to testify because he would only be analyzing "the causes of racial segregation in residence." A judge is not qualified to make such a determination but under present procedures is required to do so. The continuity of law and the citation of precedent are at odds with the use of scientific knowledge as evidence. Scientific work involves a process of continuous revision, and the reader will have noted that some of the research I have cited which questions or contradicts evidence offered in the Detroit trial was published after 1972. But in legal proceedings precedent cases are invoked as support for social science generalizations. For example, when a question was raised concerning the impact of a school boundary change upon the racial composition of the surrounding neighborhood, the litigants in the Detroit trial accepted as supporting evidence the citation in *Swann* of these alleged effects. But the fact that one court decision, or a hundred such decisions, proclaim a social science generalization does not add to its scientific validity. Science concedes nothing to extra-scientific authority and considers its own findings, no matter how carefully derived, as tentative, partial, and forever subject to rejection or revision.

Judge Roth's exclusion of the testimony of Dr. David Armor, for the suburbs, during the hearings on a metropolitan remedy is a case in point. The Armor deposition was the only instance during the entire course of the Detroit proceedings where evidence questioning the academic and attitudinal benefits of racial mixture was presented.[46] Judge Roth, however, ruled it inadmissible and characterized it as part of the "efforts of the intervenors to suggest a new rationale for a return to the discredited 'separate but equal' policy." His footnote here is instructive.

In the main such proof entirely misses the point: the violation here found has to do with school segregation caused in substantial part by force of public authority and action; yet the intervening defendants' questions and offers of proof speak mainly to educational theory and recent and sometimes contradictory research about narrowly measured educational effects, mostly on achievement test scores, of quite limited beginnings of racial or socioeconomic integration of various types and as compared with the effects of dollar or other resource inputs and continued segregation. This court does not understand, however, that such research, from the *Coleman Report* to its many reanalyses, formed the primary bases for the *Brown* decision or any of its progeny. . . . Citation to such research, either in support or rejection of school desegregation, misses the primary point: insofar as pupil assignments are concerned, the system of public schooling in every state must be operated in a racially nondiscriminatory unified fashion; until that objective is met, the very system of public schooling constitutes an invidious racial classification. The adoption of an education theory having the effect of maintaining a pattern of de jure segregation is therefore impermissible. (Whether such theories, research, or evidence on educational quality or inequality form the basis for requiring judicial intervention and relief in the absence of a finding of de jure segregation is a question this court need not face.)

In any event, the Court of Appeals for the Sixth Circuit held, on June 19, 1970, that greater, not less, desegregation is the proper manner to alleviate the problem of disparity in achievement.[47]

Note how the scientific question of whether desegregation reduces disparity of achievement is first declared irrelevant. This is logical and requires only that one be convinced first, that school segregation exists, and second, that it has been caused in substantial degree by government. But Judge Roth then declares that any "education theory having the effect of maintaining a pattern of de jure segregation" is not permissible. A court ruling cannot make a scientific theory "impermissible"; only an adequate amount of negative evidence can cause an explanation to be discarded. Perhaps the wording was unfortunate: the judge may have meant only that the Armor testimony was no longer relevant because a ruling of segregation de jure had already been rendered. The final paragraph of the ruling, however, tells us that the issue had been settled two years earlier, when the appeals court decided that "greater, not less desegregation" will alleviate the racial disparity in achievement. Courts cannot establish the validity of a scientific generalization, and hold to it in the face of (possibly) massive empirical refutation—a common fate of such propositions in science.

Improvements in Procedure

There is no satisfactory solution to the problems I have tried to reveal in this chapter. These difficulties are not restricted to the judicial use of evidence from the social sciences. The potential hazards of certain substances in industry, the acceptable degree of risk in nuclear energy plants, the contribution that an imperfect part in a car makes to an accident—these familiar controversies are all from the physical sciences. Edmond Cahn was correct to remind us that the courts must "proceed . . . at the risk of error,"[48] but they should at least know the extent of uncertainty and disagreement. Judges need to hear the best evidence that social science can muster. While the absence of opposing views is no guarantee that the conclusion reached is correct—everyone may be wrong—judges seem not to realize that the very existence of opposing conclusions in science is a sign that there is something seriously wrong with the evidence being presented. Disagreement is normal in law, and adversary procedures where both sides state their case reflect this. But the aim of science is agreement on evidence, and there are not "two sides" to validated scientific generalizations.

Nevertheless, within the limits of the "irresolvable tension" between scientific truth and judicial authority, there is room for much improvement in the use of social science evidence in judicial proceedings.[49] The scientific community is able to provide much better evidence than most that has been offered in these school cases, and judges can be helped to became wiser consumers of social science testimony.

There is a large literature on this topic. Twenty years ago Will Maslow suggested that important trials be monitored by representatives of the learned societies who would appraise the testimony and prepare evaluations for the court.[50] This task would be much more to the liking of those academics who refuse to participate in adversary proceedings. Frank C. J. McGurk suggested at about the same time that joint committees of the American Bar Association and the professional society of the discipline involved assume the task of collecting evidence from scholars of contrasting perspectives when there are important controversies.[51] (He also noted the need for these societies to support and encourage the appearance of experts whose unpopular testimony might subject them to abuse.) Harold L. Korn has suggested the use of written instead of oral presentations on some topics, called for changes in "evidentiary rules which . . . stifle inquiry," and noted the need for panels of neutral scholars to determine who qualifies as an expert on what subjects.[52] Jack B. Weinstein's suggestion of a "devil's advocate"[53] seems particularly appropriate for the presentation of negative evidence on the benefits of integration if the courts would hear it.

Some proposals aim to remove certain functions from adversary procedures altogether. Paul Rosen suggests that a "judicial research agency" be established to enhance "the Supreme Court's fact-finding capabilities."[54] Arthur S. Miller and Jerome A. Barron offer a valuable and comprehensive review of the problems faced by the Supreme Court's growing needs for better information and make a number of interesting proposals for improvement.[55] It seems to me, however, that the need for such reform is much more urgent at the trial court level. The appeals courts themselves do not hear expert testimony. They proceed on the basis of the briefs submitted by the litigants, the responses of counsel to the questions the judges ask, and, of course, the trial record. It is hard to see how they could possibly study very many of the voluminous transcripts before them. When I consider how long it took me to study the trial record in a single case, it seems unreasonable to expect the appellate courts to review such records even in selected cases, and they would not be able to verify the accuracy of the factual and social science testimony even if they read it carefully.

No matter how high the standard of scientific testimony, judges must continue to bear the burden of making decisions that, in the last analysis, are based upon value choices. Knowledge may contribute to a wiser choice by helping those charged with decisionmaking to discard false premises.[56] But few, if any, social scientists would agree with Kenneth Clark's contention that "moral laws" can be established or verified by the methods of scientific inquiry.[57] Science at its best can only reveal the relations between various factors or the probable consequences of certain kinds of changes. It has no means of validating or verifying value choices, for "factual premises cannot yield a normative conclusion."[58] Justice Learned Hand understood this very well when he said: "one can sometimes say what effect a proposal will have . . . just as one can foretell how much money a tax will raise and who will pay it. But when that is done one has come only to the kernel of the matter, which is the choice between what will be gained and what will be lost. The difficulty here does not come from ignorance, but from the absence of any standard, for values are incommensurable."[59]

The Warren court would surely have ruled against the right of public schools to exclude black children because of their race even if social scientists told them they could not produce evidence to prove the benefits of integrated as compared with segregated classrooms.

But Justice Holmes might not have ruled to permit compulsory sterilization if he had not been so impressed with the pseudoscience of the eugenics movement. And if Judge Roth had not been persuaded of both the inestimable benefits of racially mixed classrooms and the feasibility of the busing remedy, he would probably not have used the only lever available to him to trigger such an outcome: the finding that racial concentration in Detroit schools was substantially produced by state action. Whether one would consider such an outcome better than what did happen is a matter of value judgments, some of which are considered in the following chapter.

CHAPTER 20
Busing as a Public Issue

"The task we are called upon to perform," said Judge Roth, "is a social one which society has been unable to accomplish. In reality our Courts are called upon in these school cases to attain a goal through the educational system by using a law as a lever."[1] The attempt to use the constitutional protection against racial discrimination as a way of achieving permanent racial mixture in the nation's classrooms has been fraught with difficulties. The overwhelming majority of public school students in the United States attend the school nearest their homes. Since most children who live near each other are of the same race, the only way to create mixed schools is to divorce school assignment from residential location. Instead of walking, students must be transported, hence "busing." The term has come into the language as a short and convenient abbreviation for a rather complex concept—assigning students to schools on a racial basis so as to create roughly proportionate mixtures instead of assigning them on a geographic basis, which necessarily reflects the racial homogeneity of most neighborhoods.

Although the courts define the present school cases as applications of the *Brown* case, the public response has been quite different. Ten years before *Brown* almost one-third of the nation favored an end to compulsory segregation; within two years after the ruling that proportion had increased to almost one-half.[2] Support for the principle of integrated public schools, in the sense of open access without regard to race, is very substantial today.[3] By contrast, opposition to involuntary racial dispersion is very high among whites, wins the support of less than a majority of blacks, remains quite constant over the years, and tends to persist after busing orders are imposed.[4] Repeated opinion surveys since busing began in Pontiac, Michigan, for example, show that between 75 and 80 percent of whites continue to oppose the program.[5] Although some proponents attribute opposition to busing to the pervasiveness of racism, opinions about it seem generally unrelated to prejudice or beliefs about civil rights, as these are usually measured.[6] Such findings may be explained away by some advocates as showing only that virtually everyone is a racist or that the public is stupid: Gordon Foster, commenting on a vote of the Florida electorate that expressed opposition to segregated schools, favored equal educational opportunity, but opposed involuntary dispersion, concluded that it illustrated George Bernard Shaw's observation: "One simpleton; one vote."[7]

Instead of a serious consideration of the reasons why most people who oppose busing also say they favor desegregated schools, many of the arguments used by its proponents erect and then destroy a series of straw men: e.g., busing is widely used to transport children to private schools and by public schools in rural and suburban areas; it is used everywhere to transport handicapped children without any public outcry. Figures on numbers of children and duration of ride are offered; the U.S. Commission on Civil Rights, in a joking spirit, points out that students have even been transported to school in boats and airplanes.[8] One may well wonder whether this disingenuous approach represents a deliberate misunderstanding of the obvious fact that transportation and "busing" are not synonyms. Private school use is entirely voluntary: it is up to the parents to decide whether a school is worth a large fee and a long ride. If they decide in the negative, they change schools. To accuse people like this of hypocrisy when they object to involuntary reassignment is like making such a charge against one who prays at home but objects to compulsory religious services in school.

Rural school consolidation was enacted in response to commonsensical considerations: students in sparsely populated areas must be transported to the nearest school; children who are crippled must go to school on a bus. Busing programs of this sort bear no resemblance to compulsory programs of student dispersion to alter the racial composition of schools. A particularly ill-chosen line of argument widely used by proponents of busing programs cites the injustice imposed upon Negro students before 1954 in the South, when they were transported past schools near their homes to more distant ones designated for blacks. No one objected to that, the argument runs, so why the present hue and cry? Early civil rights supporters, many of them white, *did* object, at a time when objection was not always easy. The reference to past wrongs also suggests that some kind of compensation for past evils must be made, but who is to be compensated and who is to pay? The issue is unclear, especially in the light of assurances that busing programs benefit everyone. In fact, busing appeals neither to the self-interest of most people nor to their sense of justice. More and more, the program must rely solely upon submission to legal authority, but the law involved is unclear to those who do not understand the legal basis and unconvincing to many who do.

In earlier years busing advocates made extravagant claims for academic improvement and attitudinal benefits for students of both races, claims similar to some offered by expert witnesses on education during the Detroit trial. As late as 1972 the U.S. Commission on Civil Rights assured the public that "in one desegregated system after another the [achievement] gap is being closed,"[9] a claim quite without support. After considerable damage to their credibility, proponents have retreated to the position that racial dispersion will not depress the academic achievement of majority children, nor will it intensify white attrition in cities. Even these claims, however, are open to question. (Assurance that students of higher achievement will not be adversely affected by such changes is based on results from standardized tests. Such tests, of course, do not reflect the fact that more advanced materials can be offered in a class in which more proficient students predominate.) If white parents are persuaded of the importance of contact with higher-achieving peers (this is the basis of most claims for the improved achievement of black students), they will surely want this advantage for their own children. Busing programs generally increase the social class heterogeneity of the classroom much beyond what would be found in a mixed neighborhood, where the cost of housing acts as something of a screening process. Advantaged children thus will encounter larger proportions of students with both learning and disciplinary problems; their parents would oppose this even if no racial difference were involved. Some kinds of behavior are so feared that even if the statistical probability of occurrence is very low parents will go to great lengths to avoid it if they can. Some analysts have characterized this response as class rather than race prejudice. But it is hard to see why recognition of these group differences in behavior is considered legitimate description when offered by social scientists and "prejudice" when offered by ordinary citizens.[10] In sum, if parents do not know of, or do not understand, the hypothesis that the presence of a majority of advantaged peers in a child's classroom is helpful, they will think student dispersion plans are senseless. But if they believe in the enhancing effect of such a majority, they will resist losing this benefit for their own children.

Unsubstantiated claims for the positive effects of busing on academic achievement still persist, but they are now usually attributed to others rather than vouched for by those who circulate them: "In several cities the Commission on Civil Rights has been told of inner city schools that have been improved magically and almost overnight when the district launched a busing program."[11] Reports of improvement are not reported as verified information (although these data would have been available to the Civil Rights Commission) but thus: "According to Geraldine Johnson, a teacher . . . math and reading scores of both majority and minority students rose."[12]

Parents who see advantages in small schools or in proximity to schools, which makes access and involvement in school affairs easier, are told that these concerns are baseless. In a report addressed to parents in 1972, the Civil Rights Commission assured them, with doubtful accuracy, that the "educational trend in recent years has been . . . toward larger schools which can provide better facilities and a broader curriculum."[13] As for local control and parental participation, the Commission declared in a report of five years later that there was no reason why metropolitan busing should preclude "structures which will maximize parental participation in school affairs"; local control and the influence of parents, said the Commission, can be preserved and even enhanced.[14] Surely these statements are an affront to common sense.

But advocates of busing programs no longer contend that they be evaluated in terms of their contribution to academic progress, improved race relations, or parental satisfaction and participation. More and more the success of busing orders is defined in terms of peaceful compliance—the mere absence of violent resistance. This has become an end in itself, described by the Civil Rights Commission as "effective desegregation."[15] The volume of protest and violent resistance, however, is an unreliable indicator. When opposition seems hopeless or when there is no appropriate target against which to direct resentment, people, whether white or black, may not reveal their bitterness. Commitments to law and order and distaste or even fear of overt protest may inhibit such displays. Many white Americans once interpreted the earlier passivity of blacks as willing submission, ignoring the warnings of social scientists and civil rights leaders that silence did not necessarily mean consent. In a nationwide study of a number of school systems that have been "desegregated" as a result of court orders or on their own initiative, the Commission declared that "there is one conclusion that stands out above all others: desegregation works." This seems to mean only that reassignment has proceeded without violence. Although there are some unsubstantiated claims of improved racial understanding, more parental participation, and better academic performance by black children as a result, these are described by the Commission as "byproducts."[16] The Commission repeatedly stressed that "desegregation" is a "constitutional imperative." This would be a sound position if ending racial discrimination were truly the nature of the present effort, rather than moving to a system of school assignment by race.

In the absence of persuasive appeals to self-interest, busing advocates must rely upon submission to authority and obedience to law. Such reliance, however, requires first, that the law be clear and comprehensible, and second, that it appear just and legitimate to a substantial proportion of citizens.[17] Obligations that do not appeal to self-interest are often endorsed, albeit grudgingly, if they are obviously fair. People may grumble about paying income tax and specific provisions of the tax laws, but they generally accept the principle of such laws. White residents in transition neighborhoods whom I have studied, unhappy at the in-movement of blacks, would often say to interviewers, "Well, I don't like it—but they've got a right, same as anyone else." The principle of formal racial disregard, which most people took to be the essence of the *Brown* decision, like that of antidiscrimination legislation in employment and housing, has a clarity, a simplicity, and a universality that strongly appeals to one's sense of justice. In his paper on the *Swann* ruling Owen Fiss grappled with the problem of the public understanding and acceptance of the judicial rationale used in the present school cases:

The Court will want to avoid the appearance of picking on the South. . . . This appearance is derived from the fact that segregated patterns of student attendance are not less severe in Northern cities than in Southern ones. Under *Charlotte-Mecklenburg*, Southern school systems are obliged to eliminate those patterns and to achieve the greatest possible degree of integration. But there is no similar judgment about those patterns in the North. A complicated analysis of causation might, under the *Charlotte-Mecklenburg* theory, serve to justify the differential treatment afforded these otherwise identical patterns. But such an analysis is not likely to be understood or even believed by most people. And no national institution can afford to be unresponsive to the popular pressures.[18]

But the rationale now used by the courts (that racial concentration is created by acts of racial discrimination by school authorities) is both more complicated and less convincing. The average citizen seems to have little difficulty in understanding the difference between a Jim Crow railroad car and a bus that carries only black passengers because it is serving a black neighborhood. Yet in both instances a pattern of racial concentration exists. A problem of public understanding exists only because some busing proponents are so convinced of the evil of racially concentrated schools that they have been willing to use a contrived and unconvincing rationale to enlist judicial power to alter this pattern.

Twenty-five years after *Brown,* the task of ascertaining whether or not racial discrimination is being practiced by a school system ought to proceed in the same fashion in both North and South, and such an investigation may not be easy. But I see no way of avoiding it: whether in schools, employment, or housing, the test of numbers is not adequate. Prior to World War II, for example, Jews were severely discriminated against in admission to many professional schools, in which they were nevertheless permitted to enroll in considerably greater proportions (often the quota was 10 percent of applicants) than their percentage of the national population of 3 percent. Neither under- nor over-representation of a group is a proof of discriminatory treatment. Fiss correctly asserts that the true concern of the courts in the recent school cases is the existence of racial concentration, not its cause, and this is why an honest and strict policy of racial disregard by school systems is viewed by proponents of busing as an ineffective remedy. Adherence to a color-blind policy will not produce the degree of mixture they desire. But because nothing in the Constitution bars minority preponderance in public facilities, those wishing to eliminate such imbalance have cloaked their efforts in an elaborate and unconvincing rationale purporting to show that this racial concentration is caused by discrimination in the school system.

The clarity and simplicity of the principle of universal citizenship, with its underlying appeal to a norm of fairness, gave *Brown* an unassailable moral authority. Blacks demanded to be treated exactly as other citizens—nothing more, but nothing less. The present school cases lack the qualities which marked *Brown*, and the more they are discussed and explained the more striking is their questionable logic and factual basis. Consider, for example, one of the many efforts of the U.S. Commission on Civil Rights to persuade citizens that busing orders are a constitutional requirement: "Given the tightly segregated neighborhoods in most American communities desegregation is simply not possible in many localities without busing and is not likely to be for years to come. Where courts have ordered . . . busing they have done so for a sound reason: namely, that a violation of the Constitution must have an effective remedy."[19]

But if it is segregated neighborhoods that make desegregated schools impossible, what are we to think of statements by the Commission (and in court rulings) that attribute segregation to school system violations?[20] What is the violation of the Constitution to which the Commission refers? If the condition of racial concentration were itself a violation of the Constitution, there would be no need for a trial. It is also hard to see how a school system can be found guilty of failing to accomplish what the Civil Rights Commission itself says is usually impossible without metropolitan-wide busing. No city school system can implement such a plan on its own, and it is not a constitutional requirement unless and until each suburb has been found guilty of de jure segregation.

This confusion, or misrepresentation, is reflected in the public statements of both proponents and opponents of busing and has created a miasma of obfuscation and misunderstanding, a strange kind of shadow-boxing with neither side articulating the issues clearly. Persons in public life, when pressed for their views, often say that busing is justified only as a last resort, or should be done within reason, or used as a remedy if no other way can be found, or used only in order to remedy constitutional violations. They seem not to understand that courts can order busing only after they find that the constitution has been violated. Perhaps this contention that northern schools are racially concentrated because of cheating by school authorities is so outlandish and far-fetched that people who hear it simply do not understand it. If schools must be mixed, transportation is a first, last, and only resort, since so few children live in mixed neighborhoods. After a court has ruled that racial concentration has been in large measure caused by school authorities, desegregation, defined as the creation of racially unidentifiable schools, can be ordered. "Racially unidentifiable" means schools of racial proportions not too dissimilar from the racial makeup of the school district. This is precisely what people have in mind when they conclude that the "desegregation" remedy now means racial balancing, and this deduction is confirmed when, in cities under remedy orders, lists of proposed racial percentages for each school are released to the public. But busing proponents, mindful of congressional limitations on such efforts, generally deny that racial balance is their aim.[21] The Commission on Civil Rights contends that public opinion polls about busing are defective because respondents are often asked whether they favor plans to achieve racial balance, while "desegregation, not racial balance, is the goal."[22] This is not honest, and I think must contribute to people's suspicion that someone is trying to deceive them. Another distinction without a difference is made by Gordon Foster: "measures to remedy past discrimination would have the same effect as a statistically random assignment of pupils and school personnel in terms of race. This would not constitute racial balancing but would simply make for assignments within a nonidentifiable racial range."[23]

In less public settings, people may be more candid; thus Flannery, the plaintiffs' co-counsel in *Milliken*, stated at a university conference: "Most educators and lawyers feel that racial balancing, by any other name, is what is required."[24] Recently, in a newspaper column, the long-time head of the NAACP referred to the well-established principle that "racially unbalanced school systems are not constitutional."[25] It is hard to believe that the man who led the organization during its period of aggressive court actions against northern school systems does not realize that this is not true; perhaps he would like people to think that the condition of racial imbalance is itself a constitutional violation. In 1974 Carl Rowan wrote that due to "white fright and flight" black children predominated in the public schools of many cities, and concluded, "Jim Crow still lives!" thus equating state-imposed exclusion with the effect of residential trends.[26] Other public figures have added to the confusion, for example, former President Gerald Ford: "Forced busing to achieve racial balance is not the proper way to get quality education." Judicial busing orders have nothing to do with "quality education"; there is no constitutional requirement for this worthy but elusive aim.

The concern of constitutional scholars that a court's decision be rational, understandable, and intellectually satisfying bespeaks their recognition that reason is not absent from human judgment even when the topic in question arouses strong feelings. The judicial opinion seeks to confer rationality upon judicial decisions, a function widely recognized in the literature.[27] Law journals are filled with papers searching for an adequate basis for the abolition of what used to be called de facto segregation, and both proponents and skeptics have indicated their criticism of the present rationale.[28]

There is something gravely defective about a legal concept—de jure segregation—which equates a Jim Crow system in the old South, where the mingling of black and white school staff and students was forbidden by law, with the actions of Detroit's pro-integration leadership struggling, in a predominantly black system, to maintain mixed schools as one neighborhood after the next undergoes transition as a result of residential movements. The search for rationality is not confined to legal scholars or professors. I take very seriously as a factor in human behavior the wish to make sense out of the buzzing confusion of public statements and messages in the media. An institution that lacks the legitimation of popular consent has a special concern to avoid appearing arbitrary. Judges, however, do not have to offer explanations of their rulings to those most directly affected by them. In the fall of 1974 I observed attorneys trying to explain to groups of Detroit parents, many of whom had attended mixed schools in the city, that the system was segregated de jure "just like the South used to be." Cited as an example was the construction of the very school building in which one of these meetings was being held; the neighborhood had been white when the building was begun but became racially mixed soon after. How did building this school violate the Constitution, someone asked. I wondered how the judges of the Sixth Circuit would have responded to such questions. In response to an attorney's warning that the district court might require each school to be made approximately 25 percent white, a parent asked: "Is that the percentage the Supreme Court thinks is the best for education?" The lawyer replied, quite accurately: "Oh, no. It has nothing to do with *that*." The audience was obviously bewildered.

It is unfortunate that there have not been more intensive studies of the public understanding of and response to busing orders. Sociologists who would scorn explanations of student protests and urban violence which rely so heavily upon "failures of law-enforcement" either attribute anti-busing protests largely to such failures, or are content with analyses that do little more than label the offenders as bigots. An astonishing theory of democratic government was asserted by Judge Wright in *Hobson:*

Judicial deference to [legislative] judgments is predicated in the confidence courts have that they are just resolutions of conflicting interests. This confidence is often misplaced when the vital interests of the poor and of racial minorities are involved . . . because of the abiding danger that the power structure—a term which need carry no disparaging or abusive overtones—may incline to pay little heed to even the deserving interests of the politically voiceless and invisible minority.[29]

My evaluation is that most people think busing is unjust. If this is accurate, why do they believe that it is? Do they recognize that such dispersion greatly increases social class heterogeneity in schools? To what extent, if any, is there concern that busing may permanently institutionalize student assignment by race? Judicial rulings that attribute racially concentrated schools to actions of the leaders of a school system contain a strong accusatory element. Detroiters, for example, must, it seems to me, conclude either that their once-lauded school officials were masters of deceit or that the courts were engaged in some kind of legal hocus-pocus. "Deliberate and purposeful segregation of black and white children," the charge in *Milliken,* cannot occur in a fit of absent-mindedness. A member of the Civil Rights Commission, for example, recently characterized the actions of school boards found guilty of de jure segregation as "premeditated and carefully devised manipulation to maintain separate school systems,"[30] a baffling accusation, given the fact that most children live in racially homogeneous neighborhoods.

My own impression is that the public believes busing is ordered by judges because "integration" is thought to upgrade the school performance of black children, but they are puzzled by courts continuing to order dispersion in the light of recent reports that such may not be the case. Further, in order to avoid the affront to self-esteem implicit in the contention that predominantly black schools are detrimental to learning, busing programs are often presented to black parents with some version of the "hostage theory": good schools, that is, schools of equal resources, including teachers who do their job, can only be assured when enough white families use them to assure that adequate resources are made available. But since research indicates that equal school resources will not guarantee equal achievement, this false expectation simply encourages a search for other scapegoats when this one is no longer available. There is already a considerable literature containing charges of teacher prejudice against black children, attacking ability grouping, charging unequal rates of disciplinary actions against black students, and so on, to explain the failure of busing programs to improve academic achievement.

Busing orders do not appeal to self-interest. They lack the moral authority of simple justice, and the attempt to wrap them in the mantle of *Brown* has not helped the busing cause. But reasonable proponents, while conceding these defects, often insist that this remedy, with all of its shortcomings, has one prime virtue that other approaches lack: it is practical. Yet if the actions of school authorities were really a substantial cause of racially concentrated schools, or if the opposition to dispersion were based entirely on irrational fears, racism, and faulty estimates of self-interest, a busing program would have some assurance of success built into it as it proved itself in action. But a program that would be bitterly resented if all concerned were white is not likely to be more successful because some participants are black.

The fallacious empirical basis used by the courts to justify classifying Northern school imbalance as the product of de jure segregation means that unless a permanent system of racial quotas in school assignment is institutionalized, the remedy offered by busing will be short-lived in most cases. Whether the courts are victims of misinformation or are acting as conscious architects of a social policy utilizing a lever that they know to be an artifice makes no difference. If the diagnosis of the causes of school racial concentration is erroneous, the remedy will be ineffective.

Neighborhoods change. Busing may intensify the processes involved in middle-class attrition, both black and white. It is unfortunate that almost all the controversy on this subject has been couched in terms of accelerated exodus: "white flight."[31] In order to maintain the school racial proportions developed at the start of a busing plan, the sorting-out processes that produced the existing residential patterns would have to be reversed.[32] If they continue much as before, even without acceleration, racial imbalance in the schools will be regenerated. A permanent system of student assignment by racial quotas would have to be instituted, with continuous redistricting or reapportionment to correct these imbalances. Even then (depending on the percentages in the original plan), some schools or systems will once again become predominantly black as whites under-choose, while blacks over-choose, some residential areas. In order to avoid the regeneration of racial imbalance, busing would have to alter the patterns of residential behavior of both races in sufficient numbers to overcome the destabilizing effects of the differential birth rate of blacks and whites;[33] the constraints of economic limitations and housing discrimination on black residential mobility; varying degrees of own-group clustering by white ethnic groups as well as by blacks; middle-class avoidance of areas with or near large numbers of poor (mostly black) households in response to social class differences as well as to prejudice; new national migration trends suggesting that some white middle-class households are avoiding older metropolitan areas of the Northeast and Midwest in favor of other regions and smaller and less central locations;[34] and increased use of non-public schools by prosperous families of both races, a disturbing trend of which we have increasing evidence.[35]

It must be borne in mind that the starting condition for most busing orders is an entrenched pattern of large, racially concentrated, residential areas. There is little indication that busing programs will disestablish them.[36] Those who have argued that busing does not worsen racial residential divisions, i.e., that white flight is not intensified by busing, usually attribute white out-movement to grim social and economic conditions such as violent crime, housing abandonment, deteriorated city services, and massive unemployment.[37] But this suggests an even more pessimistic outlook, for such conditions can hardly be expected to change as a result of busing unless one subscribes to an especially naive version of the hostage theory: if one's children cannot escape contact with the city, parents will do something to cure its ills. Social problems of this magnitude, however, are not ameliorated within a time span relevant to a child's school experience, and those who can, will withdraw from or avoid such settings for their children.

It is true that if one accepts the NAACP's definition of desegregation as a school system of racial proportions reasonably similar to those of the overall public school population, regardless of what those proportions are, none of this makes any difference. (A motive for the NAACP insistence on using statistical proportions as a definition of desegregation may be the potential for use of this principle in employment, housing, and college admissions.[38]) But thus far the courts appear unwilling to abandon the belief that school desegregation should involve a substantial white presence. They have also indicated their probable refusal to order continuous reapportionment to correct racial imbalances created after busing has been in existence for some time. It is this uncertainty over the very meaning of desegregation that is reflected in, for example, the response of the Sixth Circuit to NAACP objections to the DeMascio remedy in Detroit. The appeals court's ruling reveals how cloudy is the constitutional imperative under which the court is acting. The judiciary falters as it rules on the Northern school cases because the courts seek, by strained logic and inadequate evidence, to move far beyond their original purpose of eliminating mandatory segregation—yet try to maintain the appearance of doing only that, in order to maintain continuity with the 1954 ruling. They attempt to graft mechanisms for achieving stable integration onto constitutional principles intended to strike down state-imposed racial separation. A judicial command to cease racial discrimination need entail no concern for achieving certain racial proportions and no thought as to how long racial mixture will continue to exist. Anti-discrimination orders thus logically and properly take no heed of adverse white reaction. But an enduring racial mixture cannot be secured by issuing judicial commands: to quote the late impresario Sol Hurok, "If they don't want to come nothing will stop them."

At the present time a prime reason for the continuation of these rulings is the power of precedent. Once having defined the policies of the Detroit system as de jure segregation, it is not easy to see how judges elsewhere can, without glaring inconsistency, avoid similar rulings when suits are brought in other cities. In addition, as more busing programs stemming from earlier court orders are executed, the desegregation business grows in size. Until I observed the proliferation of jobs associated with the publications, record-keeping, inspectors, monitors, workshops, and training programs that come to a city under a busing order, I had thought that the mechanics of the matter were inconsequential, but these activities do create a considerable constituency that has a commitment to the program and a vested interest in continuing it. A more important factor in staying on the present course is the reluctance of so many civil rights advocates who have become dubious or even negative about the effects of busing to say so publicly because of their loyalty to the symbol of a movement so long cherished. It is awkward and unpleasant to be associated with an opposition first identified with lawless violence by extremists. Anti-busing opinions labor under the burden of this stigma (a factor used adroitly by proponents) and have only recently acquired a degree of legitimacy.[39] In advance of a ruling, civil rights supporters find the easiest course is to wait and see how the courts decide; after the ruling, the law must be obeyed.

Perhaps the recent decisions that appear to require evidence of segregative intent will provide the rationale needed for those judges who would like to shift gears as they observe the educational ineffectiveness and doubtful feasibility of busing.[40] But a "social policy dressed in Constitutional attire" (to use a phrase from Frank Goodman [1972]) does not readily reflect new knowledge and more accurate appraisals of its consequences; it is the essence of such rights that they must not depend on such cost-benefit calculations. Having insisted, for example, that school systems must not be influenced by concern over white attrition, judges are not likely to devote much attention to signs that in many instances busing programs will mean distributing ever-dwindling proportions of those white children whose parents find it difficult to avoid the program. Courts have become prisoners of their own doctrine that dispersion is imposed only to correct racial concentration resulting from constitutional violations and therefore must be limited to those school systems found guilty of such acts.

A social policy imposed as a constitutional right is one that is deprived of revision and opposition through normal political processes. The courtroom lacks both the safeguards of the academy and the restraints of the legislature. I count it more a strength than a weakness that within a democratic society some substantial degree of public support is ordinarily required before major social policy changes can be instituted. In the case of court-ordered busing for constitutional violations which are not understood, people are compelled to submit to a remedy which a great many detest but over which they have no control save by individual action that may require a heavy financial burden. Resistance is wrong as well as futile; constitutional amendment is almost impossible and is certainly unwise. A resentment that lacks a realistic and appropriate target against which opposition can be peacefully and legitimately directed is thus engendered. This is a serious burden upon American society, and tends to generate irrational scapegoating responses.

The costs of the busing effort may be indicated in a summary fashion (I am disregarding financial costs here, although in some places they are considerable).

1. Suspicion and cynicism about government have been fed by decisions that ascribe racial imbalance to deliberate acts of discrimination by school officials of both races; those who reject this contrived causal theory will have lessened confidence in the courts. So too will those who believe that courts order busing to improve the academic performance of black students, yet persist in this course despite a steady flow of inconclusive findings. My own impression is that busing orders in heavily black school systems such as Detroit are viewed by the public as senseless and incomprehensible.

2. To the extent that black parents believe claims for the impact of mixture upon their children's academic performance, hopes thus engendered will generally be proved false.

3. If my surmise that busing programs in predominantly black school systems will be short-lived is correct, there will be a strong sense that people have been subjected to a disliked dislocation to no purpose.

4. If ways are found (it is hard to imagine what they might be) to include large numbers of affluent families in a busing program, many will retreat to private schools, with a loss to the public system of vigorous and articulate critics as well as influential sources of support. It would be ironic if a program to increase classroom diversity transformed the system into an institution used mainly by the disadvantaged.

5. Poor and working-class households will suffer some loss from the erosion of their ties to the nearby elementary school. One need not endorse the extravagant claims of the community control movement to acknowledge the importance of easy access to and familiarity with the school that one's young children attend. Dispersion plans that "share the burden of busing" by frequent school changes are painfully obtuse and disregardful of parents' concerns and children's wishes. The neighborhood school does function, especially for poor people, both as a useful conduit to communication with the larger society and as an aid to social integration within it.[41] The impairment of these ties, brought about by busing to more distant schools, is not easily measurable, but I think the loss is not trivial.

6. The integrity of the academic community has been injured and the reputation of social science tarnished by the eagerness of some to

serve this cause in a propagandistic manner and the willingness of so many others to remain silent in the face of unfounded claims by their colleagues.

7. Although the loyalty to the civil rights movement of many segments of the leadership of the old labor-liberal coalition has generally prevented open breaks, it is no secret that there has been internal disaffection. Making busing a symbol of the civil rights movement, while it has inhibited some from opposing the program, has contributed little to busing's success. My judgment is that, over all, it has hurt the effort to achieve racial equality more than it has helped. The greatest resource of the civil rights movement has been its unassailable moral integrity; this treasure has been sadly dissipated by the Northern school cases, with their dubious research, contrived evidence, and public double-talk.

In this country the complex of legal protections collectively described as "civil rights" is often confused with the volume of interracial contact. Support for civil rights may be revealed in both words and deeds, but the amount of actual interracial association in which a person is involved is not a good measure or indicator of such sentiments. Neither empirical evidence nor logic confirms the view that commitment to civil rights and volume of interracial contact are manifestations of a single dimension. I have emphasized earlier in this book the absence of any consistent relationship between belief in civil rights and residence in a racially mixed neighborhood; the same is true for sending one's children to racially mixed schools. Although the occasional crusader uses an area or a school as a setting for demonstrating devotion to civil rights causes, these instances are statistically rare.

Minorities are generally indifferent to the amount of actual contact which they have with members of a majority group, but they (correctly) detect the overwhelming importance of civil rights guarantees to their protection and security.[42] For example, though most blacks do not prefer to live in predominantly white neighborhoods, virtually all blacks and all proponents of civil rights consider free access to such a neighborhood to be an indispensable aspect of citizenship. One's support of an organization's right to exist or of a journal to publish has no necessary relationship to a wish to join the organization or read the journal. In a study of black students' preference for attending black high schools, James Bolner and A. Vedlitz concluded that "Negro pupils favor desegregation overwhelmingly as an abstract principle" but not in practice.[43] But desegregation is a principle the existence of which can be tested in various ways; it is not a synonym for substantial interracial mixture. It means that access is open to all on the same terms; it does not take into account any group characteristic that may cause one to seek out or avoid some or even most of the group's members, depending on a number of situational factors. The exercise of civil rights means that the prerogatives of citizenship shall not be withheld because of group characteristics; it does not require one to assert (sometimes contrary to considerable evidence) that such differences do not exist or that human beings must cultivate a bland indifference toward them. Bolner and Vedlitz concluded, like some others who have studied this matter, that the previous experience of segregated living had distorted the responses of black students and made free choice impossible. Of course, all of our sociocultural experiences shape and constrain our behavior, but why some are considered distortions and an interference with free choice is not entirely clear. The suggestion that in the absence of constraints neither class nor ethnicity would shape associational preferences seems unreasonable. If groups exist and subcultures are real, human behavior will be influenced by them.

In the early years of the civil rights movement one could predict that in every group discussing these issues there would be at least one person whose opposition to fair employment laws or open occupancy requirements would begin with the protestation: "Some of my best friends are Negroes (or Jews, or whatever), but. . . ." Commitment to equal protection for all citizens often has little to do with interethnic friendliness, real or alleged. As wars are not prevented by ethnic festivals or visits to other nations, support for civil rights has an uncertain relationship to interracial association. Before the Nazi period, Germany had one of the highest rates of intermarriage between Jews and Gentiles in the world, but this did not protect its Jews against the consequences of the erosion of democratic institutions, an erosion that occurred despite high Jewish occupational attainment and left them defenseless.

Interethnic relationships may be generated as a consequence or byproduct of association in efforts toward common goals—in, for example, a trade union. But there is little to suggest that friendships can be contrived in order to produce the conditions that often create them. Rich people may take the *Wall Street Journal*, but giving poor people a subscription to it will not make them rich.

Since social class mixture even within ethnic groups tends to be avoided, it is hard to see why such heterogeneous association between ethnic groups should be considered a goal which is either attainable or urgently required. Harvey Molotch, reflecting upon his study of various attempts to create a racially mixed area in Chicago, concluded: "Integration before equality is putting the cart before the horse."[44] Molotch was not talking about open housing but about the achievement of stable racially mixed neighborhoods. Reasonable socioeconomic parity is a necessary, although not a sufficient, precondition for harmonious interaction, but personal contact is far too weak a variable to have much of an effect upon the condition of inequality.

There is a small but influential group of people whose support for busing has been based on their fear that racially homogeneous association, even when it occurs within a framework of strict protection against discrimination, jeopardizes civil rights by perpetuating the racial separation that the Kerner Commission found so menacing.[45] It is hard to tell whether this is a valid concern. I think that black economic improvement, together with vigilant protection against discrimination, will inevitably generate varying degrees of racial mixture in different segments of our lives. The danger that such changes will be too slow in coming seems to me considerably less than the dangers inherent in the present strategy. Using a complex, contrived, and unconvincing rationale that compels racial mixture in classrooms by "proving" that imbalance results from unconstitutional discrimination weakens faith in that document, while it jeopardizes the creation of coalitions needed for so many important social reforms. For example, I often wonder what the outcome would have been if the vast amount of effort expended on the busing venture had been invested in an effort to win support for educational resource allocation on a basis of need, while offering financial aid to systems which encourage student dispersion on a voluntary basis. The struggle to win and then to implement busing orders has badly strained some important political alliances, especially those involving white working-class groups, and there is some evidence that this course of action has impaired our capacity, never strong enough, to strive in other ways for a more just and humane society.

The principle of formal racial disregard is a powerful safeguard. Any minority group that abandons it for the sake of a temporary advantage is risking precious moral capital. In the last analysis, what protects a group from those who, because of their power and numbers, could, if they wished, injure or destroy it is not what is written in a document. Many written constitutions all over the world speak of equal treatment but are, as it is said, only scraps of paper. Adherence to these norms of protection of all citizens by our laws involves a system of established institutional restraints that prohibits unequal treatment on a basis of race, ethnicity or religion. Such a system endures because a sufficiently large group of people believe that it is legitimate, that it is just. This sense of justice, weak and undependable though it often proves to be, is ultimately all we have.

APPENDIX A
Excerpts from Judge Roth's Ruling

Ronald BRADLEY et al., Plaintiffs, v. William G. MILLIKEN et al.,
Defendants, DETROIT FEDERATION OF TEACHERS, LOCAL
#231, AMERICAN FEDERATION OF TEACHERS, AFL-CIO,

Defendant-Intervenor,
and Denise Magdowski et al., Defendants-Intervenors.

Civ. A No. 35257.

United States District Court, E. D. Michigan, S. D.

Sept. 27, 1971.

338 F. Supp. 582 (1971).

Ruling on Issue of Segregation

ROTH, District Judge.

This action was commenced August 18, 1970, by plaintiffs, the Detroit Branch of the National Association for the Advancement of Colored People[1] and individual parents and students, on behalf of a class later defined by order of the Court dated February 16, 1971, to include "all school children of the City of Detroit and all Detroit resident parents who have children of school age." Defendants are the Board of Education of the City of Detroit, its members and its former superintendent of schools, Dr. Norman A. Drachler, the Governor, Attorney General, State Board of Education and State Superintendent of Public Instruction of the State of Michigan. In their complaint, plaintiffs attacked a statute of the State of Michigan known as Act 48 of the 1970 Legislature on the ground that it put the State of Michigan in the position of unconstitutionally interfering with the execution and operation of a voluntary plan of partial high school desegregation (known as the April 7, 1970, Plan) which had been adopted by the Detroit Board of Education to be effective beginning with the fall 1970 semester. Plaintiffs also alleged that the Detroit Public School System was and is segregated on the basis of race as a result of the official policies and actions of the defendants and their predecessors in office.

---

1. The standing of the NAACP as a proper party plaintiff was not contested by the original defendants and the Court expresses no opinion on the matter.
Note: appendix page numbers in [brackets] represent page numbers of Judge Roth's ruling as published and as cited in the Notes to this volume.

Additional parties have intervened in the litigation since it was commenced. The Detroit Federation of Teachers (DFT), which represents a majority of Detroit Public School teachers in collective bargaining negotiations with the defendant Board of Education, has intervened as a defendant, and a group of parents has intervened as defendants.

Initially the matter was tried on plaintiff's motion for preliminary injunction to restrain the enforcement of Act 48 so as to permit the April 7 Plan to be implemented. On that issue, this Court ruled that plaintiffs were not entitled to a preliminary injunction since there had been no proof that Detroit has a segregated school system. The Court of Appeals found that the "implementation of the April 7 Plan was thwarted by State action in the form of the Act of the Legislature of Michigan" (433 F.2d 897, 902), and that such action could not be interposed to delay, obstruct or nullify steps lawfully taken for the purpose of protecting rights guaranteed by the Fourteenth Amendment.

The plaintiffs then sought to have this Court direct the defendant Detroit Board to implement the April 7 Plan by the start of the second semester (February, 1971) in order to remedy the deprivation of constitutional rights wrought by the unconstitutional statute. In response to an order of the Court, defendant Board suggested two other plans, along with the April 7 Plan, and noted priorities, with top priority assigned to the so-called "Magnet Plan." The Court acceded to the wishes of the Board and approved the Magnet Plan. Again, plaintiffs appealed but the appellate court refused to pass on the merits of the plan. Instead, the case was remanded with instructions to proceed immediately to a trial on the merits of plaintiffs' substantive allegations about the Detroit School System 438 F.2d 945 (6th Cir. 1971).

Trial, limited to the issue of segregation, began April 6, 1971, and concluded on July 22, 1971, consuming 41 trial days, interspersed by several brief recesses necessitated by other demands upon the time of Court and counsel. Plaintiffs introduced substantial evidence in support of their contentions, including expert and factual testimony, demonstrative exhibits and school board documents. At the close of plaintiffs' case, in chief, the Court ruled that they had presented a prima facie case of state imposed segregation in the Detroit Public Schools; acccordingly, the Court enjoined (with certain exceptions) all further school construction in Detroit pending the outcome of the litigation.

The State defendants urged motions to dismiss as to them. These were denied by the Court.

At the close of proofs intervening parent defendants (Denise Magdowski, et al.) filed a motion to join, as parties, 85 contiguous "suburban" school districts—all within the so-called Larger Detroit Metropolitan area. This motion was taken under advisement pending the determination of the issue of segregation.

It should be noted that, in accordance with earlier rulings of the Court, proofs submitted at previous hearings in the cause, were to be and are considered as part of the proofs of the hearing on the merits.

In considering the present racial complexion of the City of Detroit and its public school system we must first look to the past and view in perspective what has happened in the last half century. In 1920 Detroit was a predominantly white city—91%—and its population younger than in more recent times. By the year 1960 the largest segment of the city's white population was in the age range of 35 to 50 years, while its black population was younger and of childbearing age. The population of 0–15 years of age constituted 30% of the total population of which 60% were white and 40% were black. In 1970 the white population was principally aging—45 years—while the black population was younger and of childbearing age. Childbearing blacks equaled or exceeded the total white population. As older white families without children of school age leave the city they are replaced by younger black families with school age children, resulting in a doubling of enrollment in the local neighborhood school and a complete change in student population from white to black. As black inner city residents move out of the core city they "leap-frog" the residential areas nearest their former homes and move to areas recently occupied by whites.

The population of the City of Detroit reached its highest point in 1950 and has been declining by approximately 169,500 per decade since then. In 1950, the city population constituted 61% of the total population of the standard metropolitan area and in 1970 it was but 36% of the metropolitan area population. The suburban population has increased by 1,978,000 since 1940. There has been a steady out-migration of the Detroit population since 1940. Detroit today is principally a conglomerate of poor black and white plus the aged. Of the aged, 80% are white.

If the population trends evidenced in the federal decennial census for the years 1940 through 1970 continue, the total black population in the City of Detroit in 1980 will be approximately 840,000, or 53.6% of the total. The total population of the city in 1970 is 1,511,000 and, if past trends continue, will be 1,338,000 in 1980. In school year 1960–61, there were 285,512 students in the Detroit Public Schools of which 130,765 were black. In school year 1966–67, there were 297,035 students, of which 168,299 were black. In school year 1970–71 there were 289,743 students of which 184,194 were black. The percentage of black students in the Detroit Public Schools in 1975–76 will be 72.0%, in 1980–81 will be 80.7% and in 1992 it will be virtually 100% if the present trends continue. In 1960, the non-white population, ages 0 years to 19 years, was as follows:

0–4 years	42%
5–9 years	36%
10–14 years	28%
15–19 years	18%

In 1970 the non-white population, ages 0 years to 19 years, was as follows:

0–4 years	48%
5–9 years	50%
10–14 years	50%
15–19 years	40%

The black population as a percentage of the total population in the City of Detroit was:

(a)	1900	1.4%
(b)	1910	1.2%
(c)	1920	4.1%
(d)	1930	7.7%
(e)	1940	9.2%
(f)	1950	16.2%
(g)	1960	28.9%
(h)	1970	43.9%

The black population as a percentage of total student population of the Detroit Public Schools was as follows:

(a)	1961	45.8%
(b)	1963	51.3%
(c)	1964	53.0%
(d)	1965	54.8%
(e)	1966	56.7%
(f)	1967	58.2%

(g) 1968   59.4%
(h) 1969   61.5%
(i) 1970   63.8%

For the years indicated the housing characteristics in the City of Detroit were as follows:

(a) 1960   total supply of housing units was 553,000
(b) 1970   total supply of housing units was 530,770

The percentage decline in the white students in the Detroit Public Schools during the period 1961–1970 (53.6% in 1960; 34.8% in 1970) has been greater than the percentage decline in the white population in the City of Detroit during the same period (70.8% in 1960; 55.21% in 1970), and correlatively, the percentage increase in black students in the Detroit Public Schools during the nine-year period 1961–1970 (45.8% in 1961; 63.8% in 1970) has been greater than the percentage increase in the black population of the City of Detroit during the ten-year period 1960–1970 (28.9% in 1960; 43.9% in 1970). In 1961 there were eight schools in the system without white pupils and 73 schools with no Negro pupils. In 1970 there were 30 schools with no white pupils and 11 schools with no Negro pupils, an increase in the number of schools without white pupils of 22 and a decrease in the number of schools without Negro pupils of 62 in this ten-year period. Between 1968 and 1970 Detroit experienced the largest increase in percentage of black students in the student population of any major northern school district. The percentage increase in Detroit was 4.7% as contrasted with—

New York	2.0%
Los Angeles	1.5%
Chicago	1.9%
Philadelphia	1.7%
Cleveland	1.7%
Milwaukee	2.6%
St. Louis	2.6%
Columbus	1.4%
Indianapolis	2.6%
Denver	1.1%
Boston	3.2%
San Francisco	1.5%
Seattle	2.4%

In 1960, there were 266 schools in the Detroit School System. In 1970, there were 319 schools in the Detroit School System.

In the Western, Northwestern, Northern, Murray, Northeastern, Kettering, King and Southeastern high school service areas, the following conditions exist at a level significantly higher than the city average:

(a) Poverty in children
(b) Family income below poverty level
(c) Rate of homicides per population
(d) Number of households headed by females
(e) Infant mortality rate
(f) Surviving infants with neurological defects
(g) Tuberculosis cases per 1,000 population
(h) High pupil turnover in schools

The City of Detroit is a community generally divided by racial lines. Residential segregation within the city and throughout the larger metropolitan area is substantial, pervasive and of long standing. Black citizens are located in separate and distinct areas within the city and are not generally to be found in the suburbs. While the racially unrestricted choice of black persons and economic factors may have played some part in the development of this pattern of residential segregation, it is, in the main, the result of past and present practices and customs of racial discrimination, both public and private, which have and do restrict the housing opportunities of black people. On the record there can be no other finding.

Governmental actions and inaction at all levels, federal, state and local, have combined, with those of private organizations, such as loaning institutions and real estate associations and brokerage firms, to establish and to maintain the pattern of residential segregation throughout the Detroit metropolitan area. It is no answer to say that restricted practices grew gradually (as the black population in the area increased between 1920 and 1970), or that since 1948 racial restrictions on the ownership of real property have been removed. The policies pursued by both government and private persons and agencies have a continuing and present effect upon the complexion of the community—as we know, the choice of a residence is a relatively infrequent affair. For many years FHA and VA openly advised and advocated the maintenance of "harmonious" neighborhoods, *i.e.*, racially and economically harmonious. The conditions created continue. While it would be unfair to charge the present defendants with what other governmental officers or agencies have done, it can be said that the actions or the failure to act by the responsible school authorities, both city and state, were linked to that of these other governmental units. When we speak of governmental action we should not view the different agencies as a collection of unrelated units. Perhaps the most that can be said is that all of them, including the school authorities, are, in part, responsible for the segregated condition which exists. And we note that just as there is an interaction between residential patterns and the racial composition of the schools, so there is a corresponding effect on the residential pattern by the racial composition of the schools.

Turning now to the specific and pertinent (for our purposes) history of the Detroit school system so far as it involves both the local school authorities and the state school authorities, we find the following:

During the decade beginning in 1950 the Board created and maintained optional attendance zones in neighborhoods undergoing racial transition and between high school attendance areas of opposite predominant racial compositions. In 1959 there were eight basic optional attendance areas affecting 21 schools. Optional attendance areas provided pupils living within certain elementary areas a choice of attendance at one of two high schools. In addition there was at least one optional area either created or existing in 1960 between two junior high schools of opposite predominant racial components. All of the high school optional areas, except two, were in neighborhoods undergoing racial transition (from white to black) during the 1950s. The two exceptions were: (1) the option between Southwestern (61.6% black in 1960) and Western (15.3% black); (2) the option between Denby (0% black) and Southeastern (30.9% black). With the exception of the Denby-Southeastern option (just noted) all of the options were between high schools of opposite predominant racial compositions. The Southwestern-Western and Denby-Southeastern optional areas are all white on the 1950, 1960, and 1970 census maps. Both Southwestern and Southeastern, however, had substantial white pupil populations, and the option allowed whites to escape integration. The natural, probable, foreseeable and actual effect of these optional zones was to allow white youngsters to escape identifiably "black" schools. There had also been an optional zone (eliminated between 1956 and 1959) created in "an attempt to separate Jews and Gentiles within the system," the effect of which was that Jewish youngsters went to Mumford High School and Gentile youngsters went to Cooley. Although many of these optional areas had served their purpose by 1960 due to the fact that most of the areas had become predominantly black, one optional area (Southwestern-Western affecting Wilson Junior High graduates) continued until the present school year (and will continue to affect 11th and 12th grade white youngsters who elected to escape from predominantly black Southwestern to predominantly white Western High School). Mr. Hendrickson, the Board's general fact witness, who was employed in 1959 to, *inter alia*, eliminate optional areas, noted in 1967 that: "In operation Western appears to be still the school to which white students escape from predominantly Negro surrounding schools." The effect of eliminating this optional area (which affected only 10th graders for the 1970–71 school year) was to decrease Southwestern from 86.7% black in 1969 to 74.3% black in 1970.

The Board, in the operation of its transportation to relieve overcrowding policy, has admittedly bused black pupils past or away from closer white schools with available space to black schools. This practice has continued in several instances in recent years despite the Board's avowed policy, adopted in 1967, to utilize transportation to increase integration.

With one exception (necessitated by the burning of a white school), defendant Board has never bused white children to predominantly black schools. The Board has not bused white pupils to black schools despite the enormous amount of space available in inner-city schools. There were 22,961 vacant seats in schools 90% or more black.

The Board has created and altered attendance zones, maintained and altered grade structures and created and altered feeder school patterns in a manner which has had the natural, probable and actual effect of continuing black and white pupils in racially segregated schools. The Board admits at least one instance where it purposefully and intentionally built and maintained a school and its attendance zone to contain black students. Throughout the last decade (and presently) school attendance zones of opposite racial compositions have been separated by north-south boundary lines, despite the Board's awareness (since at least 1962) that drawing boundary lines in an east-west direction would result in significant integration. The natural and actual effect of these acts and failures to act has been the creation and perpetuation of school segregation. There has never been a feeder pattern or zoning change which placed a predominantly white residential area into a predominantly black school zone or feeder pattern. Every school which was 90% or more black in 1960, and which is still in use today, remains 90% or more black. Whereas 65.8% of Detroit's black students attended 90% or more black schools in 1960, 74.9% of the black students attended 90% or more black schools during the 1970–71 school year.

The public schools operated by defendant Board are thus segregated on a racial basis. This racial segregation is in part the result of the discriminatory acts and omissions of defendant Board.

In 1966 the defendant State Board of Education and Michigan Civil Rights Commission issued a Joint Policy Statement on Equality of Educational Opportunity, requiring that

"Local school boards must consider the factor of racial balance along with other educational considerations in making decisions about selection of new school sites, expansion of present facilities. . . . Each of these situations presents an opportunity for integration."

Defendant State Board's "School Plant Planning Handbook" requires that

"Care in site locations must be taken if a serious transportation problem exists or if housing patterns in an area would result in a school largely segregated on racial, ethnic, or socio-economic lines."

The defendant City Board has paid little heed to these statements and guidelines. The State defendants have similarly failed to take any action to effectuate these policies.

Exhibit NN reflects construction (new or additional) at 14 schools which opened for use in 1970–71; of these 14 schools, 11 opened over 90% black and one opened less than 10% black. School construction costing $9,222,000 is opening at Northwestern High School which is 99.9% black, and new construction opens at Brooks Junior High, which is 1.5% black, at a cost of $2,500,000. The construction at Brooks Junior High plays a dual segregatory role: not only is the construction segregated, it will result in a feeder pattern change which will remove the last majority white school from the already almost all-black Mackenzie High School attendance area.

Since 1959 the Board has constructed at least 13 small primary schools with capacities of from 300 to 400 pupils. This practice negates opportunities to integrate, "contains" the black population and perpetuates and compounds school segregation.

The State and its agencies, in addition to their general responsibility for and supervision of public education, have acted directly to control and maintain the pattern of segregation in the Detroit schools. The State refused, until this session of the legislature, to provide authorization or funds for the transportation of pupils within Detroit regardless of their poverty or distance from the school to which they were assigned, while providing in many neighboring, mostly white, suburban districts the full range of state supported transportation. This and other financial limitations, such as those on bonding and the working of the state aid formula whereby suburban districts were able to make far larger per pupil expenditures despite less tax effort, have created and perpetuated systematic educational inequalities.

The State, exercising what Michigan courts have held to be its "plenary power" which includes power "to use a statutory scheme, to create, alter, reorganize or even dissolve a school district, despite any desire of the school district, its board, or the inhabitants thereof," acted to reorganize the school district of the City of Detroit.

The State acted through Act 48 to impede, delay and minimize racial integration in Detroit schools. The first sentence of Sec. 12 of the Act was directly related to the April 7, 1970, desegregation plan. The remainder of the section sought to prescribe for each school in the eight districts criterion of "free choice" (open enrollment) and "neighborhood schools" ("nearest school priority acceptance"), which had as their purpose and effect the maintenance of segregation.

In view of our findings of fact already noted we think it unnecessary to parse in detail the activities of the local board and the state authorities in the area of school construction and the furnishing of school facilities. It is our conclusion that these activities were in keeping, generally, with the discriminatory practices which advanced or perpetuated racial segregation in these schools.

It would be unfair for us not to recognize the many fine steps the Board has taken to advance the cause of quality education for all in terms of racial integration and human relations. The most obvious of these is in the field of faculty integration.

Plantiffs urged the Court to consider allegedly discriminatory practices of the Board with respect to the hiring, assignment and transfer of teachers and school administrators during a period reaching back more than 15 years. The short answer to that must be that black teachers and school administrative personnel were not readily available in that period. The Board and the intervening defendant union have followed a most advanced and exemplary course in adopting and carrying out what is called the "balanced staff concept"—which seeks to balance faculties in each school with respect to race, sex and experience, with primary emphasis on race. More particularly, we find:

1. With the exception of affirmative policies designed to achieve racial balance in instructional staff, no teacher in the Detroit Public Schools is hired, promoted or assigned to any school by reason of his race.

2. In 1956, the Detroit Board of Education adopted the rules and regulations of the Fair Employment Practices Act as its hiring and promotion policy and has adhered to this policy to date.

3. The Board has actively and affirmatively sought out and hired minority employees, particularly teachers and administrators, during the past decade.

4. Between 1960 and 1970, the Detroit Board of Education has increased black representation among its teachers from 23.3% to 42.1%, and among its administrators from 4.5% to 37.8%.

5. Detroit has a higher proportion of black administrators than any other city in the country.

6. Detroit ranked second to Cleveland in 1968 among the 20 largest northern city school districts in the percentage of blacks among the teaching faculty and in 1970 surpassed Cleveland by several percentage points.

7. The Detroit Board of Education currently employs black teachers in a greater percentage than the percentage of adult black persons in the City of Detroit.

8. Since 1967, more blacks than whites have been placed in high administrative posts with the Detroit Board of Education.

9. The allegation that the Board assigns black teachers to black schools is not supported by the record.

10. Teacher transfers are not granted in the Detroit Public Schools unless they conform with the balanced staff concept.

11. Between 1960 and 1970, the Detroit Board of Education reduced the percentage of schools without black faculty from 36.3% to 1.2%, and of the four schools currently without black faculty, three are specialized trade schools where minority faculty cannot easily be secured.

12. In 1968, of the 20 largest northern city school districts, Detroit ranked fourth in the percentage of schools having one or more black teachers and third in the percentage of schools having three or more black teachers.

13. In 1970, the Board held open 240 positions in schools with less than 25% black, rejecting white applicants for these positions until qualified black applicants could be found and assigned.

14. In recent years, the Board has come under pressure from large segments of the black community to assign male black administrators to predominantly black schools to serve as male role models for students, but such assignments have been made only where consistent with the balanced staff concept.

15. The numbers and percentages of black teachers in Detroit increased from 2,275 and 21.6%, respectively, in February, 1961, to 5,106 and 41.6%, respectively, in October, 1970.

16. The number of schools by percent black of staffs changed from October, 1963 to October, 1970 as follows:

Number of schools without black teachers—decreased from 41, to 4.

Number of schools with more than 0%, but less than 10% black teachers—decreased from 58, to 8.

Total number of schools with less than 10% black teachers—decreased from 99, to 12.

Number of schools with 50% or more black teachers—increased from 72, to 124.

17. The number of schools by percent black of staffs changed from October, 1969 to October, 1970, as follows:

Number of schools without black teachers—decreased from 6, to 4.

Number of schools with more than 0%, but less than 10% black teachers—decreased from 41, to 8.

Total number of schools with less than 10% black teachers—decreased from 47, to 12.

Number of schools with 50% or more black teachers—increased from 120, to 124.

18. The total number of transfers necessary to achieve a faculty racial quota in each school corresponding to the system-wide ratio, and ignoring all other elements is, as of 1970, 1,826.

19. If account is taken of other elements necessary to assure quality integrated education, including qualifications to teach the subject area and grade level, balance of experience, and balance of sex, and further account is taken of the uneven distribution of black teachers by subject taught and sex, the total number of transfers which would be necessary to achieve a faculty racial quota in each school corresponding to the system-wide ratio, if attainable at all, would be infinitely greater.

20. Balancing of staff by qualifications for subject and grade level, then by race, experience and sex, is educationally desirable and important.

21. It is important for students to have a successful role model, especially black students in certain schools, and at certain grade levels.

22. A quota of racial balance for faculty in each school which is equivalent to the system-wide ratio and without more is educationally undesirable and arbitrary.

23. A severe teacher shortage in the 1950s and 1960s impeded integration-of-faculty opportunities.

24. Disadvantageous teaching conditions in Detroit in the 1960s—salaries, pupil mobility and transiency, class size, building conditions, distance from teacher residence, shortage of teacher substitutes, etc.—made teacher recruitment and placement difficult.

25. The Board did not segregate faculty by race, but rather attempted to fill vacancies with certified and qualified teachers who would take offered assignments.

26. Teacher seniority in the Detroit system, although measured by system-wide service, has been applied consistently to protect against involuntary transfers and "bumping" in given schools.

27. Involuntary transfers of teachers have occurred only because of unsatisfactory ratings or because of decrease of teacher services in a school, and then only in accordance with balanced staff concept.

28. There is no evidence in the record that Detroit teacher seniority rights had other than equitable purpose or effect.

29. Substantial racial integration of staff can be achieved, without disruption of seniority and stable teaching relationships, by application of the balanced staff concept to naturally occurring vacancies and increases and reductions of teacher services.

30. The Detroit Board of Education has entered into successive collective bargaining contracts with the Detroit Federation of Teachers, which contracts have included provisions promoting integration of staff and students.

The Detroit Board has, in many other instances and in many other respects, undertaken to lessen the impact of the forces of segregation and attempted to advance the cause of integration. Perhaps the most obvious one was the adoption of the April 7 Plan. Among other things, it has denied the use of its facilities to groups which practice racial discrimination; it does not permit the use of its facilities for discriminatory apprentice training programs; it has opposed state legislation which would have the effect of segregating the district; it has worked to place black students in craft positions in industry and the building trades; it has brought about a substantial increase in the percentage of black students in manufacturing and construction trade apprenticeship classes; it became the first public agency in Michigan to adopt and implement a policy requiring affirmative act of contractors with which it deals to insure equal employment opportunities in their work forces; it has been a leader in pioneering the use of multi-ethnic instructional material, and in so doing has had an impact on publishers specializing in producing school texts and instructional materials; and it has taken other noteworthy pioneering steps to advance relations between the white and black races.

[1,2] In conclusion, however, we find that both the State of Michigan and the Detroit Board of Education have committed acts which have been causal factors in the segregated condition of the public schools of the city of Detroit. As we assay the principles essential to a finding of de jure segregation, as outlined in rulings of the United States Supreme Court, they are:

1. The State, through its officers and agencies, and usually, the school administration, must have taken some action or actions with a purpose of segregation.

2. This action or these actions must have created or aggravated segregation in the schools in question.

3. A current condition of segregation exists.

We find these tests to have been met in this case. We recognize that causation in the case before us is both several and comparative. The principal causes undeniably have been population movement and housing patterns, but state and local governmental actions, including school board actions, have played a substantial role in promoting segregation. It is, the Court believes, unfortunate that we cannot deal with public school segregation on a no-fault basis, for if racial segregation in our public schools is an evil, then it should make no difference whether we classify it de jure or de facto. Our objective, logically, it seems to us, should be to remedy a condition which we believe needs correction. In the most realistic sense, if fault or blame must be found it is that of the community as a whole, including, of course, the black components. We need not minimize the effect of the actions of federal, state and local governmental officers and agencies, and the actions of loaning institutions and real estate firms, in the establishment and maintenance of segregated residential patterns—which lead to school segregation—to observe that blacks, like ethnic groups in the past, have tended to separate from the larger group and associate together. The ghetto is at once both a place of confinement and a refuge. There is enough blame for everyone to share.*

---

*Conclusions of Law follow.

APPENDIX B
Chronology of the Detroit Case

1956	Samuel Brownell becomes superintendent of schools.
1959	Norman Drachler is appointed head of the Community Relations Division; later in the year is made an assistant superintendent of schools.
1960	Detroit School Board's adherence to color-blind, nondiscriminatory policy is reaffirmed.
1962	Citizens Advisory Committee on Equal Educational Opportunities completes a two-year study; releases the first count of Detroit public school pupils by race; as of 1961 the system was 46 percent black.
1964	A liberal pro-integration majority now prevails on the Detroit School Board, and board policy begins to shift from emphasis on racial disregard to emphasis on policies which further racial integration.
1966	Drachler is named acting superintendent. Arthur Johnson, former director of the Detroit NAACP and first deputy director of the Michigan Commission on Civil Rights, is named deputy superintendent.
1969	State legislature passes Act 244, decentralizing Detroit schools.
1970	*April 7:* Detroit School Board adopts a desegregation plan altering the attendance boundaries of half of Detroit's high schools, resulting in a public outcry and a campaign to recall those board members who backed the plan.
	July: state legislature passes Act 48, which nullifies the April 7 Plan.
	August: Board of Education members who supported the April 7 Plan are recalled. NAACP files suit challenging the constitutionality of Act 48 and asking for restoration of April 7 Plan.
	September: Federal District Court Judge Stephen Roth denies the NAACP request.
	October: Sixth Circuit Court of Appeals rules unconstitutional that portion of Act 48 barring implementation of the April 7 Plan.
	December: Judge Roth selects a voluntary magnet desegregation plan offered by the Detroit School Board.
1971	*April 6:* NAACP suit charging Detroit schools with intentional and official racial segregation comes to trial before Judge Roth.
	July: Drachler resigns; Charles Wolfe is appointed superintendent of schools. Trial ends.
	September: Judge Roth rules that Detroit schools are segregated de jure.
1972	*February:* Detroit School Board decides to support a metropolitan desegregation remedy.

313

March: hearings on a Detroit-only remedy are held; Judge Roth rules that no Detroit plan can desegregate Detroit schools. Suburbs are then admitted as intervenors, and hearings on a metropolitan remedy begin.

June: Judge Roth selects a remedy involving Detroit and fifty-two suburban school districts in the tri-county area, involving about 780,000 children.

December: a three-justice panel of the Sixth Circuit Court of Appeals affirms Roth's ruling of segregation de jure in Detroit and his conclusion that the desegregation remedy must not be confined to the city of Detroit.

1973   *June:* the ruling is affirmed *en banc,* i.e., by the full Sixth Circuit, three members dissenting.

1974   *February:* U.S. Supreme Court hears oral arguments on appeals by the State of Michigan and the suburbs concerning the metropolitan remedy.

July: The United States Supreme Court rules (5 to 4) that because only Detroit had been found guilty of de jure segregation the remedy must be confined to the city. The Detroit School Board is ordered to desegregate its schools. Judge Roth dies before the Supreme Court decision is issued.

1975   *January:* Judge Robert DeMascio is assigned to the case.

April: hearings on plans for the desegregation remedy begin before Judge DeMascio; he appoints three experts to assist him: Wilbur Cohen, Francis Keppel, and John Finger.

August: Judge DeMascio issues guidelines for revision of plans submitted by Detroit School Board and by plaintiffs; guidelines include numerous educational components to "eradicate the effects of past discrimination."

1975–76   A series of court orders is issued on various aspects of the remedy, including student and teacher assignments, educational components, a code of student conduct, community participation, and the appointment of a fifty-five-member monitoring commission.

1976   *January:* public schools now about 75 percent black; reassignment of some 28,000 students begins; about 22,000 of these must be bused.

August: in response to strong criticism from NAACP, Sixth Circuit Court of Appeals reviews student assignment portion of the remedy and remands it to the judge for further desegregation.

1977   *June:* U.S. Supreme Court unanimously upholds the educational components in Judge DeMascio's order, over the objections of the State of Michigan concerning its obligation to pay a large share of these costs.

1978   Judge DeMascio declines to expand busing in view of declining proportion of white students; NAACP appeals to Sixth Circuit for program's expansion.

1980   The Sixth Circuit Court of Appeals orders expansion of Detroit busing program, although fewer than 15 percent of students are white, and suggests that Judge DeMascio remove himself from the case. NAACP hails decision but also announces intention to reopen litigation for city-suburban busing remedy. Detroit Board of Education, now predominantly black, votes to appeal Sixth Circuit's order to the U.S. Supreme Court.

Notes

Introduction

Note: the references throughout the text to the record of the trial in 1971 before Judge Stephen Roth, *Bradley v. Milliken*, are identified as "T." The transcripts of the 1972 hearings before Judge Roth on plans to integrate the schools are cited in similar fashion: "T, DR," for "Detroit Remedy" or Detroit-only desegregation plans, and "T, MR," for "Metropolitan Remedy" or metro-area desegregation plans. The reader is reminded that oral testimony is not expected to have the precision, sentence structure, or grammatical niceties of written statements. Those who have heard tape recordings of their own conversations have learned to expect these differences.

1. *People ex rel. Workman v. Board of Education of Detroit*, 18 Michigan (1869).
2. *Bradley v. Milliken*, 338 F. Supp. 582 (E.D. Mich. 1971); hereafter cited as *Bradley v. Milliken* (1971). See Appendix A for Judge Roth's ruling.
3. *Brown v. Board of Education*, 347 U.S. 483 (1954). For a summary of cases leading up to it see Read (1975), p. 8; also Bell (1976), pp. 472–77.
4. Cited in Friedman (1969), p. 375, from transcript of the oral argument before the Supreme Court.
5. For a brief summary of some forms of resistance offered to *Brown* in the South, see *New York University Law Review* (1971), pp. 1083–90; Read (1975), pp. 10–20.
6. The prompt desegregation of the dual system in Washington, D.C., was initially praised by civil rights supporters (see, e.g., Knoll [1959]), but the schools became predominantly black as a consequence of residential movements and the increased use of private schools.
7. See Taeuber and Taeuber (1965), p. 45; Palen (1975), pp. 216, 218; and Clotfelter (1975), p. 268. See also Roof, in Schwirian (1974), pp. 592–93; and Schnore and Evenson (1966).
8. See *Brown v. Board of Education*, at 494–95. For the meaning of the *Brown* ruling, see, for example, Bloch (1965); Rosen (1972), chs. 7–8; Cahn (1955); Wechsler (1959); Pollak (1959); Van Den Haag (1960); Richter (1972), pp. 423–35; Goodman (1972); Dimond (1972); Kirp and Yudof (1974); and the work of Fiss (1965, 1971, 1974, 1975, 1976).
9. Richter (1972), p. 436.
10. *U.S. v. Jefferson County Board of Education*, 372 F.2d 836 (5th Cir. 1966). For a helpful discussion of the importance of this case and the second Jefferson County ruling, *U.S. v. Jefferson County Board of Education*, 380 F.2d 385 (5th Cir. 1967), see Read (1975), pp. 23–28.
11. *U.S. v. Jefferson County Board of Education* (1966), at 887–88.
12. *Ibid.*, at 876. The doubtful empirical nature of this contention is also noted by Goodman (1972, p. 294) in his masterful monograph on Northern-style school segregation.

315

13. *Green v. County School Board*, 391 U.S. 430 (1968); Read (1975), p. 30.
14. See Wolf (1972) for illustrations of some of these claims.
15. Taylor, Benjes, and Wright (1975), p. 72.
16. *Swann v. Charlotte-Mecklenburg Board of Education*, 402 U.S. 1 (1971). See Fiss (1971) for a brilliant analysis of the "contrived" nature of this theory of the causes of racial imbalance and the hazards of such an approach as compared with a more straightforward one suggested by the same author (Fiss 1975).
17. Grant (1971), p. 63. See also Pilo (1975).
18. During the Drachler administration applications from students for transfers to open enrollment schools were not accepted if racial concentration would be increased thereby.
19. See Grant (1971), pp. 66–77, for an excellent account of these events.
20. *Detroit Free Press*, February 16, February 20, April 3, 1971.
21. *Ibid.*, March 3, March 12, March 13, March 15, March 16, March 18, March 19, March 20, March 31, 1971.
22. *Ibid.*, April 18, April 27, May 24, 1970.
23. Ruling of the District Court, December 1970. Judge Roth was not, as Bolner and Shanley (1974, p. 40) state, a black man, nor was he Jewish, as some might conclude from his name. He was of Hungarian Catholic background.
24. Conference of October 4, 1971.
25. *Milliken v. Bradley*, 418 U.S. 717 (1974).
26. *Bradley v. Milliken* (1971), at 592.

Overview, Part I

1. *Bradley v. Milliken*, 338 F. Supp. (E.D. Michigan 1971) (hereafter cited as *Bradley v. Milliken* [1971]), at 587.
2. *Ibid.*, at 592.
3. *Bradley v. Milliken*, 484 F.2d (6th Cir. 1973) (hereafter cited as *Bradley v. Milliken* [1973]), at 242.
4. See Grant (1971, 1975); also Pilo (1975), pp. 403–4: "The Detroit public schools under Drachler's leadership and with the support of a majority of the Board aggressively pursued a policy of racial integration unrivaled in any Northern city."
5. *Deal v. Cincinnati Board of Education*, 396 F.2d 55 (1966).
6. Cahn (1961), p. 129.
7. The hearings on desegregation remedies, held several months after the trial, also contained a large amount of testimony on residential behavior. See Chapter 17 below.

Chapter 1

1. This presentation was largely the work of the lawyers from the Harvard University Center for Law and Education; see T, p. 684.
2. *Bradley v. Milliken* (1971), at 787. But this depends on one's interpretation of the meaning of the phrase "relatively infrequent." Bayley (1976, pp. 62–63) asserts that the average American moves fourteen times in his lifetime. A commonly accepted estimate is that about 20 percent of American households move each year; see the U.S. Advisory Commission on Civil Disorders *Report* (1968), pp. 244–45; Molotch (1972), pp. 151, 172.
3. See Palen (1975), pp. 216–18; Taeuber and Taeuber (1965), p. 3. Clotfelter (1975) shows how ending Jim Crow schools in the South increased racial residential concentration.

4. Litwack (1961), pp. 169–70.
5. Taueber and Taeuber (1965), pp. 54–55.
6. *Ibid.*, p. 39. A condition of total separation by race would yield an index of 100.
7. Katzman (1973), p. 67. See also Burgess (1928) on the severity of residential segregation in Chicago after World War I.
8. See Allen (1971); Rex and Moore (1967), pp. 246–47; Davison (1966), p. 110; Deakin (1964).
9. McKee (1963).
10. Grier and Grier (1967), p. 531.
11. See, for example, Deutsch and Collins (1951) and Wilner, Walkely and Cook (1955). In any case, the units in public housing projects represented such a tiny fraction of the overall housing supply that their impact on the segregation index was minimal.
12. For descriptions of such programs, see Wolf and Lebeaux (1969), pp. 84–89; Molotch (1972), ch. 6. Two instances of reported success are the Ludlow area, near Cleveland (see Diekhoff [1969]), and Oak Park, near Chicago (see *Time*, October 31, 1977, pp. 16–21; *Newsweek*, October 17, 1977, p. 47).
13. For further details, see the National Committee against Discrimination in Housing newsletter, *Trends*, for January–February, 1974.
14. Terreberry, in Wolf and Lebeaux (1969); Cagle and Deutscher (1970); Davis (1965).
15. See Schelling (1971). Aaron (1972, p. 17) also notes that residential segregation can occur without discrimination.

Chapter 2

1. Taeuber (1970), p. 12.
2. Taeuber and Taeuber (1965), p. 23.
3. Wolf (1972), p. 173.
4. Brink and Harris (1964), pp. 158–59.
5. *Ibid.*, pp. 161–62. See also National Academy of Sciences (1972), pp. 10–11.
6. Marx (1967), pp. 175–76.
7. Bradburn, Sudman, and Gockel (1971), p. 134.
8. Campbell and Schuman (1968), p. 15.
9. Schuman and Hatchett (1974), p. 7.
10. Hermalin and Farley (1973), p. 608. Morrill (1965, p. 360) also finds that blacks usually prefer a larger proportion of their own group than is "readily acceptable to whites. Thus a fundamental dilemma arises." Duncan, Schuman, and Duncan (1973, p. 108) reports that their 1971 data show that 66 percent of black Detroiters prefer a neighborhood "mixed half and half." Only 2 percent stated a preference for an area that was "mostly white."
11. See Hermalin and Farley (1973), p. 598, for a summary of these data.
12. Kantrowitz (1973), p. 77. That this wish is difficult to achieve because most blacks are poor is shown in Erbe (1975), p. 812.
13. Downs (1970), p. 74, n. 23.
14. Gans, in Haar (1972), pp. 90–92.
15. Gans (1969), p. 380. See also Chapter 1, nn. 11–12, above.
16. Watts et al. (1964), p. 8.
17. *Ibid.*, pp. 10–11.
18. Davis (1965), pp. 209–15.
19. Grier and Grier (1964), p. 14.
20. Bradburn, Sudman, and Gockel (1971).
21. U.S. Advisory Commission on Civil Disorders (1968), p. 396.

22. Hauser (1966), p. 96. See also Berger (1966); Perry and Feagin (1972), pp. 438–39.
23. Rapkin and Grigsby, in Frieden and Morris, eds. (1968), p. 160.
24. Glazer (1971).
25. Quoted in Friedman (1969), p. 239.
26. See Simpson and Yinger (1972), pp. 232–33. I have suggested elsewhere that the earlier insistence of American sociologists that there is no distinctive subculture associated with black Americans arose from their desire to discredit racist or stereotyped conceptions of Negroes (see Wolf [1972], p. 175). For another explanation see Metzger (1971); see also Fein (1971, pp. 50–51), who asserts that "black culture has been with us all along. . . . most were unable to accept [it] as recently as a decade ago." After considering some factors in its development he concludes that "even if the expression of the new allegiance is, in its origins, primarily a reaction-formation, its authenticity grows with each passing day."
27. Gordon (1964).
28. Singer (1962), pp. 419–32; Isaacs (1963).
29. Broom and Glenn (1966), p. 199. See also Blauner, in Rose, ed. (1970).
30. Suttles (1968), p. 136.
31. Molotch (1972), pp. 176–77.
32. Myrdal (1944), pp. 189–90, 193, 386–88. But he saw "Negro culture" solely as a "distorted" or "pathological development of . . . American culture" (p. 928).
33. See Tilly (1974), pp. 265–67. A similar process occurs in the search for a job; see Granovetter (1973).
34. Molotch (1972), p. 17. See also Molotch (1972b, p. 683), in which he notes that blacks will pay more than whites in areas near existing black settlement. A similar point is made by Pascal (1970, p. 416). He observes that not many blacks are willing to pay the higher price which many whites will pay for dwellings distant from black neighborhoods. Muth (1969) describes this as blacks' lesser aversion to living near other blacks.

Chapter 3

1. *Bradley v. Milliken* (1971), at 592. There was also a reference at 588 to the use of optional zones to separate Jewish and non-Jewish children. This evaluation, which I believe to be an unwitting distortion of Jewish self-segregation tendencies, is discussed in Chapter 14 below.
2. See Gordon (1964) for a discussion of this topic.
3. See Granovetter (1973); Tilly (1974), pp. 265–67; Laumann (1973).
4. As noted, Thurgood Marshall, arguing for the NAACP before the Supreme Court in *Brown*, specifically rejected this perspective. See also Glazer (1971).
5. Gordon (1964), pp. 77–81.
6. Studies show that various white ethnic groups vary markedly in the rate at which their residential concentration diminishes. See Beshers, Laumann, and Bradshaw (1964), p. 487.
7. Lieberson (1962), pp. 680–81; Agocs (1977).
8. Rosenthal (1960).
9. On Detroit, see Grossberg (1971), p. 57 and Agocs (1977). See Tilly (1974), p. 272.
10. Clark (1970).
11. Parenti (1969), p. 281.
12. Wolfinger (1965), p. 897. See also Levine and Herman (1972) and Darroch and Marston (1971). The latter found that socioeconomic status did not account for ethnic residential concentrations among whites.
13. Agocs and Thompson (1973), pp. 1–2. See also Agocs (1977).

14. Sandberg (1974, p. 71) concludes that "although declining in intensity, ethnicity is measurable . . . and continues to have meaning in the lives of large numbers [of Polish-Americans] into the fourth generation, even in a region [Los Angeles] far removed from areas of original settlement."
15. *Ibid.*, p. viii. See also Guest and Weed (1976), a recent study of three metropolitan areas, for further evidence of the persistence of a considerable degree of white ethnic clustering.
16. Both Lieberson (1973) and Glazer (1971) note the possible significance of this factor. The absence of generation data for blacks is noted by Taeuber and Taeuber (1964), p. 378.
17. Kantrowitz (1969). See also Bleda (1975).
18. Kantrowitz (1969), pp. 693–94.
19. Kantrowitz (1973), pp. 76–79.
20. Taeuber (1970), pp. 13–15.
21. Birch et al. (1975), pp. 35–36.
22. *Ibid.*

Chapter 4

1. For studies that are in general agreement with Taeuber, see Farley (1975), pp. 882–85; Kain (1969); Schnore and Sharp, in Hadden et al., eds. (1967). See Farley (1975, p. 884) for estimates of the proportion of blacks that would be living in various suburbs if location were based solely on income. But these proportions are often much smaller than those favored by blacks (see poll data reported in Chapter 2).
2. Grier and Grier (1964), p. 16.
3. Gans, in Haar (1972), pp. 90–92; Gans (1969), p. 384.
4. Pascal (1967). For a detailed enumeration of black economic disadvantages in the housing market not reflected by rentals paid, see especially pp. 67–90 of Pascal's study.
5. Zelder (1970a), p. 94; Zelder (1970b), pp. 268–70.
6. Downs (1973), ch. 12.
7. Lansing, Clifton, and Morgan (1969), p. 67.
8. Bell (1974), pp. 55–58.
9. Warren (1968), pp. 6–24.
10. Wolf and Lebeaux (1969), p. 52. See also Molotch (1972), p. 176.
11. Connolly (1973), pp. 104–9.
12. Wolfe and Blood (1960). The comparable proportion for whites in 1955 was 43 percent. In addition, four-fifths of the blue-collar blacks were in the lower-status categories, as compared with only half of the whites. Deskins (1972, p. 198) cites census data for 1950 showing that if both black men and black women workers are included, 14 percent of the black work force was in some type of white-collar employment, but more than half of this group were in the clerical or sales category.
13. Erbe (1975), pp. 803, 812.
14. Pascal (1967), pp. 6–8. The use of the term "prejudice" to include (as Pascal does) aversion to lower-class behavior as well as irrational hostility to persons on the basis of their race obscures an important distinction. See Campbell (1967); Mackie (1973); Petersen (1958).
15. *Bradley v. Milliken* (1971), at 586.
16. Gans (1968), p. 282 (Gans' italics).
17. Gans (1972), p. 86.
18. Downs (1970), p. 34.

19. See, for example, Levine (1971). It was reported several years ago (Hermalin and Farley [1973], p. 597) that two-thirds of whites thought "Negroes have a right to live wherever they can afford to"; 84 percent said it "would make no difference if a Negro with the same income and education" moved onto their block.

20. See "Lafayette Park," in Wolf and Lebeaux (1969). The attempt to attract prosperous families of either race with children of high school age has been unsuccessful because of this factor.

Chapter 5

1. Pascal (1970, pp. 413–14) considers and discards this conspiratorial explanation. Molotch (1972, pp. 157–58) found no evidence of blockbusting in his study area, nor did I (Wolf and Lebeaux [1969]). See also Barresi (1972) and Muth (1969).

2. These references are to Detroit high schools, now all black. It may be noted that if, as the NAACP's expert witness asserted, all of the whites had fled the city (whether due to racist attitudes or for any other reason), it would seem difficult to attribute the schools' racial composition to constitutional violations by school authorities, as plaintiffs also alleged. No one, however, including the judge, remarked upon this inconsistency.

3. Sloane did not tell Judge Roth that when the dual school system was abolished in Washington the proportion of black students was far less than at present. Nor did he mention what a man of Roth's age who had been close to the civil rights movement might remember: the desegregation of the District schools after the 1954 Supreme Court decision was hailed nationwide not only as a welcome display of obedience to law but as a stunning example of the educational effectiveness of integration as it was then defined, i.e., the end of mandatory racial exclusion; see Knoll (1959). (The claims for educational improvement were based on the higher scholastic average in the newly mixed classrooms, with scores not classified by race, just as they were to be in the educational testimony later in the Detroit trial.) A candid account of what happened in Washington would have fulfilled Sloane's assertion that the District experience was "instructive," but it was not given, and the court was thereby deprived of highly relevant information.

4. It is not clear from the record whether Sloane, after revealing that he thought the pupil population was 46 percent black (as it had been ten years before the trial), was told of the correct racial composition, 65 percent.

5. For studies of racial transition where no "panic," "flight," or acceleration of residential mobility took place, see Molotch (1972); Guest and Zuiches (1971); Aldrich (1975); Aldrich and Reiss (1976); Wolf and Lebeaux (1969), "The Bagley Area." For an account of the difficulty found by fair housing groups attempting to find whites willing to buy in mixed areas, see Molotch (1972); Wolf and Lebeaux (1969).

6. See Fishman (1961); Wolf (1960); Aldrich and Reiss (1976), p. 864; Molotch (1972), p. 200; Bradburn, Sudman, and Gockel (1971), pp. 122–24; Wolf and Lebeaux (1969), pp. 40–41; Cataldo et al. (1973), p. 4.

7. Since I first called attention to the lack of evidence for the operation of a tipping point, many others have come to a similar conclusion. See Wolf (1963); Aldrich (1975); Stinchcombe et al. (1969); Pryor (1971); Kantrowitz (1973), p. 58; Molotch (1972), p. 163; Real Estate Research Corporation (1976), p. 10.

8. See Wolf and Lebeaux (1969), pp. 49–63.

9. See Campbell (1971, p. 125), summarizing this evidence: "The numerous comparisons we are able to make of the [racial] attitudes and perceptions of white people in the suburbs and in the cities do not show any important differences." See also Gans (1968), pp 137–39.

10. Zikmund (1975); Palen (1975), p. 420.
11. Molotch (1972), pp. 174–203. This is a dominant theme, very ably presented, in the work of Gans (1968); see, for example, pp. 172–78. See also Wolf and Lebeaux (1969), pp. 125–27, 150–51, 157–65.
12. See Bradburn, Sudman, and Gockel (1971), pp. 122–24; Morris (1973), p. 89; Lang and Lang, in Dentler, Mackler, and Warshauer (1967), p. 51.
13. Molotch (1972), pp. 83–84, 176–77; Erbe (1975); Connolly (1973); Wolf and Lebeaux (1969), "The Bagley Area"; also Sutker and Sutker (1974), p. 129.
14. Foote (1960); Wolf and Ravitz (1964); Stegman (1969); Gans, in Haar (1972), pp. 91–92.
15. See Wolf and Lebeaux (1969), pp. 53–58.

Chapter 6

1. St. John (1975), p. 9. For a comprehensive review of the literature see the valuable work by White et al. (1973). A briefer review is found in St. John. Illustrative of varying emphases are Bernstein (1961, 1965); Bruner (1971); Cazden (1976); Deutsch et al. (1967); Hess and Shipman (1965, 1968); Jencks et al. (1972); Lipset and Bendix (1964), ch. 9; Miller and Woock (1970); Mosteller and Moynihan, eds. (1972), especially the contribution by Marshall Smith, pp. 312–15; Passow (1963); Plumer, in Williams (1970); Sewell, Haller, and Ohlendorf (1970); St. John and Herriott (1966); Strodtbeck, in Passow, Goldberg, and Tannenbaum, eds. (1967), especially pp. 253–58.
2. See, for example, Douglas (1963); Pringle, Butler, and Davie (1966), especially pp. 114–15; Husen, in Swift (1970); Thorndike (1973).
3. This was, of course, the chief finding of Coleman et al. (1966), and later analyses of those data confirmed the conclusions of that report. See, for example, Smith (1972), pp. 311–12; Jencks et al. (1972). The Coleman Report summarized as follows: "The educational disadvantage with which a group begins [school] remains the disadvantage with which it finishes" (p. 273). The "widening gap" is well explained on the same page. In most parts of the nation black academic proficiency does not "deteriorate," even in the relative sense, but if, to use an analogy, one car begins at a speed of twenty miles per hour, another at thirty, and nothing occurs to change these rates of speed, the distance lost by the slower becomes greater over time (Grant [1972], p. 124). See also Baughman and Dahlstrom (1968).
4. Wolf and Lebeaux (1969), p. 291.
5. I could find nothing in the Drake (1965) history that resembled these statements. In response to a letter to Professor Drake enclosing a copy of the Green testimony, Drake said that they did not reflect his study.
6. Gans, in Greer (1972), p. 18. See also Greer (1969a, 1969b).
7. Ravitch (1974). See also Greeley (1970), p. 917; Mann, in Daly, ed. (1968), p. 19.
8. Handlin (1951), pp. 244–48.
9. Department of Research, Detroit Board of Education.
10. U.S. Commission on Civil Rights (1967), p. 80. Parents' education was used as the indicator of socioeconomic status. See also Smith (1972), pp. 247–48; Armor (1972), pp. 217, 223.
11. Goslin (1967), p. 851.
12. Wolf (1969). For a different perspective, see Fantini, Gittell, and Magat (1970).
13. See Chapter 9 below concerning the effects of racial mixture upon achievement. Note also Bonacich and Goodman (1972), pp. 34–35; Armor (1972), pp. 216–17; Hsia (1971), pp. 2, 46–47.
14. Goslin (1967).

15. Herzog et al. (1972). In 1976 C. N. Lebeaux estimated that approximately one-third of Detroit's black students came from households on public assistance.
16. Stinchcombe (1969). Trotman (1977) finds that the usual SES measures do not capture differences in the home environment of black as compared with white middle-class children.
17. Jencks et al. (1972), p. 82. See also Preston (1974).
18. Treiman and Terrell (1975), p. 191; Kantner and Zelnik (1974); also Cutright, in Rainwater (1974). A "Round-up of Research" in *Transaction* (1967) reported that whites with less than an eighth-grade education had a larger proportion of intact marriages than black college graduates.
19. For a survey of these attitudes see Schuman (1969).
20. See, for examples of ethno-religious influences on a wide variety of behavioral areas, Bales (1964); Bonacich, Light, and Wong (1977); Clark (1975); Glazer (1971a); Greeley (1969, 1974, 1975); Hardy (1974); Featherman (1971); Hiltz (1971); Katzman (1968, 1969, 1971); Kitano (1967); Lenski (1961); Lieberson (1963); Light (1972); Lipset and Bendix (1964), pp. 56, 255–57; Montero (1973); Petersen (1971); Sklare, ed. (1958); Singer (1973); Thernstrom (1968, 1969); Wolfinger (1965). But see Alba (1977) for evidence that some of these differences may not now be very marked.
21. Murdoch (1920).
22. Cited by Cohen (1970), pp. 16, 17.
23. Featherman (1971), p. 214.
24. Lesser, Fifer, and Clark (1965); Stodolsky and Lesser (1967; Lesser, in Messick (1976).
25. Gross (1967).
26. See Schwartz, in Epps, ed. (1973); Sue and Frank (1973), pp. 140–42.
27. Majoribanks (1972). See also Heller (1969) on Mexican-Americans.
28. Rosenberg (1968).
29. Rosenwaike (1973).
30. *Ibid.*, p. 68.
31. Thernstrom, in Moynihan, ed. (1968), p. 177.

Chapter 7

1. *Bradley v. Milliken* (1971), at 589.
2. See Coleman et al. (1966), pp. 296–97, for a summary of the findings. Later analyses of these and other data by Jencks et al. (1972) and Mosteller and Moynihan, eds. (1972), as well as most other research, generally confirmed this finding (see Jencks et al., pp. 84–97, for an exceptionally clear exposition). The absence of a demonstrable relationship between achievement variation and resource variation was disputed by Bowles and Levin (1968); they also disputed the Coleman Report's inference that a student's peers exerted an independent influence upon academic achievement. But these scholars specifically noted that their analysis did not demonstrate that the relationships between school resources and achievement disproved the conclusions of the Coleman Report; rather, they recommended an "agnostic" position. I know of no substantial scholarly research that would confirm the relationship between school inputs and academic achievement claimed by Green in the courtroom. For a comprehensive bibliography, see White et al. (1973).

A study done in 1971–72 of the effects of increased educational resources in 102 integrated Southern school districts showed no gains for white students at any age, none for elementary school blacks, and none for black high school girls, in contrast to results for black high school boys, which did show improvement. But the time span was too brief for great significance to be attached to these findings. See Crain (1973).

3. Both Mosteller and Moynihan, eds. (1972, p. 8), and more popular treatments, such as the excellent article by Hodgson (1973), report that the research team was astonished (Hodgson reports that Coleman was "staggered") at the relatively small differences, nationwide, in resource allocation to black and to white students. See also Coleman (1967), pp. 21–22. For data on specific differences in resource allocations, see the Coleman Report (1966), pp. 67–121; for teacher differences, see pp. 130–48.

4. See St. John and Herriott (1966).

5. Guthrie et al. (1971). During his discussion of resources Guthrie did not dwell upon the existence of marked differences in academic proficiency at the time of school entry.

6. Quoted in the *Detroit News*, January 2, 1966.

7. Letter of January 14, 1966, sent to the principal.

8. Perloff (1964), p. 9.

9. See the discussion in Chapter 6 above.

10. See Murphy and Cohen (1974) for an instructive account of the storm created in Michigan by state-wide achievement testing and its failure to show a strong relationship to resource allocation.

11. Reported in the *Detroit Free Press*, February 9, 1971.

12. Phyllis Levenstein's Mother-Child Home Program, the "Verbal Interaction Project," is the outstanding example; see Levenstein (1977).

13. Coons et al. (1970, p. 30) observed that "the basic lesson to be drawn from the experts at this point is the current inadequacy of social science to delineate with any clarity the relation between cost and quality. [But] if money is inadequate to improve education the residents of poor districts should at least have an equal opportunity to be disappointed by its failure." See Jencks et al. (1972, p. 29) for an excellent discussion of alternative bases upon which increased resources for disadvantaged children might be justified; I share their opinion that schools should not be required to prove that they increase competency but only that they make life better in the present for children from disadvantaged circumstances. See also Coons (1977).

14. Among the many contributors to basic research in intellectual development with a special interest in the effects of social and economic disadvantage are David Ausubel, Basil Bernstein, Benjamin Bloom, Jerome Bruner, Courtney Cazden, Martin Deutsch, Miriam Goldberg, Robert Hess, J. McVicker Hunt, Irwin Katz, Phyllis Levenstein, Benjamin Passamanick, Virginia Shipman, Irving Sigel, and Frederick Strodtbeck.

15. Jencks et al. (1972), pp. 155–59.

Chapter 8

1. Merton (1949), ch. 7. The classic example is the way in which the expectation of a bank failure often led, prior to deposit insurance, to a bank run, which produced a failure.

2. Rosenthal and Jacobson (1968). The distortion of the Pygmalion drama is worth mentioning. Shaw's lines are quoted by Rosenthal and Jacobson as though in support of their thesis, but in the play Eliza says that she will always be a flower girl to Professor Higgins "because he always treats me as a flower-girl." Her re-education is a stunning success, notwithstanding a continuous stream of insults and invective from Higgins, who declares that "a woman who utters such depress-

ing and disgusting sounds has no right to live," describes her to her face as a "draggle-tailed guttersnipe," etc. Eliza is described as having great native intelligence, "extraordinary quickness of ear," intense motivation (she offers to pay for her own lessons), and a willingness to subject herself to relentless and intensive drill. In short, native ability, plus an extraordinary program of compensatory education, plus severance of all ties to her native milieu, are offered as the reasons for her success, not a benign expectation that she will do well, which is the meaning that has come to be associated with the phrase Pygmalion Effect in American education.

3. There was no information in this work as to what kinds of teacher behavior, if any, accounted for the I.Q. gains (irregular and inconsistent) of some of the children predicted to "bloom." No observations of teachers, systematic or otherwise, were conducted, and in fact the teachers could not, for the most part, even remember which children had been predicted to have a learning spurt.

4. There was no such finding in the Coleman material, but apparently no one in the courtroom was aware of this. St. John (1971) notes that teachers in slum schools who have high expectations for their students tend to leave these settings (p. 429), but this consequence was never mentioned.

5. Snow (1969), pp. 197, 199. The reference to Huff is to his *How To Lie with Statistics* (New York: Norton, 1954).

6. Buckley (1968), p. 124.

7. Thorndike (1968), pp. 708, 711.

8. Claiborn (1969), pp. 382–83.

9. Dusek (1973), p. 1.

10. Fleming and Anttonen (1971), pp. 241, 250.

11. José and Cody (1971), p. 48.

12. Barber and Silver (1968a).

13. Barber et al. (1969).

14. Among the studies that have reported confirmation of some aspects of the expectancy hypothesis in schools are those of Palardy (1969), Rubovits and Maehr (1973), and Rist (1970).

15. Smith (1972), pp. 262, 268–69.

16. Fein (1971), p. 114.

17. Quoted in Friedman (1969), p. 402.

18. No distinction between "tracks" and "ability groups" was made, although some educators contend that grouping by proficiency or ability is quite different from provision of alternate curricula or tracks at the secondary school level on a basis of choice. A rather extreme form of high school tracking was found to intensify I. Q. differences (Rosenbaum, 1975).

19. 269 F. Supp. 401 (1967).

20. See, for example, Dimond (1972b, p. 31), who says that any grouping or tracking procedure that results in a disproportionate racial composition may be a suspect classification and in some states is simply illegal.

21. See Chapter 6.

22. Probably the court reporter's rendering of "this perception."

23. See Murphy and Cohen (1974) for an account of this program.

24. Jencks (1972), pp. 34, 96, 107.

25. National Education Association (1968), Heathers (1969), and Bryan (1971).

26. Borg (1966), p. 92.

27. Dyer (1968), p. 54.

28. Crain et al. (1973), pp. 85, 135.

29. Smith (1972), p. 278.

30. Throughout these proceedings, at both the trial and the remedy stages, the conten-

tion that no students would be harmed by placement in classrooms containing large proportions of pupils with educational problems went unchallenged. The basis for this, when a rationale *is* offered, is that test results show no loss to such children. But the claim is spurious when the tests are based on the attainment of standard levels of proficiency and simply do not include materials that could have been offered in other classroom settings. See Goldberg, Passow, and Justman (1966), p. 153. See also Hacker (1972), pp. 184–85.

31. Judge Roth's failure to understand that Cass Tech's singular success was due primarily to its admission requirements and classes for bright students, as well as to its special curricula, is apparent from his pre-trial comments on magnet schools (see the Introduction). NAACP counsel Lucas did characterize Cass as a "school for high track kids" in a question to Superintendent Drachler during the latter's deposition (p. 154), but this was near the end of the trial. The deposition was not taken in the courtroom, and the judge may not have read it.

32. Kirp and Yudof (1974), ch. 7. For an example of the error of attributing the cause of a condition to the instrument that detects it, see Michigan Law Review (1973, pp. 1218–19), where social science writings are cited to "prove" that bias inheres in tests that show a strong correlation between test scores and socioeconomic status. A recent empirical study of curriculum placement in city high schools (Heyns, 1974) shows that background characteristics are almost entirely mediated by differential scholastic achievement. Ethnicity and social class circumstances may produce differences in scholastic achievement, but school placement is usually based on this achievement whatever its causes may be.

Chapter 9

1. This view has not gone unchallenged by those who contend that while the right to open access on a non-discriminatory basis is self-evident, the assertion that racial mixture is a remedy for such discrimination is not. Fiss (1975) observes that it is difficult to define mixture as a remedy unless there are demonstrable benefits from it, and Goodman (1972) suggests that substantial empirical verification of such benefits seems reasonable if dispersion is to be imposed upon persons, most of them white, but including some blacks as well, who are adverse to it.

2. The frequent references to the "widening" or "worsening" gap between disadvantaged and other children as they progress through school suggest that the process of schooling itself lowers their academic proficiency. This is not the case. Rather, schools have thus far been generally unable to eliminate the deficit with which the disadvantaged learner begins, and the longer this failure continues, the farther behind the student falls. (See Chapter 6, n. 3, above for further explanation.) See also Coleman et al. (1966), p. 220.

3. See Coleman (1966). Campbell (1973) is a lucid and valuable presentation of the issues involved.

4. Coleman et al. (1966), p. 22. See Caldwell (1970), Grant (1973), and Young and Bress (1975) for discussion of some of the concerns that may have affected the writing of the summary. Hodgson (1973) offers helpful insights on the early impact of the Report.

5. Dyer (1968), p. 53.

6. Coleman (1967). But it must be noted that in some sections of his testimony before the Senate Select Committee on Equal Educational Opportunity an apparent wish to be as supportive of integration efforts as possible overcame his characteristic scholarly caution; see the committee proceedings of April 21, 1970. See also Cain and Watts (1970); Sewell, Marscuilo, and Pfautz (1967); Nichols (1968).

7. See Wilson (1959), a study that reported what Wilson called some negative "effects" (in fact, they were statistical correlations) of predominantly working-class school composition upon middle-class children. In 1973, summarizing research on the effects of race mixtures upon whites, Sheldon White concluded: "We simply do not know how and to what degree substantial school desegregation would affect white children" (p. 19). Wilson's study of Richmond, California (1969), does suggest that a predominantly lower-class school has some adverse effects on white achievement; see his fifth chapter.

8. Greeley and Rossi (1966), using the usual controls for social background, found that children who attended Catholic schools were higher achievers than those in public schools. They speculate that the decision to spend for parochial schooling may reflect some family characteristics that escape the usual SES controls used by researchers.

9. Levin (1968), p. 67.

10. St. John (1970).

11. Mosteller and Moynihan, eds. (1972), present a number of scholarly analyses of the Coleman Report data. See also Averch et al. (1972), p. 148; Grant (1972); Jencks (1972); and White (1973). The last of these presents a comprehensive summary of research. While cautiously positive on the probable enhancing effects of higher-status peers upon low achievers, White concludes that since the "measured outcomes of desegregation are not likely to be sufficiently large to compel desegregation as a strictly educational strategy, it would be more fruitful if desegregation were debated and judged in social and political terms" (p. 20, Appendix IIA).

12. Dimond (1972a), p. 46.

13. See Hsia, on Evanston (1971), and Armor (1972, 1973). In a ten-year study of Riverside busing, Gerard and Miller (1975) failed to find academic gains for black children there. A remarkable but little-known work was done on schools in Oakland, California, by Spaulding (1967); longitudinal data on black children in mixed and black classrooms did not show any effects from classroom composition (p. 109).

14. St. John (1975), p. 36.

Chapter 10

1. Coleman et al. (1966), p. 280.

2. *Ibid.*, p. 320.

3. Jencks et al. (1972), pp. 35, 154. Crain (1971) found that black children who attended predominantly white northern schools had higher levels of aspiration than those who attended schools that were predominantly black. His findings may reflect the characteristics of the minority of black families who live in predominantly white neighborhoods.

4. Wolf and Lebeaux (1969), p. 563.

5. See Zirkel and Moses (1971), p. 260; for a review of research, see pp. 253–54.

6. Rosenberg and Simmons (1971), pp. 24–25.

7. Coleman et al. (1966), pp. 288, 324.

8. McCarthy and Yancey (1971).

9. Heiss and Owens (1972), p. 369.

10. Asher and Allen (1969), p. 164.

11. Hsia (1971), pp. 4, 94, 107.

12. St. John (1971), p. 594.

13. St. John (1975), p. 53.

14. Powell (1973), pp. 256, 280–81. The findings to which Guthrie referred in his testimony, quoted above (T, pp. 4121–22), do not appear in this book, which had

not been published at the time. Perhaps he was referring to other (unpublished) research.

15. Porter (1971), pp. 85–86.
16. *Ibid.*, pp. 101–7.
17. *Ibid.*, pp. 200–212.
18. See Simpson and Yinger (1972); Davis (1966); and St. John (1975), especially pp. 58–60.
19. See Wolf (1972–73), p. 169, referring to the Allport (1958) proposition; Williams et al. (1964), pp. 191, 219; Simpson and Yinger (1972), p. 683. St. John's 1975 book is of great value, especially ch. 4.
20. See, for example, Dentler and Elkin's study of prejudice among sixth-graders, in which the following items were used as measures of "anti-Negro bias": "Many Negro children like to use bad words"; "Negro boys are tougher than white boys when they get mad"; "A lot of Negro children don't do their homework at all"; etc. (Dentler and Elkins, in Dentler, Mackler, and Warshauer [1967]). Despite the colloquial language, these are empirical propositions with general support in the sociological literature. Indeed, the authors themselves, in the same article, observe that "intelligence and reading ability . . . increases as per cent Negro [in school] decreases," a statement which, if offered in simpler words by the children in the study, would have been categorized as an indicator of prejudice. Not surprisingly, bias, as these researchers measured it, was lower in all-white schools than in predominantly black or "unsegregated" (their term) ones (pp. 63–73). In a study reported in the same volume, Lang and Lang found that opposition to a school pairing program for integration was greater among parents who had lived in a racially mixed area than among those who had not (Lang and Lang [1967], p. 51). Greeley and Rossi did not find graduates of overwhelmingly white Catholic schools to be more prejudiced than graduates of non-Catholic schools (Greeley and Rossi [1966], pp. 121–24). See also Mackie (1973) and Campbell (1967).
21. Beginning with the work of Richard LaPiere (1934), there has been a continuous stream of research and controversy on the question of the relationship between opinion statements and other types of behavior. See Blumer (1955), Rose (1956), and Deutscher (1966) for efforts at formulating the general principles involved in these relationships. There is also a voluminous literature of surveys and syntheses of a host of empirical studies: see, e.g., Wicker (1969), who concluded: "Taken as a whole these studies suggest that it is considerably more likely that attitudes will be unrelated to overt behavior than that attitudes will be closely related to action . . . . only rarely can as much as 10% of the variance in overt behavioral measures be accounted for by attitudinal data" (p. 65). See also Amir (1969).
22. See Schuman (1969) for opinion data showing that only a small proportion of people now believe that group differences in behavior are of biological origin.
23. St. John (1975), p. 80. See also a review of research by Carithers, who states: "There is no general agreement about the effects of interracial contact. . . . We simply do not know what happens to whom under what conditions of school desegregation" (1970, pp. 41–45). Wolf and Simon (1975) is one of several recent studies that found no improvement in interracial relations among children after several years of a busing program.

Chapter 11

1. There is a substantial literature on this subject; see, e.g., Altshuler (1970); Fantini, Gittell, and Magat (1970); Glazer (1969); Goldbloom (1969); Mayer (1969); and Ravitch (1972). A *New York Times* headline of March 18, 1970, read: "Drive to Decentralize Schools Gains over U.S." See also Bell (1976).

2. See Fein (1971) for a valuable analysis; also Eisinger (1973); Hamilton (1968); Haskins (1969).
3. See Cohen (1969); Kirp (1970), especially pp. 1365–66; Grant (1971), on the events in Detroit; also Dimond (1970); Pindur (1972).
4. Wolf (1969).

Overview, Part III

1. *Bradley v. Milliken* (1971), at 593.
2. *Bradley v. Milliken* (1973), at 242.
3. *Deal v. Cincinnati Board of Education*, 369 F.2d 55 (6th Cir. 1966).
4. Fiss (1971), p. 705.
5. *Ibid.* Whether or not this concern justifies the use of a contrived theory is for the reader to decide.
6. *Bradley v. Milliken* (1971), at 592.
7. This laudatory section began: "It would be unfair for us not to recognize the many fine steps the Board has taken to advance the cause of quality education for all in terms of racial integration and human relations" (*ibid.*, at 589, and continuing at 590–92).
8. *Ibid.*, at 588.
9. *Bradley v. Milliken* (1973), at 227–32.
10. *Bradley v. Milliken* (1971), at 588.
11. *Bradley v. Milliken* (1973), at 222–27. Some references to optional areas are also included in these pages.
12. *Bradley v. Milliken* (1971), at 587, 588.
13. *Bradley v. Milliken* (1973), at 232–35.

Chapter 12

1. *Bradley v. Milliken* (1973), at 237.
2. Detroit, Michigan, Board of Education, *Findings and Recommendations of the Citizens Advisory Committee on Equal Educational Opportunities* (1962), p. x. The chairman of the subcommittee on school facilities was Damon Keith, later a federal district judge. In the Pontiac school case he declared the system segregated de jure on grounds similar to those used in Detroit.
3. *Bradley v. Milliken* (1971), at 589.
4. See recommendations of the Citizens Advisory Committee on School Needs, quoted in Detroit Public Schools, *Inventory of Facility Needs* (1972), p. 12.
5. *Bradley v. Milliken* (1971), at 588, citing the joint policy statement on equality of educational opportunity of the Board of Education of the State of Michigan and the Michigan Civil Rights Commission, April 23, 1966.
6. *Ibid.*, citing the state Board of Education, *School Plant Planning Handbook*. Since housing costs tend to be quite similar within a small area, the notion that proper siting of walk-in schools could avoid socioeconomic homogeneity is without foundation.
7. Quoted by Kaplan, in Hill and Feeley, eds. (1968), p. 154.
8. Fiss (1971), p. 704, n. 13, quoting from *Swann*.

Chapter 13

1. "For some years it was a Board of Education policy to transport classrooms of black children intact to white schools where they were educated in segregated classes" (*Bradley v. Milliken* [1973], at 230).

2. *Ibid.*, at 230–32.
3. *Bradley v. Milliken* (1971), at 588. The comments quoted are the sole reference to this matter to be found in Judge Roth's ruling, but the appeals court greatly elaborated upon it.
4. *Bradley v. Milliken* (1973), at 221.
5. *Ibid.*, at 227–30.
6. During the 1966–1967 school year the busing policy was altered from one of racial disregard to one that gave the superintendent some discretion. If otherwise feasible, he could transport students past the nearest school with space, if integration would not be enhanced there, to another school where a better racial mix would be obtained (T, pp. 2815–16, 3402).
7. Parents had been assured repeatedly that as soon as the Ruthruff school addition was completed those who wished to do so could transfer their children back to Ruthruff (*Minutes of the Detroit Board of Education*, May 27, 1969, pp. 727–29). The parents' protest and demands to be returned to Ruthruff was supported by the NAACP (p. 727). These minutes also confirm school records as to the numbers involved (p. 727).
8. Foster also discussed the busing in 1960 from the almost half-black Jefferson Junior High to the all-black Hutchins (T, pp. 1489–1500). Since the bypassing of white schools with unused capacity was not an issue in this case, and since the appeals court listed the Jefferson–Hutchins case as a rezoning rather than a busing violation, it is not included here.
9. *Bradley v. Milliken* (1971), at 588. The defendants' expert witness offered as an excuse the fact that compensatory education programs in inner-city schools required sharply reduced class size (T, pp. 3186–87). This is true, but there is no evidence whatever that, regardless of available space, children from better residential areas would have been reassigned to inner-city schools. Superintendent Drachler in his deposition referred to the uproar from parents of both races created by any hint of transportation to a "worse," i.e., poorer, neighborhood (T, Drachler Deposition, June 28, 1971, p. 50).

Chapter 14

1. *Bradley v. Milliken* (1971), at 587–88.
2. *Bradley v. Milliken* (1973), at 232.
3. After World War II and throughout the 1950s civil rights organizations in Michigan made strenuous and generally successful efforts to have government agencies drop racial designations on their records. No racial count was taken in the schools until 1961, when opinions on this question began to change.
4. From the testimony of Foster and Henrickson, we have ascertained the dates of the elimination of the various optional zones:

Zone	Year Eliminated	Source
1. Northwestern–Chadsey	1960	T, p. 1432
2. Central–Northern	1961	T, p. 1428
3. Northwestern–Northern	1962	T, p. 1430
4. Central–Mackenzie	1962	T, p. 1418, 3121–22
5. Southeastern–Denby	1962	T, p. 3154
6. Thomas–Greusel	1962	T, p. 3159–60
7. Chadsey–Mackenzie	1963	T, p. 3151

Zone	Year Eliminated	Sources
8. Northwestern–Western	1963	T, pp. 1438–39
	(partial)	
	1964	
	(partial)	
	1965	
	(complete)	
9. Southwestern–Western	1970	T, pp. 1467, 1469, 3426
	(partial)	
	1971	
	(complete)	

These elimination dates were confirmed in the testimony of a witness for the plaintiffs, William Lamson (T, pp. 1227–47).

5. Plaintiffs' Exhibit 128A, Joint Appendix Volume IX B, pp. 333–44.
6. A careful study would be required to establish why some black students, even in 1970–1971, were using the transfer-to-white options available to them under the open school policy, while others were not.
7. See Plaintiffs' Exhibit 128A, pp. 340, 352.
8. See Wolf and Lebeaux (1969) on the Bagley area and Lafayette Park.
9. Both court decisions noted that the defendants' witness had substantiated the discriminatory nature of the Western–Southwestern option (Henrickson stated that it "can be said to have frustrated integration . . . over the decade" [T, p. 3421]). It was never brought out during the trial that Western was widely regarded as a model of a successful multiethnic school. Both Western (approximately 40 percent black and 20 percent Hispanic) and its surrounding neighborhood were lauded by civil rights groups and received considerable media coverage as examples of stable integration.
10. *Bradley v. Milliken* (1971), at 588.
11. *Milliken v. Bradley*, 418 U. S. 717 (1974), at 785. The majority opinion, at 725, also accepted this finding. The ruling that Detroit was segregated de jure was not appealed before the Supreme Court by any party.

Chapter 15

1. *Bradley v. Milliken* (1971), at 588.
2. *Bradley v. Milliken* (1973), at 222–27.
3. *Ibid.*, at 222–26.
4. One proposal was to eliminate the Chadsey–Mackenzie option and assign the all-black Sherrill students to Chadsey, which still had a white majority but had a larger proportion of blacks than Mackenzie. The other was to eliminate the Central–Mackenzie option and assign the predominantly black Winterhalter and McKerrow students to the almost all-black Central.
5. *Bradley v. Milliken* (1973), at 225.
6. *Ibid.*, at 227.
7. *Ibid.*
8. *Bradley v. Milliken* (1971), at 588.
9. The Sixth Circuit ruling did not specify the number of discriminatory feeder pattern alterations but merely listed the schools involved. From the record we determined the actual number of changes to be ten. The ruling first cited testimony on four schools involved in two violative changes (the Vernor–Vandenberg changes, which are discussed next in the text). An additional twenty-four schools were listed

(excluding Higginbotham and Courville), which the record indicates were involved in eight changes. Hence there were ten feeder changes (twelve, if Higginbotham and Courville, in which no segregatory changes were specified, according to the record, are included).

10. During 1960 and 1961 the board was in process of firming up its school boundaries and providing uniform articulation patterns. In explaining the changes that occurred in those years, Henrickson mentioned other factors as well, e.g., elimination of dangerous or circuitous routes; in every case, however, considerations of capacity were involved.

11. *Bradley v. Milliken* (1973), at 226.

12. *Bradley v. Milliken* (1971), at 588.

13. Taeuber (1975), p. 835.

14. Farley (1975), pp. 166, 180.

15. *Bradley v. Milliken* (1973), at 250.

16. *Bradley v. Milliken* (1971), at 588.

17. *Ibid*.

18. Sheldon and Glazier (1965), pp. 75–76. Similar assessments have been offered by even the most fervent proponents of court-ordered racial reassignment, including the U. S. Commission on Civil Rights; see *Racial Isolation in the Schools* (1967), p. 154; Pettigrew, in Katz and Gurin, eds. (1969), p. 95.

Chapter 16

1. See Richter (1972) for a discussion of the acts of school systems which the courts may use to support the causal theory of government responsibility for racially imbalanced schools.

2. *Milliken v. Bradley*, 418 U. S. 717 (1974), at 779 (Justice White dissenting).

3. *Bradley v. Milliken* (1973), at 241, 242.

4. *Swann v. Charlotte–Mecklenburg Board of Education, 402 U.S. 1 (1971), at 20–21.*

5. *Bradley v. Milliken* (1971), at 587. Perhaps this doctrine, cited in *Swann*, was a carryover from some of the old Southern school cases, for it seems reasonable that in the Jim Crow South, where black children were legally restricted to certain schools, school location would have some influence on household location. But Justice Thurgood Marshall's dissent in *Milliken* incorporates a very strange application of the "corresponding effect" doctrine to the Northern situation: "The state's creation, through de jure acts of segregation, of a growing core of all-Negro schools inevitably acted as a magnet to attract Negroes to the areas served by such schools and to deter them from settling either in other areas of the city or in the suburbs" (*Milliken v. Bradley*, 418 U. S. 717 [1974], at 805). It is indeed surprising that Justice Marshall believed that all-black schools were so attractive to Detroit's black parents that they rejected other residential locations in order to place their children in these schools.

6. See, for example, "Lafayette Park," in Wolf and Lebeaux (1969).

7. See "The Bagley Area" in *ibid*.; Molotch (1972); Bradburn, Sudman, and Gockel (1971), ch. 9.

8. See Palen (1975), pp. 216, 218; also Clotfelter (1975), pp. 263–68.

9. Suttles (1968), pp. 58–59; Real Estate Research Corporation (1976).

10. Blumberg and Lalli (1966), p. 130.

11. Gerard and Miller (1975, p. 47) report that between 1965 and 1971 fifteen black families in Riverside, California, had moved into "predominantly Anglo areas." In Evanston, Illinois, Berry et al. found no evidence of change in the usual patterns of racial transition (in Schwartz [1976], pp. 234–35).

12. See, for example, Pettigrew and Green (1976); Rossell (1975–76). This is the essence of the "white flight" controversy.
13. This statement, along with other similarly unsupported "social science" generalizations, was quoted in the 1973 ruling of the Sixth Circuit Court of Appeals, at 234, for example.
14. U. S. Commission on Civil Rights (1967), p. 154. The evidence for the relative stability of city-wide and metropolitan remedies is considered in Chapter 17 below.
15. Quoted in *ibid*. See also Sheldon and Glazier (1965); Farley and Taeuber (1974), p. 905; and Farley (1975), pp. 169, 193.
16. "The Bagley Community Council," in Wolf and Lebeaux (1969).
17. Pettigrew (1969), p. 95.
18. Taeuber's prepared statement is quoted from part 5, p. 2731, of the August 25 hearings of the Senate Select Committee on Equal Educational Opportunity (1970).
19. *Ibid.*, p. 2747.
20. Hanley (1974) also made this point (pp. 130–31).
21. Taeuber (1975), pp. 843–44.
22. Katzman (1973), pp. 67–79.
23. As late as 1967, for example, the Illinois Supreme Court held unconstitutional the provision of the state's Armstrong Act which called for student assignment on a racial basis to achieve integration, declaring: "Although today a court might rule that the state is required to consider race in a benign way, tomorrow this might well prove a precedent for a much less happy result. . . . We hold that programs to create equal educational opportunities must under the equal protection clause of the fourteenth amendment . . . be administered without regard to race" (quoted by Hill and Feeley, in Hill and Feeley, eds. [1968], pp. 102–3). For an excellent discussion of this issue, see Kaplan (1963).

Chapter 17

1. From the "Colloquy of Court and Counsel, October 4, 1971," Vol. 1a, p. 217, of the *Joint Appendix, Pleadings*.
2. For a helpful discussion of the concerns that influenced NAACP strategy, see Beer (1975). Louis Beer was an associate of George Roumell, who replaced Bushnell as Board attorney.
3. Mosteller and Moynihan (1972).
4. Coleman et al. (1966), p. 307.
5. Bailey (1970), p. 31.
6. See Justice Weick's dissent in *Bradley v. Milliken* (1973), at 268–69, for a description of the conditions of suburban participation; see also the Supreme Court ruling in *Milliken v. Bradley* (1974), at 731.
7. See Judge Roth's "Findings of Fact and Conclusions of Law on Detroit-Only Plans of Desegregation," dated March 28, 1972, Vol. 16, pp. 456–60.
8. The 1970 census showed 9.5 percent of persons in the Detroit S.M.S.A. to be college graduates and 19 percent to have some college training: 6 percent of adults in the city of Detroit were found to be college graduates. It is true that parents of schoolchildren would be younger and would be more likely to have some college education than others, but according to data supplied by the State Board of Education approximately 10 percent of school-age children in the area attended non-public schools. Most of these children were from more prosperous households, while lower-income families contributed somewhat disproportionately to public school enrollment.

9. Suburban counsel began to quote from a Coleman paper which had just been published: "There is not sufficient evidence to show that the kinds of benefits to lower-SES class children that come from a . . . heterogeneous school cannot also be provided by other means" (Coleman [1972], pp. 15–16, quoted in T, MR, pp. 1389–90). Coleman's criticism of judicial busing orders which were based on the assumption that racial concentration alone constitutes educational inequality (see pp. 13–14) was not quoted.

10. There is little longitudinal research on this matter. A study that has such data found some unfavorable effects; see Justman, in Passow, Goldberg, and Tannenbaum (1967); see also Inbar (1976).

11. *Detroit News*, July 28, 1971. For a study of crime in and near urban schools, see Lalli and Savitz (1977); their data were gathered in 1971.

12. Palen (1975), p. 152.

13. Stegman (1969), p. 28.

14. *Ibid.*, p. 25; Michelson (1968).

15. See Orfield (1974–75), pp. 781–82. The declining school population in some all-white suburbs near Detroit had caused the closing of some elementary schools by 1976.

16. Data on these trends are now available; see *Mobility of the Population of the U. S., Series P-20, No. 285 (March 1970–1975)*. Survey data suggest that these movements reflect long-standing wishes to be "farther away from the center of things"; see Michelson (1968), p. 39.

17. The use of private schools in some southern districts under busing orders is described as "a mass movement" that has "drastically altered racial balances in the public schools"; see Giles, Cataldo, and Gatlin (1975), p. 22; also Clotfelter (1976), pp. 29–30. The latter notes that "the available evidence gives no reason to believe that there will be significant declines."

18. See n. 8 above.

19. From "Findings of Fact and Conclusions of Law in Support of Ruling on Desegregation Area and Development of Plan, June 14, 1972."

20. *Milliken v. Bradley* (1974).

21. See his *Memorandum Opinion and Remedial Decree* of July 3, 1975, and *Memorandum and Order*, November 4, 1975.

22. Quoted in *Detroit Free Press*, August 17, 1975.

23. Quoted in *National Observer*, September 6, 1975.

24. *Bradley v. Milliken*, U. S. Sixth Circuit Court of Appeals, No. 75-2018, August 4, 1976.

25. *Detroit Free Press*, September 7, 1977.

Chapter 18

1. After this chapter was written I read Professor Charles L. Black's comments in 1970 before the Senate Select Committee on Equal Educational Opportunity, in which he warned that school desegregation is endangered by defining it. He drew a comparison with the law's "wise" refusal to define fraud: "there are few things more certain to play into the hands of segregationists than the giving to them of neat formulas with which, and only with which, they have to comply in order to put themselves beyond the reach of the whole equity of the Constitution" (p. 2221). The refusal to define a term because there is a strategic advantage to doing so is a sharp contrast to the norms of science. It would appear that the plaintiffs in the school cases have been following Black's advice.

2. See Rader (1970); Dimond (1972a); Fiss (1974); Goodman (1972); Horowitz and Karst (1969); Kurland (1968); Read (1975); and Yudof (1973).
3. *Milliken v. Bradley* (1974), at 746.
4. "Findings of Fact and Conclusions of Law on Detroit-Only Plans of Desegregation," March 28, 1972, affirmed by the Sixth Circuit Court of Appeals in *Bradley v. Milliken* (1973), at 244.
5. *Ibid*.
6. Yudof (1973), p. 439.
7. The use by government of racial classifications for purportedly benign purposes was of doubtful legality for many years (see Chapter 16, n. 23, above). Benign quotas to maintain or secure racial mixture in public housing were ruled unconstitutional in a case involving New York.
8. Flannery (1972).
9. Levin and Moise (1975), p. 106. Justice Thurgood Marshall's dissent in *Milliken*, at 801, also stated that "Detroit-only desegregation would be a futile exercise leading only to white flight," but it was a violation of the Constitution for the Detroit Board of Education to come to this conclusion.
10. *Bradley v. Milliken*, August 4, 1976, p. 7.
11. *Ibid.*, p. 14.
12. *Ibid.*, p. 16.
13. *Ibid.*, p. 17.
14. *Ibid*. I believe that the Sixth Circuit wanted to give judicial support to the plaintiffs' position that, following a finding of de jure segregation, pupil reassignment to create schools of roughly similar racial composition cannot depend on whether some believe that the black proportion is "too high."
15. Friedman (1969), p. 47. See also *ibid.*, pp. 49, 375.
16. Rosen (1972), p. 27.

Chapter 19

1. Cahn (1955), pp. 157–58, 167. See Coons (1977), esp. pp. 56–59.
2. For various aspects of the use of social science evidence in *Brown*, see Black (1960); Cahn (1955, 1956, 1962), pp. 127–33; Clark (1960); Friedman (1969); Gregor (1963a and b); Heyman (1961); Kalven, in Hazard (1968); Kelly (1964); Konvitz (1958); Levin and Moise (1975), pp. 52–54; Rosen (1972); and Wechsler (1959).
3. Among the few social scientists to express criticisms of the quality of the material and concern about its use as a basis for such an important decision were Berger (1957) and Van Den Haag (1960). See also Berns (1963).
4. Clark (1963), p. 38. See also Clark, quoted in the *New York Times*, June 11, 1972; Clark (1973, 1976).
5. *New York Times*, June 11, 1972.
6. *Ibid*.
7. John Davis, counsel for the southern school systems, called attention during the *Brown* litigation to the fact that the Clarks' famous doll studies, for example, did not support the conclusion drawn from them (see Friedman [1969], pp. 58–59). I doubt that any sociologists knew of Davis' criticism; if they had, they might have dismissed anything from such a suspect source. Much later, Horowitz (1970, p. 7) observed that the research cited in *Brown* could "barely pass as a college term paper." Criticism of this kind was quite rare, however, probably because of fear that such candor might harm civil rights efforts; see Wolf (1972).
8. *Hobson v. Hansen*, 269 F. Supp. 401 (1967).
9. *Ibid.*, at 419.

10. *Ibid.*, at 420. Since I have not read the trial record, I cannot say whether Coleman was quoted correctly.
11. *Ibid.*, at 482, 484, 491, 514.
12. *Ibid.*, at 514.
13. Ibid., at 407.
14. *Ibid.*, at 504.
15. *Ibid.*, at 497. Horowitz (1977) has a superb discussion of this case.
16. Dimond (1972a), p. 46.
17. *Bradley v. School Board of City of Richmond*, 338 F. Supp. 67 (E. D. Va. 1972). See also Craven (1975). The plaintiffs' expert on education, Robert Green, is also quoted in another Michigan ruling, *Oliver v. Kalamazoo Board of Education*, 368 F. Supp. 143 (W. D. Mich. 1973).
18. *Keyes v. School District No. 1*, 313 F. Supp. 51 (D. Colo. 1970).
19. *Hart v. Community School Board of Brooklyn, N.Y.*, 383 F. Supp. 699 (1974), at 714, 725, 728–29, 731, 739, 744–45, 746–47.
20. *Reed v. Rhodes*, 422 F. Supp. 708 (1976).
21. See Rosen (1972), p. 28, for a discussion of this influence.
22. *Buck v. Bell*, 274 U.S. 200 (1927). The impact of the then-popular eugenics movement is seen in a comment by Oliver Wendell Holmes (1915), p. 3: "Wholesale social regeneration . . . cannot be affected appreciably by tinkering with the institution of property but only by taking in hand life and trying to build a race."
23. For somewhat contrasting views see Fiss (1971, 1974, 1975) and Goodman (1972).
24. Yudof (1973), pp. 456–64. This excellent paper is a most valuable contribution.
25. *Ibid.*, p. 457.
26. The plaintiffs' co-counsel in *Milliken*, J. Harold Flannery (1972), asserts that Northern school segregation is caused by "readily quantifiable, observable, empirically demonstrable forces, more often than not involving school authorities" (p. 17). Later (p. 21) he revises this assessment: "it's very difficult to quantify the segregationist effect of school board policies and practices going back over the years." It is astonishing that sociologists and demographers have not challenged this analysis of racial concentration in schools. My original research proposal to the Ford Foundation did not include a study of the causal adequacy of the evidence used to support this "theory" of school segregation because, like others, I did not then think of it in those terms. It was only after studying the trial record that I gradually began to understand the nature of this approach.
27. Murphy and Pritchett (1961), p. 317, observe that "the judicial fact-finding process, a highly ritualized trial by battle of wits, is not used in any other area of human activity . . . where there is need to determine facts or verify data."
28. *Bradley v. Milliken*, at 585 (see Appendix A), gives the black proportion in Detroit in 1920 as 9 percent, a figure not reached until almost twenty years later. But a table on the next page has 4 percent, the correct proportion.
29. *Ibid.*
30. *Ibid.*
31. Quoted by Levin and Hawley (1975), p. 3.
32. See Henry Levin (1975), p. 234, for some astute comments on this subject.
33. Piehler et al. (1974), p. 1091.
34. The president of the American Sociological Association, Alfred McClung Lee, sought in 1976 to persuade the A.S.A. executive council to censure James Coleman. His attempt failed. Nathaniel Jones, general counsel for the NAACP, described Coleman as a "fraud . . . thoroughly repudiated by his colleagues" (*Detroit Free Press*, December 8, 1975). Dr. Kenneth Clark charged that Coleman had "deliberately misled" the public (Clark [1976], p. 5). Antagonism to Coleman may have been kindled by his cautions regarding court-ordered busing programs (see

Coleman [1972]), but it became intense after his research in 1975 on "white flight" and after a deposition of his was used by an anti-busing group in Boston that same year.

On June 13, 1972, the *Washington Post* reported that David Armor's Harvard office had been the target of vandalism after he gave a deposition (May 24, 1972) on behalf of suburban defendant-intervenors in the Detroit metropolitan remedy hearings. The *Post* quoted praise of Armor's research from colleagues who asked not to be identified for fear of reprisals or condemnation, while officials of the Detroit and the Boston branches of the NAACP characterized Armor as a "racist" (*Detroit News*, May 25, 1972). The *Wall Street Journal* on March 7, 1974, reported efforts to discourage publication of findings by Harold Gerard on the questionable effects of racial dispersion in the schools of Riverside, California, and the opposition to publication of the work of Gerald Lesser on ethnic differences in patterns of cognitive functioning. Lesser (1976) states that his 1968 study remains unreported because his colleagues were "adamant" in their belief that publication would tend to invite the misuse of its findings for "racist causes" (p. 145).

A similar policy was advocated by one of the speakers at a University of Michigan conference on school desegregation and the law: "If your news people can't find anything good to say about the desegregation of schools tell them to keep their opinions to themselves" (see University of Michigan, School of Education [1972], p. 68). Christopher Jencks' research on the effect of school variables, including peer effects, was described by Kenneth Clark as revealing "racial biases" (Clark [1973], p. 82).

35. Earlier efforts by civil rights groups to obliterate racial designations on government records and to refrain from gathering such data even for research were widespread. See Nesbitt ([1960–61], p. 66) for a reference to the American Civil Liberties Union's attempt to have the United States Census Bureau cease collecting information involving race because "to do so raises the specter of some threatened discrimination." During the trial Judge Roth misinterpreted the Detroit Citizens Advisory Committee on Equal Educational Opportunities report of 1962 as having recommended racial balance in teacher assignment (T, p. 4338). In fact, such a policy was unthinkable at that time; see pp. IX and 81 of the report. The entire stress of the civil rights movement during this period was one of insistence on racial disregard in employment, but no one made this clear to Judge Roth, leaving him to conclude that a commitment to racial balance had been ignored for several years before the trial. For examples of the NAACP's earlier support of color-blind geographic school assignment, see its official organ, *Crisis* —for example, issues of November, 1946, January, 1949, June–July, 1955, and November, 1956.

36. The extent to which "intent to segregate" need be demonstrated and what evidence is required to demonstrate such intent is still unclear and is much discussed in the law journals. See, for example, Read (1975), pp. 41–43; Marshall (1975). Some later court rulings during 1977 suggest that this requirement may be more important in future cases. Failure to declare a goal of integration has been cited as support for charges of de jure segregation, but so has the failure to implement a declared goal. See *Hobson v. Hansen*, 269 F. Supp. 401 (1967), at 441, wherein Judge J. Skelly Wright characterized as "indifference and inaction" the failure of the District of Columbia School Board (in an overwhelmingly black school system) to "install actual integration as an objective of administration policy."

37. School officials who ignore these strictures do so at their peril. For example, when Superintendent Harold Spears of San Francisco openly referred to societal disadvantages, such as family size and deviant speech patterns, that make language skills more difficult to acquire, civil rights groups responded as if he had added "insult to injury"; see Kaplan, in Hill and Feeley, eds. (1968), p. 68.

38. Piehler et al. (1974) report that technical experts in product liability cases find adversary proceedings "personally degrading."
39. Moore (1972), pp. 95–96.
40. Kelly (1962), p. 14. The problem of distortion due to pressure for advocacy in the testimony of physical scientists is recognized by Piehler et al. (1974), p. 1092. See also Rose, in Lazarsfeld, ed. (1967); Wolfgang (1974).
41. Kelly (1962), p. 21; Kelly (1965).
42. Weinberg (1976), p. 23.
43. Even a copy of a court's ruling often costs more than one hundred dollars. Because of the format of a trial, evidence on a given topic may be found throughout. For example, to know all that was told to Judge Roth on the subject of residential segregation, the full trial record and the transcript of the remedy hearings must be read. The cost of such a copy would be about ten thousand dollars.
44. *Deal v. Cincinnati Board of Education*, 369 F.2d 55 (6th Cir. 1966).
45. See Beer (1975). Although a careful review of the trial record by the appellate courts would have revealed internal inconsistencies in the evidence, these courts are even less suited to the task of ascertainment of facts than a district court. See Katz (1971). Murphy and Pritchett (1961) note how rarely appellate courts challenge the factual determinations of the trial judge (p. 315).
46. Deposition of David Armor, May 24, 1972.
47. *Findings of Fact and Conclusions of Law in Support of Ruling on Desegregation Area and Development of Plan* (E.D. Mich. June 14, 1972), C.A. 35257.
48. Cahn (1963), p. 1037, quoting James Fitzjames Stephens. A discussion of the differing degrees of certainty that can reasonably be expected in law and science follows.
49. Berns (1963), p. 212. See also Hazard (1967), pp. 74–75. See Horowitz (1977). This splendid book appeared after my own analysis had been completed.
50. Maslow (1959–60), p. 245.
51. McGurk (1959–60).
52. Korn (1966), p. 1094.
53. Weinstein (1966), p. 243.
54. Rosen (1972), p. 201; see also Rosen (1977).
55. Miller and Barron (1975).
56. Katz (1971, p. 55) observes that the Supreme Court is "simply not adequately equipped to operate as an independent fact-finding agency . . . nor can it take into account, except under very limited circumstances . . . any information that is not contained in the Record on Appeal or in the briefs of counsel." For an excellent analysis of the relationship between social science research and policy concerning school desegregation, see Cohen and Weiss (1976).
57. See n. 4 above.
58. Kalven, quoting Edwin Patterson, in Hazard, ed. (1968), p. 67.
59. Hand (1977), p. 161; the quotation is from an address of 1942.

Chapter 20

1. Judge Roth, cited at 261, in *Bradley v. Milliken* (1973), Colloquy of Court with Counsel, October 4, 1971, from *Joint Appendix*, Volume 4, pp. 454–55.
2. Sheatsley (1967), pp. 304–7.
3. Greeley and Sheatsley (1971), pp. 13–19, 25–27, 34. Davis (1973).
4. See Gallup poll of September 9, 1973; Harris poll, reported in *Detroit Free Press*, November 23, 1972; Gallup Opinion Index of 1975.
5. Slawski (1977). In Pontiac the proportion of whites opposed to busing remains

about the same as when it began, although the loss of a substantial number of white households the first year was, at the time, thought to represent actions of those parents most opposed to busing. In view of the steady percentage (75) of whites opposed to busing, this interpretation is now generally discarded.

6. See Kelley (1974); Cataldo et al. (1975), p. 4.
7. Foster (1974), p. 131.
8. U.S. Commission on Civil Rights (1972), p. 5.
9. *Ibid.*, p. 16. On p. 19 the Commission reported: "Berkeley and Louisville found that both majority and minority pupils gained," though court-ordered busing did not come to Louisville until after 1972, the year of this report. The Commission has persisted in claims for post-busing gains in Berkeley, California (see U.S. Commission on Civil Rights [1976], p. 113), despite the absence of supporting evidence. A report by the Berkeley Board of Education was summarized by the *Berkeley Gazette* of March 17, 1976: "Minority students' test scores lag further and further behind white students' scores." The board also reported increased racial isolation of students and growing problems of school safety.
10. Giles, Gatlin, and Cataldo (1976).
11. U.S. Commission on Civil Rights (1972), p. 15.
12. U.S. Commission on Civil Rights (1976), p. 58. Miss Johnson is cited again in the Commission's report on Minneapolis (1977a).
13. U.S. Commission on Civil Rights (1972), p. 12.
14. U.S. Commission on Civil Rights (1977), pp. 49–50, 144.
15. U.S. Commission on Civil Rights (1976), pp. i, 152, 163. Sympathetic media treatment often reflects this usage; e.g., *Time* for September 27, 1976, reported that the school system of Birmingham, Alabama, was "integrating smoothly" by means of rezoning, pairing, and the use of magnet schools. The article then noted that since this program began the public school population had shifted from 50 percent to 70 percent black.
16. *Ibid.*, pp. 152–53.
17. See Kurland (1968) for incisive analysis of the requirements for a feasible ruling.
18. Fiss (1971), p. 705.
19. U.S. Commission on Civil Rights (1972), p. 10.
20. U.S. Commission on Civil Rights (1977), p. 82. On p. 56 the Commission states: "No one . . . dispute[s] . . . that given a continuation of current migration trends . . . central city schools will become increasingly black and Hispanic . . . whether or not they are required to be desegregated. Yet . . . courts will have . . . to require desegregation of central city schools . . . because . . . it has been demonstrated that public schools have been segregated as a result of deliberate policies of school officials."
21. For an account of congressional attempts to prevent compulsory racial balancing in schools, see Georgetown Law Journal (1972), pp. 1282, 1287–88.
22. U.S. Commission on Civil Rights (1973), p. 1.
23. Foster (1974), p. 130.
24. University of Michigan, School of Education (1972), p. 19.
25. *Detroit News*, May 5, 1977.
26. *Detroit News*, May 19, 1974.
27. See Rosen (1972), especially pp. 165–72.
28. Owen Fiss (1971, 1974, 1975, 1976) exemplifies the proponents, Frank Goodman (1972) the skeptics.
29. *Hobson v. Hansen*, 269 F. Supp. (D.C. 1967), at 507–8. For a more detailed and sophisticated presentation of what seems to me the same thesis, see Dworkin (1977), especially p. 30.
30. Saltzman (1976). During the oral argument before the Supreme Court in *Milliken*,

the plaintiffs' co-counsel, Flannery, responding to a question by one of the justices, declared that racial discrimination by the Detroit system occurred "right up to the very time of the trial"; thus these violations were not categorized as past history.

31. See, for example, the papers in the symposium on school desegregation and white flight held by the National Institute of Education in August, 1975; also Rossell (1975–76); Coleman et al. (1975); Pettigrew and Green (1976). See Armor (1976), pp. 7–11, for a summary of research.

32. None of the 1977 reports of the U.S. Commission on Civil Rights on demographic change in desegregated public school systems throughout the nation showed any such reversal, and nearly all showed some degree of continued white attrition. See Berry et al., in Schwartz, ed. (1976, pp. 234–35), on the regeneration of imbalance in the Evanston schools after busing.

33. See Orfield (1974–75).

34. See U.S. Census, *Mobility of the Population of the U.S.*, Series P-20, No. 285 (March 1970–75). A popularized summary of these trends was featured in *Time* on March 15, 1976. Survey data suggest that these movements are the actualization of long-standing inclinations to be "farther away from the center of things"; see Michelson (1968), p. 39.

35. The effects of withdrawal to private schools in some Southern districts has been noted by, e.g., Giles, Cataldo, and Gatlin (1975) and by Clotfelter (1976); see Chapter 17, n. 17, above. See also Lord (1975).

36. The Kentucky Commission on Human Rights recently (1977) attributed black suburbanization to a program that encourages black residential relocation to avoid busing. But the numbers involved are as yet small, and the movement is similar to that which occurred in other cities without this incentive.

37. For example, Rossell (1975–76, p. 688) and Orfield (1975), pp. 49–51.

38. For a valuable and incisive evaluation of the broad application of this principle, see Glazer (1975).

39. See, for example, Norman Cousins' "Busing Reconsidered," *Saturday Review*, January 24, 1976.

40. For an appraisal critical of these rulings, see Bannon (1977). See Graglia (1976) for an astute legal analysis of the defects in the judicial effort to secure racially mixed schools.

41. A study of a very poor black neighborhood in Detroit showed that the local elementary school was the only formal institution people "felt close to" (Wolf and Lebeaux [1969], pp. 256, 277–89, 562).

42. For an excellent statement of this perspective, written many years ago, see Syrkin (1964).

43. Bolner and Vedlitz (1971), pp. 320–21.

44. Molotch (1972), p. 222.

45. U.S. Advisory Commission on Civil Disorders (1968), p. 1.

Bibliography

Aaron, Henry J. *Shelter and Subsidies*. Washington, D.C.: Brookings Institution, 1972.

Agocs, Carol. *Ethnic Neighborhoods in City and Suburb: Metropolitan Detroit, 1940–1970*. Ph.D. dissertation, Wayne State University, 1977.

Agocs, Carol, and Thompson, Bryan. "The Ethnic Structure of Metropolitan Detroit, 1950–1970: An Analysis of Spatial and Social Change." Wayne State University, Center for Urban Studies, September, 1973.

Alba, Richard. "Social Assimilation among American Catholics." *American Sociological Review*, Volume 41, No. 6, 1977.

Aldrich, Howard. "Ecological Succession in Racially Changing Neighborhoods: A Review of the Literature." *Urban Affairs Quarterly*, Volume 10, No. 3, March 1975.

Aldrich, Howard, and Reiss, Albert J., Jr. "Continuities in the Study of Ecological Succession: Changes in the Race Composition of Neighborhoods and Their Businesses." *American Journal of Sociology*, Volume 81, No. 4, 1976.

Allen, Sheila. *New Minorities, Old Conflicts*. New York: Random House, 1971.

Allport, Gordon. *The Nature of Prejudice*. Garden City, New York: Doubleday Anchor, 1958.

Altshuler, Alan A. *Community Control: The Black Demand for Participation in Large American Cities*. New York: Pegasus, 1970.

Amir, Yehuda. "The Contact Hypothesis in Ethnic Relations." *Psychological Bulletin*, Volume 71, No. 5, 1969.

Armor, David J. "The Evidence on Busing." *The Public Interest*, No. 28, Summer 1972.

———. "The Double Double Standard: A Reply." *The Public Interest*, No. 30, Winter 1973.

———. *Sociology and School Busing Policy*. Santa Monica, Calif.: Rand, 1976.

Asher, Steven, and Allen, Vernon, "Racial Preference and Social Comparison Processes." *Journal of Social Issues*, Volume 25, No. 1, 1969.

Averch, Harvey A., et al. *How Effective Is Schooling? A Critical Review and Synthesis of Research Findings*. Santa Monica, Calif.: Rand, 1972.

Bailey, Stephen, *Disruption in Urban Public Secondary Schools*. Washington, D.C.: National Association of Secondary School Principals, 1970.

Bales, Robert F. "Cultural Differences in Rates of Alcoholism." *Quarterly Journal of Studies on Alcohol*, Volume 6, 1946.

341

Bannon, John. "Legitimizing Segregation." *Civil Rights Digest*, Volume 9, No. 4, Summer 1977.

Barber, Theodore X., and Silver, Maurice J. "Fact, Fiction and the Experimenter Bias Effect." *Psychological Bulletin Monograph*, Volume 70, No. 6, December 1968a.

———. "Pitfalls in Data Analysis and Interpretations: A Reply to Rosenthal." *Psychological Bulletin Monograph*, Volume 70, No. 6, December 1968b.

Barber, Theodore X., et al. "Five Attempts To Replicate the Experimenter Bias Effect." *Journal of Consulting and Clinical Psychology*, Volume 33, No. 1, 1969.

Barresi, Charles M. "Racial Transition in an Urban Neighborhood." *Growth and Change*, Volume 3, July 1972.

Baughman, Earl E., and Dahlstrom, Grant W. *Negro and White Children*. New York: Academic Press, 1968.

Bayley, David H. "Learning About Crime—the Japanese Experience." *The Public Interest*, No. 44, Summer 1976.

Beer, Louis D. "The Nature of the Violation and the Scope of the Remedy: An Analysis of *Milliken v. Bradley* in Terms of the Evaluation of the Theory of the Violation." *Wayne Law Review*, Volume 21, No. 3, March 1975.

Bell, Derrick A., Jr. "Serving Two Masters: Integration Ideals and Client Interests in School Desegregation Litigation." *Yale Law Journal*, Volume 85, No. 4, March 1976.

Bell, Duran. "Indebtedness of Black and White Families." *Journal of Urban Economics*, Volume 1, No. 1, January 1974.

Berger, Bennett. "Suburbia and the American Dream." *The Public Interest*, No. 2, Winter 1966.

Berger, Morroe, "Desegregation, Law and Social Science." *Commentary*, Volume 23, May 1957.

Berns, Walter. "Law and Behavioral Science." *Law and Contemporary Problems*, Volume 28, No. 1, Winter 1963.

Bernstein, Basil. "Language and Social Class." *British Journal of Sociology*, Volume 11, No. 3, September 1960.

———. "Social Class and Linguistic Development: A Theory of Social Learning." In *Education, Economy and Society*, edited by A. H. Halsey, J. Floud, and A. Anderson. Glencoe, Ill.: Free Press, 1961.

———. "A Sociolinguistic Approach to Social Learning." In *Penguin Survey of the Social Sciences*, edited by J. Gould. Baltimore, Md.: Penguin Books, 1965.

Berry, Brian, et al. "Attitudes toward Integration: The Role of Status in Community Response to Racial Change." In *The Changing Face of the Suburbs*, edited by Barry Schwartz. Chicago: University of Chicago Press, 1976.

Beshers, J. M.; Laumann, Edward O.; and Bradshaw, B. S. "Ethnic Congregation, Segregation, Assimilation and Stratification." *Social Forces*, Volume 62, May 1964.

Birch, David, et al. "Research Project on Neighborhood Evolution and Decline." Cambridge, Mass., Harvard-M.I.T. Joint Center for Urban Studies, 1975.

Black, Charles L., Jr. "The Lawfulness of the Segregation Decision." *Yale Law Journal*, Volume 69, January 1960.

Blauner, Robert. "Black Culture: Myth or Reality?" In *Americans from Africa*, edited by Peter Rose. New York: Atherton, 1970.

Bleda, Sharon E. "Bases of Ethnic Residential Segregation: Recent Patterns in American Metropolitan Areas." Paper presented at the annual meeting of the American Sociological Association, San Francisco, 1975.

Bloch, Charles J. "Does the Fourteenth Amendment Forbid De Facto Segregation?" *Case Western Reserve Law Review*, Volume 16, 1965.

Bloom, Benjamin S. *Stability and Change in Human Characteristics*. New York: John Wiley, 1964.

Blumberg, Leonard, and Lalli, Michael. "Little Ghettoes: A Study of Negroes in the Suburbs." *Phylon*, Volume 27, No. 2, Summer 1966.

Blumer, Herbert. "Attitudes and the Social Act." *Social Problems*, Volume 3, No. 2, October 1955.

Bolner, James, and Shanley, Robert. *Busing: The Political and Judicial Process*. New York: Praeger, 1974.

Bolner, James, and Vedlitz, A. "The Affinity of Negro Pupils for Segregated Schools." *Journal of Negro Education*, Voume 40, No. 4, Fall 1971.

Bonacich, Edna, and Goodman, Robert. *Deadlock in School Desegregation: A Case Study of Inglewood, California*. New York: Praeger, 1972.

Bonacich, Edna; Light, Ivan H.; and Wong, Charles Choy. "Koreans in Business." *Society*, Volume 14, No. 6, September–October 1977.

Borg, Walter R. *Ability Grouping in the Public Schools: A Field Study*. Dembar Educational Research Services. Madison, Wis.: 1966.

Bowles, Samuel, and Levin, Henry. "The Determinants of Scholastic Achievement: An Appraisal of Some Recent Evidence." *Journal of Human Resources*, Volume 3, No. 1, Winter 1968.

Bradburn, Norman M.; Sudman, Seymour; and Gockel, Galen L. *Side by Side: Integrated Neighborhoods in America*. Chicago: Quadrangle Books, 1971.

Brink, William, and Harris, Louis. *The Negro Revolution in America*. New York: Simon and Schuster, 1964.

Broom, Leonard, and Glenn, Norval D. "Negro-White Differences in Reported Attitudes and Behavior." *Sociology and Social Research*, Volume 50, January 1966.

Bruner, Jerome. "Poverty and Childhood." In *The Conditions of Educational Equality*, edited by Sterling M. McMurrin. Supplemental paper 34. Committee for Economic Development, 1971.

Bryan, Miriam M. *Ability Grouping: Status, Impact, and Alternatives*. TM Report 3. Washington, D.C.: Educational Resources Information Center (ERIC), 1971.

Buckley, James J. "Who Is Pygmalion, Which Is Galatea?" *Phi Delta Kappan*, Volume 50, 1968.

Burgess, Ernest W. "Residential Segregation in American Cities." *Annals of the American Academy of Political and Social Science*, Volume 140, November 1928.

Cagle, Laurence T., and Deutscher, Irwin. "Housing Aspirations: The Relocation of Poor Families." *Social Problems*, Volume 18, No. 2, Fall 1970.

Cahn, Edmond. "Jurisprudence." *New York University Law Review*, Volume 30, 1955.

———. "The Lawyer, the Social Psychologist and the Truth." *New York University Law Review*, Volume 182, 1956.

———. *The Predicament of Democratic Man*. New York: Dell, 1962.

———. "Fact Skepticism: An Unexpected Chapter." *New York University Law Review*, Volume 38, December 1963.

Cain, Glen G., and Watts, Harold W. "Problems in Making Policy Inferences from the Coleman Report." *American Sociological Review*, Volume 35, No. 2, April 1970.

Caldwell, Catherine. "Social Science as Ammunition." *Psychology Today*, Volume 4, September 1970.

Campbell, Angus. *White Attitudes toward Black People*. Ann Arbor: Institute for Social Research, University of Michigan, 1971.

Campbell, Angus, and Schuman, Howard. *Racial Attitudes in Fifteen American Cities*. Ann Arbor: Survey Research Center, Institute for Social Research, University of Michigan, 1968.

Campbell, Donald T. "Stereotypes and the Perception of Group Differences." *American Psychologist*, Volume 22, 1967.

Campbell, Ernest Q. "Defining and Attaining Equal Educational Opportunity in a Pluralistic Society." *Vanderbilt Law Review*, Volume 26, 1973.

Carithers, M. W. "School Desegregation and Racial Cleavage, 1954–70, A Review of the Literature." *Journal of Social Issues*, Volume 26, No. 4, 1970.

Cataldo, Everett, et al. "Desegregation and White Flight." *Integrated Education*, Volume 13, No. 1, January 1975.

Cazden, Courtney B. "Subcultural Differences in Child Language." *Merrill-Palmer Quarterly*, Volume 12, No. 3, July 1966.

———. "The Situation: A Neglected Source of Social Class Differences in Language Use." *Journal of Social Issues*, Volume 26, No. 2, Spring 1970.

Claiborn, William. "Expectancy Effects in the Classroom." *Journal of Educational Psychology*, Volume 60, No. 5, 1969.

Clark, Dennis. "Toward Assimilation or Ethnic Identity?" *Urban and Social Change Review*, Volume 4, No. 1, Fall 1970.

Clark, Kenneth B. "The Desegregation Cases: Criticism of the Social Scientists' Role." *Villanova Law Review*, Volume 5, Winter 1960.

———. *Prejudice and Your Child*. Boston: Beacon Press, 1963.

———. "Social Policy, Power, and Social Science Research." *Perspectives on Inequality*, Harvard Educational Review Reprint Series 8. Cambridge, Mass: Harvard Educational Review, 1973.

———. "Social Science, Constitutional Rights, and the Courts." In *Education, Social Science and the Judicial Process: An International Symposium*. Washington, D.C.: National Institute of Education, U.S. Department of Health, Education, and Welfare, 1976.

Clark, Terry N. "The Irish Ethic and the Spirit of Patronage." *Ethnicity*, Volume 2, Summer 1975.

Clotfelter, Charles T. "Spatial Re-Arrangement and the Tiebout Hypothesis: The Case of School Desegregation." *Southern Economic Journal*, Volume 42, No. 2, October 1975.

———. "School Desegregation, 'Tipping' and Private School Enrollment." *Journal of Human Resources*, Volume 11, No. 1, 1976.

Cohen, David K. "The Price of Community Control." *Commentary*, July 1969.

———. "Immigrants and the Schools." *Review of Education Research*, Volume 40, February 1970.

Cohen, David K., and Weiss, Janet A. "Social Science and Social Policy: Schools and

Race." In *Education, Social Science and the Judicial Process*, edited by Ray C. Rist and Ronald J. Anson. New York: Teachers College Press, 1977.

Coleman, James S. "Equal Schools or Equal Students?" *The Public Interest*, No. 4, Summer 1966.

———. "Toward Open Schools." *The Public Interest*, No. 9, Fall, 1967.

———. "Coleman on the Coleman Report." *The Educational Researcher*, Volume 1, No. 3, March 1972.

———. "Rawls, Nozick and Educational Equality." *The Public Interest*, No. 43, Spring 1976.

Coleman, James S.; Campbell, Ernest Q.; et al. *Equality of Educational Opportunity*. Washington, D.C.: U.S. Department of Health, Education, and Welfare, 1966.

Coleman, James S., et al. *Trends in School Segregation 1968–1973*. Washington, D.C.: The Urban Institute, 1975.

Connolly, Harold. "Black Movement into the Suburbs." *Urban Affairs Quarterly*, Volume 9, September 1973.

Coons, John E. "Recent Trends in Science Fiction: *Serrano* among the People of Number." In *Education, Social Science and the Judicial Process*, edited by Ray C. Rist and Ronald J. Anson. New York: Teachers College Press, 1977.

Coons, John E.; Cline, William H., III; and Sugarman, Stephen. *Private Wealth and Public Education*. Cambridge, Mass.: Harvard University Press, 1970.

Cousins, Norman. "Busing Reconsidered." *Saturday Review*, January 24, 1978.

Crain, Robert L. "School Integration and the Academic Achievement of Negroes." *Sociology of Education*, Volume 44, Winter 1971.

Crain, Robert, et al. *Southern Schools: An Evaluation of the Effects of the Emergency School Assistance Program and of School Desegregation*. Chicago, Ill.: National Opinion Research Center, 1973.

Craven, J. Braxton, Jr. "Further Judicial Commentary: The Impact of Social Science Evidence on the Judge: A Personal Comment." *Law and Contemporary Problems*, Volume 39, No. 1, Winter 1975.

Cutright, Philips. "Historical and Contemporary Trends in Illegitimacy." In *Deviance and Liberty*, edited by Lee Rainwater. Chicago, Ill.: Aldine, 1974.

Darroch, Gordon A., and Marston, Wilfred G. "The Social Class Basis of Ethnic Residential Segregation: The Canadian Case." *American Journal of Sociology*, Volume 77, No. 3, November 1971.

Davis, F. James. "The Effects of a Freeway Displacment on Racial Housing Segregation in a Northern City." *Phylon*, Volume 26, No. 3, Fall 1965.

Davis, James A. "The Campus as a Frog Pond. . . ." *American Journal of Sociology*, Volume 72, No. 1, July 1966.

———. "Busing." In *Southern Schools: An Evaluation of the Effects of the Emergency School Assistance Program and of School Desegregation*, Volume 2. Chicago, Ill.: National Opinion Research Center, 1973.

Davison, Robert B. *Black British: Immigrants to England*. Oxford: Oxford University Press, 1966.

Deakin, Nicholas. "Residential Segregation in Britain: A Comparative Note." *Race*, Volume 6, No. 1, July 1964.

Dentler, Robert A., and Elkins, Constance. "Intergroup Attitudes, Academic Performance and Racial Composition." In *The Urban R's*, edited by Robert A. Dentler, Bernard Mackler, and Mary Ellen Warshauer. New York: Praeger, 1967.

Deskins, Donald, Jr. *Residential Mobility of Negroes in Detroit*. Ann Arbor: Department of Geography, University of Michigan, 1972.

Detroit, Michigan, Board of Education. *Findings and Recommendations of the Citizens Advisory Committee on Equal Educational Opportunities*. Detroit: Board of Education, 1962.

Deutsch, Martin, et al. *The Disadvantaged Child*. New York: Basic Books, 1967.

Deutsch, Morton, and Collins, Mary Evans. *Interracial Housing: A Psychological Evaluation of a Social Experiment*. Minneapolis: University of Minnesota Press, 1951.

Deutscher, Irwin. "Words and Deeds." *Social Problems*, Volume 13, No. 2, Winter 1966.

Diekhoff, John C. "My Fair Ludlow." *The Educational Forum*, Volume 33, No. 3, March 1969.

Dimond, Paul R. "Reform of the Government of Education: A Resolution of the Conflict between 'Integration' and 'Community Control.'" *Wayne Law Review*, Volume 16, No. 4, Fall 1970.

―――. "School Segregation in the North: There Is But One Constitution." *Harvard Civil Rights-Civil Liberties Law Review*, Volume 7, No. 1, January 1972a.

―――. "The Law of School Classification." *Inequality in Education*, No. 12, July 1972b.

Douglas, J. W. B. *The Home and the School*. London: MacGibbon and Kee, 1963.

Downs, Anthony. *Urban Problems and Prospects*. Chicago: Markham, 1970.

―――. *Opening Up the Suburbs: An Urban Strategy for America*. New Haven, Conn.: Yale University Press, 1973.

Drake, William E. *The American School in Transition*. Englewood Cliffs, N.J.: Prentice-Hall, 1955.

Duncan, Otis; Schuman, Howard; and Duncan, Beverly. *Social Change in a Metropolitan Community*. New York: Russell Sage Foundation, 1973.

Dusek, Jerome B. "Teacher and Experimenter Bias Effects on Children's Learning and Performance." Paper presented at the annual meeting of the American Sociological Association. New York City, 1973.

Dworkin, Ronald M. "Social Sciences and Constitutional Rights: The Consequences of Uncertainty." In *Education, Social Science and the Judicial Process*, edited by Ray C. Rist and Ronald J. Anson. New York: Teachers College Press, 1977.

Dyer, Henry. "School Factors and Equal Educational Opportunity." *Harvard Educational Review*, Volume 38, No. 1, Winter 1968.

Eisinger, Peter. "Support for Urban Control-Sharing at the Mass Level." *American Journal of Political Science*, Volume 17, No. 4, November 1973.

Erbe, Brigitte Mach. "Race and Socioeconomic Segregation." *American Sociological Review*, Volume 40, No. 6, December 1975.

Fantini, Mario; Gittell, Marilyn; and Magat, Richard. *Community Control and the Urban School*. New York: Praeger, 1970.

Farley, Reynolds. "Suburban Persistence." *American Sociological Review*, Volume 29, No. 1, February 1964.

―――. "Population Trends and School Segregation in the Detroit Metropolitan Area." *Wayne Law Review*, Volume 21, No. 3, March 1975.

———. "Residential Segregation and Its Implications for School Integration." *Law and Contemporary Problems*, Volume 39, No. 1, Winter 1975.

Farley, Reynolds, and Taeuber, Alma F. "Racial Segregation in the Public Schools." *American Journal of Sociology*, Volume 79, No. 4, January 1974.

Featherman, David L. "The Socioeconomic Achievement of White Religious-Ethnic Subgroups: Social and Psychological Explanations." *American Sociological Review*, Volume 36, No. 2, April 1971.

Fein, Leonard T. *The Ecology of the Public Schools: An Inquiry into the Public Schools*. Indianapolis, Ind.: Pegasus, 1971.

Fishman, Joshua. "Some Social and Psychological Determinants of Intergroup Relations in Changing Neighborhoods." *Social Forces*, Volume 40, October 1961.

Fiss, Owen M. "Racial Imbalance in the Public Schools: The Constitutional Concepts." *Harvard Law Review*, Volume 78, No. 3, January 1965.

———. "The Charlotte-Mecklenburg Case—Its Significance for Northern School Desegregation." *University of Chicago Law Review*, Volume 38, No. 4, Summer 1971.

———. "School Desegregation: The Uncertain Path of the Law." *Philosophy and Public Affairs*, Volume 4, No. 1, Fall 1974.

———. "The Jurisprudence of Busing." *Law and Contemporary Problems*, Volume 39, No. 1, Winter 1975.

———. "Groups and the Equal Protection Clause." *Philosophy and Public Affairs*, Volume 5, No. 2, Winter 1976.

Flannery, J. Harold. "Unconstitutional Segregation and Court-Ordered Desegregation." In *Proceedings of Conference on School Desegregation and the Law*. Ann Arbor: University of Michigan School of Education, May 1972.

Fleming, Elyse S., and Anttonen, Ralph G. "Teacher Expectancy Or My Fair Lady." *American Educational Research Journal*, Volume 8, No. 2, March 1971.

Foote, Nelson, et al. *Housing Choices and Housing Constraints*. New York: McGraw-Hill, 1960.

Foster, Gordon. "*Milliken v. Bradley:* Implications for Desegregation Centers and Metropolitan Desegregation." In *Milliken v. Bradley: The Implications for Metropolitan Desegregation*. Washington, D.C.: U.S. Commission on Civil Rights, 1974.

Friedman, Leon, ed. *Argument: The Oral Argument before the Supreme Court in Brown v. Board of Education of Topeka 1952–55*. New York: Chelsea House, 1969.

Gans, Herbert. *People and Plans*. New York: Basic Books, 1968.

———. *The Levittowners*. New York: Vintage, 1969.

———. "The Future of the Suburbs." In *The End of Innocence: A Suburban Reader*, edited by C. Haar. Glenview, Ill.: Foresman and Co., 1972.

Georgetown Law Journal. Note: "Merging Urban and Suburban School Systems." *Georgetown Law Journal*, Volume 60, No. 5, May 1972.

Gerard, Harold B., and Miller, Norman. *School Desegregation*. New York: Plenum Publishing Corp., 1975.

Giles, Micheal W.; Cataldo, Everett F.; and Gatlin, Douglas S. "Desegregation and the Private School Alternative." In *Symposium on School Desegregation and White Flight*, edited by Gary Orfield. Washington, D.C.: U.S. Department of Health, Education, and Welfare, National Institute of Education, August 1975.

Giles, Micheal W.; Gatlin, Douglas S.; and Cataldo, Everett F. "Racial and Class

Prejudice: Their Relative Effects on Protest against School Desegregation." *American Sociological Review*, Volume 41, No. 2, April 1976.

Glazer, Nathan. "For White and Black, Community Control Is the Issue." *New York Times*, April 27, 1969.

————. "Blacks and Ethnic Groups: The Difference and the Political Difference It Makes." *Social Problems*, Volume 18, No. 4, Spring 1971a.

————. "Paradoxes of Health Care." *The Public Interest*, No. 22, Winter 1971b.

————. *Affirmative Discrimination*. New York: Basic Books, 1975.

Goldberg, Miriam; Passow, A. H.; and Justman, Joseph. *The Effects of Ability Grouping*. New York: Teachers College Press, 1966.

Goldbloom, Maurice J. "The New York School Crisis." *Commentary*, Volume 47, January 1969.

Goodman, Frank I. "De Facto School Segregation: A Constitutional and Empirical Analysis." *California Law Review*, Volume 60, No. 2, March 1972.

Gordon, Milton. *Assimilation in American Life*. New York: Oxford University Press, 1964.

Goslin, David A. "The School in a Changing Society." *American Journal of Orthopsychiatry*, Volume 37, October 1967.

Graglia, Lino A. *Disaster by Decree*. Ithaca, N.Y.: Cornell University Press, 1976.

Granovetter, Mark S. "The Strength of Weak Ties." *American Journal of Sociology*, Volume 78, No. 6, May 1973.

Grant, Gerald. "Essay-Review of 'On Equality of Educational Opportunity.' " *Harvard Educational Review*, Volume 42, No. 1, February 1972.

————. "Shaping Social Policy: The Politics of the Coleman Report." *Teachers College Record*, Volume 75, No. 1, September 1973.

Grant, William R. "Community Control vs. Integration—The Case of Detroit." *The Public Interest*, No. 24, Summer 1971.

————. "The Detroit School Case: An Historical Overview." *Wayne Law Review*, Volume 21, No. 3, March 1975.

Greeley, Andrew M. "A Note on Political and Social Differences among Ethnic College Graduates." *Sociology of Education*, Volume 42, No. 1, Winter 1969.

————. "Comment on Educational Expectations." *American Sociological Review*, Volume 35, No. 5, October 1970.

————. "Political Participation among Ethnic Groups in the U.S.: A Preliminary Reconnaissance." *American Journal of Sociology*, Volume 80, No. 1, July 1974.

————. "Ethnicity and Racial Attitudes." *American Journal of Sociology*, Volume 80, No. 4, January 1975.

Greeley, Andrew M., and Rossi, Peter H. *The Education of Catholic Americans*. Chicago, Ill.: Aldine Publishing Co., 1966.

Greeley, Andrew M., and Sheatsley, Paul. "Attitudes toward Racial Integration." *Scientific American*, December 1971.

Greer, Colin. "Immigrants, Negroes and the Public Schools." *The Urban Review*, Volume 3, No. 3, January 1969a.

————. "Public Schools: Myth of the Melting Pot." *Saturday Review*, Volume 52, November 15, 1969.

————. *The Great School Legend*. New York: Basic Books, 1972.

Gregor, A. James. "The Law, Social Science and School Segregation." *Case Western Reserve Law Review*, Volume 14, 1963a.

————. "The Law and Social Science: A Reply to O. C. Lewis." *Case Western Reserve Law Review*, Volume 15, 1963b.

Grier, Eunice, and Grier, George. "Obstacles to Desegregation in American Urban Areas." *Race*, Volume 6, No. 1, July 1964.

————. "Equality and Beyond: Housing Segregation in the Great Society." In *The Negro American*, edited by Talcott Parsons and Kenneth B. Clark. Boston: Beacon Press, 1967.

Gross, Morris. *Learning Readiness in Two Jewish Groups*. New York: Center for Urban Education, 1967.

Grossberg, Sidney. "Factors in Historical and Participation Identification of Detroit Area Jews." Ph.D. dissertation, Wayne State University, 1971.

Guest, Avery M., and Weed, James A. "Ethnic Residential Segregation: Patterns of Change." *American Journal of Sociology*, Volume 81, No. 5, March 1976.

Guest, Avery M., and Zuiches, J. "Another Look at Residential Turnover in Urban Neighborhoods." *American Journal of Sociology*, Volume 77, No. 3, November 1971.

Guthrie, James W., et al. *Schools and Inequality*. Cambridge, Mass.: MIT Press, 1971.

Hacker, Andrew, Commentary on Coleman's Paper. In *Integration of the Social Sciences through Policy Analysis*, edited by James C. Charlesworth. American Academy of Political and Social Science monograph 14. Philadelphia: American Academy of Political and Social Science, 1972.

Hamilton, Charles. "Race and Education: A Search for Legitimacy." *Harvard Educational Review*, Volume 38, No. 4, 1968.

Hand, Learned. *The Spirit of Liberty*, 3d ed. Chicago: University of Chicago Press, 1977.

Handlin, Oscar, *The Uprooted*. Boston: Little, Brown, and Co., 1951.

Hanley, John W., Jr. "Keys v. School District No. 1: Unlocking the Northern Schoolhouse Door." *Harvard Civil Rights-Civil Liberties Law Review*, Volume 9, No. 1, January 1974.

Hardy, Kenneth R. "Social Origin of American Scientists and Scholars." *Science*, Volume 185, No. 4150, August 9, 1974.

Haskins, Kenneth. "The Case for Local Control." *Saturday Review*, January 11, 1969.

Hauser, Philip. "Demographic Factors in the Integration of the Negro." In *The Negro American*, edited by Talcott Parsons and Kenneth B. Clark. Boston: Beacon Press, 1966.

Hawley, Amos H., and Rock, Vincent P., eds. *Segregation in Residential Areas*. Washington, D.C.: National Academy of Sciences, 1973.

Hazard, Geoffrey C., Jr. "Limitations on the Uses of Behavioral Science in the Law." *Case Western Reserve Law Review*, Volume 19, No. 1, 1967.

Heathers, Glen. "Grouping." In *Encyclopedia of Educational Research*, edited by Robert L. Ebel. New York: Macmillan, Volume 1, 1969.

Heiss, Jerold, and Owens, Susan. "Self Evaluations of Blacks and Whites." *American Journal of Sociology*, Volume 78, No. 2, September 1972.

Heller, Celia. "Class as an Explanation of Ethnic Differences in Upward Mobility." In *Structured Social Inequality*, edited by Celia Heller. New York: Macmillan, 1969.

Hermalin, Albert I., and Farley, Reynolds. "The Potential for Residential Integration in Cities and Suburbs." *American Sociological Review*, Volume 38, No. 5, October 1973.

Herzog, Elizabeth, et al. "But Some Are More Poor Than Others: SES Differences in a Pre-School Program." *American Journal of Orthopsychiatry*, Volume 42, No. 1, January 1972.

Hess, R. D., and Shipman, Virginia. "Early Experience and the Socialization of Cognitive Modes in Children." *Child Development*, Volume 36, No. 4, December 1965.

Hess, R. D.; Shipman, Virginia; et al. *The Cognitive Environments of Urban Preschool Children*. Chicago: University of Chicago Press, 1968.

Heyman, Ira M. "The Chief Justice, Racial Segregation and the Friendly Critics." *California Law Review*, Volume 49, No. 1, March 1961.

Heyns, Barbara. "Social Selection and Stratification within Schools." *American Journal of Sociology*, Volume 79, No. 6, May 1974.

Hill, Roscoe, and Feeley, Malcolm. "Comparative Analysis of the Eight Cities." In *Affirmative School Integration: Efforts to Overcome De Facto Segregation in Urban Schools*. Beverly Hills, Calif.: Sage Publications, 1968.

Hiltz, Roxanne S. "Black and White in the Consumer Financial System." *American Journal of Sociology*, Volume 76, No. 6, May 1971.

Hodgson, Godfrey. "Do Schools Make a Difference?" *Atlantic Monthly*, March 1973.

Holmes, Oliver Wendell. "Ideals and Doubts." *Illinois Law Review*, Volume 10, No. 1, May 1915.

Horowitz, Donald L. *The Courts and Social Policy*. Washington, D.C.: Brookings Institution, 1977.

Horowitz, Harold, and Karst, Kenneth L. *Law, Lawyers and Social Change*. Indianapolis, Ind.: Bobbs-Merrill, 1969.

Horowitz, Irving L. "Social Science Mandarinism: The Policy-Making Myth and the Problem of Legitimacy." In *Social Science and Public Policy*, edited by Daniel L. Knapp and Walter E. Schafer. Eugene: Lila Acheson Wallace School of Community Service and Public Affairs, 1970.

Hsia, Joyjia, *Integration in Evanston, 1967–1971: A Longitudinal Evaluation*. Evanston, Ill.: Educational Testing Service, August 1971.

Hunt, J. McV. "Has Compensatory Education Failed? Has It Been Attempted?" *Harvard Educational Review*, Volume 39, No. 2, Spring 1969.

Husen, Torsten. "The Effect of School Structure upon Utilization of Ability: The Case of Sweden and Some International Comparisons." In *Basic Readings in the Sociology of Education*, edited by David F. Swift. Boston, Mass.: Routledge and Kegan Paul, 1970.

Inbar, Michael. *The Vulnerable Age Phenomenon*. New York: Russell Sage Foundation, 1976.

Isaacs, Harold. *The New World of Negro Americans*. New York: Viking, 1963.

Jencks, Christopher, et al. *Inequality*. New York: Harper and Row, 1972.

José, Jean, and Cody, John J. "Teacher-Pupil Interaction as It Relates to Attempted Changes in Teacher Expectancy of Academic Ability and Achievement." *American Educational Research Journal*, Volume 8, No. 1, January 1971.

Justman, Joseph. "Stability of Academic Aptitude and Reading Test Scores of Mobile and Non-Mobile Disadvantaged Children." In *Education of the Disadvantaged; A Book of Readings*, edited by Harry A. Passow, Miriam Goldberg, and Abraham J. Tannenbaum. New York: Holt, Rinehart, and Winston, 1967.

Kain, John F., ed. *Race and Poverty*. Englewood Cliffs, N.J.: Prentice-Hall, 1969.

Kalven, Harry, Jr. "The Quest for the Middle Range: Empirical Inquiry and Legal Policy." In *Law in a Changing America*, edited by Geoffrey C. Hazard, Jr. Englewood Cliffs, N.J.: Prentice-Hall, 1968.

Kantner, John F. and Zelnik, Melvin. "Sexual Experiences of Young Unmarried Women in the U.S." In *Deviance and Liberty*, edited by Lee Rainwater. Chicago, Ill.: Aldine Publishing Co., 1974.

Kantrowitz, Nathan. "Ethnic and Racial Segregation in the New York Metropolitan Area, 1960." *American Journal of Sociology*, Volume 74, No. 6, May 1969.

_____. *Ethnic and Racial Segregation in the New York Metropolis: Residential Patterns among White Ethnics, Blacks, and Puerto Ricans*. New York: Praeger, 1973.

Kaplan, John. "Segregation Litigation and the Schools—Part II: The General Northern Problem." *Northwestern University Law Review*, Volume 58, No. 2, May–June 1963.

_____. "San Francisco." In *Affirmative School Integration*, edited by Roscoe Hill and Malcolm Feeley. Beverly Hills, Calif.: Sage Publications, 1968.

Katz, Michael. "The Unmasking of Dishonest Pretensions: Toward an Interpretation of the Role of Social Science in Constitutional Litigation." *American Sociologist*, Volume 6, June 1971.

Katzman, David. *Before the Ghetto: Black Detroit in the 19th Century*. Urbana, Ill.: University of Illinois Press, 1973.

Katzman, Martin T. "Discrimination, Subculture and the Economic Performance of Negroes, Puerto Ricans and Mexican Americans." *American Journal of Economics and Sociology*, Volume 27, No. 4, October 1968.

_____. "Opportunity, Subculture and the Economic Performance of Urban Ethnic Groups." *American Journal of Economics and Sociology*, Volume 28, No. 4, October 1969.

_____. "Urban Racial Minorities and Immigrant Groups: Some Economic Comparisons." *American Journal of Economics and Sociology*, Volume 30, No. 1, January 1971.

Kelley, Jonathan. "The Politics of School Busing." *Public Opinion Quarterly*, Volume 38, Spring 1974.

Kelly, Alfred H. "An Inside View of *Brown v. Board*." *Congressional Record - Senate*. Volume 108, September 1962. Pp. 19021–26.

_____. "The School Desegregation Case." In *Quarrels That Have Shaped the Constitution*, edited by John Garraty. New York: Harper and Row, 1964.

_____. "Clio and the Court: An Illicit Love Affair." In *The Supreme Court Review*, edited by Philip B. Kurland. Chicago: University of Chicago Press, 1965.

Kentucky Commission on Human Rights. *Housing Desegregation Increases as Schools Desegregate in Jefferson County*. Louisville, Ky., May, 1977.

Kirp, David L. "Community Control, Public Policy and the Limits of Law." *Michigan Law Review*, Volume 68, June 1970.

Kirp, David L., and Yudof, Mark G. *Educational Policy and the Law*. Berkeley: McCutchan Publishing Corp., 1974.

Kitano, Harry. *Japanese-Americans*. Englewood Cliffs, N.J.: Prentice-Hall, 1967.

Knoll, Ervin. "Washington: Showcase of Integration." *Commentary*, 27, No. 3, March 1959.

Konvitz, Milton R. "The Use of Intelligence in the Advancement of Civil Rights." In *Aspects of Liberty*, edited by M. R. Konvitz and C. Rossiter. Ithaca, N.Y.: Cornell University Press, 1958.

Korn, Harold L. "Law, Fact and Science in the Courts." *Columbia Law Review*, Volume 66, No. 6, 1966.

Kurland, Philip B. "Equal Educational Opportunity: The Limits of Constitutional Jurisprudence Undefined." *University of Chicago Law Review*, Volume 35, No. 4, Summer 1968.

Lalli, Michael, and Savitz, Leonard D. "The Fear of Crime in the School Enterprise, and Its Consequences." In *Conflicts and Tensions in the Public Schools*, edited by Eleanor P. Wolf. Beverly Hills, Calif.: Sage Publications, 1977.

Lang, Kurt, and Lang, Gladys. "Resistance to School Desegregation: A Case Study of Backlash among Jews." In *The Urban R's*, edited by Robert A. Dentler, Bernard Mackler, and Mary Ellen Warshauer. New York: Praeger, 1967.

Lansing, John B.; Clifton, Charles W.; and Morgan, James N. *New Homes and Poor People*. Ann Arbor, Mich.: Institute for Social Research, University of Michigan, 1969.

LaPiere, Richard. "Attitudes vs. Actions." *Social Forces*, Volume 13, No. 2, December 1934.

Laumann, Edward O. *The Bonds of Pluralism: The Form and Substance of Urban Social Networks*. New York: Wiley, 1973.

Lawton, Stephen B., and Curtner, Gregory L. "Black Schools, White Schools: A Descriptive Analysis of School Attendance Patterns in Detroit." Toronto: The Ontario Institute for Studies in Education, 1972.

Lenski, Gerhard. *The Religious Factor*. Garden City, N.Y.: Doubleday, 1961.

Lesser, Gerald S. "Cultural Differences in Learning and Thinking Styles." In *Individuality in Learning*, edited by Samuel Messick. San Francisco: Jossey-Bass, 1976.

Lesser, Gerald S.; Fifer, Gordon; and Clark, Donald H. *Mental Abilities of Children From Different Social Class and Cultural Groups*. Monographs of the Society for Research in Child Development, Volume 30, No. 4, 1965.

Levenstein, Phyllis. "The Mother-Child Home Program." In *The Preschool in Action*, edited by M. C. Day and R. K. Parker. Boston, Mass.: Allyn and Bacon, 1977.

Levin, Betsy, and Hawley, Willis D. Foreword. *Law and Contemporary Problems*, Volume 39, No. 1, Winter 1975.

Levin, Betsy, and Moise, Philip. "School Desegregation Litigation in the Seventies and the Use of Social Science Evidence: An Annotated Guide." *Law and Contemporary Problems*, Volume 39, No. 1, Winter 1975.

Levin, Henry M. "What Difference Do Schools Make?" *Saturday Review*, January 20, 1968.

———. "Education, Life Chances, and the Courts: The Role of Social Science Evidence." *Law and Contemporary Problems*, Volume 39, No. 1, Winter 1975.

Levine, Irving M., and Herman, Judith. "The Life of White Ethnics." *Dissent*, Volume 19, No. 1, Winter 1972.

Levine, Robert A. "The Silent Majority, Neither Simple nor Simple-Minded." *Public Opinion Quarterly*, Volume 35, No. 4, 1971.

Lieberson, Stanley. "Suburbs and Ethnic Residential Patterns." *American Journal of Sociology*, Volume 67, No. 6, May 1962.

──────. "Generational Differences among Blacks in the North." *American Journal of Sociology*, Volume 79, No. 3, November 1973.

Light, Ivan. *Ethnic Enterprise in America: Business and Welfare among Chinese, Japanese and Blacks*. Berkeley: University of California Press, 1972.

Lipset, Seymour, and Bendix, Reinhard. *Social Mobility in Industrial Society*. Berkeley: University of California Press, 1964.

Litwack, Leon F. *North of Slavery: The Negro in the Free States, 1790–1860*. Chicago: University of Chicago Press, 1961.

Lord, J. Dennis. "School Busing and White Abandonment of Public Schools." *Southeastern Geographer*, Volume 15, No. 2, 1975.

Mackie, Marlene. "Ariving at Truth by Definition: The Case of Stereotype Inaccuracy." *Social Problems*, Volume 20, No. 4, Spring 1973.

Mann, Arthur. "A Historical Overview." In *The Quality of Inequality*, edited by Charles U. Daly. Chicago: University of Chicago Center for Policy Study, 1968.

Marjoribanks, Kevin. "Ethnic and Environmental Influences on Mental Abilities." *American Journal of Sociology*, Volume 78, No. 2, September, 1972.

Marshall, Margaret. "The Standard of Intent: Two Recent Michigan Cases." *Journal of Law and Education*, Volume 227, No. 4, 1975.

Marx, Gary T. *Protest and Prejudice*. New York: Harper and Row, 1967.

Maslow, Will. "How Social Scientists Can Shape Legal Processes." *Villanova Law Review*, Volume 5, No. 2, Winter 1959–60.

Mayer, Martin. "The Full and Sometimes Very Surprising Story of Ocean Hill, the Teachers Union and the Teacher Strikes of 1968." *New York Times Magazine*, February 2, 1969.

McCarthy, John D., and Yancey, William L. "Uncle Tom and Mr. Charlie: Metaphysical Pathos in the Study of Racism and Personal Disorganization." *American Journal of Sociology*, Volume 76, No. 4, January 1971.

McGurk, Frank C. J. "The Law, Social Science and Academic Freedom—A Psychologist's View." *Villanova Law Review*, Volume 5, Winter 1959–60.

McKee, James B. "Changing Patterns of Race and Housing." *Social Forces*, Volume 41, March 1963.

McMurrin, Sterling M., ed. *The Conditions for Educational Equality*. Supplementary paper 34. New York: Committee for Educational Development, 1971.

Merton, Robert K. *Social Theory and Social Structure*. Glencoe, Ill.: Free Press, 1949.

Metzger, Paul L. "American Sociology and Black Assimilation: Conflicting Perspectives." *American Journal of Sociology*, Volume 76, No. 4, January 1971.

Michelson, William. "Most People Don't Want What Architects Want." *Trans-action*, Volume 37, July-August 1968.

Michigan Law Review. "Segregation of Poor and Minority Children into Classes for the Mentally Retarded by the Use of I.Q. Tests." *Michigan Law Review*, Volume 7, No. 6, May 1973.

Miller, Arthur S., and Barron, Jerome A. "The Supreme Court, the Adversary System and the Flow of Information to the Justices: A Preliminary Inquiry." *Virginia Law Review*, Volume 61, No. 6, 1975.

Miller, Harry L., and Woock, Roger R. *Social Foundations of Urban Education*. Hinsdale, Ill.: Dryden, 1970.

Miller, Norman, and Gerard, Harold B. "How Busing Failed in Riverside." *Psychology Today*, Volume 10, No. 1, June 1976.

Molotch, Harvey L. *Managed Integration*. Berkeley: University of California Press, 1972a.

———. "Why Neighborhoods Change: A Reply to Whom It May Concern." *American Journal of Sociology*, Volume 78, No. 3, November 1972b.

Montero, Darrel M. "Assimilation and Educational Achievement: The Case of Second Generation Japanese-Americans." Paper read at the annual meeting of the American Sociological Association, New York City, August 1973.

Moore, Barrington, Jr. *Reflections on the Causes of Human Misery*. Boston: Beacon, 1972.

Morrill, Richard. "The Negro Ghetto: Problems and Alternatives." *Geographical Review*, Volume 55, July 1965.

Morris, David C. "Racial Attitudes of White Residents in Integrated and Segregated Neighborhoods." *Sociological Focus*, Volume 6, No. 2, Spring 1973.

Mosteller, Frederick, and Moynihan, Daniel P., eds. *On Equality of Educational Opportunity*. New York: Random House, 1972.

Murdoch, Katherine. "A Study of Race Differences in New York City." *School and Society*, Volume 11, No. 266, January 1920.

Murphy, Jerome T., and Cohen, David K. "Accountability in Education—the Michigan Experience." *The Public Interest*, No. 36, Summer 1974.

Murphy, Walter B., and Pritchett, Herman C. *Courts, Judges and Politics*. New York: Random House, 1961.

Muth, Richard F. *Cities and Housing*. Chicago: University of Chicago Press, 1969.

Myrdal, Gunnar, et al. Washington, D.C.: National Academy of Sciences, 1972. *An American Dilemma*. New York: Harper and Row, 1944.

National Academy of Sciences. *Freedom of Choice in Housing*. Washington, D.C.: National Academy of Sciences, 1972.

National Advisory Commission on Civil Disorders. *Report of the National Advisory Commission on Civil Disorders*. New York: Bantam Books, 1968.

———. *Supplemental Studies for the National Advisory Commission on Civil Disorders*. Washington, D.C.: U.S. Government Printing Office, 1968.

National Committee against Discrimination in Housing. *Trends*, Volume 18, No. 1, January-February 1974.

National Education Association. *Ability Grouping*. Research Summary 1968–53. Washington, D.C.: National Education Association, 1968.

National Opinion Research Center. *Southern Schools: An Evaluation of the Effects of the Emergency School Assistance Program and of School Desegration*. 2 vols. Chicago: National Opinion Research Center, 1973.

Nesbitt, George B. "Misconceptions in the Movement for Civil Rights in Housing." *Journal of Intergroup Relations*, Volume 21, No. 1, Winter 1960–61.

New York University Law Review. Note. "School Busing and Desegregation: The Post-Swan Era." *New York University Law Review*, Volume 46, December 1971.

Nichols, Robert C. "Review of the U.S. Commission on Civil Rights, 'Racial Isolation in the Public Schools.' " *American Educational Research Journal*, Volume 5, No. 4, November 1968.

Orfield, Gary. "Federal Policy, Local Power, and Metropolitan Segregation." *Political Science Quarterly*, Volume 89, No. 4, Winter 1974–75.

————. "White Flight Research: Its Importance, Perplexities and Possible Policy Implications." In *Symposium on School Desegregation and White Flight*, edited by Gary Orfield. Washington, D.C.: National Institute of Education, U.S. Department of Health, Education, and Welfare, 1975.

Palardy, Michael J. "What Teachers Believe—What Children Achieve." *Elementary School Journal*, Volume 69, No. 7, April 1969.

Palen, J. John. *The Urban World*. New York: McGraw-Hill, 1975.

Parenti, Michael. "Ethnic Politics and the Persistence of Ethnic Identification." In *Ethnic Group Politics*, edited by H. A. Bailey, Jr., and E. Katz. Columbus, Ohio: Merrill, 1969.

Pascal, Anthony H. *The Economics of Housing Segregation*. Santa Monica, Calif.: Rand, 1967.

————. "The Analysis of Residential Segregation." In *Financing the Metropolis: Public Policy in Urban Economics*, edited by J. P. Crecine. Beverly Hills, Calif.: Sage Publications, 1970.

Passow, Harry A., ed. *Education in Depressed Areas*. New York: Teachers College Press, 1963.

————. *Urban Education in the 1970's: Reflections and a Look Ahead*. New York: Teachers College Press, 1971.

Passow, Harry A.; Goldberg, Miriam; and Tannenbaum, Abraham J., eds. *Education of the Disadvantaged: A Book of Readings*. New York: Holt, Rinehart and Winston, 1967.

Perry, David C., and Feagin, Joe R. "Stereotyping in Black and White." In *People and Politics in Urban Society*, edited by Harlan Hahn. Beverly Hills, Calif.: Sage Publications, 1972.

Petersen, William. "Prejudice in American Society." *Commentary*, Volume 26, October 1958.

————. *Japanese Americans*. New York: Random House, 1971.

Pettigrew, Thomas F. "The Negro and Education: Problems and Proposals." In *Race and the Social Sciences*, edited by Irwin Katz and Patricia Gurin. New York: Basic Books, 1969.

Pettigrew, Thomas F., and Green, Robert L. "School Desegregation in Large Cities: A Critique of the Coleman White Flight Thesis." *Harvard Educational Review*, Volume 46, No. 1, February 1976.

Piehler, Henry R., et al. "Product Liability and the Technical Expert." *Science*, December 20, 1974.

Pilo, Marvin. "A Tale of Two Cities." *Education and Urban Society*, Volume 7, No. 4, August 1975.

Pindur, Wolfgang. "Legislative and Judicial Roles in the Detroit School Decentralization Controversy." *Journal of Urban Law*, Volume 50, No. 1, August 1972.

Plumer, Davenport. "A Summary of Environmentalist Views and Some Educational Implications." In *Language and Poverty*, edited by Frederick Williams. Chicago: Markham, 1970.

Pollak, Louis. "Racial Discrimination and Judicial Integrity: A Reply to Professor Wechsler." *University of Pennsylvania Law Review*, Volume 108, No. 1, November 1959.

Porter, Judith D. R. *Black Child, White Child*. Cambridge, Mass.: Harvard University Press, 1971.

Powell, Gloria. *Black Monday's Children*. New York: Appleton-Century-Crofts, 1973.

Preston, Samuel H. "Differential Fertility, Unwanted Fertility and Racial Trends in Occupational Achievement." *American Sociological Review*, Volume 39, No. 4, August 1974.

Pringle, M. L. Kellmer; Butler, N. R.; and Davie, R. *11,000 Seven Year Olds*. London: Longmans, 1966.

Pryor, Fredrick L. "An Empirical Note on the Tipping Point." *Land Economics*, Volume 47, No. 4, November 1971.

Rader, R. M. "Demise of the Neighborhood School Plan." *Cornell Law Review*, Volume 55, No. 4, April 1970.

Rapkin, Chester, and Grigsby, W. "The Prospect for Stable Interracial Neighborhoods." In *Urban Planning and Social Policy*, edited by Bernard J. Frieden and Robert Morris. New York: Basic Books, 1968.

Ravitch, Diane. "Community Control Revisited." *Commentary*, Volume 53, No. 2, February 1972.

———. *The Great School Wars*. New York: Basic Books, 1974.

Read, Frank T. "Judicial Evolution of the Law of School Integration since *Brown v. Board of Education*." *Law and Contemporary Problems*, Volume 39, No. 1, Winter 1975.

Real Estate Research Corporation. *Stability of Racial Mix in Illinois Schools*. Office of Education of the State of Illinois, April 1976.

Rex, John, and Moore, Robert. *Race, Community and Conflict: A Study of Sparkbrooke*. Oxford: Oxford University Press, 1967.

Richter, Robert I. "School Desegregation after *Swann*: A Theory of Government Responsibility." *University of Chicago Law Review*, Volume 39, No. 2, Winter 1972.

Rist, Ray. "Student Social Class and Teacher Expectations: The Self-Fulfilling Prophecy in Ghetto Education." *Harvard Educational Review*, Volume 40, No. 3, 1970.

Rist, Ray, and Anson, Ronald J. eds. *Education, Social Science, and the Judicial Process*. New York: Teachers College Press, 1977.

Roof, Clark W. "Residential Segregation of Blacks and Racial Inequality in Southern Cities: Toward a Causal Model." In *Comparative Urban Structure*, edited by Kent P. Schwirian. Lexington, Mass.: D. C. Heath, 1974.

Rose, Arnold. "Intergroup Relations vs. Prejudice." *Social Problems*, Volume 4, No. 2, December 1956.

———. "The Social Scientist as an Expert Witness in Court Cases." In *The Uses of Sociology*, edited by Paul Lazarsfeld, William H. Sewell, and Harold L. Wilensky. New York: Basic Books, 1967.

Rosen, Paul. *The Supreme Court and Social Science.* Urbana: University of Illinois Press, 1972.

———. "Social Science and Judicial Policy Making." In *Using Social Research in Public Policy Making,* edited by Carol H. Weiss. Lexington, Mass.: D. C. Heath, 1977.

Rosenbaum, James A. "The Stratification of Socialization Processes." *American Sociological Review,* Volume 40, No. 1, February 1975.

Rosenberg, Morris. *Society and the Adolescent Self-Image.* Princeton: Princeton University Press, 1968.

Rosenberg, Morris, and Simmons, Roberta G. *Black and White Self-Esteem: The Urban School Child.* Arnold and Caroline Rose Monograph Series. Washington, D.C.: American Sociological Association, 1971.

Rosenthal, Erich. "Acculturation without Assimilation." *American Journal of Sociology,* Volume 66, No. 3, November 1960.

Rosenthal, Robert, and Jacobson, Lenore. *Pygmalion in the Classroom.* New York: Holt, Rinehart, and Winston, 1968.

Rosenwaike, Ira. "Inter-Ethnic Comparisons of Educational Attainment." *American Journal of Sociology,* Volume 79, No. 1, July 1973.

Rossell, Christine H. "School Desegregation and White Flight." *Political Science Quarterly,* Volume 90, No. 4, Winter 1975–76.

Rubovits, Pamela, and Maehr, Martin L. "Pygmalion, Black and White." *Journal of Personality and Social Psychology,* Volume 25, No. 2, 1973.

St. John, Nancy. "Desegregation and Minority Group Performance." *Review of Educational Research,* Volume 40, No. 1, February 1970.

———. "The Elementary Classroom as a Frog Pond: Self-Concept, Sense of Control and Social Context." *Social Forces,* Volume 49, June 1971.

———. "Diversity in Urban Schools." In *Encyclopedia of Education,* edited by Lee C. Deighton. New York: Macmillan, 1971b.

———. *Desegregation Outcomes for Children.* New York: John Wiley and Sons, 1975.

St. John, Nancy, and Herriott, Robert. *Social Class and the Urban School.* New York: John Wiley and Sons, 1966.

Saltzman, Murray, Member, U.S. Civil Rights Civil Commission. Letter to the editor, *Saturday Review,* April 17, 1976.

Sandberg, Neil C. *Ethnic Identity and Assimilation: The Polish-American Community.* New York: Praeger, 1973.

Schelling, Thomas G. "On the Ecology of Micromotives." *The Public Interest,* No. 25, Fall 1971.

Schnore, Leo F., and Evenson, Philip C. "Segregation in Southern Cities." *American Journal of Sociology,* Volume 72, No. 1, 1966.

Schnore, Leo F., and Sharp, Harry. "The Changing Color of Our Big Cities." In *Metropolis in Crisis,* edited by Jeffrey K. Hadden, Louis H. Masotti, and Calvin J. Larson. Itasca, Ill.: F. E. Peacock, 1967.

Schnore, Leo F.; Andre, Carolyn D.; and Sharp, Harry. "Black Suburbanization 1930–1970." In *The Changing Face of the Suburbs,* edited by Barry Schwartz. Chicago: University of Chicago Press, 1976.

Schuman, Howard. "Sociological Racism." *Trans-action,* Volume 7, No. 2, December 1969.

Schuman, Howard, and Hatchett, Shirley. *Black Racial Attitudes: Trends and Complexities*. Ann Arbor: Survey Research Center, Institute for Social Research, University of Michigan, 1974.

Schwartz, Audrey J. "The Culturally Advantaged: A Study of Japanese-American Pupils." In *Race Relations*, edited by Edgar G. Epps. Cambridge, Mass.: Winthrop, 1973.

Sewell, William H.; Haller, Archibald; and Ohlendorf, George W. "The Educational and Early Occupational Status Achievement Process." *American Sociological Review*, Volume 35, No. 6, December 1970.

Sewell, William H.; Marscuilo, L.; and Pfautz, Howard. "Review Symposium on the Coleman Report." *American Sociological Review*, Volume 32, No. 3, June 1967.

Sheatsley, Paul. "White Attitudes toward the Negro." In *The Negro American*, edited by Talcott Parsons and Kenneth B. Clark, Boston, Mass.: Beacon Press, 1967.

Sheldon, Eleanor B., and Glazier, Raymond A. *Pupils and Schools in New York City*. New York: Russell Sage Foundation, 1965.

Simpson, George, and Yinger, Milton J. *Racial and Cultural Minorities*. New York: Harper and Row, 1972.

Singer, David. "Profile of the Jewish Academic, Some Recent Studies." *Midstream*, Volume 19, June-July 1973.

Singer, Lester. "Ethnogenesis and Negro-Americans Today." *Social Research*, Volume 29, No. 4, Winter 1962.

Sklare, Marshall, ed. *The Jews: Social Patterns of an American Group*. Glencoe, Ill.: Free Press, 1958.

Slawski, Edward J. "Pontiac Parents: For Busing or Integration?" In *Conflicts and Tensions in the Public Schools*, edited by Eleanor P. Wolf. Beverly Hills, Calif.: Sage Publications, 1977.

Smith, Brewster M. "Race Differences." *Science*, Volume 163, January 31, 1969.

Smith, Marshall. "Equality of Educational Opportunity: The Basic Findings Reconsidered." In *Equality of Educational Opportunity*, edited by F. Mosteller and D. P. Moynihan. New York: Random House, 1972.

Snow, Richard E. "Unfinished Pygmalion." *Contemporary Psychology*, Volume 14, No. 4, April 1969.

Spaulding, Sheila. *Analysis of Data Concerning Graduates of the Public Schools of Oakland, California*. Oakland, Calif.: Dumbarton Research Council, 1967.

Stegman, Michael A. "Accessibility Models and Residential Location." *Journal of the American Institute of Planners*, Volume 35, No. 1, January 1969.

Stinchcombe, Arthur L. "Environment: The Cumulation of Effects Is Yet To Be Understood." *Harvard Educational Review*, Volume 39, No. 3, Summer 1969.

Stinchcombe, Arthur L.; McDill, Mary; and Walker, Dollie. "Is There a Racial Tipping Point in Changing Schools?" *Journal of Social Issues*, Volume 25, No. 1, 1969.

Stodolsky, Susan S., and Lesser, Gerald. "Learning Patterns in the Disadvantaged." *Harvard Educational Review*, Volume 37, No. 4, Fall 1967.

Strodtbeck, Frederick L. "The Hidden Curriculum in the Middle-Class Home." In *Learning and the Educational Process*, edited by J. D. Krumboltz. Chicago: Rand McNally, 1965.

Sue, Derald W., and Frank, Austin C. "A Typological Approach to the Study of

Chinese and Japanese American College Males." *Journal of Social Issues*, Volume 29, No. 2, 1973.

Sutker, Solomon and Sarah S., eds. *Racial Transition in the Inner Suburb*. New York: Praeger, 1974.

Suttles, Gerald D. *The Social Order of the Slum: Ethnicity and Territory in the Inner City*. Chicago: University of Chicago Press, 1968.

Syrkin, Marie. "Can Minorities Oppose *De Facto* Segregation?" *Jewish Frontier*, Volume 31, September 1964.

Taeuber, Karl E. *Patterns of Negro-White Residential Segregation*. Santa Monica, Calif.: Rand, January 1970.

————. "Demographic Perspectives on Housing and School Segregation." *Wayne Law Review*, Volume 21, No. 3, March 1975.

Taeuber, Karl E., and Taeuber, Alma F. *Negroes in Cities: Residential Segregation and Neighborhood Change*. Chicago, Ill.: Aldine, 1965.

Taylor, William; Benjes, John E.; and Wright, Eric E. "School Desegregation and White Flight: The Role of the Courts." *Symposium on School Desegregation and White Flight*, edited by Gary Orfield. Washington, D.C.: National Institute of Education, U.S. Department of Health, Education, and Welfare, August 1975.

Terreberry, Shirley. "Household Relocation: Residents' Views." In *Change and Renewal in an Urban Community*, by Eleanor P. Wolf and Charles N. Lebeaux. New York: Praeger, 1969.

Thernstrom, Stephen. "Poverty in Historical Perspective." In *On Understanding Poverty*, edited by D. P. Moynihan. New York: Basic Books, 1968.

————. "Immigrants and WASPS: Ethnic Differences in Occupational Mobility in Boston 1880–1940." In *Nineteenth Century Cities*, edited by Stephen Thernstrom and Richard Sennett. New Haven: Yale University Press, 1969.

Thorndike, Robert L. "Review of Robert Rosenthal and Lenore Jacobson, *Pygmalion in the Classroom*." *American Educational Research Journal*, Volume 5, No. 4, November 1968.

————. *Reading Comprehension Education in Fifteen Countries*. New York: John Wiley and Sons, 1973.

Tilly, Charles, *An Urban World*. Boston, Mass.: Little, Brown, 1974.

Time, March 15, September 27, 1976, October 31, 1977.

Trans-action. "Round-Up of Current Research." *Trans-action*, Volume 4, No. 5, April 1967.

Treiman, Donald, and Terrell, Kermit. "Sex and the Process of Status Attainment." *American Sociological Review*, Volume 40, No. 2, April 1975.

Trotman, Frances Keith. "Race, IQ and the Middle Class." *Journal of Educational Psychology*, Volume 69, No. 3, June 1977.

U.S. Advisory Commission on Civil Disorders. *Report*. New York: Bantam Books, 1968.

U.S. Commission on Civil Rights. *Racial Isolation in the Schools*. 2 vols. Washington, D.C.: U.S. Commission on Civil Rights, 1967.

————. *Your Child and Busing*. Washington, D.C.: U.S. Commission on Civil Rights, 1972.

———. *Public Knowledge and Busing Opposition*. Washington, D.C.: U.S. Commission on Civil Rights, March 1973.

———. *Milliken v. Bradley: The Implications for Metropolitan Desegregation*. Washington, D.C.: U.S. Commission on Civil Rights, 1974.

———. *Desegregation of the Nation's Public Schools*. Washington, D.C.: U.S. Commission on Civil Rights, August 1976.

———. *Statement on Metropolitan School Desegregation*. Washington, D.C.: U.S. Commission on Civil Rights, February 1977a.

———. *School Desegregation in Minneapolis, Minnesota*. A Staff Report. Washington, D.C.: U.S. Commission on Civil Rights, May 1977b.

U.S. Congress. Senate. Select Committee on Equal Educational Opportunity. *Hearings on Equal Educational Opportunity: Part 5—De Facto Segregation and Housing Discrimination*. 91st Cong., 2d sess., August 25, 26, 27, September 1, 1970.

University of Michigan, School of Education. *Developments in School Desegregation and the Law—Program for Educational Opportunity*. Proceedings of a conference held at the Program for Educational Opportunity, University of Michigan, Ann Arbor, May 17–19, 1972.

Van Den Haag, Ernest. "Social Science Testimony in the Desegregation Cases." *Villanova Law Review*, Volume 6, No. 1, Fall 1960.

Warren, Donald R. *A Comparative Study of Life Styles and Social Attitudes of Middle Income Whites and Negroes in Detroit*. Detroit: Detroit Urban League, 1968.

Watts, Lewis; Freeman, Howard E.; Hughes, Helen M.; Morris, Robert; and Pettigrew, Thomas F. *The Middle-Income Negro Family Faces Urban Renewal*. Waltham, Mass.: Brandeis University, Florence Heller Graduate School for Advanced Studies in Social Welfare, for the Department of Commerce and Development, Commonwealth of Massachusetts, 1964.

Wechsler, Herbert. "Toward Neutral Principles of Constitutional Law. *Harvard Law Review*, Volume 73, No. 1, November 1959.

Weinberg, Alvin M. "The Many Dimensions of Scientific Responsibility." *Bulletin of the Atomic Scientists*, Volume 32, No. 9, November 1976.

Weinstein, Jack B. "Some Difficulties in Devising Rules for Determining Truth in Judicial Trials." *Columbia Law Review*, Volume 66, No. 2, February 1966.

White, Sheldon H., et al. *Federal Programs for Young Children: Review and Recommendations*. Vol. 1: *Goals and Standards of Public Programs for Children*. Washington, D.C.: U.S. Department of Health, Education, and Welfare, 1973.

Wicker, Allan W. "Attitudes versus Actions." *Journal of Social Issues*, Volume 25, No. 4, 1969.

Williams, Frederick, ed. *Language and Poverty: Perspectives on a Theme*. New York: Academic Press, 1970.

Williams, Robin, et al. *Strangers Next Door*. Englewood Cliffs, N.J.: Prentice-Hall, 1964.

Wilner, Daniel M.; Walkley, Rosabelle P.; and Cook, Stuart W. *Human Relations in Interracial Housing*. Minneapolis: University of Minnesota Press, 1955.

Wilson, Alan B. "Residential Segregation of Social Classes and Aspirations of High School Boys." *American Sociological Review*, Volume 24, No. 6, December 1959.

———. "Social Stratification and Educational Achievement." In *Education in Depressed Areas*, edited by A. Harry Passow. New York: Teachers College Press, 1963.

――――. *The Consequences of Segregation: Academic Achievement in a Northern Community*. Berkeley, Calif.: Glendessary Press, 1969.

Wolf, Eleanor P. "Racial Transition in a Middle Class Area," *Journal of Intergroup Relations*, Volume 1, No. 3, Summer 1960.

――――. "The Tipping Point in Racially Changing Neighborhoods." In *Urban Planning and Social Policy*, edited by Bernard Freiden and Robert Morris. New York: Basic Books, 1968.

――――. "Community Control of Schools as Ideology and Social Mechanism." *Social Science Quarterly*, Volume 50, No. 3, December 1969.

――――. "Civil Rights and Social Science Data." *Race*, Volume 13, July 1972.

Wolf, Eleanor P., and Lebeaux, Charles N. *Change and Renewal in an Urban Community*. New York: Praeger, 1969.

Wolf, Eleanor P., and Ravitz, Mel J. "Lafayette Park: New Residents in the Core City." *Journal of the American Institute of Planners*, Volume 30, No. 3, August 1964.

Wolf, Robert L., and Simon, Rita J. "Does Busing Improve the Racial Interactions of Children?" *Educational Researcher*, Volume 4, No. 1, January 1975.

Wolfe, Donald, and Blood, Robert. "Negro-White Differences in Working-Class Marriage." Paper read at the annual meeting of the American Sociological Association, New York City, 1960.

Wolfgang, Marvin E. "The Social Scientist in Court." *Journal of Criminal Law and Criminology*, Volume 65, No. 2, 1974.

Wolfinger, Raymond E. "The Development and Persistence of Ethnic Voting." *American Political Science Review*, Volume 59, No. 4, December 1965.

Young, Beloine Whiting, and Bress, Grace Billings. "Coleman's Retreat and the Politics of Good Intentions." *Phi Delta Kappan*, Volume 57, No. 3, November 1975.

Yudof, Mark. "Equal Educational Opportunity and the Courts." *Texas Law Review*, Volume 51, No. 3, March 1973.

Zelder, Raymond E. "Racial Segregation in Urban Housing Markets." *Journal of Regional Science*, Volume 10, No. 1, 1970a.

――――. "Residential Desegregation, Can Nothing Be Accomplished?" *Urban Affairs Quarterly*, Volume 5, No. 3, March 1970b.

Zikmund, Joseph, II. "Sources of the Suburban Population: 1955–1960 and 1965–70." *Publius: The Journal of Federalism*, Volume 5, No. 1, Winter 1975.

Zirkel, Percy A., and Moses, E. G. "Self-Concept and Ethnic Group Membership among Public School Students." *American Education Research Journal*, Volume 8, No. 2, March 1971.

Index

363

Eleanor P. Wolf is a professor of sociology at Wayne State University. She is the author, with Charles N. Lebeaux, of *Change and Renewal in an Urban Community* and has written widely on residential behavior, education, and intergroup relations. This research on the utilization of social science materials in school desegregation proceedings was supported by the Ford Foundation.

The book was designed by Robert L. Nance. The typeface for the display and text is Caledonia, designed by W. A. Dwiggins about 1938. The book is printed on IP's Bookmark and the book is bound in Holliston Mills Crown Linen over binder's boards. Manufactured in the United States of America.